1, 2, & 3 JOHN

1, 2, & 3 JOHN

ZONDERVAN
Exegetical Commentary
ON THE
New Testament

KAREN H. JOBES

CLINTON E. ARNOLD
General Editor

 ZONDERVAN®

ZONDERVAN

1, 2, and 3 John
Copyright © 2014 by Karen H. Jobes

ISBN 9780310518013 (ebook)

Requests for information should be addressed to:
Zondervan, 3900 *Sparks Dr. SE, Grand Rapids, Michigan 49546*

Library of Congress Cataloging-in-Publication Data

Jobes, Karen H.
    1, 2, and 3 John / Karen H. Jobes.
       p. cm.—(Zondervan exegetical commentary series on the New Testament)
    Includes index.
    ISBN: 978-0-310-24416-5 (hardcover)
    1. Bible. Epistles of John-Commentaries. I. Title. II. Title: First, Second, Third John.
  BS2805.53.J63   2013
  227'.94077—dc23   2013020160

Cover design: Tammy Johnson
Interior design: Beth Shagene

Printed in the United States of America

---

19 20 21 22 23 24 25 /LSCC/ 25 24 23 22 21 20 19 18 17 16 15 14 13 12 11 10 9 8 7 6 5 4 3

Dedicated to the memory of
Patty Comber
(1949 – 2012)

The world is a lonelier place without you, dear friend.

Contents

Series Introduction

This generation has been blessed with an abundance of excellent commentaries. Some are technical and do a good job of addressing issues that the critics have raised; other commentaries are long and provide extensive information about word usage and catalogue nearly every opinion expressed on the various interpretive issues; still other commentaries focus on providing cultural and historical background information; and then there are those commentaries that endeavor to draw out many applicational insights.

The key question to ask is: What are you looking for in a commentary? This commentary series might be for you if

- you have taken Greek and would like a commentary that helps you apply what you have learned without assuming you are a well-trained scholar.
- you would find it useful to see a concise, one- or two-sentence statement of what the commentator thinks the main point of each passage is.
- you would like help interpreting the words of Scripture without getting bogged down in scholarly issues that seem irrelevant to the life of the church.
- you would like to see a visual representation (a graphical display) of the flow of thought in each passage.
- you would like expert guidance from solid evangelical scholars who set out to explain the meaning of the original text in the clearest way possible and to help you navigate through the main interpretive issues.
- you want to benefit from the results of the latest and best scholarly studies and historical information that help to illuminate the meaning of the text.
- you would find it useful to see a brief summary of the key theological insights that can be gleaned from each passage and some discussion of the relevance of these for Christians today.

These are just some of the features that characterize the new Zondervan Exegetical Commentary on the New Testament series. The idea for this series was refined over time by an editorial board who listened to pastors and teachers express what they wanted to see in a commentary series based on the Greek text. That board consisted of myself, George H. Guthrie, Constantine R. Campbell, Thomas R. Schreiner, and Mark L. Strauss along with Zondervan senior editor at large Verlyn Verbrugge, and former Zondervan senior acquisitions editor Jack Kuhatschek. We also enlisted a board of consulting editors who are active pastors, ministry leaders, and seminary professors to help in the process of designing a commentary series that will be useful to the church. Zondervan senior acquisitions editor Katya Covrett has now been shepherding the process to completion.

We arrived at a design that includes seven components for the treatment of each biblical passage. What follows is a brief orientation to these primary components of the commentary.

Literary Context

In this section, you will find a concise discussion of how the passage functions in the broader literary context of the book. The commentator highlights connections with the preceding and following material in the book and makes observations on the key literary features of this text.

Main Idea

Many readers will find this to be an enormously helpful feature of this series. For each passage, the commentator carefully crafts a one- or two-sentence statement of the big idea or central thrust of the passage.

Translation and Graphical Layout

Another unique feature of this series is the presentation of each commentator's translation of the Greek text in a graphical layout. The purpose of this diagram is to help the reader visualize, and thus better understand, the flow of thought within the text. The translation itself reflects the interpretive decisions made by each commentator in the "Explanation" section of the commentary. Here are a few insights that will help you to understand the way these are put together:

1. On the far left side next to the verse numbers is a series of interpretive labels that indicate the function of each clause or phrase of the biblical text. The corresponding portion of the text is on the same line to the right of the label. We have not used technical linguistic jargon for these, so they should be easily understood.
2. In general, we place every clause (a group of words containing a subject and a predicate) on a separate line and identify how it is supporting the principal assertion of the text (namely, is it saying when the action occurred, how it took place, or why it took place?). We sometimes place longer phrases or a series of items on separate lines as well.

3. Subordinate (or dependent) clauses and phrases are indented and placed directly under the words that they modify. This helps the reader to more easily see the nature of the relationship of clauses and phrases in the flow of the text.

4. Every main clause has been placed in bold print and pushed to the left margin for clear identification.

5. Sometimes when the level of subordination moves too far to the right — as often happens with some of Paul's long, involved sentences! — we reposition the flow to the left of the diagram, but use an arrow to indicate that this has happened.

6. The overall process we have followed has been deeply informed by principles of discourse analysis and narrative criticism (for the Gospels and Acts).

Structure

Immediately following the translation, the commentator describes the flow of thought in the passage and explains how certain interpretive decisions regarding the relationship of the clauses were made in the passage.

Exegetical Outline

The overall structure of the passage is described in a detailed exegetical outline. This will be particularly helpful for those who are looking for a way to concisely explain the flow of thought in the passage in a teaching or preaching setting.

Explanation of the Text

As an exegetical commentary, this work makes use of the Greek language to interpret the meaning of the text. If your Greek is rather rusty (or even somewhat limited), don't be too concerned. All of the Greek words are cited in parentheses following an English translation. We have made every effort to make this commentary as readable and useful as possible even for the nonspecialist.

Those who will benefit the most from this commentary will have had the equivalent of two years of Greek in college or seminary. This would include a semester or two of working through an intermediate grammar (such as Wallace, Porter, Brooks and Winbery, or Dana and Mantey). The authors use the grammatical language that is found in these kinds of grammars. The details of the grammar of the passage, however, are discussed only when it has a bearing on the interpretation of the text.

The emphasis on this section of the text is to convey the meaning. Commentators examine words and images, grammatical details, relevant OT and Jewish background to a particular concept, historical and cultural context, important text-critical issues, and various interpretational issues that surface.

Theology in Application

This, too, is a unique feature for an exegetical commentary series. We felt it was important for each author not only to describe what the text means in its various details, but also to take a moment and reflect on the theological contribution that it makes. In this section, the theological message of the passage is summarized. The authors discuss the theology of the text in terms of its place within the book and in a broader biblical-theological context. Finally, each commentator provides some suggestions on what the message of the passage is for the church today. At the conclusion of each volume in this series is a summary of the whole range of theological themes touched on by this book of the Bible.

Our sincere hope and prayer is that you find this series helpful not only for your own understanding of the text of the New Testament, but as you are actively engaged in teaching and preaching God's Word to people who are hungry to be fed on its truth.

Clinton E. Arnold, general editor

Author's Preface

It is an interesting time to be writing a commentary on any book in the Johannine corpus, for Johannine studies have been shifting, the consensus among scholars of the past thirty years is crumbling, and a new one has not yet emerged. Because the letters of John cannot be interpreted independently of the Fourth Gospel, the currents of Johannine gospel scholarship have largely directed interpretation of the letters as well.

Johannine scholarship has shifted away from the twentieth-century approaches that were largely shaped by Bultmann's existentialist, demythologizing philosophy of hermeneutics, aided by the methodologies of source and redaction criticisms. The dominant approach to Johannine studies for the last few decades perceived difficulties with John's gospel that were thought to be solved by an elaborate reconstruction of its redactional history with one or more corresponding historical scenarios involving the Johannine community. Scholars such as Martyn, Kysar, and Brown dominated the field in the second half of the twentieth century with their theories for the composition of John's gospel and letters that focused more on the conjectured issues of the late first-century Johannine community, supposedly expelled from Jewish synagogues, than on the life and teachings of Jesus.[1]

As an alternative approach, scholars began to apply methods of new literary criticism to John's gospel, initiated largely by Alan Culpepper in his *Anatomy of the Fourth Gospel: A Study in Literary Design*.[2] Literary criticism brought new insights to light about the structure and composition of the gospel, but they still stood next to theories of its redaction and basically followed Bultmann's approach of considering it story rather than history. By the time the Jesus Seminar, led by Robert Funk, published *The Five Gospels: The Search for the Authentic Words of Jesus: New Translation and Commentary* in the early 1990s, any historical value of John's gospel had been dismissed by the majority of NT scholars.

Conservative, evangelical scholars, such as D. A. Carson, Leon Morris, Craig

---

1. See Robert Kysar, "The Expulsion from the Synagogue: The Tale of a Theory," in *Voyages with John: Charting the Fourth Gospel* (Waco, TX: Baylor University Press, 2005), 237–45, and "Charting the Voyages: An Autobiographical Introduction," ibid., 1–6.

2. In the series Foundations and Facets: New Testament (R. Funk, ed.; Philadelphia: Fortress, 1983).

Blomberg, and Andreas Köstenberger, continued to defend the historical reliability of a gospel that claimed to be centrally concerned with witnessing to the truth, even while they recognized the literary qualities of this gospel that are clearly different from the Synoptics. By recognizing that truth is not exhausted by historical facts alone, many of the alleged problems of John's gospel — problems such as dischronologized events, apparent redactional seams, and theological tensions — can be put to rest. These features that explain the significance of the facts might be expected especially in a telling of Jesus' life that even early Christians recognized as a "spiritual" (Gk. *pneumatikon*) gospel (Eusebius quoting Clement of Alexander, *Hist. eccl.*, 6.14.7).

The present commentary attempts to position itself by several distinctives:

1. I work from the reasoned assumption that the author of John's letters either was the same person who authored the Fourth Gospel or was a close associate of that writer. Many of the assumptions of twentieth-century scholarship that led to a conclusion that the author could not have been the apostle John are not shared by this writer.

2. I hold to the thesis that, while the letters must be allowed their own voice, they cannot be properly understood without reference to John's gospel as the interpretive framework for the metaphors, images, and theology common to both.

3. While I allow that a close associate of the beloved disciple may have put an already essentially complete gospel into its final form, I do not assume an extended compositional history for the Fourth Gospel into which the production of each of the three Johannine letters must be placed. This commentary wishes to distance itself from the more speculative reconstructions of the Johannine community that were based on assumptions of an extensive redactional history of the gospel as the historical background against which the letters are interpreted, and therefore will not systematically engage interpreters whose work has characteristically relied on such reconstructions.

4. The more recent arguments for a nonpolemical reading of 1 John have provided a needed refocus for the intent of the letters, which this commentary shares. While I recognize that the letters were written during a time of schism and confusion in the Johannine churches, no specific reconstruction of the heresy is attempted or assumed. The truths presented in the letters could argue against a variety of christological heresies that may or may not have been forms of Gnosticism, Docetism, or Cerinthianism. There is not sufficient evidence to reconstruct the false teaching with such specificity, and so it seems wisest to refrain from doing so. The letters speak to a variety of false beliefs, many of which are still with us today.

Acknowledgments

This commentary has been several years in the making, and many people have influenced the shape it has taken. The author thanks Katya Covrett, senior acquisitions editor at Zondervan, and Clint Arnold, series editor for the Zondervan Exegetical Commentary on the New Testament series, for inviting me to contribute this volume. And thanks are also due to Verlyn Verbrugge for his editing work that improves this volume. My former pastor and friend, Diana Trautwein, encouraged me to take on another commentary and has been a constant source of encouragement and support along the way. I have benefited from my students in the exegesis courses on John's letters that I have taught since 2005 in the Biblical Exegesis program in Wheaton's Graduate School. They have not let me avoid some of the harder questions about these brief NT books.

My teaching assistants during these years have each contributed in helpful ways. I especially acknowledge the contributions of Cassandra Blackford (2005 – 2006), Charlie Trimm (2010 – 2011), Jon Hoglund (2011 – 2012), Jeremy Otten (2012 – 2013), and Chris Smith (Fall 2013), who helped to index this volume. My husband, Dr. Forrest Jobes, has continued to express the Ephesians 5 kind of love that has enabled me to spend such a large part of our life writing this volume. I am grateful to the Lord for all of these people and the rich blessing each has been in my life.

Abbreviations

Abbreviations for books of the Bible, pseudepigrapha, rabbinic works, papyri, classical works, and the like are readily available in sources such as *The SBL Handbook of Style* and are not included here.

AB	Anchor Bible
ABR	*Australian Biblical Review*
abt.	about
ACCS	Ancient Christian Commentary Series
ACNT	Augsburg Commentary on the New Testament
AE	*Luther's Works.* St. Louis: Concordia; Philadelphia: Fortress, 1955 – [American Edition].
ANTC	Abingdon New Testament Commentaries
BCBC	Believers Church Bible Commentary
BDAG	*A Greek – English Lexicon of the New Testament and Other Early Christian Literature*, third edition, rev. and ed. Frederick W. Danker.
BDF	*A Greek Grammar of the New Testament and Other Early Christian Literature*, trans. and ed. Robert W. Funk.
BECNT	Baker Exegetical Commentary on the New Testament
Bib	*Biblica*
BSac	*Bibliotheca sacra*
BST	The Bible Speaks Today
BT	*The Bible Translator*
BTNT	Biblical Theology of the New Testament
CBQ	*Catholic Biblical Quarterly*
CEB	Common English Bible
CurBS	*Currents in Research: Biblical Studies*
ESV	English Standard Version
EvQ	*Evangelical Quarterly*
GTJ	*Grace Theological Journal*
ICC	International Critical Commentary
IVPNTC	The IVP New Testament Commentary Series
JBL	*Journal of Biblical Literature*

JETS	*Journal of the Evangelical Theological Society*
JGRChJ	*Journal of Greco-Roman Christianity and Judaism*
JPT	*Journal of Pentecostal Theology*
JRS	*Journal of Roman Studies*
JSNT	*Journal for the Study of the New Testament*
JSNTSup	Journal for the Study of the New Testament: Supplement Series
JTS	*Journal of Theological Studies*
LN	J. P. Louw and Eugene A. Nida, *Greek – English Lexicon of the New Testament: Based on Semantic Domains.* New York: United Bible Societies, 1989.
LNTS	Library of New Testament Studies
LS	Henry G. Liddell and Robert Scott, *Greek – English Lexicon.* Oxford: Clarendon Press, 1972.
MNTC	The Moffatt New Testament Commentary
NAC	New American Commentary
NASB	New American Standard Bible
NBBC	New Beacon Bible Commentary
NCBC	New Century Bible Commentary
Neot	*Neotestamentica*
NET	New English Translation
NETS	The New English Translation of the Septuagint
NICNT	New International Commentary on the New Testament
NIDNTT	*New International Dictionary of New Testament Theology*, ed. Colin Brown, 4 vols. Grand Rapids: Zondervan, 1975 – 1978.
NIV	New International Version
NIVAC	New International Version Application Commentary
NJB	New Jerusalem Bible
NKJV	New King James Version
NovT	*Novum Testamentum*
NRSV	New Revised Standard Version
NTC	The New Testament in Context
NTL	New Testament Library
NTS	*New Testament Studies*
PNTC	Pillar New Testament Commentary
P. S. I.	Pubblicazione della società italiana per la ricerca dei papiri greci e latini in Egitto: Papiri greci e latini, ed. G Vitelli et al., 14 vols. (1912 –).
RSV	Revised Standard Version
SBLDS	SBL Dissertation Series
SCJ	*Stone-Campbell Journal*
Sem	*Semeia*

SJT	*Scottish Journal of Theology*
SP	Sacra pagina
SPAW	Sitzungsberichte der Preussischen Akademie der Wissenschaften.
TDNT	*Theological Dictionary of the New Testament*, ed. G. Kittel and G. Friedrich, 10 vols. (1964 – 76).
TNTC	Tyndale New Testament Commentaries
TynBul	*The Tyndale Bulletin*
WBC	Word Biblical Commentary
WTJ	*Westminster Theological Journal*
ZEB	*Zondervan Encyclopedia of the Bible,* ed. Merrill C. Tenney, rev. Moisés Silva, 5 vols. Grand Rapids: Zondervan, 2009.
ZTK	*Zeitschrift für Theologie und Kirche*

Introduction to 1, 2, and 3 John

The three books of the NT that have come to us as 1, 2, and 3 John are so similar to each other that much that can be said of any one of them can be said about all three. Thus, this introduction will address those features of these books that are common to all three. The commentary on each of the three also is prefaced by a brief introduction that addresses issues specific to each letter.

Significance of the Letters

Before turning to historical matters, the question of why bother studying these books should be considered. Their presence in the NT, of course, demands the attention of those who believe the Bible to be God's Word. But what is the significance of these three brief letters toward the back of our Bibles?

Do you want to know God? Is the truth about God important to you? Knowing God truly is the overarching theme of both John's gospel and letters. In a world that was already filled with conflicting religions and philosophies, a world in that respect similar to our own, Jesus said, "Now this is eternal life: that they *know* you, the only true God, and Jesus Christ, whom you have sent" (John 17:3, italics added). Jesus defines eternal life as knowing God, for it is only through responding to God's self-revelation to humankind that any of us can come to know him and enjoy life with him both now and throughout eternity. That's a pretty significant issue for every person in any place in history.

Furthermore, Jesus claims that there is only one true God, the God who sent Jesus Christ into the world. There are many different, and often conflicting, views of God in various cultures today. We live in spiritually confusing times, especially as every culture becomes more religiously diverse. Many believe that it doesn't matter what you believe about a higher power as long as you believe it sincerely. But can any and all religions be true — everything from Eastern ideas about reincarnation to "new age" spirituality to beliefs taught in the sacred synagogues, mosques, and temples across North America and around the world? John wrote these three brief letters in a spiritually confusing time when there were conflicting theologies about Jesus Christ in order to assure his readers of their eternal life after death because they truly knew God in Christ. What could be more significant than that?

Authorship and Provenance

Church tradition from the earliest days of Christianity has ascribed these letters to John, commonly believed to be the apostle John — one of Jesus' chosen twelve, the son of Zebedee, and "the disciple whom Jesus loved" of John's gospel. But note that neither the text of the gospel nor that of the letters bears John's name, or any name. Second and Third John are from the pen of "the elder," who is not further identified. The letters and gospel are anonymous to us, but the Christians who originally received them undoubtedly knew the identity of the author, and it is likely on the ancient testimony of those believers that the letters have been ascribed to John.

But John (Gk. Ἰωάννης) was a common name at the time, and early in Christian history some came to doubt if "the elder" was the same man as the author of 1 John and John's gospel. Modern scholarship has complicated the issue even further with most NT scholars rejecting the identity of the beloved disciple as the apostle John and conjecturing as many as five different author/redactors for the gospel and letters.

The earliest ascription of authorship to John comes from Polycarp, bishop of Smyrna (d. AD 156), and from Papias, a contemporary of Polycarp, whose writings survive only as quotations in the later writings of Irenaeus and Eusebius. Both Polycarp and Papias lived in the greater vicinity of Ephesus in western Asia Minor, the location to which the apostle John is said to have fled at about the time when the Romans destroyed the temple in Jerusalem (AD 70), taking Mary the mother of Jesus with him. There he presumably lived for the rest of his long life, on into the reign of Trajan, the Roman emperor who ruled the empire from AD 98 to 117. Irenaeus (AD 175 – 195), bishop of Lyon, was born in Asia Minor and as a child personally knew Polycarp, who is said to have been appointed bishop of Smyrna by eyewitnesses of the Lord Jesus. Irenaeus says that John, the disciple of the Lord who was with Jesus in the upper room, wrote the gospel while living in Ephesus (*Haer.* 3.1.2). Even though such sources are subject to the same historical scrutiny as other ancient documents, this is a remarkable chain of historical witnesses enjoyed by no other NT book.

The witness of Papias is more complicated and has been the subject of more debate, for his writings are preserved only in those of Eusebius, whose interpretation of Papias's words raised the possibility of two men named John, one authoring the gospel and another, the elder John, the letters and the book of Revelation (*Hist. eccl.* 3.39.3 – 17). Papias mentions John twice, once as a "disciple of the Lord" and again as an "elder." But Eusebius overlooked the fact that even when Papias refers to Peter and James, he doesn't at first call them "apostles" but "elders," suggesting that the two titles were not mutually exclusive in Papias.[1] But ever since the fourth century when Eusebius wrote, there has been debate in the church about the authorship of

---

1. For a fuller discussion, see Karen H. Jobes, *Letters to the Church: A Survey of Hebrews and the General Epistles* (Grand Rapids: Zondervan, 2011), 399 – 407.

the three letters attributed in the NT to "John" and about who is buried in "John's tomb" in Ephesus.

Although the issue of authorship will not likely ever be known with certainty, the author of these letters clearly claims to be a bearer of the apostolic teaching about Jesus that was based on eyewitness testimony about his public ministry, death, and resurrection. The relationship between the three letters and between them and the gospel (see discussions below) indicates that the same author likely wrote all three letters, and he was also either the author of the gospel or a close associate. These letters insist that this apostolic testimony trumps any reinterpretation of Jesus by those who were not commissioned by him and who were far removed from personal knowledge of him.

Historical Situation: Anti-Gnostic Reading or Nonpolemical Reading?

As with every letter in the NT, we must infer the historical setting of John's letters and the reason they were written from the contents of the letters themselves, an innately subjective interpretive task that we undertake with little other information. It is difficult to read any text without making some assumptions about the situation for which it was written, when and where the author lived, and how to relate references in the text to the "real world." But just as a color sample placed against one background can appear as if it changes color when placed against a different background, the assumptions readers bring to what they read can make a big difference in how they understand the meaning of the text. Thus, it is important to continually check our assumptions about the historical background of the biblical books. It is clear that some disagreement has disrupted the churches under the author's purview and spiritual authority, and that he is concerned to reassure his congregations of their salvation as they adhere to the teachings and beliefs about Jesus that the author represents.

The major themes of right belief about Jesus, a right attitude toward sin, and interpersonal relationships characterized by love are clear, but why the author has chosen to discuss these particular topics is not. He reinforces his authority as a bearer of the apostolic teaching about the revelation of God in Jesus Christ, which implies that the source of truth about God in Christ was in some dispute. But the author writes with the intent of a pastor to care for his people rather than as an apologist to argue directly against those who have left the Johannine church(es). As Brooke wrote, "It is probably true that the writer never loses sight altogether of the views of his opponents in any part of the Epistle. But it is important to emphasize the fact that, in spite of this, the real aim of the Epistle is not exclusively, or even primarily, polemical."[2]

---

2. Alan Brooke, *A Critical and Exegetical Commentary on the Johannine Epistles* (ICC; Edinburgh: T&T Clark, 1912), xxvii.

Nevertheless, scholarship throughout the late nineteenth and twentieth centuries spent much time and ink on reconstructing the more specific nature of the false teaching with the assumption that it had an antinomian impulse motivated by (proto-)gnostic tendencies.[3] The gnostic assumption was developed in the twentieth century by Rudolf Bultmann,[4] after which time the three letters were routinely read against the specific christological error of Docetism, which derived from the application of gnostic thought to the gospel of Jesus Christ, and against licentious living, which was one conclusion of gnostic thought applied to Christian living. Read through this lens, the verbs of sense in the prologue of 1 John were taken to drive home the physicality of Jesus as a real human being, as also was his coming in flesh (1 John 4:2; 2 John 7).

The late twentieth and early twenty-first centuries have brought another perspective that has been gaining ground, that these letters should *not* be read as a direct polemic against Docetism or its specific Ephesian expression, Cerinthianism.[5] Tradition teaches that Cerinthus was a contemporary of John in Ephesus and taught that the divine nature descended upon the ordinary man Jesus at his baptism and departed from him in Gethsemane, a view referred to as adoptionism by modern theologians. (See commentary 1 John 2:19.) Offering several factors that argue against a presumed gnostic background, Lieu writes, "Granted that this framework of interpretation has the compelling advantage of allowing, at least superficially, a consistent exegesis of the whole letter, the question must be asked how far it is valid and true to the thought and function of 1 John."[6]

This recent nonpolemical view is a needed corrective to Johannine scholarship that has depended so heavily on identifying what the secessionists believed and why they left (1 John 2:19), and to refocus the discussion in terms that sit better with the author's own statements about why he wrote. His concern was to shepherd those in his spiritual care to remain within the bounds of orthodoxy rather than to directly address the heresy(-ies) that disrupted the church(es); that makes it difficult to reconstruct with specificity the problems being addressed. It does free interpreters to focus their attention on how John defines orthodoxy, which in fact implicitly argues against not only Cerinthianism, Docetism, and Gnosticism more broadly, but many heresies through the centuries and in our own time.

---

3. E.g., this approach is seen in J. Lias, *The First Epistle of St. John: With Exposition and Homiletical Treatment* (Chicago: A. C. McClurg, 1887), 132, adopted and developed by William Alexander, *The Expositor's Bible,* 1903, available at http://hdl.handle.net/2027/uva.x002599581 (accessed 1 March 2012).

4. Rudolf Bultmann, *The Johannine Epistles* (Hermeneia; trans. R. Philip O'Hara with Lane C. McGaughy and Robert W. Funk; Philadelphia: Fortress, 1973), 38, 46, 47.

5. Judith M. Lieu, "'Authority to Become Children of God': A Study of 1 John." *NovT* 23 (1981): 210–28; Hansjörg Schmid,

"How to Read the First Epistle of John Non-polemically," *Bib* 85 (2004): 24; Terry Griffith, *Keep Yourselves from Idols: A New Look at 1 John* (JSNTSup 233; Sheffield: Sheffield Academic, 2002); idem, "A Non-polemical Reading of 1 John: Sin Christology and the Limits of Johannine Christianity," *TynBul* 49 (1998): 253–76; Daniel Streett, *They Went Out from Us: The Identity of the Opponents in First John* (Berlin: De Gruyter, 2011).

6. Lieu, "Authority to Become," 210.

Nevertheless, it is clear from John's letters that he was arguing *against* some serious misunderstanding and distortion of the gospel. Given the likely setting in Ephesus and the likely date of the letters, the influence of Greek philosophical assumptions, perhaps combined with a misunderstanding of the promises of John's gospel, had produced beliefs that were, perhaps unwittingly, opposed to the gospel of Jesus Christ (i.e., they were "anti-Christ" beliefs).

Relationship of the Letters to John's Gospel

It remains true that although 1 John's primary purpose was not polemical, the schism within the community was the immediate occasion of the letter, and the origins of that schism are to be seen in those elements in the thought of the community of 1 John that necessitated both the christological and the moral debate. It is when we trace *the roots of these elements to the Fourth Gospel* that we can understand better the problem and the achievement of I John.[7]

The similarities between John's letters and the Fourth Gospel indicate some relationship between them.

Some Similarities between John's Gospel and the Epistles of John

Gospel of John	1 John	2 John	3 John
John 1:1 In the beginning was the Word, and the Word was with God, and the Word was God. *John 1:14* The Word became flesh and made his dwelling among us. *John 15:26* "When the Advocate comes, whom I will send to you from the Father — the Spirit of truth who goes out from the Father — he will testify about me. *John 15:27* And you also must testify, for you have been with me from the beginning.	*1 John 1:1* What was from the beginning, what we have heard, what we have seen with our eyes, what we have perceived, and our hands have touched — this we proclaim about the Word of Life.		
John 3:21 But whoever lives by the **truth** comes into the light	*1 John 1:6* If we say,"We have fellowship with him." and walk in the darkness, we lie and we do not do the **truth**.	*2 John 4* I rejoice greatly because I have found some of your children walking in the **truth**.	*3 John 3* I rejoice greatly when brothers come and tell of your **truth** — how you are walking in the truth.
John 1:5 The light shines in the darkness, and the darkness has not overcome it.	*1 John 2:8* … because the darkness is passing away and the true light is already shining.		

---

7. Ibid., 225 (italics added).

Gospel of John	1 John	2 John	3 John
John 8:12 When Jesus spoke again to the people, he said, "I am the light of the world. Whoever follows me will never walk in darkness, but will have the light of life."	*1 John 1:5* And this is the message that we have heard from him and announce to you: God is light, and there is no darkness in him at all. *1 John 2:9* The one who says, "I am in the light," and hates their brother or sister is still in the darkness.		
John 1:12 – 13 Yet to all who did receive him, to those who believed in his name, he gave the right to become children of God — children born not of natural descent, nor of human decision or a husband's will, but born of God.	*1 John 5:1* Everyone who believes that Jesus is the Christ has been born of God.		
John 15:12 My command is this: Love each other as I have loved you.	*1 John 3:23* And this is his command: to believe in the name of his Son, Jesus Christ, and to love one another, just as he gave the command to us.	*2 John 5* And now I ask you, lady — not as writing you a new command, but [as writing a command] that we have had from the beginning — that we love one another	
John 15:7 If you remain in me and my words remain in you, ask whatever you wish, and it will be done for you.	*1 John 3:24* And the one who keeps his commands remains in him [God], and he himself in them; and in this way we know that he remains in us: from the Spirit, whom he gave to us.	*2 John 9* Everyone who goes beyond and does not remain in the teaching of Christ does not have God. The one who remains in the teaching [of Christ], this one has both the Father and the Son.	
John 13:34 A new command I give you.	*1 John 2:8* Yet I am writing to you a new command.		
John 14:16 And I will ask the Father, and he will give you another **advocate** to help you and be with you forever.	*1 John 2:1* But if someone should sin, we have a *paraclete* with the Father — the righteous Jesus Christ.		

Gospel of John	1 John	2 John	3 John
John 17:3 Now this is eternal **life**: that they **know** you, the only true God, and Jesus Christ, whom you have sent.	*1 John 2:25* And this is the promise that he himself promised us — eternal **life**. *1 John 5:11* And this is the testimony: that God has given eternal **life** to us and this **life** is in his Son.		
John 14:6 Jesus answered, "I am the way and the truth and the life. No one comes to the Father except through me."	*1 John 2:23* No one who denies the Son has the Father either. The one who acknowledges the Son has the Father also.		
	1 John 2:18 Children, it is the last hour, and just as you heard that **antichrist** is coming, even now many have become antichrists, and so we know that it is the last hour.	*2 John 7* Many deceivers have gone into the world, those who do not confess Jesus Christ coming in the flesh; such a person is the deceiver and the **antichrist**.	
John 13:30 As soon as Judas had taken the bread, he went out. And it was night.	*1 John 2:19* They have gone out from us, but they were not of us.		
John 20:31 But these are written that you may believe that Jesus is the Messiah, the Son of God, and that by believing you may have life in his name.	*1 John 5:13* These things I write to you who believe in the name of the Son of God so that you might know that you have eternal life.		

If these similarities did not originate with the same author, then the two authors stand closely in the same tradition about Jesus and probably personally knew one another. Despite some differences that can probably be accounted for by their different genres, the letters of John and the gospel of John are closer in language, style, dualistic worldview, and theology than they are to any other NT books. Painter observes that the similarities between the gospel and letters are closer than between other books of the NT known to have the same author, such as Luke and Acts or 1 and 2 Thessalonians.[8]

---

8. John Painter, *1, 2, and 3 John* (SP 18; Collegeville, MN: Liturgical, 2002), 68; see his extensive discussion of this issue, pp. 58–74; also I. Howard Marshall, *The Epistles of John* (NICNT; Grand Rapids: Eerdmans, 1978), 31–42.

The obvious similarities raise the methodological question of whether we should allow, and deliberately use, the Fourth Gospel to influence our exegesis of these letters. For instance, should the referent or sense of a particular term in the letters be defined by the occurrence of the same term in the gospel? While the overall similarities compel us in that direction, the different purposes for which the gospel and letters were written may caution against too quickly equating the sense of the two. In fact, some interpreters suggest that it was a misunderstanding and misuse of John's gospel that gave rise to the false teaching in the Johannine church(es), and that the letters use the same terms as the gospel but with the intent of correcting heresy. This, of course, assumes that the gospel was written and circulated first, that problems developed in its interpretation and use, and that the letters followed.

Thatcher presents another option, that although the letters and gospel arose from the same historical moment and tradition, the controversy developed before the Fourth Gospel was written while the Johannine teaching about Jesus was still in oral form.[9] Thatcher proposes that the letters were written to quell the controversy in the absence of an authoritative, written narrative of Jesus' life. In Thatcher's view the controversy called John's gospel into existence. Although this theory is interesting and creative, it seems that the letters correlate so well to the gospel in its written form that the oral tradition would have had to be essentially identical to John's gospel.

Relationship and Date of the Three Letters

A similar question can be raised about the sequence and relationship between the three letters themselves. The themes, style, and vocabulary are so similar between 1 and 2 John that it is hard to imagine they didn't come from the same hand. And the similarities between 2 John and 3 John — both being from "the elder," whose main concern was when to extend Christian hospitality (3 John) and when not to (2 John) — join them as two sides of the same coin. (See Introduction to 2 and 3 John.) This observation has led commentators to propose a number of theories about the sequence in which these letters were written.

Strecker thinks 1 John originated independently of and later than 2 and 3 John, a view held also by Marshall, who structures his commentary by addressing the books in that order.[10] Johnson proposes that all three were written by the same person at the same time and delivered as a package.[11] By that theory, Demetrius carried a letter of introduction to Gaius (3 John), along with a letter to be read in Gaius's church (2 John) as an introduction to the sermon to be delivered (1 John). Painter believes

---

9. Tom Thatcher, *Why John Wrote a Gospel: Jesus – Memory – History* (Louisville: Westminster John Knox, 2006).

10. Georg Strecker, *The Johannine Letters: A Commentary on 1, 2, and 3 John* (Hermeneia; Minneapolis: Fortress, 1995), 3; Marshall, *Epistles of John.*

11. Luke Timothy Johnson, *The Writings of the New Testament: An Interpretation* (rev. ed.; Minneapolis: Fortress, 1999), 560 – 61.

all three were written by the elder, and probably in the order in which they appear in the NT, a view shared by this writer.[12] I propose the scenario that 1 John was written and preached in the elder's home church soon after the schism. But because the secessionists had gone out, taking their false teaching with them potentially to other churches in the area, John sends 1 John to other churches with a cover letter (2 John) to "the chosen lady and her children." For whatever reason, Diotrephes refuses to receive the bearers of 2 and 1 John, and so the elder turns to his friend Gaius for support, sending Demetrius with a letter of introduction in hand (3 John). While it is almost impossible to study John's letters without imagining some such situation, any scenario must be held lightly and not allowed to dictate exegesis, for we simply do not know the details of the circumstances that relate these books to one another.

If we assume that John's gospel was written about AD 85–90 and that the letters followed after the gospel had been in circulation for some time, the letters probably date from about AD 90–95, making them perhaps the last books of the NT to have been written. The gospel of John and the three letters of John appear to have been written to people within the same geographical area (probably the Roman province of Asia, which we know as the westernmost region of Turkey). The Christians named in 3 John knew each other personally, suggesting a network of churches in the same region that had frequent and routine contact. The reason 3 John, such a brief note written to one person, Gaius, was preserved is probably that it is an important part of the same story for which 1 John and 2 John were written. Therefore, we are warranted to read these three letters in light of each other and to read the letters in light of the gospel of John.

The Place of John's Letters in the Chronology of New Testament History

Historical-grammatical exegesis is the methodological approach used by most evangelical biblical scholars. That means interpreting the text within its original historical context and paying close attention to the actual words, syntax, and structure of the text in its original language. Notice that this is not how the church reads the Bible, generally speaking. Devotional and liturgical reading tends to dehistoricize the text by being largely unaware of its historical setting and by reading the Bible as translated into a modern language.

It is certainly true, though often not considered by the general reader, that the books of the NT were not written in the order in which they appear in the NT canon. And so at the start of study, it is helpful to consider where in the chronology of NT history a book was written, and what was happening at that time that might inform

12. Painter, *1, 2, and 3 John*, 52; as also Raymond E. Brown, *The Epistles of John* (AB; New York: Doubleday, 1982), 30; Colin G. Kruse, *The Letters of John* (PNTC; Grand Rapids: Eerdmans, 2000), 7–8.

exegesis of the book. Then further, it is helpful to consider why the book appears in the sequence in which it does in the NT. Surely there was some rhyme and reason for the books to have been placed in the canonical order we find them in.

All books of the NT refer to events that happened in the first century of this era (i.e., AD 1 – 100, as the modern calendar numbers years), such as the life of Jesus, the spread of the gospel, and issues that arose in the infant churches. The NT books were themselves written in the second half of that century. The NT as a whole is focused on one person who lived in the early third of the first century, Jesus of Nazareth, and the significance of his life, death, and resurrection. The Gospels telling that story were written some decades later and so are concerned, first, with the events of Jesus' lifetime recorded but, second, with what was happening in the churches to which each gospel was addressed and which shaped their content. Thus, it is appropriate to consider what was happening in the church(es) that were the original recipients of John's gospel, most likely the last gospel to be written.

The NT letters are different from these narrative accounts of the life of Jesus because each letter addressed pressing issues of the moment rather than recounting events from a previous time period. The authors of the letters are addressing real questions, issues, and circumstances that are pressing at that moment of time. Consequently, they allow us to distinguish three periods of the first century and place the events and the origin of the books within each period: (1) Jesus' lifetime, during which no NT books were written; (2) a period of great expansion of the gospel throughout the Roman empire (AD 33 – 60); (3) a period of doctrinal and ecclesial unification (c. AD 60 – 100). The gospel and letters of John were written within this last period, when the church at large faced huge issues, such as organized persecution of Christians by the Roman government, heresy infiltrating the church (especially from the various Greek philosophies), and a crisis of church leadership, especially as the apostles died and the Lord had not returned.

John's letters reflect the second and third issues: heresy and a crisis of leadership. False teachers had emerged from the elder's own church(es), and their beliefs were challenging his apostolic leadership. If the elder was John son of Zebedee, he was likely elderly and the last living apostle. As the church stood on the brink of an uncertain future in the midst of a transition to church leaders who were not apostles, there was no more critical issue than where the truth about Jesus Christ was to be found. The elder argues that Christian leadership is essentially conservative, preserving and passing to the next generation the teaching of the apostles whom the Lord himself had chosen. Innovation in Christian belief and practice had to be bounded by apostolic orthodoxy. This is relevant in every generation of the church until the Lord returns.

Canonicity

In principle, each of the books of the NT was endued with its normative, authoritative value as soon as the ink dried, by virtue of having been written by a divinely inspired, apostolic author. But it still took time for each book that ultimately is listed in the NT canon to be recognized as such, especially when the text began to circulate beyond the original readers and churches to which each was written. Raymond Brown summarizes:

> By the mid-second century ideas, themes, and even slogans of the Johannine Epistles (or, at least, of I John) were being cited in other Christian works. But no one of the proposed similarities consists of a verbatim citation, so that it is still very difficult to be certain that any of the mentioned authors had the text of a Johannine Epistle before him.[13]

Nevertheless, it is likely that the text of 1 John was available to Polycarp (AD 69–155), who lived in Smyrna, a city in the region of Ephesus. Polycarp's *Letter to the Philippians* 7:1 (written prior to AD 140) contains a clear parallel with 1 John 4:2–3 and 2 John 7, "Everyone who does not confess Jesus Christ to have come in the flesh is antichrist," though he does not attribute it to John or his letters. There may be other, less obvious allusions to John's letters in texts written before AD 175,[14] but the earliest certain attestation of all three of these letters that has survived is from Origen (c. AD 250), who wrote that John "left also an epistle of a very few lines and, it may be, a second and a third, for not all say that these [the second and third] are genuine" (quoted in Eusebius, *Hist. eccl.* 6.25.10). The apostolic authorship of 1 John was apparently unquestioned, and Eusebius lists it among the recognized books (see Introduction to 2 and 3 John for a discussion of the evidence from Irenaeus, who quotes both 1 and 2 John as if they were one book, which suggests they may have circulated together). All three letters were recognized as canonical by the fourth century and are included in Athanasius's canon list (AD 367).

---

13. Brown, *Epistles of John*, 9.   14. Ibid., 6–9. See pp. 5–13 for a more complete survey of the ancient evidence.

Select Bibliography

Commentaries

Akin, Daniel L. *1, 2, 3 John*. NAC 38. Nashville: Broadman & Holman, 2001.

Bray, Gerald, ed. *James, 1 – 2 Peter, 1 – 3 John, Jude*. ACCS 11. Downers Grove, IL: InterVarsity Press, 2000.

Brooke, A. E. *A Critical and Exegetical Commentary on the Johannine Epistles*. ICC. Edinburgh: T&T Clark, 1912.

Brown, Raymond E. *The Epistles of John*. AB 30. New York: Doubleday, 1982.

Bultmann, Rudolf. *The Johannine Epistles*. Hermenia. Translated by R. Philip O'Hara with Lane C. McGaughy and Robert W. Funk. Philadelphia: Fortress, 1973.

Burge, Gary M. *The Letters of John*. NIVAC. Grand Rapids: Zondervan, 1996.

Calvin, John. *Commentaries on the Catholic Epistles*. Translated by John Owen. Vol. 22 of *Calvin's Commentaries*. Grand Rapids: Baker, 1999.

Culpepper, R. Alan. *The Gospel and Letters of John*. Nashville: Abingdon, 1998.

Dodd, C. H. *The Johannine Epistles*. MNTC. London: Hodder and Stoughton, 1946.

Grayston, Kenneth. *The Johannine Epistles*. NCBC. Grand Rapids: Eerdmans, 1984.

Kruse, Colin G. *The Letters of John*. PNTC. Grand Rapids: Eerdmans, 2000.

Lieu, Judith M. *I, II, & III John: A Commentary*. NTL. Louisville: Westminster John Knox, 2008.

Marshall, I. Howard. *The Epistles of John*. NICNT. Grand Rapids: Eerdmans, 1978.

McDermond, J. E. *1, 2, 3 John*. BCBC. Harrisonburg, VA: Herald, 2011.

Ngewa, Samuel. "1 John," "2 John," "3 John." Pages 1529 – 38 in *The Africa Bible Commentary*. Edited by T. Adeyemo. Grand Rapids: Zondervan, 2006.

Painter, John. *1, 2, and 3 John*. SP 18. Collegeville, MN: Liturgical, 2002.

Schnackenburg, Rudolf. *The Johannine Epistles: A Commentary*. Translated by Reginald and Ilse Fuller. New York: Crossroad, 1992.

Schuchard, Bruce G. *1 – 3 John*. Concordia Commentary. St. Louis: Concordia, 2012.

Smalley, Stephen S. *1, 2, 3 John*. WBC 51. Waco, TX: Word, 1984.

Smith, D. Moody. *First, Second, and Third John*. Interpretation. Louisville: John Knox, 1991.

Stott, John. *The Epistles of John*. TNTC. Grand Rapids: Eerdmans, 1964.

Strecker, Georg. *The Johannine Letters: A Commentary on 1, 2, and 3 John*. Hermeneia. Minneapolis: Fortress, 1995.

Thatcher, Tom. "1 John," "2 John," "3 John." Pages 414 – 538 in *The Expositor's Bible Commentary*, vol. 13. Rev. ed. Edited by Tremper Longman III and David E. Garland. Grand Rapids: Zondervan, 2006.

Thomas, John Christopher. *The Pentecostal Commentary on 1 John, 2 John, 3 John*. Cleveland, TN: Pilgrim, 2004.

Thompson, Marianne Meye. *1 – 3 John*. IVPNTC. Downers Grove, IL: InterVarsity Press, 1992.

Von Wahlde, Urban C. *The Gospel and Letters of John*. 3 vols. Grand Rapids: Eerdmans, 2010.

Williamson, Rick. *1, 2, & 3 John: A Commentary in the Wesleyan Tradition*. NBBC. Kansas City: Beacon Hill, 2010.

Witherington, Ben III. *A Socio-Rhetorical Commentary on Titus, 1 – 2 Timothy and 1 – 3 John*. Vol. 1: *Letters and Homilies for Hellenized Christians*. Downers Grove, IL: InterVarsity Press, 2006.

Yarbrough, Robert W. *1 – 3 John*. BECNT. Grand Rapids: Baker Academic, 2008.

1 John

Bass, Christopher D. *That You May Know: Assurance of Salvation in 1 John*. NAC Studies in Bible and Theology 5. Nashville: Broadman & Holman, 2008.

Brickle, Jeffrey E. *Aural Design and Coherence in the Prologue of 1 John*. London: T&T Clark, 2012.

Callow, John. "Where Does 1 John 1 End?" Pages 393 – 406 in *Discourse Analysis and the New Testament: Approaches and Results*. Edited by Stanley E. Porter and Jeffrey T. Reed. JSNTSup 170. Sheffield: Sheffield Academic, 1999.

Carson, D. A. "The Three Witnesses and the Eschatology of 1 John." Pages 216 – 32 in *To Tell the Mystery: Essays on New Testament Eschatology in Honor of Robert H. Gundry*. Edited by Thomas E. Schmidt and Moisés Silva. JSNTSup 100. Sheffield: Sheffield Academic, 1994.

Coetzee, J. C. "The Holy Spirit in 1 John." *Neot* 13 (1979): 43 – 67.

De Boer, Martinus. "The Death of Jesus Christ and His Coming in the Flesh (1 John 4:2)." *NovT* 33 (1991): 326 – 46.

Dudrey, Russ. "1 John and the Public Reading of Scripture." *SCJ* 6 (Fall 2003): 235 – 55.

Edwards, M. J. "Martyrdom and the First Epistle of John." *NovT* 31 (1989): 164 – 71.

Griffith, Terry. *Keep Yourselves from Idols: A New Look at 1 John*. JSNTSup 233. Sheffield: Sheffield Academic, 2002.

———. "A Non-polemical Reading of 1 John: Sin, Christology and the Limits of Johannine Christianity." *TynBul* 49 (1998): 253 – 76.

Hills, Julian. " 'Little Children, Keep Yourselves from Idols': 1 John 5:21 Reconsidered." *CBQ* 51 (1989): 285 – 310.

Kim, Jintae. "The Concept of Atonement in 1 John: A Redevelopment of the Second Temple Concept of Atonement." PhD diss., Westminster Theological Seminary, 2003.

———. "The Concept of Atonement in Hellenistic Thought and 1 John." *JGRChJ* 2 (2001 – 2005): 100 – 116.

Kruse, Colin G. "Sin and Perfection in 1 John." *ABR* 51 (2003): 60 – 70.

Lieu, Judith M. " 'Authority to Become Children of God': A Study of 1 John." *NovT* 23 (1981): 210 – 28.

———. "Us or You? Persuasion and Identity in 1 John." *JBL* 127 (2008): 805 – 19.

Longacre, Robert. "Towards an Exegesis of 1 John Based on the Discourse Analysis of the Greek Text." Pages 271 – 86 in *Linguistics and New Testament Interpretation: Essays on Discourse*

Analysis. Ed. David Alan Black. Nashville: Broadman, 1992.

Michaels, J. Ramsey. "By Water and Blood: Sin and Purification in John and First John." Pages 149–62 in *Dimensions of Baptism: Biblical and Theological Studies.* Edited by Stanley E. Porter and Anthony R. Cross. London: Sheffield Academic, 2002.

Moberly, R. W. L. "'Test the Spirits': God, Love, and Critical Discernment in 1 John 4." Pages 296–307 in *The Holy Spirit and Christian Origins: Essays in Honor of James D. G. Dunn.* Edited by Graham Stanton, Bruce Longenecker, and Stephen Barton. Grand Rapids: Eerdmans, 2004.

Olsson, Birger. "First John: Discourse Analyses and Interpretations." Pages 369–91 in *Discourse Analysis and the New Testament: Approaches and Results.* Edited by Stanley E. Porter and Jeffrey T. Reed. JSNTSup 170. Sheffield: Sheffield Academic, 1999.

Schmid, Hansjörg. "How to Read the First Epistle of John Non-polemically." *Bib* 85 (2004): 24–41.

Scholer, David M. "Sins Within and Sins Without: An Interpretation of 1 John 5:16–17." Pages 230–46 in *Current Issues in Biblical and Patristic Interpretation.* Edited by Gerald F. Hawthorne. Grand Rapids: Eerdmans, 1975.

Streett, Daniel R. *They Went Out from Us: The Identity of the Opponents in First John.* Berlin: De Gruyter, 2011.

Sugit, J. N. "I John 5:21: ΤΕΚΝΙΑ, ΦΥΛΑΞΑΤΕ ΕΑΥΤΑ ΑΠΟ ΤΩΝ ΕΙΔΩΛΩΝ." *JTS* 36 (1985): 386–90.

Tan, Randall K. J. "Should We Pray for Straying Brethren? John's Confidence in 1 John 5:16–17." *JETS* 45 (2002): 599–609.

Thatcher, Tom. "'Water and Blood' in Anti-Christ Christianity (1 John 5:6)." *SCJ* 4 (2001): 235–48.

Washburn, David I. "Third Class Conditions in First John." *GTJ* 11 (1990): 221–28.

Watson, Duane F. "'Keep Yourselves from Idols': A Socio-Rhetorical Analysis of the *Exordium* and *Peroratio* of 1 John." Pages 281–302 in *Fabrics of Discourse: Essays in Honor of Vernon K. Robbins.* Edited by David B. Gowler, L. Gregory Bloomquist, and Duane F. Watson. Harrisburg: Trinity Press International, 2003.

Yarid, John R. "Reflections of the Upper Room Discourse in 1 John." *BSac* 160 (2003): 65–76.

2 and 3 John

Akin, Daniel L. "Truth or Consequences: 2 John 1–13." *Faith & Mission* 23, no. 1 (2005): 3–12.

Campbell, Barth L. "Honor, Hospitality and Haughtiness: The Contention for Leadership in 3 John." *EvQ* 77 (2005): 321–41.

Floor, Sebastiaan. "A Discourse Analysis of 3 John." *Notes on Translation* 4, no. 4 (1990): 1–17.

Funk, Robert W. "The Form and Structure of II and III John." *JBL* 86 (1967): 424–30.

Lee, Chee Chiew, "The ἐκλεκτῇ κυρίᾳ of 2 John: A Metaphor for the Church and Its Theological Implications for the Contemporary Church." ThM thesis, Singapore Bible College, 2005.

Lieu, Judith M. *The Second and Third Epistles of John: History and Background.* Edinburgh: T&T Clark, 1986.

Malherbe, Abraham J. "The Inhospitality of Diotrephes." Pages 222–32 in *God's Christ and His People: Studies in Honour of Nils Alstrup Dahl.* Edited by Jacob Jervell and Wayne A. Meeks. Oslo: Universitetsforlaget, 1977.

Malina, Bruce J. "The Received View and What It Cannot Do: III John and Hospitality." *Sem* 36 (1986): 181–83.

Mitchell, Margaret M. "'Diotrephes Does Not Receive Us': The Lexicographical and Social Context of 3 John 9–10." *JBL* 117 (1998): 299–320.

Watson, Duane F. "A Rhetorical Analysis of 2 John according to Greco-Roman Convention." *NTS* 35 (1989): 104–30.

———. "A Rhetorical Analysis of 3 John: A Study in Epistolary Rhetoric." *CBQ* 51 (1989): 479–501.

General

Anderson, John L. *An Exegetical Summary of 1, 2, and 3 John*. Dallas: SIL, 1992.

Bauckham, Richard. *Jesus and the Eyewitnesses*. Grand Rapids: Eerdmans, 2006.

Chapman, John. "'We Know That His Testimony Is True.'" *JTS* 31 (1930): 379–86.

Culy, Martin M. *I, II, III John: A Handbook on the Greek Text*. Waco, TX: Baylor University Press, 2004.

Gundry, Robert H. *Jesus the Word according to John the Sectarian*. Grand Rapids: Eerdmans, 2002.

Haas, C., M. de Jonge, and J. L. Swellengrebel. *The Letters of John*. UBS Handbook Series. New York: United Bible Societies, 1972.

Harnack, Adolf von. *"Das 'Wir' in den Johanneischen Schriften."* SPAW. Berlin: Akademie der Wissenschaften, 1923.

Jackson, Howard M. "Ancient Self-Referential Conventions and Their Implications for the Authorship and Integrity of the Gospel of John." *JTS*, n.s. 50 (1999): 1–34.

Klauck, Hans-Josef, with Daniel P. Bailey. *Ancient Letters and the New Testament: A Guide to Context and Exegesis*. Waco, TX: Baylor University Press, 2006.

Köstenberger, Andreas J. *A Theology of John's Gospel and Letters*. BTNT. Grand Rapids: Zondervan, 2009.

Kysar, Robert. "The Expulsion from the Synagogue: The Tale of a Theory." Pages 237–45 in *Voyages with John: Charting the Fourth Gospel*. Waco, TX: Baylor University Press, 2005.

Lindars, Barnabas, Ruth B. Edwards, and J. M. Court, eds. *The Johannine Literature*. Sheffield: Sheffield Academic, 2000.

Menken, Maarten J. J. "Envoys of God's Envoy: On the Johannine Communities." *Proceedings of the Irish Biblical Association* 23 (2000): 45–60.

Pate, C. Marvin. *The Writings of John*. Grand Rapids: Zondervan, 2011.

Sloyan, Gerard S. *Walking in the Truth: Perseverers and Deserters: The First, Second, and Third Letters of John*. NTC. Valley Forge, PA: Trinity Press International, 1995.

Thatcher, Tom. *Why John Wrote a Gospel: Jesus – Memory – History*. Louisville: Westminster John Knox, 2006.

Trebilco, Paul. *The Early Christians in Ephesus from Paul to Ignatius*. Grand Rapids: Eerdmans, 2004.

Introduction to 1 John

Genre and Purpose

We know 1 John originated in a written form because the verb "I/we write [γράφω] these things" occurs more than a dozen times in reference to the letter (e.g., 1 John 1:4; 2:1; 5:13). Yet this document does not have the form of personal correspondence since it lacks an address and salutation and a letter closing. Because of this, there was once an attempt to call such a writing an "epistle" in distinction from a letter, but scholars have largely abandoned that distinction. Furthermore, the structure shows characteristics suggesting the author intended it to be read or performed aloud (see Structure, below). Most likely it originally served as a sermon in the author's church, and it was then circulated to other outlying churches in the area.

Socio-rhetorical analysis leads to the conclusion that 1 John was written with the purpose of "increasing audience adherence to the Johannine tradition and assuring its continued fellowship with the Johannine community, God, and Christ," and that the letter can be categorized as epideictic rhetoric, targeted to increase the audience's adherence to values it already holds.[1] Specifically, the author is keen to convince his readers to continue in their faith in Jesus Christ despite the disruption and confusion caused by members of the community who have left the church (2:19).

The false theology of the secessionists may have been especially confusing because it used the same language as and originated out of the Johannine tradition itself. "This [secessionist] theology has much in common with the author's own and appeals to the same stock of tradition that he does, a tradition to which we have access through the Gospel of John. In short, the author writes against the background of a Johannine thoughtworld that he assumes is familiar to both his readers and his opponents."[2] The author's purpose is then to untwist distorted understandings of statements found in John's gospel and to correct errant theology, in order to keep his readers aligned with the truth that has been revealed in Jesus Christ.

---

1. Duane F. Watson, "'Keep Yourselves from Idols': A Socio-Rhetorical Analysis of the *Exordium* and *Peroratio* of 1 John," in *Fabrics of Discourse: Essays in Honor of Vernon K. Robbins* (ed. David B. Gowler, L. Gregory Bloomquist, and Duane F. Watson; Harrisburg, PA: Trinity Press International, 2003), 282, 284.

2. Martinus De Boer, "The Death of Jesus Christ and His Coming in the Flesh (1 John 4:2)," *NovT* 33 (1991): 331.

Structure

The structure of 1 John is difficult to outline because its thought is circular more than linear. It returns to the same intertwined themes — sin, love, and sound Christology — again and again, developing each further in light of what has been said of the other two. Walter Moberly observes:

> John's pattern of thinking does not involve sequential logic in the manner of a conventional argument so much as the literary equivalent of musical variations on a theme — a constant circling around the basic issue, coming at it from a variety of angles, developing now this aspect and now that aspect, balancing one statement with another to clarify what is and is not entailed, returning to a point already made so that it may be seen afresh in the light of what has been said subsequently.[3]

Duane Watson argues that "the repetitive and emphatic nature of 1 John is explained by the author's use of Greco-Roman amplification techniques," which function to "strengthen adherence to traditional and honorable truths" — in this case clarifying the Johannine tradition "through repetition and emphasis of themes and topics, drawing subtle distinctions between Johannine tradition and its aberrant forms as taught by the secessionists."[4] The resulting structure helps the audience to see more clearly where their allegiance should be.

Attempts by modern scholars to describe and outline the structure of 1 John depend on the methodology employed. John's letters have been subjected most frequently to analysis based on semantic discourse analysis, which observes criteria such as spanning, boundaries, coherence, and marked prominence.[5] Discourse analysis concludes with different structures than, for instance, that revealed by the method of classical Greco-Roman rhetoric, but even the results of discourse analysis vary widely.[6] Relatively recent recognition of the aural design of a text intended to be read aloud suggests other structures.[7] Exegetical outlines display yet other features of the text, and virtually no two exegetes segment their commentaries exactly the same way. Partly this is because there are several janus verses in 1 John, verses that bridge two sections and can be grouped with either. We must also recognize that with human

---

3. R. W. L. Moberly, "'Test the Spirits': God, Love, and Critical Discernment in 1 John 4," in *The Holy Spirit and Christian Origins: Essays in Honor of James D. G. Dunn* (ed. G. Stanton, B. Longenecker, and S. Barton; Grand Rapids: Eerdmans, 2004), 298.

4. Duane F. Watson, "Rhetorical Criticism of Hebrews and the General Epistles since 1978," *CurBS* 5 (1997): 198.

5. See Grace E. Sherman and John C. Tuggy, *A Semantic and Structural Analysis of the Johannine Epistles* (Dallas: SIL, 1994); David J. Clark, "Discourse Structure in 3 John," *BT* 57 (July 2006): 109 – 15; Sebastiaan Floor, "A Discourse Analysis of 3 John," *Notes on Translation* 4, no. 4 (1990): 1 – 17; Birger

Olsson, "First John: Discourse Analyses and Interpretations," in *Discourse Analysis and the New Testament: Approaches and Results* (ed. Stanley E. Porter and Jeffrey T. Reed; Sheffield: Sheffield Academic, 1999), 369 – 91; Robert Longacre, "Towards an Exegesis of 1 John Based on the Discourse Analysis of the Greek Text," in *Linguistics and New Testament Interpretation: Essays on Discourse Analysis* (ed. David Alan Black; Nashville: Broadman, 1992), 271 – 86.

6. Watson, "'Keep Yourselves from Idols,'" 281 – 302.

7. Jeffrey E. Brickle, *Aural Design and Coherence in the Prologues of First John* (LNTS 465; London: T&T Clark, 2012).

communication being what it is, no discourse follows exactly the principles of either its contemporaneous conventions or, much less, the theories of modern scholarship.

Modern analyses using various methodolgies have shown that 1 John is a carefully crafted work. Based on discourse analysis Callow concludes in his analysis of 1 John 1 that "not only is this a strongly structured piece of writing, but it is also lexically cohesive."[8] Brickle concludes from an aural analysis of the sound patterns in the prologue of 1 John that "while John did not strive to meet classical standards ... he clearly demonstrates the ability to compose in an aurally and rhetorically powerful manner."[9] The outline offered below is the result of this writer's exegetical understanding of the book, consulting the results of various other methodologies along the way.

Outline of 1 John

   I. John Claims the Authority of the Apostolic Witness (1:1 – 4)
      A. John's Claim to Accurate Historical Knowledge (1:1)
      B. The Appearance of the Eternal Life (1:2)
      C. John's Goal of Fellowship (1:3)
      D. Making the Joy of Fellowship Complete (1:4)
  II. Announcement of the Message (1:5 – 10)
      A. God Is Light (1:5)
      B. First Two Contrasting Conditional Clauses (1:6 – 7)
      C. Second Two Contrasting Conditional Clauses (1:8 – 9)
      D. Fifth Conditional Clause: If We Say That We Have Not Sinned ... (1:10)
 III. Dealing with Sin (2:1 – 6)
      A. Bringing the Topic of Sin to Bear on His Readers (2:1 – 2)
      B. Knowing God Means Avoiding Sin by Keeping His Commands (2:3 – 6)
 IV. Love, Light, and Darkness (2:7 – 11)
      A. The Continuity of John's Teaching with Jesus' Teaching (2:7 – 8)
      B. The Relationship of Love and Hate to the Light and Darkness Duality (2:9 – 11)
  V. Children, Fathers, and Young Men (2:12 – 14)
      A. Children, Your Sins Are Forgiven (2:12)
      B. Fathers, You Know Him Who Is from the Beginning (2:13a – c)
      C. YoungMen, You Have Overcome the Evil One (2:13d – f)
      D. Children, You Know the Father (2:14a – c)
      E. Fathers, You Know Him Who Is from the Beginning (2:14d – f)
      F. Young Men, You Are Strong (2:14g – k)
 VI. Love for World Is Contrary to Love for Father (2:15 – 17)
      A. Command Not to Love the World (2:15)

---

8. J. Callow, "Where Does 1 John 1 End?" *JSNT* 170 (1999): 397.

9. Brickle, *Aural Design*, 109.

1 John 1:1 – 4

Literary Context

This opening prologue of the book provides the foundation for its message by introducing the authority of its author, who bears the eyewitness testimony of Jesus, the Word who is Life. According to the conventions of Greco-Roman rhetoric, these verses function to make the audience attentive and well disposed to receive the message that follows. They introduce the major topic of the letter, assure the readers of eternal life, and encourage them to continue in the beliefs and values they already hold. The possible allusion to idolatry stands in contrast to the truth about God revealed in Jesus Christ and forms an inclusio with the final command in 5:21, "Children, keep yourselves from idols."

→ **I. John Claims the Authority of the Apostolic Witness (1:1 – 4)**
    A. John's Claim to Accurate Historical Knowledge (1:1)
    B. The Appearance of the Eternal Life (1:2)
    C. John's Goal of Fellowship (1:3)
    D. Making the Joy of Fellowship Complete (1:4)
  II. Announcement of the Message (1:5 – 10)
    A. God Is Light (1:5).
    B. First Two Contrasting Conditional Clauses (1:6 – 7)
    C. Second Two Contrasting Conditional Clauses (1:8 – 9)
    D. Fifth Conditional Clause: If We Say That We Have Not Sinned . . . (1:10)

Main Idea

The truth about Jesus Christ begins with his being an actual person in human history who chose witnesses to explain the true significance of his life, death, and resurrection. This opening invites readers to join the fellowship of like-minded belief by following and remaining in the teaching about Christ given by those who have the authority to speak spiritual truth.

Translation

1 John 1:1–4

1a	list/object of 3c	What was from the beginning,
b	list/object of 3c	what we have heard,
c	list/object of 3c	what we have seen with our eyes,
d	list/object of 3c	what we have perceived, and
e	list/object of 3c	our hands have touched —
f	reference of 3c	this we proclaim about the Word of Life.

2a	assertion	**The Life appeared,**
b	assertion	and **we have seen [it],**
c	assertion	and **testify [to it],**
d	assertion	and **proclaim to you the eternal Life,**
		which was with the Father and
		has appeared to us.
e	assertion	
3a	object	What we have seen and
b	object	have heard,
c	assertion	**we proclaim also to you,**
d	purpose	so that you also may have fellowship with us.
e	assertion	And indeed our fellowship is with the Father and
		with his Son, Jesus Christ.

4a	assertion	And **these things we write**
b	purpose	so that our joy may be complete.

Structure

The opening of 1 John is perhaps the most unusual in the biblical corpus, for no other book begins with a relative pronoun, "what" (ὅ), as its first word. In fact, there are four neuter singular relative pronouns in the opening verse, and the main verb doesn't appear until verse 3 ("we proclaim," ἀπαγγέλλομεν). The unusual word order that fronts this string of pronouns with respect to their verbs highlights the message of the testimony and adds rhetorical impact by emphasizing the object of proclamation, the gospel of Jesus Christ.

> *What* was from the beginning,
> *what* we have heard,
> *what* we have seen with our eyes,
> *what* we have perceived,
> and our hands have touched —
> this we proclaim about the Word of Life. (italics added)

The structure of this testimony is centered on the assertion that the Life has appeared and that "we have seen" it and now we "testify" and" proclaim" it (v. 2).

Following this assertion, the neuter singular accusative relative pronoun "what" (ὅ) resumes the claim of having seen and heard what is being announced in the following content of the letter (v. 3a). The "so that" (ἵνα) clause in v. 3d-e states the purpose of the announcement, that recipients might have fellowship with "us," a fellowship that is with the Father and his Son, Jesus Christ.

The use of the first person plural pronoun raises an exegetical debate well known to interpreters of 1 John about the identity of the referent (see Explanation of the Text). The verbs of sensory perception ("have heard," "have seen," "have touched") make a claim that the message is based on firsthand testimony to the Word of Life, though not necessarily eyewitness testimony of the earthly Jesus, since the relative pronoun is neuter, not masculine, as would be required to refer to Jesus or to the noun "word" (λόγος). Perhaps the author is thinking of the gospel message, which could be referred to as a neuter noun (εὐαγγέλιον), or the more absract idea of the significance of Jesus' life, death, and resurrection.

The final statement of the letter opening states one, though not the only, purpose for writing (taking "these things" [ταῦτα] to refer to all that is to follow), that the joy resulting from the Word of Life might be made complete. Textual variants make it uncertain whether John wrote "our" joy or "your" joy (see discussion in Explanation of the Text).

Although the Greek of this passage is relatively easy, its meaning is more difficult to discern. Raymond Brown has described the syntax of the passage as "a grammatical obstacle course"[1] because the relationship of various parts of the passage to each other — which is smoothed out in English translation — is not straightforward in the Greek. These first four verses form one long sentence in the Greek text, made more difficult by two parenthetical statements.

Exegetical Outline

→ **I. John Claims the Authority of the Apostolic Witness (1:1 – 4)**

    A. John claims to have accurate historical knowledge about the Word of Life and its significance (1:1)

    B. The eternal Life that was with the Father has appeared (1:2)

        1. John testifies to it (1:2a – c)

        2. He proclaims it to his readers (1:2d)

    C. John announces what he has seen and heard so that those who hear might have fellowship with John and with God the Father and his Son, Jesus Christ (1:3)

    D. John writes to make the joy of fellowship complete (1:4)

---

1. Brown, *Epistles of John*, 152.

Explanation of the Text

1:1 What was from the beginning, what we have heard, what we have seen with our eyes, what we have perceived, and our hands have touched — this we proclaim about the Word of Life (Ὃ ἦν ἀπ᾽ ἀρχῆς, ὃ ἀκηκόαμεν, ὃ ἑωράκαμεν τοῖς ὀφθαλμοῖς ἡμῶν, ὃ ἐθεασάμεθα καὶ αἱ χεῖρες ἡμῶν ἐψηλάφησαν περὶ τοῦ λόγου τῆς ζωῆς). This opening verse of the prologue to 1 John forms an essential foundation for understanding the rest of the letter, but it is fraught with exegetical issues. Although the Greek of 1 John is often said to be the easiest in the NT, the syntax of this first verse and its relationship to the rest of the passage is not straightforward. There are at least five exegetical issues that must be considered in an attempt to understand what is being said here:

(1) the referent of the neuter relative pronouns (ὅ) and their relationships to each other
(2) the meaning of "from the beginning" (ἀπ᾽ ἀρχῆς)
(3) the purpose of the repeated verbs of sensory experience
(4) the identity of the first person plural pronoun "we"
(5) the meaning of the genitive in the phrase "the Word of Life."

It is worth the time and effort to discuss each of these in some detail to have the clarity needed to understand the rest of the letter.

(1) Given that the author is basing his authority on the eyewitness source of his knowledge, it may seem natural to read this opening verse as a claim that the "we" subject of the verbal forms refers to one or more eyewitnesses of the earthly life of Jesus. In other words, to paraphrase, "we have heard Jesus, we have seen Jesus with our own eyes, we have looked at him (while he taught and performed miracles), and our hands have touched him." But the Greek does not allow this direct reference to the person of Jesus. It is somewhat surprising to find *neuter* relative pronouns rather than the masculine pronouns, which would be grammatically required if John were referring directly to hearing, seeing, and touching Jesus. It seems the author is not referring directly to the person of Jesus, but is thinking more broadly of the gospel message centered on Jesus, which could be referred to with the neuter noun ("gospel," εὐαγγέλιον), even though he doesn't use that word. Or perhaps he was using the relative pronoun of general reference to point to all that had been involved generally with knowing Jesus.[2]

Some interpreters understand the referent to be "the message preached by Jesus during his ministry and that message as later proclaimed by the Johannine tradition-bearers."[3] Brickle's recent work on the aural design of this prologue, intended to be read aloud in its original church setting, has suggested that the repetition of the neuter relative pronoun is part of "three key aural patterns (ὅ/καί/vowel-μεν)" that by design aid the listener's understanding and memory.[4]

Although the author is basing his knowledge on the eyewitness source, he is apparently referring to Jesus in categories that go beyond what one could have known about Jesus from mere physical observation, with phrases such as "what was from the beginning" and "the eternal Life, which was with the Father and has appeared to us." The author seems to be making a distinction here similar to

---

2. Perhaps similar to the English construction, "What you said was very good," where "what" is a pronoun referring generally to all that was said.

3. E.g., Watson, " 'Keep Yourselves from Idols,' " 297.
4. Brickle, *Aural Design*, 108 – 10.

the distinction between physical event and its significance that we find in the signs of John's gospel. Yes, the seven signs are miracles, but they function as signs only as their revelatory significance is perceived. Some people saw only what Jesus did but failed to perceive its significance; those who did perceive the significance are said to have put their faith in Jesus (e.g., John 2:11). And so the neuter relative pronouns suggest a perception of Jesus with all the truth he brings that goes beyond mere sensory perception.

(2) There is some question about the relationship of the four relative pronouns to each other. Many interpreters take all four as the direct objects of the verb in verse 3, "we proclaim" (ἀπαγγέλλομεν). Others construe the first pronoun (ὅ) to function as the nominative subject of the predicate "was from the beginning" (ἦν ἀπ' ἀρχῆς) with the three relative clauses that follow in apposition: we proclaim what was from the beginning, namely, what we have heard, what we have seen with our eyes, what we have perceived and our hands have handled.[5]

Either way, John is stressing the message about Jesus, which was "from the beginning" (ὃ ἦν ἀπ' ἀρχῆς). This raises the question, the beginning of what? The prepositional phrase "from the beginning" (ἀπ' ἀρχῆς) is used eight times in this brief letter (1:1; 2:7, 13, 14, 24 [2x]; 3:8, 11) and twice in 2 John (vv. 5, 6), as well as twice in John's gospel (8:44; 15:27). Interpreters see a number of options for the referent of "the beginning" in John's writings:

(1) the preexistence of the Son, echoing John 1:1 ("In the beginning was the Word ...") and, indirectly, Gen 1:1 ("in the beginning ...")

(2) the beginning of a Christian's life at conversion to faith in Christ

(3) the beginning of God's redemptive work in human history

(4) the beginning of the Christian gospel, defined as:

(a) the conception and birth of Jesus, or

(b) the beginning of Jesus' public ministry, or

(c) the beginning of the preaching of the gospel after Jesus' resurrection

The prologue of 1 John is obviously similar to that of John's gospel, with both mentioning a "beginning" in their first verse. Although some object to allowing John's gospel and letters to mutually interpret each other, the extent of the parallels and correspondences seems to demand that the metaphors, images, and theology of the letters be understood within the framework of the Fourth Gospel (see Relationship of the Letters to John's Gospel in the Introduction to 1, 2, and 3 John).

John's gospel begins with the famous statement "in the beginning was the Word" (ἐν ἀρχῇ ἦν ὁ λόγος), which alludes to Gen 1:1, "in the beginning God made the heavens and the earth" (Gk. LXX, ἐν ἀρχῇ ἐποίησεν ὁ θεὸς τὸν οὐρανὸν καὶ τὴν γῆν). Both statements are made in reference to the creation, for John 1:3 goes on to explain: "Through him all things were made; without him nothing was made that has been made." Furthermore, both John 1:1 and Gen 1:1 LXX use the same prepositional phrase, "in the beginning" (ἐν ἀρχῇ). The situation in 1 John 1:1 is somewhat different, where there is no mention of creation and the prepositional phrase is "from the beginning" (ἀπ' ἀρχῆς). Construing 1 John 1:1 in light of John 1:1 and Gen 1:1 means that what "we" have heard, have seen, and have touched is the message about the Word (ὁ λόγος), who was the agent of creation.

This understanding is supported by the prepositional phrase "*about* the Word of Life. The Life

5. Stephen S. Smalley, *1, 2, 3 John* (WBC 51; Waco, TX: Word, 1984), 3; Martin M. Culy, *I, II, III John: A Handbook on the Greek Text* (Waco, TX: Baylor University Press, 2004), 2.

appeared" (περὶ τοῦ λόγου τῆς ζωῆς … ἡ ζωὴ ἐφανερώθη), which modifies all three neuter relative clauses. Moreover, in verse 2, the Life that appeared "was with the Father" (ἦν πρὸς τὸν πατέρα), another echo of John 1:1, where the same preposition (πρός) is used in reference to God ("the Word was with God"). The interpretation that "what was from the beginning" in 1 John 1:1 is a reference that ties the gospel to the preexistent Christ seems to sit well with the use of the same prepositional phrase in 1 John 2:13, 14, which refers to "the One who is from the beginning" (τὸν ἀπ' ἀρχῆς).[6] The allusion to the primeval history of Genesis is also mentioned in 1 John 3:8 with the reference to the devil, who has been sinning "from the beginning" (ἀπ' ἀρχῆς).

But other occurrences of this prepositional phrase in 1 John more clearly refer to the beginning of the Christian lives of the readers (2:7, 24; 3:11; 2 John 6, and possibly v. 5 as well).[7] Following this option would mean that what "we" have heard, and seen, and touched is also the truth that Christians have known since the first day they came to believe in Christ. First John 2:7 uses "beginning" in a reference to the start of one's Christian life: "Dear friends, I am not writing to you a new command but an old command, which you have had from the beginning [ἀπ' ἀρχῆς]. The old command is the message that you have heard."

Another option is to take "beginning" to refer to the beginning of the Christian gospel, when Jesus himself first began to preach and perform miracles, when the Word who is "the Life appeared" (1:2).[8] This interpretation accords well with John 15:26 – 27, where Jesus promises his disciples,

"When the Advocate [παράκλητος] comes, whom I will send to you from the Father — the Spirit of truth who goes out from the Father — he will testify about me. And you also must testify, *for you have been with me from the beginning*" (ἀπ' ἀρχῆς; italics added). Jesus made this promise on the night before he died, during the Passover meal that he celebrated as his Last Supper with the Twelve. Jesus' use of ἀπ' ἀρχῆς here offers convincing evidence that in 1 John 1:1 – 4, John claims to represent the apostolic witness about the life and ministry of Jesus as witnessed from its beginning. When understood in this way, it is a claim either that the author was an eyewitness of Jesus, or that he is among those who preserve and teach the true apostolic message about Jesus received from the eyewitnesses. This claim would underscore the authority of the letter, highlighting the apostolic witness as older and more reliable than the newer ideas that were making inroads, because it was based on accurate knowledge of the historical Jesus.

The Johannine corpus is well known for its abundant wordplays and double entendres, and the use of "from the beginning" in 1 John 1:1 is probably meant to suggest more than one sense. The Word who was with God and who was God in the beginning at the creation is, in 1:1 – 2, the Word who is the Life that was revealed in the man Jesus, whom "we" have heard, and seen, and touched during his incarnation[9] (see discussion below on the phrase "Word of Life"). Thus, while the temporal focus of 1:1 is on the lifetime of Jesus, it alludes to his preexistence and reminds the readers of what they have believed since the beginning of their faith in Christ.

---

6. Gary M. Burge, *The Letters of John* (NIVAC; Grand Rapids: Zondervan, 1996), 53; Marshall, *Epistles of John*, 100 – 101; Smalley, *1, 2, 3 John*, 5; D. Moody Smith, *First, Second, and Third John* (Interpretation; Louisville: John Knox, 1991), 36.

7. Strecker, *Johannine Letters*, 8 – 9.

8. Kruse, *Letters of John*, 51; Marianne Meye Thompson,

1 – 3 John (IVPNTC; Downers Grove, IL: InterVarsity Press, 1992), 37 – 38.

9. So Bruce Schuchard's comment that it refers to "a starting point in past history" of the work of the Creator. See *1 – 3 John* (Concordia Commentary; St. Louis: Concordia, 2012), 66 n.46.

(3) Of the five major exegetical issues in this verse, the third is the repetition of verbs of sensory experience — "what we have heard, what we have seen with our eyes, what we have perceived, and our hands have touched" (ὃ ἀκηκόαμεν, ὃ ἑωράκαμεν τοῖς ὀφθαλμοῖς ἡμῶν, ὃ ἐθεασάμεθα καὶ αἱ χεῖρες ἡμῶν ἐψηλάφησαν) — which emphasizes both the physicality of the Word who is Life and the eyewitness knowledge of Jesus as the source of the author's testimony.

The two references to the sense of sight ("we have seen," "we have perceived"; ἑωράκαμεν and ἐθεασάμεθα) are especially puzzling, unless the two verbs of sight are somewhat different in their sense. The first is clearly a verb of sensory perception, seeing "with our eyes" (τοῖς ὀφθαλμοῖς ἡμῶν). The second verb, "what we have perceived" (θεάομαι), can also be used of a perception that is nonsensory, to see something "above and beyond what is merely seen with the eye,"[10] which suggests that the author has perceived the true significance of Jesus' life, death, and resurrection that goes beyond what could be seen with the eyes. This use of the verb "what we have perceived" can be seen in every other instance of the verb in the letters and gospel (John 1:14, 32, 38; 4:35; 6:5; 11:45; 1 John 4:12, 14), both where a physically visible object is in view (e.g., John 4:35) and where the perception requires an understanding that goes beyond the physical (e.g., 1 John 4:14).

The spiritual truth of the gospel is not simply the historical facts of Jesus' person, teaching, and miracles. Consider the difference between these two statements: "Jesus of Nazareth died on a cross in Jerusalem" and "Jesus *Christ* died on a cross in Jerusalem *for our sin*." The first states certain facts about the man Jesus that anyone present at that moment could have witnessed and that are corroborated by historians of the period, such as Tacitus and Suetonius, and the Jewish historian Josephus.[11] The second statement is an interpretation of the significance of Jesus' death — a statement about his identity as the Messiah and what he accomplished by dying on the cross — a truth that must be received in faith. It is a statement of the orthodox tradition that forms the heart of the Christian gospel.

This idea of a perception that goes beyond physically seeing is similar to the use of the term "sign" (σημεῖον) in John's gospel to refer not just to a miracle Jesus performed, but also to the *significance* of that miracle. The verb translated "touch" here (ψηλαφάω) is also used in Heb 12:18 in a reference to Mount Sinai, where God revealed himself in tangible manifestations that could be felt or touched. It also alludes to the episode of Thomas and the resurrected Jesus, when Thomas refused to believe unless he touched Jesus' resurrected body (John 20:25). Although a different verb is used there, John implies that those who have not touched Jesus (like Thomas) but believe the message of those who have (the disciples who saw him) are the blessed who have not seen and yet believe (John 20:29).

Some interpreters do not see any reference to an eyewitness experience in this verse at all, and instead see the verbs of perception here as an allusion to Isa 59:9 – 10 and/or Ps 15 "with its vivid mockery of the idols of the nations, who 'have eyes and will not see, have ears and will not hear, have noses and will not smell, have hands and will not touch [ψηλαφάω].'"[12] A similar heaping up of the verbs of sensory perception is found Ps 115:3 – 7:

> Our God is in heaven;
> he does whatever pleases him.

---

10. BDAG, *s.v.* θεάομαι.

11. Tacitus, *Ann.* 15.44; Suetonius, *Claud.* 25.4; Josephus, *Ant.* 20.200 – 203.

12. Judith M. Lieu, *I, II, & III John: A Commentary* (NTL; Louisville: Westminster John Knox, 2008), 40.

But their idols are silver and gold,
    made by human hands.
They have mouths, but cannot speak,
    eyes, but cannot see.
They have ears, but cannot hear,
    noses, but cannot smell.
They have hands, but cannot feel,
    feet, but cannot walk,
    nor can they utter a sound with their throats.

In contrast to the deceptive knowledge of the divine that the ancient world sought through idols made by craftsmen (and that our modern world seeks through intangible gods of our own making), 1 John 1:1 holds out the truth about God as revealed in Jesus Christ. Most relevant to John's purposes would be the next line of this psalm, "Those who make them will be like them, *and so will all who trust in them*" (Ps 115:8, emphasis added). In contrast to those who consult lifeless idols and know nothing, the apostles have seen, and heard, and touched the source of true knowledge of God, and they now proclaim that knowledge.

Moreover, the phrase "from the beginning" may also be echoing traditional language that is found in extrabiblical writings to refer to idols that were not "from the beginning" (e.g., Wis 14:12 – 13). In contrast to idols, Hab 1:12 speaks of the true God as being from the beginning, using the same phrase "from the beginning" (ἀπ᾽ ἀρχῆς) in its ancient Greek translation: "Are you not from the beginning, O Lord, my holy God? So we shall not die" (NETS). In this intriguing variation from the MT, God's eternality is given as the basis of eternal life for God's people, the very topic that John wishes to assure his readers about (1 John 5:13). The Hebrew text reads, "My God, my Holy One, you will never die," which is a congenial statement in light of the resurrection of Jesus, who was "from the beginning."

If there is any allusion to idols in the opening of 1 John, it is indeed subtle, at least to modern readers. But the strength of this argument is that the closing verse of the letter, "Children, keep yourselves from idols" (5:21), is resolved from an abruptly puzzling ending to an intelligible inclusio, exhorting readers to remain in the apostolic teaching if they wish to have true knowledge of God.[13]

(4) A fourth factor of major exegetical significance in this opening verse is John's use of the first plural form of the verbs, "what *we* have heard … *we* have seen … *we* have touched." This long-standing debate is about whether the "we" is a true plural, referring to some group of people whom the author considered himself to represent (such as the apostolic eyewitnesses or the Johannine community), or whether it is a singular reference to only the author himself, similar to the "editorial" or "magisterial" we in English.[14] If it is a genuine plural, then is it an associative "we," which defines the author and his readers as one group together? Or is it the dissociative "we," which defines a group composed of the author and unspecified peers, but excludes the readers?

The first person *singular* pronoun occurs only fourteen times, either explicit in the text or implied by the verb form, in 1 John (2:1, "my," μου; *passim*, first singular forms of "I write," γράφω). But there are almost a hundred occurrences of verbs in the first plural form with the implied subject "we" and another more than fifty occurrences of an inflected form of the first person personal pronoun "we" (e.g., ἡμῖν, ἡμᾶς). Most of these are inclusive (or associative) plurals, where the author is including himself together with the readers. For instance, 1 John 1:9, "If *we* confess our sins, he is faithful and righteous, to forgive *our* sins and to cleanse *us* from all unrighteousness" (italics added). The au-

---

13. Watson, " 'Keep Yourselves from Idols,' " 297.

14. See *The Chicago Manual of Style*, 16th edition, 5.45, and *The Oxford American College Dictionary*, ad loc.

thor would no doubt include himself in that group (though one could imagine a dissociative "we" for rhetorical purposes even in such instances).

But if the "we" of 1:1 – 4 is a true plural, an inclusive "we" does not work well there because the "we" of which the author is a member has fellowship with God the Father and his Son, Jesus Christ, and he writes so that "you may have" (or continue to have) that fellowship too (1:3d). If the plural is genuine, it must be a dissociative use, where the author is identifying himself with a group of whom the readers are *not* necessarily a part.

Reading the "we" as a genuine plural, some scholars take it to be a direct reference to the apostles, who were eyewitnesses of Jesus' life, death, and resurrection — a small and elite group indeed. On this view, the neuter relative pronoun would refer to the eyewitnesses' whole experience of Jesus, such as his teaching, miracles, and the like.[15] Perhaps the majority of NT scholars who take the first plural as a genuine plural read it as referring to the "Johannine community," a group of undetermined number who faithfully preserved the teaching of an eyewitness of Jesus, who was probably the "beloved disciple" of John's gospel. For those who would identify the beloved disciple as the apostle John, the Johannine community preserved the eyewitness testimony of the apostle after his death — that is, what he had heard, and seen, and touched concerning the Word of Life from the beginning. In this view, the neuter relative pronouns refer to the Johannine tradition vicariously experienced, an indirect witness to the testimony of the beloved disciple of John's gospel. Others, who see no relation between "John's" gospel and "John's" letters, consider each book to be an independent reworking of the common tradition to which the neuter relative pronoun refers.[16]

But 1 John was clearly written by one person, even if he was representative of a group, because he most often uses the first person singular when referring to his writing, for instance, in 2:1, "These things I write to you" (ταῦτα γράφω ὑμῖν). The fact that the author uses both "we write" and "I write" to refer to one and the same letter strongly tilts the "we" in 1:1 – 4 in the direction of a singular reference.

There are a few reasons an author might use the plural pronoun as a singular self-reference. Although this usage is found in modern writings, similar instances can be found in ancient texts as well. The plural of majesty (i.e., authority) would imply that the author had well-recognized authority over his readers; it was a form often used by royalty. The editorial "we" implies no authority of the author over the readers, but is a convention used where "I" would sound too self-focused. Its use borders on the rhetorical "we," meant to create "a sense of corporate unity and of continuity reaching beyond the present situation and players."[17] Judith Lieu, for instance, considers the plural "we" to be a device to "deflect attention away from the author as if he were speaking only on his own authority" and to create "a sense of corporate unity and of continuity" into which the readers are invited.[18] She considers the "we" to refer to the singular author, who is a bearer of the orthodox Jesus tradition, though not an eyewitness himself.

Greek writers such as Demosthenes and Thucydides often referred to themselves with the plural form "we," creating the sense of the narrator's involvement with the story and consequently their reliability in reporting it, a factor that might inform the use of the first person plural in John's gospel, especially in John 21:24.[19] The first person

---

15. For instance, Robert W. Yarbrough, *1 – 3 John* (BECNT; Grand Rapids: Baker Academic, 2008), 35.

16. See, e.g., Lieu, *I, II, & III John*, 8.

17. Ibid., 39.

18. Ibid.

19. William Sanger Campbell, "The Narrator as 'He,' 'Me,' and 'We': Grammatical Person in Ancient Histories and in the Acts of the Apostles," *JBL* 129 (2010): 385 – 407, esp. 403 – 4.

plural form also implies a sense of familiarity that draws readers into the text, to become personally involved and share a sense of purpose with the author. As William Campbell writes, "The bond that readers develop with the first person plural narrator engenders a more compassionate and appreciative stance toward the narrator and, therefore, acceptance of the narrator's perspective and an empathetic reading."[20] While Campbell's research centered in narrative, it is easy to see how similar aims could be achieved by use of the first plural in discourse (and his argument may be more directly relevant to the "we" in John's gospel narratives).

Adolf von Harnack, John Chapman, and, more recently, Howard Jackson have each argued that the "we" in the epilogue of the gospel of John (21:24) refers to the singular author because the singular and plural first person forms are often found interchanged in ancient writings beyond the NT; this suggests that 1 John 1:1–4 should be read similarly.[21] Jackson observed that in formally registered public documents found among the papyri, such as contracts, deeds, wills, and affidavits, the body of the document was written in third person but an appendix included a reference in first person to the testator, witness, or other legal agent involved. John's gospel is centrally concerned with providing an authoritative witness to the story of Jesus and may have imitated that convention, even though it is unlikely the gospel was ever formally registered as a public document. First John is similarly concerned with the testimony based on the eyewitness source.

More recently, Richard Bauckham has argued persuasively that the "we" in the epilogue of John's

gospel (and elsewhere) and in 1 John 1:1–4 is the singular "we" of "authoritative testimony."[22] If the "we" were so understood, John's gospel would be read as a deposition of eyewitness testimony with a self-reference to the witness in John 21:24. Given the similarities of John's gospel and 1 John, the "we" in the opening verses of the letter would be understood as a singular reference to the author, using the "we" of authoritative testimony. This understanding sits well with the function of the opening verses, which certainly seek to establish authority for the teaching that follows in the body of the letter. If the "we" of John 21:24 is in fact singular, it largely undercuts the reigning theory of the last thirty years or more, which has read it as a reference to a Johannine community behind the epilogue of the Fourth Gospel and the opening verses of 1 John.

The identity of the "we" here cannot be decided with certainty, but the singular "we" of authoritative testimony has much to recommend it. If the author were an eyewitness of the historical Jesus such as the apostle John (which Bauckham denies),[23] the basis of his authoritative "we" of testimony would nevertheless be his membership in the group of apostolic eyewitnesses, even if the "we" is not a direct reference to that group. In other words, even an apostolic eyewitness could use the singular "we" for his rhetorical purposes. But the singular "we" of authoritative testimony does not completely rule out the possibility of an author who, although not himself an eyewitness, nevertheless stood in the genuine apostolic tradition that had its origin with the eyewitnesses (much like Mark's relationship to Peter or Luke's to Paul).

Regardless of whether the plural pronoun refers

---

20. Ibid., 404.

21. Adolf von Harnack, *"Das 'Wir' in den Johanneischen Schriften"* (SPAW; Berlin: Academie der Wissenschaften, 1923), 96–113; John Chapman, "'We Know That His Testimony Is True,'" *JTS* 31 (1930): 379–87; Howard M. Jackson, "Ancient Self-Referential Conventions and Their Implications for the

Authorship and Integrity of the Gospel of John," *JTS*, n.s. 50 (1999): 1–34.

22. Richard Bauckham, *Jesus and the Eyewitnesses: The Gospels as Eyewitness Testimony* (Grand Rapids: Eerdmans, 2006), 369–83.

23. Ibid., 412.

to the author alone or to him as a member of a group, the author claims to speak the true, apostolic message about Jesus Christ with the apostolic authority of those who have experienced God's revelation through Jesus from the beginning. The issue of who has the authority to speak spiritual truth is raised throughout John's letters because it was written at a time (late first century) and a place (outside Palestine) in which Greek ideas were making heretical inroads in the churches. These opening verses include an implied invitation to the readers to embrace the author's message (his authoritative testimony) if they wish to enjoy the fellowship of truly knowing God.

(5) John's concern was to proclaim with authority what he knew "about the Word of Life" (περὶ τοῦ λόγου τῆς ζωῆς) to his readers. The final exegetical issue of this verse involves determining the referent of the "Word of Life," specifically, how to construe *logos*. Is this "Word of Life" a reference to Jesus himself as the living Word of God, echoing the opening of John's gospel?[24] Or does it refer to the "message of life" proclaimed about him?

How one understands the referent of "word" (λόγος) will also influence the sense of the genitive "of life." Does the author mean to say that the word *is* life, using an epexegetical genitive? Or is life an attribute of the word, i.e., a life-giving word (adjectival attributive genitive)? Or is "of life" an objective genitive, where "life" serves as the content of the message — in other words, that the message is about life (which requires the word to be impersonal). On the one hand, remember that the neuter relative pronouns in this verse cannot refer to the person of Jesus himself, but go beyond the historical person of Jesus to the true significance of his death and resurrection. The gospel consists not only of the historical facts about Jesus, but the divine interpretation of the meaning of his life,

death, and resurrection. Since v. 1 is in the context of proclamation (vv. 2–3), the phrase "Word of Life" could refer to the gospel message about Christ, who has brought eternal life to humankind.

On the other hand, 1 John is concerned with the topic of the assurance of eternal *life* (5:13; see The Theology of John's Letters). While John's gospel states that the Word became incarnate, 1 John 1:2 says that the *Life* appeared, the Life that had been with the Father. What was seen, and heard, and touched is "about the Word" (περὶ τοῦ λόγου), but then the genitive "of Life" (τῆς ζωῆς) becomes the *subject* of the next statement, "the Life appeared," an apparent reference to the incarnation (v. 2). This suggests that the phrase "Word of Life" is a transition intended to bridge the Word of John's prologue with the Life of 1 John, and it can be taken as epexegetical, meaning the "Word who is Life." This reading echoes Jesus' statement in John's Gospel, "I am ... *the life*" (John 11:25; 14:6). While some interpreters would cite this difference between the gospel and 1 John as evidence that two authors are at work, using similar terms but meaning something different by them, it is more likely that because of his emphasis on the assurance of eternal life, John wishes to point to the Word who *is* eternal Life as the grounds for assurance about eternal life.

John accomplishes much in this opening verse. First, he claims a source of knowledge that cannot be matched by those who did not have access to, or who chose to ignore, the apostolic eyewitness. Second, "what was from the beginning" had become a physical reality capable of being heard, being seen, and being touched. This statement speaks to the issues of who has the authority to speak about Christ and true Christology, both major issues later in the letter. The issue of authority hinges on the question of who knows the truth about Jesus — those he

---

24. See, e.g., Yarbrough, *1–3 John*, 38.

chose to be with him during his lifetime and bear witness after his death or those who had no such direct access or calling. Clearly, the more reliable witnesses would be the apostles chosen by Jesus because they walked with him during his earthly ministry and witnessed his resurrection. The apostolic tradition is what they passed on to others about who Jesus is and what his life meant. That is the reliable apostolic tradition preserved in the NT, written either by the eyewitnesses themselves or by their closest colleagues (e.g., Luke with Paul, Mark with Peter).

But over time new interpretations of the significance of Jesus emerged from other sources as the gospel message interacted with people who had come into the church from different backgrounds and who were distorting the apostolic tradition under various influences, such as Greek philosophy and pagan beliefs. Just as the Bible is used and misused by countless people today, those who can legitimately claim the authority of the truth about Jesus are those who embrace the reliability of the NT, where the apostolic tradition has been preserved.

The second claim of this verse is about the content of the apostolic tradition concerning the true nature of Jesus. Those who were with him during his public ministry and were privy to his teaching about himself knew that he was a physical being, fully human. As ideas emerged after his resurrection about the spiritual presence and reality of the Christ, the significance of the full humanity of Jesus began to recede. After all, for those living beyond the lifetime of Jesus, ourselves included, it is his *spiritual* presence that is most real to us. We do not now have direct contact with Jesus in any physical form. In the history of Christian thought, the depreciation of the humanity of Jesus Christ opened the door to claims of new revelation that were other than, and sometimes contradictory to, the apostolic tradition. This issue is also present later in John's letter, with his concern about the antichrists' apparent denial that the physical man Jesus is the Christ (1 John 2:22), and that the Christ has come in the flesh (1 John 4:2 – 3; 2 John 7).

1:2 The Life appeared, and we have seen [it], and testify [to it], and proclaim to you the eternal Life, which was with the Father and has appeared to us (καὶ ἡ ζωὴ ἐφανερώθη, καὶ ἑωράκαμεν καὶ μαρτυροῦμεν καὶ ἀπαγγέλλομεν ὑμῖν τὴν ζωὴν τὴν αἰώνιον ἥτις ἦν πρὸς τὸν πατέρα καὶ ἐφανερώθη ἡμῖν). John states his role as a witness to the Life that entered human history. To "see" and "bear witness" are legal terms of the courtroom deposition, where one not only gave evidence from eyewitness experience but also vouched for the truthfulness of what others said. The issue of what is true is at the heart of testimony, and therefore it is not coincidental that truth is also a major concept within John's writings. In fact, Jesus states that the purpose of his incarnation was to testify to the truth (John 18:37b) of what he revealed about God and eternal life (1:18).

Therefore, the role of a reliable, testifying witness is arguably the major theme in John's gospel and letters, where the Greek verb "to witness" or "testify" (μαρτυρέω) occurs more than forty times. The Fourth Gospel can be seen as the story of the witnesses, starting with John the Baptist, who "came as a witness to testify concerning that light, so that through him all might believe" (John 1:7). But the events of Jesus' life brought testimony even weightier than that of John the Baptist (5:36). God himself testified about Jesus (5:37; 8:18), and in turn Jesus was a witness to what the Father said and did (12:49; 17:18).

This chain of witnesses continued with the apostles whom Jesus Christ personally chose to bear witness of him (John 15:27), and with the one whose testimony comprises John's gospel (19:35; 21:24). That theme of an unbroken line of witness is picked up again here in these opening verses of 1 John. Standing in this direct chain of witnesses, the author of 1 John faithfully executes his role as a witness, even by writing this letter: "And we have beheld and testify that the Father sent his Son [to be] the Savior of the world" (1 John 4:14).

John testifies to the Life that "appeared," that he has seen the Life, and that his writing is his testimony "about the Word of Life" (περὶ τοῦ λόγου τῆς ζωῆς, v. 1f). The testimony about the Life that has appeared originated with the Incarnate One himself. Some take the phrase "the eternal life" (τὴν ζωὴν τὴν αἰώνιον) to refer to the eternal life that became available to believers through Christ, but it is more likely primarily a statement that the Life that became incarnate had preexisted eternally "with the Father."[25] As Yarbrough notes, "in Jesus Christ what is eternal and transcendent has become palpably immanent."[26] John here makes one of the clearest statements of the eternal preexistence of Jesus Christ, raising him above any other religious teacher or prophet. But it is also true that eternal life is offered to fallen human beings through Christ when they come to faith in him and share in his eternal life, and so both ideas are in view.

John reiterates that "we have seen" (perfect tense) and "testify" (present tense) to the Life that appeared. Not only has the author seen the Life and not only does he now bear witness to it, but he also proclaims that witness to the readers of this letter, specifically that "the eternal Life, which was with the Father ... has appeared to us" in the person of Jesus Christ. As Smalley observes, these three verbs of seeing, testifying, and proclaiming "express in order the three ideas of experience, attestation and evangelism which form part of any genuine and lasting response to the gospel."[27]

1:3 What we have seen and have heard, we proclaim also to you, so that you also may have fellowship with us. And indeed our fellowship is with the Father and with his Son, Jesus Christ (ὃ ἑωράκαμεν καὶ ἀκηκόαμεν ἀπαγγέλλομεν καὶ ὑμῖν, ἵνα καὶ ὑμεῖς κοινωνίαν ἔχητε μεθ' ἡμῶν. καὶ ἡ κοινωνία δὲ ἡ ἡμετέρα μετὰ τοῦ πατρὸς καὶ μετὰ τοῦ υἱοῦ αὐτοῦ Ἰησοῦ Χριστοῦ). John extends an invitation to his readers to fellowship with him and with God. The English word "fellowship" might connote little more than coffee and donuts after church, or the large room in the church building where potluck dinners are held. But the Greek word translated "fellowship" (κοινωνία) means having not only a close relationship but also an association based on common interests and purposes. John invites his readers to enter into a relationship with God the Father and his Son, Jesus Christ, by embracing God's redemptive purposes for the world in general and for individual lives in particular, as Jesus revealed them.

Those who lived and walked with Jesus the Messiah during his earthly ministry were drawn into fellowship with him, and not just because he was the Messiah but also because he was the Son of God, his Father. The title "Son of God" has become so familiar to Christian ears as to have almost lost its meaning. It has certainly lost the shock value it must have had among the earliest hearers of the gospel. Within the pagan world, "son of god" could refer to various demigods in Greco-Roman mythology as well as to human heroes. The Roman emperor was referred to as "a son of god" and often would be divinized, sometimes even before his death.

Within the Jewish world, "son of God" had messianic connotations from the covenant promises of 2 Sam 7:14 and Ps 2:6 – 7. It was with the

---

25. See ibid., 39.
26. Ibid., 34.

27. Smalley, *1, 2, 3 John*, 9.

resurrection of Jesus that the full extent of the messianic promises was realized (Rom 1:4). God's deliverance brought by the Messiah was not just from foreign occupation but from death itself, showing Yahweh to be Creator and sovereign King in distinction from pagan deities. Furthermore, the resurrection shows Jesus to be the world's true Ruler, who has passed beyond anything the world's power can do to him and, furthermore, to his followers. Finally, Jesus' sonship shows that he and the Father share the same nature and purposes for the world.[28]

John invites his readers into the fellowship of those who recognize that the eternal Life that was with the Father has appeared on earth to be seen, and heard, and touched by human beings. The *hina* clause, "so that you also may have fellowship with us" (ἵνα καὶ ὑμεῖς κοινωνίαν ἔχητε μεθ᾽ ἡμῶν) explains that the purpose of the apostolic procla-

mation "we proclaim also to you" (ἀπαγγέλλομεν καὶ ὑμῖν) is to extend an invitation to fellowship with God and his Son, Jesus Christ. This fellowship comes to those who receive the apostolic gospel message of the significance of the Life from God, who walked among us.

Implied in this invitation is the warning that if John's readers do not continue to embrace the apostolic witness, their fellowship with John and with God and the Son cannot be sustained. This seems to be the case of those who "went out from us" (2:19), breaking fellowship with the community that John represents, and the case of those who go beyond the teaching about Christ (2 John 9). This letter then becomes both an invitation to remain in fellowship by continuing to embrace the apostolic tradition and an exhortation to reject the newer teaching of those who have departed from it.

IN DEPTH: Messiah or Christ?

One of the exegetical debates about 1 John among scholars today is how to construe the Greek word *christos* (χριστός) in reference to Jesus. The Greek adjective derives from the cognate verb *chriō* (χρίω), which means to anoint. In the OT, Messiah similarly derives from the Hebrew verb "to anoint," and so in the ancient Greek translation of the OT (the Septuagint), references to the Messiah were translated with the Greek word *christos*.

In the NT the sense of the word develops as the true nature of Jesus is progressively revealed. In the Gospels and Acts *Christos* was often used to identify Jesus as the Messiah (e.g., Matt 1:1, "This is the genealogy of Jesus the Messiah [*Christou*] the son of David, the son of Abraham"; or as in Mark 8:29, "Peter answered, 'You are the Messiah [*Christos*].'" But after the resurrection of Jesus and further illumination from the Spirit, the appellation *Christos* came to have a significance that went beyond any expectations for the Messiah of Israel.[29] It shifted from designating the title of God's anointed leader of Israel to a proper name that reflected the divine nature of the Son of God who was incarnate as Jesus Christ (e.g., Col 1:22).

28. N. T. Wright, *The Resurrection of the Son of God* (Christian Origins and the Question of God, vol. 3; Minneaplis: Fortress, 2003), 728, 731.

29. Brown, *Epistles of John*, 171 – 72.

There is debate about when, or even whether, this shift occurred. Martin Hengel thinks that even in Paul's writings *Christos* is used almost entirely as a proper name with only "a glimmer of its titular use."[30] Representing another side of the debate, N. T. Wright argues that "Jesus' Messiahship remained central and vital for Paul" and in fact persisted throughout early Christianity.[31] However, the idea of the Messiah was transformed in at least four ways, according to Wright, when applied to Jesus: (1) it lost its ethnic specificity and became relevant to all nations; (2) the messianic battle was not against worldly powers but against evil itself; (3) the rebuilt temple would be the followers of Jesus; and (4) the justice, peace, and salvation that Messiah would bring to the world would not be a geopolitical program but the cosmic renewal of all creation.[32] It is to this transformed sense of the Messiah as the Son of God himself that the appellation *Christos* refers by the time John writes his gospel and letters.

When John wrote his gospel, the sense of *Christos* as Messiah had apparently declined almost completely, at least to the Gentile ear, because in 1:41 when Andrew tells Simon (Peter) about Jesus, John reminds his readers that *Christos* once meant Messiah, "'We have found the Messiah [Μεσσίαν]' (that is, the Christ [χριστός])." This transformed sense of "Messiah" is equivalent to and interchangeable with "Son of God" in John 20:31. This shift in sense of the title *Christos* during the first century raises the question of when it should be understood, and probably translated, as Messiah and when as Christ.

More to the point for 1 John, which does John mean when he writes, "Who is the liar but the one who denies that *Jesus is the Christ*? This one is the antichrist, the one who denies the Father and the Son" (1 John 2:22, italics added)? Is the liar the person who denies that Jesus is the Messiah? Or is it those who deny the divine nature of Jesus designated by the compound name Jesus Christ? The answer to that question has far-reaching implications for understanding the historical setting and interpreting 1 John.

If John is insisting that Jesus is the Jewish Messiah against those who are waiting for another, then John's primary message goes against a Jewish audience, some of whom apparently had become Christians but then changed their mind about Jesus.[33] But if *Christos* had come to designate the divine nature of Jesus that went beyond all Jewish expectation for the Messiah, then he writes against any who deny that divine nature.

In the context of what is said about Jesus "*Christos*" in 1 John, it seems the focus is on his divine nature. First John 2:22 immediately goes on to mention denying "the Father and the Son," a reference to the divine nature of Jesus. In

30. Martin Hengel, *Studies in Early Christology* (Edinburgh: T&T Clark, 1995), 1.

31. Wright, *Resurrection of the Son of God*, 554 – 55.

32. Ibid., 563.

33. E.g., Streett, *They Went Out from Us*.

1 John 4:2, John specifies the criteria for orthodoxy, writing, "In this way you know the Spirit of God: every spirit that acknowledges Jesus *Christ* has come in the flesh is from God" (italics added). Clearly here the reference to "Christ" signifies his divine nature, for it would not have been exceptional even in Jewish thinking to think that the Messiah was a human being. Therefore, while John certainly believed that Jesus was the Messiah, his point to both Jew and Gentile is that Jesus was more than the expected Messiah. For the Messiah turned out to be God himself come to earth.

1:4 And these things we write so that our joy may be complete (καὶ ταῦτα γράφομεν ἡμεῖς ἵνα ἡ χαρὰ ἡμῶν ᾖ πεπληρωμένη). John concludes the opening of his letter with a statement of his purpose in writing. This is the first of thirteen occurrences of the verb "write" (γράφω), but the only one in the first person plural, "we write" (γράφομεν). The demonstrative pronoun "these things" (ταῦτα) most likely refers to the letter as a whole. As Watson points out, 1:4 ("these things we write") and 5:13 ("these things I write") form an inclusio for the body of the letter.[34]

The shift from the first plural in the opening of the letter to subsequent occurrences of the first singular "I write" (γράφω) suggests that the author considered himself an authoritative representative of those who bore reliable witness to the Life that had appeared. Two other statements of the purpose of the letter are given with *hina* clauses in 1 John 2:1 ("My little children, these things I write to you

so *that* you will not sin"; italics added) and 5:13 ("These things I write to you who believe in the name of the Son of God so *that* you might know that you have eternal life"; italics added). In both, the second plural indirect object ("to you") is used, which may count as evidence for the textual variant that here in 1:4 it is the readers' joy that is in view, not the author's ("and these things we write so that *your* joy may be complete").[35]

Nevertheless, given that John is writing to encourage his readers to remain within the bounds of the apostolic teaching about Jesus, their continued embrace of the author's message will complete his joy in knowing that his proclamation has not been in vain. But given the reciprocal nature of fellowship, where shared joy is one of its characteristics, either reading comes out at about the same place. The first plural "our" joy captures reference to the readers' joy if taken as an inclusive plural.

The theme of joy fulfilled is also found in John's

---

34. Watson, " 'Keep Yourselves from Idols,' " 287.

35. The textual variant here "our" (ἡμῶν) or "your" (ὑμῶν) is difficult to decide, as both external and intrinsic evidence are inconclusive. Both readings are widely attested in the manuscript witnesses and are about equally early. Scribes may have been influenced for the second person pronoun by the similar construction in John 16:24. But a variant introduced by mishearing the exemplar being read aloud or being influenced by the preceding first person pronoun (which also has a variant reading) could also account for the variant. Metzger argues

on intrinsic evidence that the first person pronoun "seems to suit best the generous solicitude of the author, whose own joy would be incomplete unless his readers shared it" (*A Textual Commentary on the Greek New Testament* [Stuttgart: Deutsche Bibelgesellschaft, 1994], 639). However, as Metzger also admits, the second person ὑμῶν is "more expected" and therefore, in Metzger's opinion, a reason why scribes would have changed it from the first person. Contra Metzger, Culy observes that "the letter is clearly to benefit the readers" and argues that the second person pronoun is original (Culy, *I, II, III John*, 9).

gospel, particularly in the Upper Room Discourse (John 3:29 [2x]; 15:11 [2x]; 16:20 – 22, 24; 17:13),[36] and also in the two other letters of John (2 John 12; 3 John 4). John's statement here echoes one of Jesus, who, on the night before he died, consoled his disciples by saying, "I have told you this so that my joy may be in you and that *your* joy may be complete" (italics added; John 15:11). If John's gospel influenced the author's choice of words here, it provides intrinsic evidence that the original reading was the second person plural.

The repetition of the verb "write" (γράφω) throughout 1 John makes it difficult to argue that this book originated as anything but in written form, despite its rhetorical features that suggest an oral delivery.[37] Given that most reading was done aloud in the first century, even written works would have been composed with consideration of how the wording sounded, and the elusive structure of 1 John may be due largely to this aural context, which is unfamiliar to readers within literary cultures.[38] Although it originated as written discourse, the letter's lack of the standard Hellenistic letter opening and of any conventional closing greetings means it could not have been a personal letter, even though traditionally it is called just that (see discussion of genre in Introduction to 1 John). Evidently the author's identity, which would have been specified in the conventional letter opening, must have been clearly known to the original recipients through other means, perhaps communicated by the courier of the letter or because it was sent with a cover letter, possibly what we know as 2 John (see Introduction to 2 John).

Socio-rhetorical analysis has shown that 1 John 1:1 – 4 functions as the *exordium* of rhetorical discourse, intended to predispose the audience to adhere to the author's viewpoint.[39] The character of an author as a perceivably good man and reliable witness is, according to Quintilian, the strongest influence at every point of the case to be made (*Inst.* 4.1.7). In this case, the origin of John's longstanding message of eyewitness testimony about the Life that appeared makes the author a reliable witness, an important factor in persuading the readers to his viewpoint. This opening establishes the author's authority to speak to the issues that he will develop in the body of the letter, specifically to speak against those who are teaching an aberrant Christology.

These opening verses of 1 John establish the author's authority to teach spiritual truth because his message is grounded in both the historical reality of Jesus Christ and his authoritative understanding of the true significance of those facts. His message is not something that he has merely dreamed up, perhaps in contrast to false teaching mentioned later in the letter. John invites his readers to the fellowship of like belief, that they might have fellowship not only with the author but also with the Father and Jesus Christ, and thereby truly know God. This will make their joy complete.

Theology in Application

It is difficult to imagine any two topics of greater relevance and importance to Christian theology and life than the authority of Scripture and the nature of Jesus

---

36. See John R. Yarid, "Reflections of the Upper Room Discourse in 1 John," *BSac* 160 (2003): 65 – 76.

37. Russ Dudrey, "1 John and the Public Reading of Scripture," *SCJ* 6 (Fall 2003): 235 – 55.

38. For a recent work on this important topic see Brickle, *Aural Design.*

39. Watson, "'Keep Yourselves From Idols.'"

Christ. The eyewitness testimony of the Twelve (with Judas replaced by the apostle Paul), whom Jesus selected to bear witness of the significance of his life, death, and resurrection, now resides in the pages of the NT. This is not to say that every NT book was written by an eyewitness of Jesus, for clearly not all were. Luke, for instance, did not see Jesus with his eyes, but he worked closely with the apostle Paul, who encountered the risen Jesus on the Damascus road. Mark, who as a young boy may actually have seen Jesus, is said to have produced his gospel from the eyewitness testimony of Peter.

The gospel of John had its origin in the eyewitness testimony of the disciple whom Jesus loved, who was likely the apostle John. James is the half brother of Jesus, who became the leader of the church in Jerusalem after Peter's departure. While the authors of some books cannot be identified with certainty, this commentary operates on the premise that the NT is the repository of the reliable and authoritative witness to the significance of the person and message of Jesus Christ. Beyond its reliability as ancient and authentic human testimony to Jesus, it is the divinely inspired Word of God, whose truth is based on the character of God himself. The NT is God's interpretation of the significance of Jesus.

The Problem of Truth in an Age of Relativism

In our day the proclamation of the gospel as the exclusive truth about Jesus Christ has fallen out of favor with many, even among those who would self-identify as Christians. The influence of cultural pressures such as rationalism and historical criticism, New Age spirituality, and radical ecumenicalism with non-Christian religions has reduced the NT to an irrelevant ancient artifact, at worst, or as simply one option for modern religion, at best. To preach the NT as the exclusive truth about Jesus Christ and his mission to reconcile humanity to God is often viewed dimly as an assertion of power and inappropriate behavior in our largely pluralistic modern society.

It can be reassuring to realize that this situation today is similar to that of the first century, when heresy made inroads into Christian communities through the influence of Greco-Roman philosophy, through the beliefs and practices of pagan religions, and under the pressure of the Roman rule to accept polytheism and pluralism in the name of the empire so that one might not be a "hater of mankind" (Suetonius, *Nero* 16). It is reassuring to realize that despite such a hostile environment, the NT and its apostolic witness have survived, bringing the true gospel message to successive generations of people from the time the ink dried on the autographs down through the centuries to our present day.

In the earliest days of the infant church, before the NT had come into existence, the mobility that allowed the gospel to travel throughout the Roman Empire in just a few decades also gave rise to the problem of conflicting interpretations of Jesus' life and the apostles' teachings that were incompatible with the truth.[40] All of the epistles preserved in the NT had some concern to define and circumscribe the boundary of truth against false claims. Now that the church has the NT, there is still the problem of interpretations of its text that bend and distort its message. Moreover, we now live in a time that manifests the further problem of a radical relativism that denies there is one truth, one meaning of a text, one orthodox interpretation of the gospel message. Nevertheless, this ancient book that preserves the voices of the Lord's apostles will continue to speak to every generation until the Lord returns. Far from being an assertion of power, the apostolic gospel is a gracious invitation to fellowship with God and his Son, Jesus Christ. Those who embrace the gospel find fellowship with one another around the Word of God and with the apostles he chose to be bearers of his revelation.

The second point of essential importance is that Jesus Christ was a real person whom many people heard, saw, and touched. While the Holy Spirit today mediates Christ's presence to his church, the work of the Spirit does not replace the incarnation of Christ as the man Jesus. In fact, it was necessary for Jesus to be born into humanity, to live a sinless life, to die a redemptive death, and to rise from the grave in final victory before the Holy Spirit could be given (John 16:7). The work of the Spirit is to testify about Jesus (15:26), not to offer a generic brand of spirituality or religious experience of the kinds so popular in our modern society. The point of 1 John 1:1 – 4 is that Jesus really was with us, that the eternally preexistent Son of God was here! God knows firsthand the joys and sorrows, the trials and temptations, the hopes and fears of being human. The gospel message of the apostles originated in their encounter with the God-man.

Ongoing Revelation from the Spirit?

Modern claims that the work of the Spirit offers the world something in addition to Jesus Christ, or other than Jesus Christ, were also preceded by such claims already in the first century. The dispute between John and those who went out from his church(es) was evidently about the true nature of Christ, with the heretics influenced by neoplatonic ideas and likely claiming some sort of truth based perhaps in a misunderstanding of the promises of the gospel of John. This opening unit of 1 John points its readers today as it did in ancient times to the inseparable truth that Jesus is who the NT says he is, and that apart from the NT, there is no true knowledge about Jesus Christ. The Spirit's work today is always in agreement with the testimony of the NT.

---

40. Judith M. Lieu, *The Second and Third Epistles of John: History and Background* (Edinburgh: T&T Clark, 1986), 129 – 30.

CHAPTER 2

1 John 1:5 – 10

Literary Context

After the author has established the basis of his authority in 1:1 – 4, this pericope opens the body of the letter by making a major theological statement, "God is light ..." (1:5), from which all of John's subsequent teaching flows. He introduces the topic of sin, one of the three major foci of the letter. (The other two are Christology and the ethical mandate to love.) Discussion of this subject extends at least through 2:6, and the topic is raised again in chapter 3. Because John chooses to introduce this topic first, one could argue that his concern about his readers' understanding of sin is prominently in mind.

    I. John Claims the Authority of the Apostolic Witness (1:1 – 4)

→ **II. Announcement of the Message (1:5 – 10)**

    A. God Is Light (1:5)

    B. First Two Contrasting Conditional Clauses (1:6 – 7)

    C. Second Two Contrasting Conditional Clauses (1:8 – 9)

    D. Fifth Conditional Clause: If We Say That We Have Not Sinned ... (1:10)

    III. Dealing with Sin (2:1 – 6)

Main Idea

God himself defines the standard of human morality and spirituality that is necessary in order to have fellowship with him, a state that John refers to as being "in the light." Sin is the opposite and violation of that standard, which makes fellowship with God impossible and is described as walking "in darkness." God sent his Son into history to die the atoning death that cleanses sin and restores fellowship with God, and so any claim that denies sin implicitly calls God a liar and is itself the essence of sin.

Translation

---

1 John 1:5–10

5a	assertion	And **this is the message**
		that we have heard from him and announce to you:

b	content	**God is light,** and
c	content	**there is no darkness in him at all.**

6a	condition	If we say,
b	content	"We have fellowship with him," and
c	condition	walk in the darkness,
d	result	**we lie**
e	result	and **we do not do the truth.**

7a	contrast	But if we walk in the light
		as he himself is in the light,
b	result	**we have fellowship with one another**
c	result	and **the blood of Jesus his Son cleanses us from all sin.**

8a	contrast & condition	If we say,
b	content	"We have no sin," then
c	result	**we deceive ourselves**
d	result	and **the truth is not in us.**

9a	condition	If we confess our sins,
b	assertion	**he is faithful and righteous,**
c	result	to forgive our sins and
d	result	to cleanse us from all unrighteousness.

10a	condition	If we say,
b	content	"We have not sinned,"
c	result	**we make him a liar**
d	result	and **his word is not in us.**

Structure

The major theological statement in 1:5 stands as a heading and foundational premise over all that follows. The author announces the message that he has heard and proclaims to his readers, that God is light, in whom there is no darkness. This statement invokes a duality between light and its opposite — darkness — which characterizes the Johannine conceptual universe and carries through the discourse. The pericope is then structured by five third class conditional clauses, each introduced by "if" (ἐάν) in verses 6, 7, 8, 9, and 10. The first and second conditional clauses form a contrasting pair (vv. 6 and 7), as do the third and fourth conditional clauses (vv. 8 and 9). The fifth conditional clause may function as a final statement that reiterates the previously stated conditions. The repetition of "if we say" (ἐὰν εἴπωμεν, vv. 6, 8, 10) creates the powerful rhetorical effect of revealing a logical progression toward the disastrous conclusion of making God a liar (v. 10). The negative "if ... then" statements are as follows:

v. 6a – c   If we say, "We have fellowship with him," and walk in the darkness ...
v. 8a – b   If we say, "We have no sin" ...
v. 10a – b If we say, "We have not sinned" ...
v. 6d – e   ... [then] we lie and we do not do the truth.
v. 8c – d   ... then we deceive ourselves and the truth is not in us.
v. 10c – d ... [then] we make him a liar and his word is not in us.

The claim to be in fellowship while sinning is a lie, which turns into self-deception when not confessed. Sustained self-deception that rationalizes sin implicitly calls God a liar and puts one on the side of darkness. The remedy that interrupts and prevents the progression is found in vv. 7c, 9d: Jesus' blood cleanses sin when it is confessed and not denied.

Exegetical Outline

→ **II. Announcement of the Message (1:5 – 10)**
    A. God is light (1:5)
    B. First two contrasting conditional clauses (1:6 – 7)
        1. If we claim to have fellowship with God ... (1:6)
        2. but if we walk in the light ... (1:7)
    C. Second two contrasting conditional clauses (1:8 – 9)
        1. If we claim to have no sin ... (1:8)
        2. [but] if we confess our sin ... (1:9)
    D. Fifth conditional clause: if we say that we have not sinned ... (1:10)

Explanation of the Text

1:5 And this is the message that we have heard from him and announce to you: God is light, and there is no darkness in him at all (Καὶ ἔστιν αὕτη ἡ ἀγγελία ἣν ἀκηκόαμεν ἀπ' αὐτοῦ καὶ ἀναγγέλλομεν ὑμῖν, ὅτι ὁ θεὸς φῶς ἐστιν καὶ σκοτία ἐν αὐτῷ οὐκ ἔστιν οὐδεμία). After establishing his authority to deliver a message that is rooted in both the historical facts about Jesus and his true significance (1:1 – 4), John transitions from the introduction about the source and authority of his teaching to its first major point: "God is light, and there is no darkness in him at all." Using the binary opposites of light and darkness from the natural world, the statement invokes a conceptual dualism that characterizes Johannine thought and that will be carried throughout 1 John. (See "In Depth: The Johannine Dualistic Framework" below.)

Light is an apt metaphor for God, for it is the first fundamental property of the universe created by God (Gen 1:1), it allows and sustains all life, it makes life far more pleasant and safer than living in the dark, and it reveals what is hidden. The statement "God is light" (ὁ θεὸς φῶς ἐστιν) is not a metaphysical statement about God, which would lead to a type of pantheism, as if the photons in the universe had some divine quality. Rather, the statement describes a fundamental axiom about God that is important for John's teaching. Just as light and darkness cannot physically coexist in the same space, John uses this duality to explain what constitutes fellowship with God and what disqualifies a person from fellowship, because sin and righteousness are as mutually exclusive as light and darkness.

The opposition of light and darkness was a ubiquitous motif in ancient religions, just as it remains today, with light representing the positive value and darkness the negative. Therefore, scholars debate which connotations associated with light the author had in mind and what he was intending to communicate about God. One could look to the OT or to ancient Jewish tradition preserved, for instance, at Qumran or in Philo's writings.[1]

The polarity between light and darkness is found in the Qumran documents as they describe the "lot" of the righteous: "And you, [O God,] created us for yourself as an eternal people, and into the *lot of light* [*wbgrl 'wr*] you cast us" (1QM 13.9, cf. 13.10). In Philo, the creation account is shown to be the root of the Jewish moral categories: "And after the shining forth of that light, perceptible only to the intellect, which existed before the sun, then its adversary darkness yielded, as God put a wall between them and separated them, well knowing *their opposite characters, and the enmity existing between their natures*" (*Opif.* 33, italics added). Philo also describes God as dwelling in pure light, which accounts for his omniscience:

> For it is impossible for us, who are but men, to foresee all the contingencies of future events, or to anticipate the opinions of others; but to *God*, as dwelling in pure *light*, all things are visible; for he, penetrating into the very recesses of the soul, is able to see, with the most perfect certainty, what is invisible to others. (*Deus* 29, italics added)

The presence of the polarity in both Qumran and Hellenistic Jewish thought shows that John is not being distinctively creative when he associates God with light and insists that those who have fellowship with God must live in the light where God is. Because this duality pervades his writings, the first, but perhaps not final, source for understanding this polarity must be John's gospel, which has twenty-three occurrences of "light" (φῶς) in sixteen verses (see John 1:4, 5, 7, 8, 9; 3:19, 20, 21; 5:35; 8:12; 9:5; 11:9, 10; 12:35, 36, 46). That gospel first refers to light in reference to the incarnation of Jesus Christ: "In him was life, and that *life* was the *light* of all mankind" (John 1:4, italics added); and, "The true light that gives light to everyone was coming into the world" (1:9). A primary association of light in John's thought seems to be life that results when one comes into the true light that has come into the world, the Lord Jesus Christ (1:12).

---

1. There are several parallel themes when 1 John is compared with material in the Dead Sea Scrolls, including light and darkness, truth and deceit, categorizing people into "sons of light" and "sons of darkness" — each category being motivated by spirit forces. This does not indicate that John was directly referring to the Qumran material, only that these categories were a common way of thinking in Jewish thought across the various forms of Second Temple Judaism. See Kruse, *Letters of John*, 32, for further discussion.

In addition to the three verses just noted, John's gospel identifies Jesus as the Light of Life in many statements (italics added):

John 1:5: The *light* shines in the darkness, and the darkness has not overcome it.

John 8:12: When Jesus spoke again to the people, he said, "I am the *light* of the world. Whoever follows me will never walk in darkness, but will have the *light* of *life*."

John 9:5: "While I am in the world, I am the *light* of the world."

John 12:35: Then Jesus told them, "You are going to have the *light* just a little while longer. Walk while you have the *light*, before darkness overtakes you. Whoever walks in the dark does not know where they are going."

John 12:36: "Believe in the *light* while you have the *light*, so that *you may become children of light*."

This association of light with *life* is apt also in 1 John with the stated purpose of the letter, to reassure its readers that they have eternal life in the name of the Son of God (5:13). But 1:5 – 10 brings out the moral aspect of the metaphor. The statement that God is light and that in him there is no darkness at all is a definition of ethical and moral goodness, for John goes on to say that those who "walk in the darkness" cannot be in fellowship with God. This thought has metaphorical coherence with the use of light as a symbol for life in John's gospel, for God is the source of life, and to have fellowship with God means to have life, as Adam and Eve did before they were deceived. When they turned away from God, the very source of life, the inevitable consequence was to suffer death. Even today when people criticize God for imposing such a harsh penalty, they fail to recognize that God did not say, "If you sin, I will kill you," but "You will die." To remove oneself from God's presence through sin is of necessity to remove oneself from the source of life, and therefore, death is the only place to go.

The identification of God with light is given as the content of the message that "we" have heard and is, therefore, the logical starting point of the duality of light and darkness in John's thinking. Living after the invention of electric lights, we rarely feel the power of this duality. But if you have ever had a power failure after sunset or experienced absolute darkness in the depths of a cave when the tour guide turned off the light, that memory may help you to feel the force of the duality. The symbol of darkness represents all that defeats life. The duality is stated explicitly with John's comment, "there is no darkness in [God] at all" (σκοτία ἐν αὐτῷ οὐκ ἔστιν οὐδεμία). Notice the two negatives "no … none" (οὐκ … οὐδεμία), emphasizing the complete absence of darkness in God. With this John draws the sharpest of lines to position God and light on one side of the duality; on the other side, darkness represents all that is not of God.

Although the statement formally introduces the topic of sin in 1:6 – 10, the statement of the message can also function as a heading for the entire letter. Everything that John will address about sin, Christology, and love throughout the letter takes its starting point from the defining idea that God is light and that in him there is no darkness. It is a summary statement of the message that John claims "we" have heard from "him." The first plural pronoun in v. 5 still functions to identify the author as an authoritative witness of the spiritual truth found in Christ. The nearest antecedent of the pronoun "him" is Jesus Christ in v. 3, preceded immediately by "the Father." John clearly claims divine revelation about God from Jesus, perhaps from Jesus' statement, "I am the light of the world" (John 8:12; 9:5). The statement need not be taken as a quotation from Jesus, but may be read as a theological summary of what Jesus taught and embodied about God as John heard it.

Both in this pericope and in John's gospel, the moral dimension of the metaphor is clear (John

11:10; 12:35, 36, 46). Jesus expected his followers to be "children of light" (12:36), children who have been given life by the Father and who therefore reflect the moral attributes of their Father. To be in darkness is to be without the light, which results in evil thoughts and behaviors that cannot claim fellowship with Jesus Christ or the Father.

The closest statements elsewhere in the Bible to "God is light, and there is no darkness in him at all" are the statements that God is "a faithful God who does no wrong" (Deut 32:4 NIV 1984) and "the LORD is upright ... there is no wickedness in him" (Ps 92:15 NIV 1984). The binary opposition of light and darkness expresses symbolically the two ways to walk — an expression that is characteristic of Jewish Second Temple tradition found, for instance, in the *Testament of Asher*: "God gave mankind two ways and two dispositions and two types of action and two manners and two goals ... two ways, of good and evil" (*T. Ash.* 1:3 – 5). A similar construction is found in Qumran's *Community Rule* and other documents from that community.

John's gospel also speaks of light as a moral category (italics added below):

John 3:19: This is the verdict: *Light* has come into the world, but people loved darkness instead of light because their deeds were evil.

John 3:20: Everyone who does evil hates the *light*, and will not come into the *light* for fear that their deeds will be exposed.

John 3:21: But whoever *lives by the truth* comes into the *light*, so that it may be seen plainly that what they have done has been done in the sight of God.

John 11:9: Jesus answered, "Are there not twelve hours of daylight? Anyone who walks in the daytime will not stumble, for they see *by this world's light*.

John 12:46: I have come into the world as a *light*, so that no one who believes in me should stay in darkness.

The primary implication of John's introductory statement about God is that, if God *is* light, then God himself by virtue of his being and character defines the moral standard of human life.

Many voices compete for the prerogative of defining morality in our times, and it was no less so in the first century. Philosophers, pagan priests and priestesses, and rulers who legislated, as well as other individuals who felt entitled to do so, made claims about moral truth, just as many people today wish to assume that prerogative (see Theology in Application). But it is only God himself, the creator and sustainer of all life, who can authoritatively define moral truth. To know God is therefore to know truth about how to live in the way that he intends. It is only within a life of obedience to God's moral truth that a relationship with God, what John calls fellowship, can be sustained. What follows in 1:6 – 2:2 is an unpacking of the implications of this theological statement that God is light for those who claim to have fellowship with him, especially for those whose lives do not bear out the truth of their profession.

IN DEPTH: The Johannine Dualistic Framework

Because God is light, everything that is the antithesis of God is darkness. John uses the mutually exclusive duality between light and darkness to order and structure his theological worldview, both in the letters and the gospel. God, who is the light of life, came into a dark world, and the darkness was not able to extinguish the light (John 1:4 – 5, 9). Starting with light and darkness, John builds a dualistic frame based on binary polarities: above and below, good and evil, truth and lies, life and death.[2] As John presents the human condition, each person is either in the light or in the darkness, which is surely a vantage point only God himself knows. For in the end, all will be sorted into only two groups, but at the present time those who are in darkness may come into the light, and some who claim to be in the light are actually still in darkness (1 John 2:9). The point John makes with his moral duality is an eschatological point, showing that one's standing with God is not always evident from a snapshot of a moment in one's life.

N. T. Wright presents four types of dualities regularly accepted in the first-century thought of mainline Judaism, three of which can be seen in John's dualistic framework: the theological/cosmological, the moral, and the eschatological.[3] The *theological/cosmological* duality observes the Creator-creation distinction and is reflected in the gospel with reference to the Word, apart from whom nothing was made that has been made, who was with God above but came into the world below (John 1:1 – 3, 10, 14).

The *moral* duality is based on the theological; if the righteous God is light, in whom there is no darkness at all, he has the authority to define human morality. Behavior that is not of God is of sin and lies in the realm of darkness. People choose darkness because their deeds are evil (John 3:19). Refusing to come into the light, they are alienated from God and will perish in their sins. It is only by coming to the light of life, Jesus Christ, that one is cleansed from sin and has fellowship with God (1 John 1:3, 7). The moral duality that John presents assigns sin to the dark side, yet he recognizes that believers in the light nevertheless do sin. It is that tension between his dualistic framework and the existential reality of sin that causes him to write as he does about Christian sin in 1 John 3:1 – 10 (esp. v. 9). He must uphold in principle both the darkness of sin and the ongoing cleansing of sin for believers in Christ. Christ came to destroy sin, and so those who follow him must not sin; but the sin of believers can be cleansed and forgiven, whereas the sin of those in darkness, who reject the light, cannot.

The *eschatological* duality is present in the Johannine framework because of its emphasis on eternal life after death. Although John does not contrast this age and the age to come explicitly, he does imply it when he writes: "The world and its desires are passing away, but the one who does the will of God remains

2. Richard B. Hays, *The Moral Vision of the New Testament: Community, Cross, New Creation: A Contemporary Introduction to New Testament Ethics* (Louisville: Westminster John Knox, 1996), 154.

3. N. T. Wright, *The New Testament and the People of God* (Christian Origins and the Question of God, vol. 1; Minneapolis: Fortress, 1992), 253, 255 – 56.

forever" (1 John 2:17). In fact, in John's thinking, believers have already passed from this life into eternal life (John 5:24). The realm of the light is present, and therefore the eschatological promise of eternal life has been realized. The eternal age is present in the life of believers, but this age, referred to in Johannine language as "the world," is passing away. Whatever good the world may offer is of temporary and transient value. As Hays points out, "it is not quite correct to describe John's worldview as a cosmic dualism, for the powers of light and darkness are not equally counterposed. There is never any doubt of God's ultimate sovereignty and triumph over evil."[4]

John presents his dualistic framework to show the theological truth of God, to discuss the human condition of life in this world, and to present the eschatological reality of eternal life after death for those who walk in the light, who find their life in the Son of God.

1:6 If we say, "We have fellowship with him," and walk in the darkness, we lie and we do not do the truth (Ἐὰν εἴπωμεν ὅτι κοινωνίαν ἔχομεν μετ' αὐτοῦ καὶ ἐν τῷ σκότει περιπατῶμεν, ψευδόμεθα καὶ οὐ ποιοῦμεν τὴν ἀλήθειαν). John begins his teaching that a profession of faith in Christ requires a life that matches it. He does not here specify what walking in the darkness entails, but based on the light/dark duality, it clearly means walking in a way that is totally antithetical to God, in whom there is no darkness at all. Therefore, any claim to be in fellowship with God while walking in darkness is clearly a lie.

"To walk" in Hebrew idiom refers to the way one lives and behaves (e.g., Gen 5:24; Deut 5:33; Ps 1:1). "To walk in the light" means allowing God's revealed will to motivate and guide one's actions and decisions. To live and behave in a way that is antithetical to God means that one is not living out the truth. In modern Western culture, "truth" is a mental, cognitive entity, but one of the distinctives of Johannine thought is that truth is not a doctrine to be believed and accepted cognitively;

it is something that must be done ("I do"; ποιέω), something to be embodied by the person claiming to have the truth (see "In Depth: 'Truth' in John's Letters," below). To do the truth means to live in accordance with God's definition of truth in all our words and decisions. Clearly John here aligns lies and self-deceit with darkness.

The present tense of the verbs "walk" (περιπατῶμεν) and "do" (ποιοῦμεν) is sometimes pressed to add the nuance of customary or habitual behavior.[5] However, tense alone cannot bear that weight. Rather, this tense is chosen to be compatible with the semantic sense of the verbs in context, which provides the nuance of customary or ongoing behavior. "To walk" as used for an idiom for living is by its nature an ongoing process. The negative added to the verb "do" (ποιοῦμεν) explains in negative terms what it means to walk in darkness, and therefore also connotes ongoing or habitual process.

Verse 6 is the first of three occurrences of the conditional, subjunctive phrase "if we say" (ἐὰν εἴπωμεν), a phrase found elsewhere in deliberative

---

4. Hays, *Moral Vision*, 154.

5. E.g., Brown, *Epistles of John*, 197.

logic (e.g., Matt 21:25 – 26//Mark 11:31 – 32//Luke 20:5 – 6; LXX 4 Kgdms 7:4). It introduces a major theme in the letter, the topic of sin's effect on fellowship with God and with each other. This third class conditional is used to present a hypothetical situation that may or may not be in direct reference to those who left the Johannine church(es) under less than amiable circumstances (1 John 2:18 – 19).

Although the third class conditional "if" (ἐάν plus a verb in the subjunctive mood in the protasis) is often taught in Greek classes as a "future probable condition" or a "general condition," this does not prohibit the idea that the conditional is a present reality in some contexts. Daniel Wallace points out the overlap between the first class conditional, often called a condition of fact (εἰ plus a verb in the indicative mood, where the protasis is assumed true at least for argument's sake), and the third class conditional.[6] Furthermore, David Washburn's study of the third class conditionals in 1 John argues that most of them (twenty-two out of twenty-eight by his count) "focus on present time."[7] The resolution need not rest solely on the syntax of the third class conditional but may lie, rather, on the rhetorical effect of the statements.

Given the repeated language, it certainly sounds as if someone was in fact saying these things, or at least was inclined to do so. The "if we say …" clauses need not be taken as direct quotes from the opponents, but may be understood as ideas that needed correction regardless of their origin. As Lieu points out, "Although 1 John was written in the wake of a schism, it does not necessarily ad-dress the causes of that schism, only perhaps its effects."[8]

Rhetorically, the phrase "if we say" achieves a definition of a group *some* of whom may say such things, whether they are the ones who went out or are still among the congregation left behind. This likely accounts for the use of "if" (ἐάν) with the subjunctive, for as Wallace points out in his comment on 1 John 1:9, this is "a present general condition in which the subject is distributive ('if any one of us'). The subjunctive is thus used because of the implicit uncertainty as to who is included in the *we*."[9] In other words, the use of "if" (ἐάν) and the subjunctive does not necessarily argue against the inference that someone or some group was actually saying these things. The repetition of the phrase certainly sounds as if John believes it is something that is in danger of being said or is actually being said. His purpose is to show the logical consequences of such thinking. The sense of the general condition extends the force of the argument beyond the present situation and people (i.e., "if we *ever* say …") and may explain why the author chose ἐάν rather than εἰ.

The referent of the first plural pronoun shifts here in verse 6. It is no longer the "we" of authoritative testimony as in 1:1 – 4 but is likely the rhetorical "we," meant to create a sense of unity based on the congenial assumption of fellowship (1:3). It softens the challenge of the more blunt "if *you* say …" by including the author rhetorically among the hypothetical offenders, expressing the unity he hopes for within his church.

---

6. Daniel B. Wallace, *Greek Grammar beyond the Basics* (Grand Rapids: Zondervan, 1996), 685.

7. David I. Washburn, "Third Class Conditions in First John," *GTJ* 11 (1990): 221 – 28, esp. 223.

8. Lieu, *I, II, & III John*, 22.

9. Wallace, *Greek Grammar*, 698 (italics original).

IN DEPTH: "Truth" in John's Letters

In our times, truth is closely associated with facts. But John's writings show a truth that goes far beyond the facts to an interpretation of the significance and entailments of the facts. The purpose of the signs in John's gospel is not only to narrate miracles of Jesus, but also to present them in such a way that the astute reader perceives the identity of Jesus as both the long-awaited Messiah and the Savior sent by God to atone for sin.

John defines truth as that which has been revealed about God and mankind through the coming of Jesus, who declared that he *is* "the truth" (John 14:6). This absolute statement is further expounded by John's use of the adjective "true" (ἀληθινός), which carries the sense of authentic, genuine, and real. In John's gospel, Jesus is "the true light" (John 1:9), "the true bread" (6:32), and "the true vine" (15:1). The truth that Jesus brings is not simply one story among many or one claim to spiritual truth, but is revelatory of God, who can be known in no other way (1:18). The incarnation creates a reality against which all other claims to truth are to be measured.

Accordingly, the challenge John puts before his readers goes beyond believing the truth. In our society, truth is a cognitive concept, something that one believes or that can be proven or falsified. John certainly emphasizes believing the truth, but truth for him goes beyond the cognitive to the way life is lived. Truth is something that should not merely have our intellectual assent but is something that believers in Christ *do*. If truth is the reality that Jesus has revealed, then it demands those who believe in him live according to that truth (1 John 1:6; 2 John 4; 3 John 4).

A central aspect of the reality Jesus Christ has revealed is that all human beings are sinners, alienated from life-giving fellowship with God. Atonement for sin is at the heart of the truth Jesus reveals, and there can be no claim to truth that overlooks sin (1 John 1:8; 2:4; 5:6). To walk in the truth means to be cleansed from sin and to stop sinning, for Jesus came to destroy sin (2:1; 3:5 – 6). In this way, the great theological truths of Christianity are related to Christian ethics. Anyone who does not love others sins against them, by John's definition (3:10, 14, 17 – 18, 23; 4:21; 5:2; 2 John 6).

Therefore, truth in John's writings refers not only to individual propositions to be believed, but to the entire revelation of God in Christ that Jesus brought into the world (see also the Theology of John's Letters).

1:7 But if we walk in the light as he himself is in the light, we have fellowship with one another and the blood of Jesus his Son cleanses us from all sin (ἐὰν δὲ ἐν τῷ φωτὶ περιπατῶμεν ὡς αὐτός ἐστιν ἐν τῷ φωτί, κοινωνίαν ἔχομεν μετ᾽ ἀλλήλων καὶ τὸ αἷμα Ἰησοῦ τοῦ υἱοῦ αὐτοῦ καθαρίζει ἡμᾶς ἀπὸ πάσης ἁμαρτίας). In contrast to claiming fellowship with God but walking in darkness, when one walks in the light as God himself is in the light, fellowship *with one another* is achieved, and one is cleansed from all sin by the blood of Jesus, God's Son.

Surprisingly, John does not say that by walking in the light one achieves fellowship *with God*, which might be expected to follow from v. 6, and this no doubt accounts for the textual variant "with him" (μετ᾽ αὐτοῦ). The more unexpected statement that mentions fellowship with "one another" (ἀλλήλων) introduces the thought that fellowship with God and fellowship in the Christian community are intimately related. Only when believers are walking in the light can we have fellowship with God, a fellowship that is embodied as fellowship with one another.

Moreover, John associates being cleansed from sin by Jesus' blood, a reference to his death, with walking in the light. The word "sin" (ἁμαρτία) makes its first appearance in the letter here. By implication, sin and walking in the darkness are associated, but cleansing from sin is associated with walking in the light. Uncleansed sin breaks fellowship with one another and with God.

After the statement that God is light (v. 5), it is striking to see the simile that John's readers are to "walk in the light as [ὡς] he [God himself] is in the light." Note that the emphatic personal pronoun "himself" (αὐτός) must refer to God, because John goes on to refer to Jesus as "his" Son. Witherington

sees this as a reference to God's behavior, which "can stand the light of day or close scrutiny."[10] The simile has biblical parallels, such as the "Lord of lords ... who lives in unapproachable light" (1 Tim 6:15 – 16). God himself is the source of the light, and those who wish to be in fellowship with him must dwell in that same light of moral truth that God has revealed in Jesus Christ.

The blood of Jesus, God's Son, cleanses those who walk in the light of God's moral truth and have fellowship with one another. "The blood of Jesus" refers to his death on the cross and argues against those who claim that it is Jesus' ethical teachings that form the heart of the Christian gospel. To walk in the light *means* to be cleansed from sin. People don't need just more good ethical instruction; rather, they need purification from all that separates them from the presence and purposes of God. Christ's atonement for sin achieves a reconciliation with God that restores fellowship.

1:8 If we say, "We have no sin," then we deceive ourselves and the truth is not in us (ἐὰν εἴπωμεν ὅτι ἁμαρτίαν οὐκ ἔχομεν, ἑαυτοὺς πλανῶμεν καὶ ἡ ἀλήθεια οὐκ ἔστιν ἐν ἡμῖν). John now begins to develop the association between sin and truth. This second pair of contrasting conditions involves one's attitude toward sin. John claims that if anyone should say that they have no sin to deal with, they are self-deceived.

The issue of self-deception regarding sin in one's Christian life is perennial. Fallen human nature leads us to rationalize our sin and thereby deny it. Vigilance all throughout life is called for, with each decision to speak or act. How many ways are there to deny sin? One might claim perfection in Christ. One might reason that anything a Christian does must be okay. Or one might simply define what one does as not sin — a phenomenon increasingly seen

---

10. Ben Witherington III, *A Socio-Rhetorical Commentary on Titus, 1 – 2 Timothy and 1 – 3 John* (vol. 1 of Letters and Homilies for Hellenized Christians; Downers Grove, IL: InterVarsity Press, 2006), 453.

in societies where what is legal is not necessarily morally righteous as God defines it.

But there is more to it: the very duality between light and darkness that John teaches raises the question of whether those who are walking in the light as believing Christians *can* sin. In John's strong duality between light and darkness, sin is on the side of darkness, and John describes no twilight that might allow for an admission of sin in the lives of light-dwellers. This could lead believing Christians to conclude that by definition they cannot sin and therefore say, "I have no sin." If the gospel of John was written before this letter, John may here be correcting a misinterpretation of the light duality found there. Thus, John will spend considerable ink in this letter explaining how the existential presence of sin in the life of Christians is related to the light-dark duality, which would seem to exclude its presence in the life of a believer (see also comments on 3:1 – 10).

Regardless of whether the denial of one's sin comes from the rationalizations of a fallen heart or from a misunderstanding of John's duality, if anyone says they have no sin, they are self-deceived and the truth revealed by Christ is not in them. John is addressing believing Christians, and yet he explains that to deny one's sin is itself an act of darkness. The truth cannot be in those who deny their sin, because by definition a Christian is one who lives by the truth that Jesus died to cleanse their sin. Thus, to reassure his readers of their eternal life (5:13), John must address the problem of ongoing sin in the Christian's life (see the Theology of John's Letters).

1:9 If we confess our sins, he is faithful and righteous, to forgive our sins and to cleanse us from all unrighteousness (ἐὰν ὁμολογῶμεν τὰς ἁμαρτίας ἡμῶν, πιστός ἐστιν καὶ δίκαιος, ἵνα ἀφῇ ἡμῖν τὰς ἁμαρτίας καὶ καθαρίσῃ ἡμᾶς ἀπὸ πάσης ἀδικίας). The alternative to denying one's sin is to confess it. Denying one's sin is inconsistent with walking in the light, which entails the recognition of sin and a willingness to confess it.

John does not specify the setting or scope for confession, but wisdom suggests that the confession of sin should be confined to those with knowledge of the sin. Confession is not a magic incantation or a ritual that in and of itself is efficacious. The efficacy of confession of sin lies not in the confessor but in the faithfulness (πιστός) and righteousness (δίκαιος) of God, whose Son's blood was shed for this very purpose (v. 7). Because the Father sent Jesus Christ to be the atonement for sin, he would be unfaithful to that purpose if he ignored the confession of sin or withheld the grace promised. John declares the impossibility of the confessor being turned away because God *is* faithful and righteous to his purposes in the atoning work of Jesus Christ, with both the intention and result (ἵνα) that he cleanses those who confess from all unrighteousness.

The language of God's faithfulness and justice reflects his covenant (cf. Exod 34:6 – 7; Deut 7:8 – 10; 32:4).[11] Under the old covenant God defined sin and specified the consequences of living in ways that defied his moral law. The provisions for atonement under the old covenant pointed ahead to the day when Christ's blood would seal the final covenant of grace. Words of new covenant promises announced by the prophet Jeremiah are echoed throughout 1 John.[12] Both the forgiveness and the cleansing promised under the new covenant (Jer 33:8 [LXX Jer 40:8]) are here declared fulfilled in Christ. Because of his gracious provision for forgiveness, God would be unfaithful to his covenant promises and consequently unjust if

---

11. Brown, *Epistles of John*, 209 – 10.
12. Jintae Kim, "The Concept of Atonement in 1 John: A Redevelopment of the Second Temple Concept of Atonement" (PhD diss., Westminster Theological Seminary, 2003), 103.

he withheld forgiveness from those who confess their sin, or if he allowed those who deny sin to stand on the same footing as those who confess.

Because of God's character and his faithfulness to his promises that Christ fulfilled, cleansing from confessed sin is assured. Clearly, John teaches that walking in the light requires ongoing cleansing from sin in order to maintain fellowship with God, a fellowship that cannot be sustained if one concludes for whatever reason that one does not have sin and consequently that cleansing is no longer needed.

1:10 If we say, "We have not sinned," we make him a liar and his word is not in us (ἐὰν εἴπωμεν ὅτι οὐχ ἡμαρτήκαμεν, ψεύστην ποιοῦμεν αὐτὸν καὶ ὁ λόγος αὐτοῦ οὐκ ἔστιν ἐν ἡμῖν). The denial of sin is itself a profound sin that implicitly calls God a liar. This fifth and final third class conditional, "if we say …" (ἐὰν εἴπωμεν …), is a summary of the content of vv. 6–9 and presses home the severity of denying sin.

The perfect tense of the verb "have sinned" (ἡμαρτήκαμεν) suggests a persistent state of denial of sin in the past that has led to the present state, rather than an individual and temporary instance. It may hint that some of John's readers were reconsidering whether atonement really is at the heart of the Christian gospel. If there was a way they could understand themselves to have never sinned either before their Christian conversion or after, the focus of their "gospel" might shift away from the cross and, perhaps, onto Jesus' teaching or life example (as in fact has happened in liberal Protestantism). When sin becomes passé, atonement is unnecessary.

I have known professing Christians, even Christian clergy, who at some point in their Christian lives decided that their understanding of God's

work in the world had matured beyond the need for a sacrificial atonement, which they consider to be a primitive idea of the ancient world that is no longer necessary in today's more sophisticated understanding of religion. Whenever one denies the need for atonement, it is an implicit presumption of one's own innocence, in effect saying, "I have not sinned."

For any who think, for whatever reason, that they have not sinned, John holds the strongest accusation. Rather than being faithful Christians, they are in fact making God a liar because God says we have sinned and he sent his Son into the world to atone for the very sin that it has become so popular to deny. As Lieu comments:

> The very fact of divine forgiveness demonstrates the reality of sin, and since God's character both defines sin and inspires the forgiveness that God offers, then any denial of sin calls into question God's fidelity and truthfulness, [and] treats God as a liar.[13]

Whether this was the actual position of those who went out from the Johannine church(es) or was only a possibility raised in the wake of their leaving, John condemns the thought in the strongest terms.

Taken to refer to an individual, the statement that God's word (λόγος) is not in "us" means that people who stand in the state of denying sin are not truly regenerate, even if they consider themselves Christian. Taken as a collective, to believe and communicate this error means that the word of God is not being preached in such a community. In either case, God's truth is not in "them" (cf. v. 8). As Strecker points out:

> The dualism of "light and darkness" (vv. 5–7) is paralleled and interpreted by the contrast of "truth and falsehood" (vv. 6, 8, 10). The accent in

---

13. Lieu, *I, II, & III John*, 59.

both instances is ethical, since ψεύδεσθαι ("lying") is identical with "not doing the truth" (οὐ ποιεῖν τὴν ἀλήθειαν) = "walking in darkness" (ἐν τῷ σκότει περιπατεῖν, v. 6).[14]

In this opening of his letter, John is building and defining the conceptual duality of light and darkness, based on the presupposition that "God is light" in v. 5. In the next section he will discuss atonement as the heart of the gospel and what it means to live as people of the light.

Theology in Application

There are three essential and related theological points made in this pericope: (1) God's nature and being define the ethical and moral standard for human life; (2) the atonement of Jesus' death is central to having fellowship with God and is therefore at the heart of the gospel; and (3) to deny the reality of sin in general or the sin in one's own life is in essence to consider God a liar and destroys relationship with him.

God Defines the Standard of Human Morality

In a culture such as ours that values independent thinking and autonomy, it is often difficult for people to acknowledge the most basic principle of Theology 101: God is God and I am not. By virtue of the fact that he is the creator of the universe and all life within it, and in his ongoing role in sustaining all he has created, God's authority extends to the spiritual and moral universe in which human beings live. John's implicit claim that it is God himself who defines spiritual light and darkness is perhaps the foremost principle that seekers and converts to Christianity need to embrace. God is entitled to set the standards for human life and to judge each person according to those standards, whether or not they recognize his existence or authority. My role as a creature of God is to bend my will to his, to walk in the light as he has defined it, and to live with the moral consequences of my decisions. Without that fundamental understanding of God's sovereign right over all human beings, one cannot truly know God, accept Christ, or have a mature spiritual nature.

The Preeminence of Jesus' Death

John's letters do not describe the physical details of Jesus' death, but they assume the atonement of Jesus' death as central to having fellowship with God. The Fourth Gospel explains more deeply the crucifixion of Jesus, his resurrection, and the impartation of the Spirit to his disciples, and is intended to bring people to faith in Jesus Christ (John 20:30 – 31). The letters are written to those who have already professed faith in a crucified Lord but who are needing reassurance of eternal life during confusing times (1 John 5:13). John points out the inherent and profound

---

14. Strecker, *Johannine Letters*, 33.

contradiction between professing to be a Christian on the one hand, and denying that sin exists in one's life on the other. As Köstenberger puts it, "Hence it is not the claim of sinlessness that carries the day but the humble confession of the need for the cleansing blood of Christ that enables believers to continue 'walking in the light' and thus to enjoy fellowship both with Jesus and with other believers."[15]

The Reality of Sin

Readers today need to hear the third point made in this passage, which declares the reality of sin. There is in modern society a rationalization about sin that prevents even the word from being used beyond the walls of the church, for sin implies a moral responsibility to God. Wrong behavior is attributed to bad parenting, genetic propensities, or lack of adequate education, or it is embraced to affirm a perceived entitlement of individuals to define moral principles for themselves. The claim that there is a God and that violation of his moral standard is sin invites harsh social disapproval in a culture that no longer believes in absolute truth and sees any such claim as a wrongful and arrogant assertion of power.

Furthermore, it is increasingly difficult to define sin in a society where what is legal is not necessarily ethical and moral by God's standards. Collectively, modern mankind has said, "We have no sin," and "We have not sinned." Unfortunately, many preachers and churches have bent under that social pressure and largely avoid the "s" word. This will no doubt continue to be one of the greatest challenges to the church's proclamation of the gospel in the years ahead. This denial of sin by society, even with the complicity of the church, is itself sin. To deny sin is to call God a liar, for God has declared his moral standard and has paid dearly for our sin by sending Jesus Christ to die as our atonement. What serious business it is to deny sin in any of the many ways we humans, starting with Adam and Eve, have found to do it!

15. Andreas J. Köstenberger, *A Theology of John's Gospel and Letters* (BTNT; Grand Rapids: Zondervan, 2009), 265.

1 John 2:1 – 6

Literary Context

This pericope continues the topic of sin that was introduced in 1:5 – 10, but moves the discussion from the more general level of "if we say . . ." to a more personal, direct address to "my little children" (τεκνία μου). This term occurs several times within the letter, most often in discussions involving the fatherhood of God. It may reflect Jesus' use of the same term in the Upper Room Discourse (John 13:33).

The opening verse of this unit states the reason that the author writes "these things" (2:1), presumably referring back to the topic of sin and confession. John switches from "if we say" to "the one who says" (vv. 4, 6), which continues the discussion of consistency in the Christian life between a profession of faith in Christ and how one lives.

    I. John Claims the Authority of the Apostolic Witness (1:1 – 4)

    II. Announcement of the Message (1:5 – 10)

➡ **III. Dealing with Sin (2:1 – 6)**

       A. Bringing the Topic of Sin to Bear on His Readers (2:1 – 2)

       B. Knowing God Means Avoiding Sin by Keeping His Commands (2:3 – 6)

    IV. Love, Light, and Darkness (2:7 – 11)

Main Idea

This section addresses the relationship between two major concepts of authentic Christian living: the need to deal rightly with sin and the expression of love for God in Christ through obedience to his command. Both of these thoughts are integral to knowing God and, consequently, to having assurance of eternal life.

Translation

---

1 John 2:1–6

1a	address	My little children,
b	assertion	**these things I write to you**
c	purpose	so that you will not sin.
d	condition	But if someone should sin,
e	assertion	**we have a *paraclete* with the Father,**
f	apposition	the righteous Jesus Christ.
2a	assertion	**He himself is the atoning sacrifice for our sins,** and
b	expansion	not for ours alone, but also
c		for the whole world.
3a	basis	And **this is how we know**
b	content	that we know him:
c	condition	if we keep his commands.
4a	assertion	**The one who says,**
	content	"I know him," and
		does not keep his commands
b	inference	**is a liar,**
c	expansion	and **the truth is not in them.**
5a	contrast	But whoever keeps his word,
b	identification	in this one
	assertion	**the love of God truly has reached its fulfillment.**
c	assertion	**This is how we know that we are in him:**
6a	exhortation	**the one who says, "I remain in him," ought also himself to walk**
b	description	just as that One walked.

Structure

These verses are part of a larger discourse unit that extends from 2:1 through 2:17. Its span is marked by the vocative "my little children" (τεκνία μου) in v. 6 and the vocative "dear friends" (ἀγαπητοί) in v. 7 that begins a smaller discourse unit. Verse 1 ("these things I write to you so that you will not sin") stands as the summary statement of the pericope.

The passage divides into two segments: vv. 1–2 and vv. 3–6 (which is further structured by the two statements in vv. 3 and 6, "this is how we know...." Each of these two statements is followed by the example of "the one who says...."

Exegetical Outline

→ **III. Dealing with Sin (2:1 – 6)**

    A. Bringing the topic of sin to bear on his readers (2:1 – 2)

        1. An admonition not to sin (2:1a-c)

        2. Reassurance if one should sin (2:1d – 2c)

            a. Jesus is the paraclete (2:1e-f)

            b. Jesus is the atoning sacrifice for sin (2:2)

    B. Knowing God means avoiding sin by keeping his commands (2:3 – 6)

        1. Keeping God's commands is the completion of God's love (2:3 – 5)

        2. Remaining in God means living as Jesus did (2:6)

Explanation of the Text

2:1 My little children, these things I write to you so that you will not sin. But if someone should sin, we have a *paraclete* with the Father, the righteous Jesus Christ (Τεκνία μου, ταῦτα γράφω ὑμῖν ἵνα μὴ ἁμάρτητε. καὶ ἐάν τις ἁμάρτῃ, παράκλητον ἔχομεν πρὸς τὸν πατέρα, Ἰησοῦν Χριστὸν δίκαιον). John states a second purpose for his letter: that his readers will not sin. This is entailed in having the joy of fellowship with God, the first stated purpose in 1:3 – 4.

After correcting anyone who might be denying or rationalizing their sin, John introduces an affectionate, conciliatory tone by addressing his readers as "my little children" (note the diminutive form of the plural, τεκνία). This vocative establishes his affection for his readers, while yet maintaining his authority to instruct them as someone older and wiser in the faith, and possibly someone who may have directly or indirectly been responsible for their conversion to Christ. Tradition holds that the apostle John left Palestine about the time of the destruction of the temple in Jerusalem in AD 70 and settled in Ephesus, from where he evangelized

and planted churches in the surrounding region. Since the gospel had been so well received through the apostle Paul, who was executed in the mid-60s, John may have chosen Ephesus to continue an apostolic witness there.

Here, for the first time in the letter, the author refers to himself in the first person singular, "I write" (γράφω), which argues against the theory that this book may have begun solely as an oral form such as a homily or speech. Clearly the author foresaw as he wrote that his words would be sent in written form to their readers, even if the letter was read aloud to them. John's intent with respect to the topic of sin is clear: he writes to warn his readers against sinning, in the many ways that sinning is possible, including a denial of sin. His explanation of sin as walking in a darkness that has no place in the Christian's life both underscores the serious nature of sin and at the same time raises questions about the existential reality of sin, especially in the lives of believers. Much of what he subsequently will say on the topic addresses this tension. The subjunctive verbal form "will not sin" (μὴ ἀμάρτητε) is required in a *hina* clause expressing purpose, but that purpose is the admonition *not* to sin, which is better expressed in English with a future, imperatival form.

As Lieu observes, "the purpose of God's forgiveness is to prompt those who experience it not to repeat the wrongs of the past."[1] But John's wisdom also leads him to acknowledge immediately the reality that "someone" will likely sin. The subjunctive in the general, third class condition, "if someone should sin" (ἐάν τις ἀμάρτῃ), allows for that reality without countermanding his prior statement that they should not sin. In that case of someone sinning, his overarching purpose to reassure his readers that they have eternal life (5:13) comes into play. He asserts that "we have" a *paraclete* with the Father, the righteous Jesus Christ (see 1:9).

The frequent use of the first person plural pronoun ("we") is distinctive of the Johannine writings. Its many occurrences in 1 John do not all have the same referent. In 1:1 – 4, regardless of whether it represents a genuine plural or stands as the author's singular self-reference, its sense is dissociative. There the author was distinguishing himself from his readers on the basis of his role as an authoritative witness to the incarnation and its significance. Here in 2:1 it is an associative or inclusive "we," for the author would certainly include himself among those for whom Jesus Christ is their *paraclete*.

The word *paraclete* (παράκλητος) is unique to the Johannine writings, but it does occur in Aquila's and Theodotion's versions in Job 16:2, replacing the cognate, παρακλήτωρ, found in Old Greek Job 16:2. There it refers to Job's supporters, as wrongheaded as they may have been. Outside the Bible, it occurs several times in Philo to refer to an eminent person "giving support to someone making a claim, or settling a dispute, or rebutting a charge,"[2] often in the context of the royal court. Philo's use of the word in the context of sacrifice for sin following restitution of an injured party is particularly of interest, for after propitiating the injured party, the guilty party is to go to the temple to ask for God's forgiveness, taking an irreproachable παράκλητος with him, which in this case is his own repentence (*Spec.* 1.237).[3]

Stoic influence in Philo casts the divine Logos as the *paraclete* who accompanies the high priest when he goes before God in the Holy of Holies on the Day of Atonement (*Mos.* 2.133 – 34).[4] In Jewish thought of that time, one's own good works were often thought to function as the *paraclete* before God's judgment.[5] Although sometimes interpreted as a legal advocate in court, it appears that it was a more general word with a broader meaning that has survived in several texts with a legal context. As Culy points out, the focus "is not so much on the ability of the [*paraclete*] παράκλητος to defend someone, but rather on the *status* of the παράκλητος, which allows him to bring about a good outcome for the one being accused" (italics original).[6]

The use of the word here echoes its occurrence in John 14:16, where Jesus says, "And I will ask the Father, and he will give you *another advocate* [παράκλητος] to help you and be with you forever" (italics added). Jesus refers to himself as the *paraclete*, or "advocate," of his disciples, and he promises the Holy Spirit will also function in that role. The "righteous Jesus Christ" (Ἰησοῦν Χριστὸν δίκαιον) is in apposition with *paraclete*. Although the Spirit is also a *paraclete*, it is the unique status of Jesus as the atoning sacrifice for sin (see 2:2) that is the

1. Lieu, *I, II, & III John*, 61.

2. Kenneth Grayston, "The Meaning of PARAKLETOS," *JSNT* 4 (1981): 72.

3. Ibid., 73.

4. Jintae Kim, "Concept of Atonement in 1 John," 97.

5. Ibid., 77.

6. Culy, *I, II, III John*, 22.

basis of his advocacy for sinners, which therefore provides consolation for anyone who sins.

2:2 He himself is the atoning sacrifice for our sins, and not for ours alone, but also for the whole world (καὶ αὐτὸς ἱλασμός ἐστιν περὶ τῶν ἁμαρτιῶν ἡμῶν, οὐ περὶ τῶν ἡμετέρων δὲ μόνον ἀλλὰ καὶ περὶ ὅλου τοῦ κόσμου). John makes a universal claim for the efficacy of Jesus' atonement both here and in 4:14, where Jesus is described as "Savior of the world" (σωτῆρα τοῦ κόσμου). If and when someone sins, our advocate is someone who has standing with the Father, the righteous Jesus Christ, because he himself (αὐτός) is the atoning sacrifice for our sins.

Brown points out that Jesus is the *hilasmos* (ἱλασμός, atonement), not the *hilastēr* (ἱλαστήρ), the one who offers the atonement.[7] How to construe and then translate the Greek word *hilasmos* here and in its only other occurrence in the NT at 4:10 is one of the perennial issues raised by this verse.[8] The word occurs six times in the LXX (Lev 25:9; Num 5:8; Ps 129:4; Ezek 44:27; Am 8:14; 2 Macc 3:33) to refer to the removal of guilt achieved by the ritual practices of Israel's ancient priesthood. The cognate noun *hilastērion* (ἱλαστηρίον) occurs frequently in the LXX Pentateuch to refer to the top covering of the ark of the covenant in ancient Israel's Most Holy Place, where blood was sprinkled on the Day of Atonement.

Older English versions translated *hilasmos* in 1 John either as "propitiation" (e.g., KJV) or "expiation" (e.g., RSV), neither of which is easily defined and understood by the average person today. Propitiation is something done to win the favor of a, usually angry, god, spirit, or person,[9] whereas expiation is directed toward nullifying an offensive act that has set in motion a train of undesirable events that has caused a breakdown in a relationship. However, the terms are not always used with clear distinction by modern authors, and more importantly, the Greek word does not clearly indicate the degree of nuance that is sought by modern theologians.

Throughout the history of the church, theologians have struggled to articulate a theory of atonement that adequately includes all the New Testament material.[10] In distinction from the Christus Victor view that atonement is achieved by Christ's victory over evil (cf. 1 Pet 3:22), or from the view that Christ's death appeases God's anger (cf. Rom 1:18), John's writings present Christ as a replacement for animal sacrifice in the temple. Early in his story of Jesus, John reports John the Baptist's exclamation, "Look, the Lamb of God!" (John 1:36), surely an allusion to the sacrificial lambs of temple sacrifice. The parallel structure of 1 John 2:1 with 1:7, 9 confirms that "Jesus Christ … the *hilasmos* for our sins" is parallel with "the blood of Jesus his Son cleanses us from all sin" (1:7) and "to cleanse us from all unrighteousness" (1:9).[11]

However, atonement for sin in John's thought is not a reference to God's anger, but to his love. "In this way is love [defined]: not that we have loved God, but that he loved us and sent his Son to be an atoning sacrifice for our sins" (4:10).[12] In Johannine thought, the cross is the exaltation of Jesus and the clearest expression of God's love. (See Theology of John's Letters.)

---

7. Brown, *Epistles of John*, 218.

8. See *NIDNTT* for an in-depth discussion of this word group in the NT, LXX, and secular Greek writers.

9. See the *Oxford American College Dictionary*, 2002.

10. For an overview of various theological views of atonement, see *The Nature of Atonement: Four Views* (ed. James Beilby and Paul R. Eddy; Downers Grove, IL: InterVarsity Press, 2006).

11. Stanislas Lyonnet, *Sin, Redemption, and Sacrifice: A Biblical and Patristic Study* (Rome: Editrice Pontificio Istituto Biblico, 1998), 149 – 50.

12. For further discussion see Yarbrough, *1 – 3 John*, 77 – 81, and Brown, *Epistles of John*, 217 – 24.

In 1 John 2:1 – 2, Jesus is called both our *paraclete* and our *hilasmos*. The meaning of this distinctive combination is to be found in Jewish thought, not Hellenistic.[13] If a Christian sins, his or her otherwise good works cannot function as the *paraclete* before the Father (πρὸς τὸν πατέρα). Only Jesus Christ, who died to atone for sin and who lives to intercede and mediate our petition for forgiveness, can fill that role.

John's further statement that Jesus is the atoning sacrifice, not only for "our" sins, but also for those of the whole "world" (κόσμος), is sometimes used to support the idea of universalism — that is, that everyone in the world will be saved by Christ's atoning sacrifice, apparently whether they know it or not. But such a thought ignores both the historical context of the book and the particular use of *kosmos* in the Johannine corpus (cf. John 3:16, which presupposes the death of Jesus and consequent forgiveness of sins). One response to claims of universalism is to argue that Christ's death is sufficient to atone for the sins of the whole world, even if only those who actually come to faith in him are saved from their sin. While that may be true, as John Calvin acknowledges, it is not what John is saying here.[14] If here it is a reference to the whole planet, consideration of the historical context in which John wrote makes a more likely interpretation to be the universal scope of Christ's sacrifice in the sense that no one's race, nationality, or any other trait will keep that person from receiving the full benefit of Christ's sacrifice if and when they come to faith.

In the ancient world, the gods were parochial and had geographically limited jurisdictions. In the mountains, one sought the favor of the mountain gods; on the sea, of the sea gods. Ancient warfare was waged in the belief that the gods of the opposing nations were fighting as well, and the outcome would be determined by whose god was strongest. Against that kind of pagan mentality, John asserts that the efficacy of Jesus Christ's sacrifice is valid everywhere, for people everywhere, that is, "the whole world." The Christian gospel knows no geographic, racial, ethnic, national, or cultural boundaries.

But "world" in John's writings is often used to refer not to the planet or all its inhabitants, but to the system of fallen human culture, with its values, morals, and ethics as a whole. Lieu explains it as that which is totally opposed to God and all that belongs to him.[15] It is almost always associated with the side of darkness in the Johannine duality, and people are characterized in John's writings as being either "of God" or "of the world" (John 8:23; 15:19; 17:6, 14, 16; 18:36; 1 John 2:16; 4:5). Those who have been born of God are taken out of that spiritual sphere, though not out of the geographical place or physical population that is concurrent with it (John 13:1; 17:15; see "In Depth: The 'World' in John's Letters" at 2:16).

Rather than teaching universalism, John here instead announces the exclusivity of the Christian gospel. Since Christ's atonement is efficacious for the "whole world," there is no other form of atonement available to other peoples, cultures, and religions apart from Jesus Christ. As Calvin comments:

> Therefore, under the word "all" he does not include the reprobate, but refers to all who would believe and those who were scattered through various regions of the earth. For, as is meet, the grace of Christ is really made clear when it is declared to be the only salvation of the world.[16]

---

13. Jintae Kim, "The Concept of Atonement in Hellenistic Thought and 1 John," *JGRChJ* 2 (2001 – 2005): 100 – 116.

14. John Calvin, *Commentaries on the Catholic Epistles* (trans. John Owen; Grand Rapids: Baker, 1999), 172 – 73.

15. Lieu, *I, II, & III John*, 65.

16. John Calvin, *The Gospel according to St. John 11 – 21 and the First Epistle of John* (trans. T. H. L. Parker; Grand Rapids: Eerdmans, 1988), 244.

2:3 And this is how we know that we know him: if we keep his commands (Καὶ ἐν τούτῳ γινώσκομεν ὅτι ἐγνώκαμεν αὐτόν, ἐὰν τὰς ἐντολὰς αὐτοῦ τηρῶμεν). John turns to a major theme of knowing God. To know God means to be in covenant with him, as God revealed through the prophet Jeremiah: "'they will all know me' … declares the LORD" (Jer 31:34). As Dodd pointed out, this is a summary statement of the new covenant promised by God, when he forgives sin and forms a people by writing the law on their hearts.[17]

To know God is to be in covenant with him, and consequently to have eternal life, as Jesus defines it in the Upper Room Discourse of John's gospel: "Now this is eternal life: that they know you, the only true God, and Jesus Christ, whom you have sent" (John 17:3). If that is the case, then John's desire to assure his readers that they have eternal life means assuring them that they do, in fact, know God truly (1 John 5:13). Therefore, knowing God, and how we know that we know God, is central to the purpose of the letter, a theme occurring eight other times in 1 John (2:4, 13; 3:1, 6; 4:6, 7, 8; 5:20).

One of the problems with religion in the Greco-Roman world was that it was impossible to know what the pagan gods and goddesses wanted from people to avert their disfavor. Pagan religion centered largely on placating the gods with the goal of avoiding any unpleasant circumstances that it was believed the gods would send in their displeasure. There was no true quest for a relationship or personal knowledge of the deities, just an appeasement of the gods to avoid their disfavor.

It was natural to extend this motive of avoiding misfortune into the sphere of life after death for those who embraced the concept. The second-century movements of various forms of Gnosticism, a modern term derived from the Greek word for knowledge (γνῶσις), offered ways of achieving deliverance of the soul after death through spiritual knowledge about oneself and one's destiny that could be gained only by mystical experience in this life. Gnosticism was not a religion, but a worldview that cut across many religions of its time.[18] Although gnostic thinking flourished much later — in the second and into the third centuries — its foundational principles, at least in embryonic form, were influential much earlier, even in the late first century.

In one of the later Christian expressions of a gnostic movement reflected in the (so-called) *Gospel of Thomas*, it was interpretations (or fabrications) of Jesus' teaching that were seen to be the central advantage of Christianity. Jesus was valued not for atonement but as a source of *gnōsis* ("knowledge"). The *Gospel of Truth*, a second-century gnostic writing, also centers on the redemption of people not out of sin and its consequences, but from ignorance and error by giving them knowledge that will benefit them in the afterlife.[19] But when the NT speaks of knowing God, a different kind of knowledge is in view. Yes, it is redemption from the ignorance and error of a fallen world, but it is knowledge of God that brings people into a personal and proper relationship with him as Creator, Redeemer, and Judge of the universe.

In sharp contrast to the value of Jesus as a source of *gnōsis* that will provide the passcodes to the afterlife, John has clearly stated the central atoning role of Jesus' death in the preceding two verses. The central truth of the Christian gospel is that God has revealed himself in the sacrificial death of his Son, which atones for the evil, immoral behavior of people — our sin. And in this way, the Son has

---

17. C. H. Dodd, *The Johannine Epistles* (MNTC; London: Hodder and Stoughton, 1946), 36 – 37.

18. Michael A. Williams, *Rethinking "Gnosticism": An Argu-*

ment for Dismantling a Dubious Category (Princeton: Princeton University Press, 1996).

19. Lieu, *I, II, & III John*, 70.

made God the Father known as a personal being (John 1:18). While Jesus' teachings are important, they are so because of his unique identity as the Son of God, who has conquered sin and death by rising from the grave, and not because he is simply a good teacher of *gnōsis*. Furthermore, *gnōsis* was a formal philosophical construct that did not strive for relationship with the creator God, whereas Jesus taught within the structure of a historical convenantal framework that had relationship with God at its heart.

Because the fundamental problem is sin, John relates the assurance of eternal life (1 John 5:13) — that we can know we have come to know God — to one's response to God's revealed will (see The Theology of John's Letters). The Father of Jesus Christ is not capricious, nor has he failed to communicate his will, as was thought in the ancient pagan world of the pantheon. He has revealed himself to mankind in various ways and at various times throughout human history (cf. Heb 1:1 – 2), but has spoken the last word in his Son. In the Bible he documented his redemptive work in human history and its significance so that all who read it may know him. The goal of God's redemptive work is to restore to himself a covenant people who will live every day of their lives in the knowledge of God's revealed will. This is a different kind of spiritual *gnōsis* than is found in the various forms of Gnosticism, even in its Christianized forms.

In keeping with the objective of reassurance, John writes that we *know* (present tense, γινώσκομεν, a reference to having confidence in the present) that we *have come to know* God (perfect tense, ἐγνώκαμεν, a reference to a past experience of God that brought us to a knowledge of him that continues in the present) — in this way (ἐν τούτῳ), a forward-pointing (cataphoric) reference to what

he says next.[20] We may find reassurance that we know God truly "if we keep his commands" (ἐὰν τὰς ἐντολὰς αὐτοῦ τηρῶμεν). Conversely, if we do not keep his commands, then we have good reason to question whether we truly know him and have eternal life.

The idea of obedience to God is central to knowledge of him, for to know him truly is to know that he is the sovereign Lord of the universe, to whom all owe obedience. To be clear, John is not teaching that obedience is necessary as a condition of knowing God; rather, it is a result of true knowledge of God and of ourselves as sinners (cf. 2 John 4 – 6). As Lieu puts it, "obedience to the commands … is the sure evidence of a knowledge of God or of Jesus that cannot otherwise be proven" to ourselves or to others.[21] In fact, as 1 John 2:4 claims, the one who claims to know God but does not keep his commands is a liar in whom there is no truth.

Before thinking about what commands John might have in mind, we should note the important point John is making, that knowing God and having fellowship with God must be expressed in how we live. There was little ethical content relevant to living in this life in the pagan religions of John's day. But a gnostic worldview did have an influence on how people lived, often a negative influence. Because of its focus on the afterlife, Gnostics believed that the material world, including our bodies, was irrelevant to their redemption at best. That view could lead to a licentious lifestyle in which the carnal and worldly urges were indulged. The alternative view in Gnosticism that the material world was evil often led to a harsh asceticism in which the body was punished by self-abuse. In sharp contrast to this kind of belief, John teaches that the kind of knowledge of God revealed in Christ must be ex-

---

20. Iver Larsen, "The Phrase ἐν τούτῳ in 1 John," *Notes on Translation* 4, no. 4 (1990): 27 – 38.

21. Lieu, *I, II, & III John*, 68.

pressed in a life lived in the here and now in obedience to "his" commands.

John's statement immediately brings at least two important questions to mind: (1) What commands? and (2) Does this reduce the Christian gospel to a form of legalism? One aspect of addressing the first question involves determining the referent of the pronoun "his" (αὐτοῦ). Are they God's commands, as for instance in the OT, or Jesus' commands as taught, for instance, in the Sermon on the Mount? The nearest antecedent in this unit of discourse is "the righteous Jesus Christ" (v. 1), and Jesus makes an appropriate referent for all similar pronouns in this unit, particularly in the admonition in v. 6 to walk as "that One" walked. Furthermore, v. 5 distinguishes between keeping "his word" (αὐτοῦ τὸν λόγον) and "the love of God" (ἡ ἀγάπη τοῦ θεοῦ). Based on this, it is likely that John had Jesus in mind throughout.

Nevertheless, when John subsequently picks up the concept of commands in 3:23 – 24, it is clearly God's commands in view: "And this is his command: to believe in the name of his Son, Jesus Christ, and to love one another, just as he gave the command to us. And the one who keeps his commands remains in him [God], and he himself in them." Furthermore, the statement in 2:5 that "this is how we know that we are in him" in the context of keeping the commands is parallel to the thought in 3:24, that the one who keeps God's commands lives in him. Consistent with Johannine thought, God's commands and Christ's commands are one (cf. John 5:19; 10:30).

So do "his commands" refer to the Ten Commandments? Is keeping the Ten Commandments a *Christian* expression of knowing God? And if so, would that be any different qualitatively from the ancient Israelite's knowledge of God? Surely Jesus kept the Ten Commandments perfectly, and John

says the one who claims to know God should walk as Jesus walked (2:6). But as Yarbrough points out, part of the issue may be the English translation of the word translated "command" (ἐντολή) as "commandment."[22] The Ten Commandments are not referred to in the LXX with this word, even though it is used many times elsewhere. Furthermore, there is no reference to keeping the Mosaic law in John's writings as there is, by way of comparison, in Paul's writings. As Lieu puts it, the commands here are "not a particular set of instructions about behavior" but "an acceptance that to be brought into and to remain in a relationship with God is to recognize and to respond to whatever God requires, simply because it is what God requires."[23] One who truly knows God recognizes his glory and excellence and obeys God's commands because they are excellent and beautiful.

Moreover, there is the clear definition of God's commands within the context of 1 John itself, corroborated by John's gospel, and that should inform our interpretation here. "And this is his command: to believe in the name of his Son, Jesus Christ, and to love one another, just as he gave the command to us" (3:23). God commands us to believe in the name of his Son (see comments on 3:23) and to love one another, just as Jesus commanded his disciples in John 13:34 – 35. The two components of this command are specifically the two major themes of John's letters. What does it mean to believe in the name of Jesus Christ? What does it mean to love one another? The answer to both questions is tightly connected to living in a way that honors God's revealed will.

2:4 The one who says, "I know him," and does not keep his commands is a liar, and the truth is not in them (ὁ λέγων ὅτι ἔγνωκα αὐτόν καὶ τὰς ἐντολὰς αὐτοῦ μὴ τηρῶν, ψεύστης ἐστίν, καὶ

---

22. Yarbrough, *1 – 3 John*, 82.　　23. Lieu, *I, II, & III John*, 69.

ἐν τούτῳ ἡ ἀλήθεια οὐκ ἔστιν). Again John states the importance of Christian profession and moral integrity. The assertion of v. 3, that we know we have come to know God if we are living out the truth God has revealed in Christ, leads John here to state its inverse. If anyone claims to have true knowledge of God but does not order their life according to God's revealed truth ("does not keep his commands"), that person is living a lie. They cannot know God while continuing to ignore his moral will.

The perfect form of the verb "I have come to know him" (ἔγνωκα) implies a continuing relationship with God based on past experience, so this remark is directed toward those who claim to be Christian but who have not learned to respond in obedience to whatever God requires.[24] Obedience to God, from whom all of life flows, is the definition of knowing him (John 17:3).

This is the third time "the truth" (ἡ ἀλήθεια) has been mentioned. In 1:6 the one who walks in darkness does not *do* the truth; in 1:8 the truth is not in those who claim to have no sin; here in 2:4 a similar statement is individualized to the one who claims to know God in Christ but is indifferent to his revealed will. Such a person does not have the truth. As Lieu observes, the words "truth" (ἀλήθεια) and "word" (λόγος) are paralleled: "the truth is not in us" (1:8) and "his word is not in us" (1:10). Here in 2:4 "truth" is put in parallel with "commands" (ἐντολάς). "The effect is not to reduce the scope of 'word' to only the command to love one another (3:11), but to elevate the idea of the command so that it is intrinsic to the message about Jesus, and about God's activity in Jesus (see 1:2)."[25]

In vv. 5 and 7, "command" will be identified with "word," which strongly suggests that "truth," "word," and "command(s)," although not exactly interchangeable in John's thoughts, are closely related. Anyone who wishes to walk authentically in the light of God cannot pick and choose which of the three is preferable. All three must be present in the believer's life. Therefore, truth in John's thought is not simply a collection of facts, but "represents the integrity and authenticity" of the entire message of redemption that God has revealed.[26] (See "In Depth: 'Truth' in John's Letters" at 1:6.)

2:5a-b But whoever keeps his word, in this one the love of God truly has reached its fulfillment (ὃς δ' ἂν τηρῇ αὐτοῦ τὸν λόγον, ἀληθῶς ἐν τούτῳ ἡ ἀγάπη τοῦ θεοῦ τετελείωται). This is the first mention of "love" (ἀγάπη), a major theme in the epistle (see "In Depth: 'Love' in John's Letters" at 4:16). Here the sense of the genitive τοῦ θεοῦ must be resolved. Is it subjective (God's love for the one who keeps his word)?[27] Or objective (human love for God)?[28] As Kruse points out, both options are clearly represented elsewhere in the letter: God's love for believers in 4:9, and the believer's love for God in 5:3.[29] In 4:12, where the sense is clearly subjective, the verb τελειόω in the perfect tense also occurs, which suggests that this is also the sense here. The statement should not be construed to mean that God's love is not complete or perfect but must be made so by human involvement. In Johannine thought, God's love, which is indeed perfect, must be lived out in the believer's life; therefore, the goal of God's love for believers is reached in the transformation of how believers treat others.

John points out that God's love for us has a goal of moral transformation. This statement stands in

---

24. Ibid., 69.

25. Ibid., 70–71.

26. Ibid., 70.

27. Bultmann, *Johannine Epistles*, 25; B. F. Westcott, *Epistles of St. John: The Greek Text with Notes* (3rd ed. [1892]; Grand Rapids: Eerdmans, 1950), 49; Yarbrough, *1–3 John*, 86.

28. Culy, *I, II, III John*, 28; Dodd, *Johannine Epistles*, 31; Kruse, *Letters of John*, 80; Marshall, *Epistles of John*, 125; Smalley, *1, 2, 3 John*, 49.

29. Kruse, *Letters of John*, 80.

contrast with v. 4, where someone was saying that they knew God in Christ but were not keeping his commands. The adverb ἀληθῶς implies that any claim for God's love in those who are not keeping his word is false. Verse 5 advances the argument in positive terms by turning our focus to the one who does keep his word. Truth is not simply a collection of facts about God or Jesus, but demands a response in lifestyle that is mindful of who God is. Commands are not simply a list of rules and regulations that reduce Christian religion to a legalistic system, but refer to believing in Jesus Christ, the Son of God, and loving one another as he taught (3:23). The "word" (λόγος) is the full message of redemption that God has revealed in Christ, not simply the words on a page.

The ambiguity of the antecedent of "his word" (αὐτοῦ τὸν λόγον), whether God or Christ, continues here. Although we have argued above that Christ is the likely referent, John's Christology, which understands the Son and the Father to be one (John 10:30), would allow God as the referent as well. But resolving the ambiguity brings an exegetical crispness: "Whoever keeps Christ's word, that is, his command that we are to love one another, truly in this one the love of God (θεοῦ) has reached its fulfillment."

Of the 116 times the noun "love" (ἀγάπη) occurs in the NT, a full quarter are found in John's writings, and more than half of those in John's writings are found in 1 John. The theme of love among believers in Christ is a major thought in John's writings, and particularly in his letters (see The Theology of John's Letters).

This discussion of "love" in John's writings helps us to further the discussion of how to construe the genitive construction "love of God" (ἡ ἀγάπη τοῦ θεοῦ) here. As noted above, scholars have argued for both options. But if, as we have already suggested, "Jesus Christ" is the antecedent of "keeps his word," then Jesus had much to say in the gospel about the believer's love for him (italics added below):

> John 14:15: "If you *love* me, keep my commands."
>
> John 14:21: "Whoever has my commands and keeps them is the one who *loves* me. The one who *loves* me will be loved by my Father, and I too will love them and show myself to them."
>
> John 14:23: Jesus replied, "Anyone who *loves* me will obey my teaching. My Father will love them."

These verses may suggest that in 1 John 2:5 we have an objective genitive, that the believer's love for God reaches its fulfillment when that person loves Christ by living out his commands.

But Jesus also says in John 14:23 that the Father will love the one who loves Christ and obeys Jesus' teaching, which suggests a subjective genitive in 1 John 2:5, God's love for the believer. There is a decided ambiguity and reciprocity in the phrase "love of God."[30] Moreover, the concept of love for Christ is extended to love for others by the fundamental command of Jesus in John's gospel (italics added):

> John 13:34: "A new command I give you: *Love one another.* As I have loved you, so you must *love one another.*"
>
> John 15:12: "My command is this: *Love each other* as I have loved you."
>
> John 15:17: "This is my command: *Love each other.*"

Living out Jesus' command to love is John's major focus when he refers to commands in this letter (italics added):

> 1 John 3:11: For this is the instruction that you heard from the beginning, that we *love one another.*

---

30. Wallace calls such a genitive a "plenary genitive." See *Greek Grammar*, 119 – 20.

1 John 3:23: And this is his command: to believe in the name of his Son, Jesus Christ, and to *love one another*, just as he gave the command to us.

1 John 4:7: Dear friends, let us *love one another*, because love is of God, and everyone who loves has been begotten of God and … knows God.

1 John 4:11: Dear friends, if God loved us like this, we also ought to *love one another*.

1 John 4:12: No one has ever seen God. If we *love one another*, God lives in us, and his love is completed in us.

2 John 5: And now I ask you, lady — not as writing you a new command but [as writing a command] that we have had from the beginning — that *we love one another*.

Taking "love of God" as an objective genitive in 1 John 2:5 produces a wonderful logical flow to John's thought that helps to understand what the verb "reached its fulfillment" (τετελείωται) means, a word that is often translated with an English phrase including "perfected" (NASB, NKJV, ESV) and "perfection" (NRSV, NJB). And the shift in 2:7 – 11 to explicitly address love for others seems to confirm that here an objective genitive is in view (see comments on 2:7). But that translation doesn't capture the sense of *teteleiōtai* in middle voice, which is more about reaching an intended goal than about meeting an impossibly high standard.[31] In other words, God in Christ has loved us by redeeming us from sin (John 3:16; 1 John 4:10), and that love has a transformative goal in the life of the believer, that they should love God, both the Father and the Son, which is expressed by love for others (John 13:34).

That transformative goal has been reached in the one who lives out the message that God has revealed, for by doing so, the believer turns from sin and begins to relate rightly to God and to others.

This does not mean that the believer has been perfected and no longer needs to continue to exercise love. Rather, when a believer loves others, the goal of God's redemptive love in that person's life has been achieved in that behavior.

Love as Jesus defined it is not an emotional response, though emotion may be involved; rather, love is the considerate treatment of others in accord with God's revealed will (cf. the parable of the good Samaritan in Luke 10:25 – 37). Brown states this idea well: "Agape is not a love originating in the human heart and reaching out to possess noble goods needed for perfection; it is a spontaneous, unmerited, creative love flowing from God to the Christian, and from the Christian to a fellow Christian."[32] This flow of love from God to the Christian believer to others comports well with what John says in 1 John 4:10 – 11: "In this way love is [defined]: not that we have loved God, but that he loved us and sent his Son [to be] an atoning sacrifice for our sins. Dear friends, if God loved us like this, we also ought to love one another." The circularity continues in 2 John 6a-b, "And this is love: that we walk according to his commands."

2:5c – 6 This is how we know that we are in him: the one who says, "I remain in him," ought also himself to walk just as that One walked (ἐν τούτῳ γινώσκομεν ὅτι ἐν αὐτῷ ἐσμεν· ὁ λέγων ἐν αὐτῷ μένειν ὀφείλει καθὼς ἐκεῖνος περιεπάτησεν καὶ αὐτὸς [οὕτως] περιπατεῖν). John here introduces the idea that Jesus, in his life on this earth, is the role model for the Christian believer. In 1:7 the significance of Jesus' death for cleansing sin was stated; here the significance of Jesus' life on this earth is presented as an example for the believer who wants "to remain" (μένειν) in him.

There is considerable debate over whether "in

---

31. For a helpful discussion of the verb τελειόω in its NT usage, see Moisés Silva, "Perfection and Eschatology in He-

brews," *WTJ* 39 (1976): 60 – 71.

32. Brown, *Epistles of John*, 254 – 55.

this way" (ἐν τούτῳ) points backward (anaphoric) or forward (cataphoric). Is it that we that we can enjoy the assurance of eternal life that comes from knowing "we are in him" because we keep the command to love others (a backward reference)? Or does "in this way" point forward to v. 6, that it is only the one who walks as Jesus walked who can authentically claim to remain in him? In a change of punctuation from NA27, the editors of the NA28 *Greek New Testament* have punctuated the verse to leave the question unresolved. Nevertheless, a number of interpreters argue that the way one knows that they are "in him" is stated in v. 6. The disagreement suggests that this expression links what has just been said about loving God by loving others with the statement that follows about remaining in him.

Kruse notes that the phrase forms an inclusio with v. 3, but also notes that the topic of being in him anticipates v. 6.[33] Culy offers the helpful data that clear cataphoric (forward-pointing) uses of the demonstrative pronoun in 1 John are usually followed by syntax that is not present here (an epexegetical *hoti* or *hina* clause), and he agrees with the editors of NA27 that the reference is anaphoric (that is, referring to a previous thought).[34] While the reference primarily points backward, it also forms a transition to the thought that follows.[35] This is reflected in the change in punctuation in NA28.

Believers in whom the love of God has attained its goal by producing love for others may know that they "are in him" (ἐν αὐτῷ ἐσμεν). John's concept of being and remaining "in him" (ἐν αὐτῷ) is comparable to the apostle Paul's foundational concept of being in Christ (e.g., Rom 8:1; 1 Cor 1:30; 15:18, 22; 2 Cor 1:21; 5:17; 12:19; Gal 3:26; 5:6; Eph 1:13; Phil

1:1; 4:21; 1 Thess 4:16). As Smalley notes, "When the writer speaks here of 'existing in him' we may conclude that a reference to Jesus is not entirely excluded. John is in fact asking how we can be sure that we are 'in' God, as he has made himself known in Christ Jesus."[36]

The syntax of the Greek is the infinitive of indirect discourse.[37] For an analogous English example, someone might say, "I know her," which when repeated to a third party would be expressed as, "She claimed *to know* her" (using the English infinitive). The similar syntax in the Greek of v. 6 means that someone might claim, "I am abiding in God/ Christ." The subject of the verb "ought" (ὀφείλει) is the entire expression "the one who says, 'I remain in him.'" What John is saying is to walk the talk. If one claims to abide in God, then one must also walk as "that One" (ἐκεῖνος) walked, an allusion to Jesus (e.g., John 1:18; 2:21; 5:11, 19). (One of the distinctive characteristics of John's writings is his frequent use of the demonstrative pronoun instead of the personal pronoun and how often he uses it, though not exclusively, to refer to God or Jesus.)

"Remain" (μένω) is a favorite Johannine verb. More than 55 percent of all occurrences of this verb in the NT are found in John's gospel and letters. Of the sixty-seven occurrences in John's gospel and letters, twenty-one of these are found in the letters in reference to the believer remaining, or abiding, in God or Christ (e.g., 1 John 2:6, 10, 14, 17, 19, 24, 27, 28; 3:6, 9, 24; 4:15; 2 John 9). The concept of remaining or abiding is an important theological theme in Johannine thought. In John's gospel, the mutual abiding of the believer in Christ and Christ in the believer is pictured beautifully in Jesus' analogy of the vine and the branches in John 15. In the letters it refers to the presence of

---

33. Kruse, *Letters of John*, 80 – 81.
34. Culy, *I, II, III John*, 29.
35. Brown, *Epistles of John*, 258.
36. Smalley, *1, 2, 3 John*, 51.
37. Wallace, *Greek Grammar*, 603.

the Spirit in the believer (1 John 3:24; 4:13), and consequently the believer's continuing belief in the gospel of Christ (1 John 4:15; 2 John 9) and their behavior toward others that expresses love for God (1 John 3:6; 4:12). The possibility of not remaining in him is also mentioned (1 John 3:6, 9; 2 John 9). In fact, John's pastoral concern that his readers remain in God as revealed in Christ is arguably the major motivation of these letters.

The background for this idea is probably to be found in the promises of a new covenant relationship (Jer 31:33; Ezek 36:26, 27) that involves a new knowledge of God and the indwelling of his Spirit that transforms the believer (cf. John 14:16 – 17). The new covenant signals a relationship to God that is characterized not by cultic observances or the legalistic performance of requirements, but by a heart that has been changed to agree truly and sincerely with God and to follow after him.

The concept of a mutual indwelling of God and the Christian believer is distinctively different from God's presence with his people in the OT, which was mediated through the tabernacle or temple (Exod 17:7; Deut 31:16 – 17; 2 Chr 6:18). The Spirit of God came upon people to equip them for specific redemptive acts, but it did not indwell them (Num 11:25; 24:2; Judg 3:10; 6:34; 11:29; 14:6, 19; 15:14; 1 Sam 10:10; 11:6; 16:13; 18:10; 19:23; 2 Chr 15:1; 20:14). To have God dwell within the believer and the believer within God is not a reference to some mystical experience, but to the fact that the believer partakes of the eternal life that characterizes God (1 John 1:2). Therefore, the earthly life of the Christian should manifest the qualities of the eternal life he or she has received.

This concept of the abiding life and love of the Christian in the Father and the Son, and their abiding presence and love in the believer, communicates that the "Christian's relationship with God is not a series of encounters but a stable, continuous way of life" that begins with the new birth (John 1:13; 3:3; 1 John 2:29; 3:9; 4:7; 5:1, 4, 18).[38] And that stable, continuous way of life with God is characterized by a vitality that is visible, just as fruit on the vine is the proof of vitality (John 15). By virtue of this new and vital life, other realities abide in the believer, such as love and the Spirit.

Because of this vital, new life that is born of God, the one who claims to remain or abide in him "ought" to walk (i.e., live) as Jesus did. So what specifically does it mean to live as Jesus did? The Jesus movement of the 1960s seemed to believe that to wear long hair and sandals encouraged one to live as Jesus did. But even "the Jesus people" recognized that to live as Jesus did goes far beyond fashion and other elements of the culture into which one happens to be born.

This new life that is based on Jesus' atoning death is for "the whole world" (2:2), and so must transcend culture in significant ways. The blood of Jesus cleanses sin, but to love God means obedience to his revealed will, which Jesus accomplished perfectly, even though it meant he had to suffer the horrors of the crucifixion. Jesus was without sin because he won the struggle in the garden of Gethsemane over whether to obey God's will and go to the cross or to turn away. Jesus won that struggle because he was completely committed to obeying God, a commitment completely motivated by love for others. To walk as "that One" walked means to live in unflinching obedience to God, which constitutes love for him and for others.

---

38. Brown, *Epistles of John*, 260.

Theology in Application

Our Need for God

God is an inescapable part of human experience. Although called by many different names and conceptualized in many different forms, some concept of deity is present in every culture. Even the atheist must hold a conscious position of rejecting God's existence, as opposed to living in a world in which there is simply no concept of God at all. And yet not every concept of deity can be true. Every human being needs to know the truth about who God is and how to have a relationship with him. While knowledge of other things may seem more relevant and pressing to some — things such as how to drive a car, balance a checkbook, make friends, and do our jobs well — knowing God is the most essential kind of human knowledge. For at the ultimate and inevitable end each of us must face, everyone will realize that there is nothing more important than knowing the God who created us and to whom we each return either in fellowship or under judgment. God wants us to know him, and he has revealed himself throughout human history, finally and most completely, in the incarnation as the human being we know as Jesus Christ.

Sin Blocks a Relationship with God

In the opening verses of the body of this letter (1:5 – 10), the apostolic author, whose knowledge of God as revealed in human form goes back to Jesus himself, establishes a basic principle: we cannot know God as God deserves to be known until sin has been defeated in our lives. It may be possible to know *about* God without dealing with our sin (and even possible to teach and preach *about* God), but it is not possible to have fellowship with God without acknowledging our sin and receiving his forgiving cleansing by the blood of Christ. As Lieu has put it, "Claiming not to have sin is not a matter of arrogant self-righteousness but of misrepresenting the very nature of God."[39]

Now in 2:1 – 6, John brings that general principle to bear more specifically on the readers of his day. Even while, on the one hand, it is itself a sin to claim one has no sin, John also needs, on the other hand, to teach that it is important not to sin. In other words, the existential reality of our sin does not give a license to indulge in it, because God has revealed that he doesn't want his creatures to sin against him or against each other.

John teaches that the proper attitude toward sin is to avoid it. But when we sin by commission or omission, whether intentionally or not, we can bring our sin to Jesus, our *paraclete* before the Father, who pleads his blood on our behalf. On that basis God will cleanse us of sin (see comments on 1:9).

---

39. Lieu, *I, II, & III John*, 57.

John also teaches the universal scope of sin and Jesus' atonement for it. Christ died not only for "our" sins, but for the sins of "the whole world." This important point is relevant to how Christians engage with other religions in our pluralistic society today. There are many points of ethics and practice that Christianity shares with the other great world religions. If Jesus were only human and nothing more, his teachings could be put on par with those of other great teachers and philosophers. And while it may be right and good at times for the Christian church to join in common cause with other religions, it must never be done in such a way as to suggest that there are many different but equivalent roads to knowing God.

Monotheism Misunderstood

A misunderstanding of the monotheism embraced by the three great world religions (Judaism, Christianity, and Islam) may confuse some so that they think we are all worshiping the same God just by different names or practices. That line of thought runs counter to what the NT teaches. When the Romans conquered the Greeks, they did not destroy Greek culture, but largely integrated it with their own. For their religious framework, this meant harmonizing the pantheon of deities by allowing that the same god or goddess was known by two different names. For instance, the Roman goddess Diana was identified with the Greek goddess Artemis, and their different functions merged.

But notice that when the apostle Paul went to evangelize the Greco-Roman world with the good news that God had become man, he did not say, "You Romans call him Jupiter, and you Greeks call him Zeus, but we call him Yaweh." Even though Paul knew there is only one God, to identify him with Zeus or Jupiter would be to mix heretical cultural notions with what God had revealed about himself. Instead Paul says, "We are bringing you good news, telling you to turn from these worthless things to the living God, who made the heavens and the earth and the sea and everything in them" (Acts 14:15). This is not to say that God does not use the religious experiences of people from various cultures to bring them to himself in a true, saving knowledge of Jesus Christ. But religious experience apart from Christ is insufficient to know God truly as he has revealed himself.

We Don't Get to Make Up Our Own Truth

The privatization and individualization of religious belief seem to lead people to believe that they are entitled to pick and choose their own religious truth. But when John states that Jesus atoned not for our sins only but also for the sins of the whole world (2:2), he excludes the argument that Jesus is truth for Christians only, but not for Jews or Muslims or atheists. Upholding the universal scope of the exclusive message of the gospel of Jesus Christ in an increasingly pluralistic world will be arguably one of the most difficult challenges to the future of the church.

Obedience Is Not Legalism

John moves from the basic principle that dealing rightly with sin is necessary for knowing God to the necessity of obedience. In 2:3 – 6 he specifies that to know God means to live as God says we should, because to think otherwise is a failure to recognize who God is and his right to have a claim on our lives. As discussed above on 2:3, God's "commands" do not refer to a list of dos and don'ts, but should be understood in light of 3:23 – 24, where God commands Christians "to believe in the name of his Son, Jesus Christ, and to love one another.... And the one who keeps his commands remains in him [God], and he ... in them." Rather than legalism, obedience means living in God and he in us.

God's love reaches out to his fallen creatures in Christ's cross, with the goal of restoring them to living rightly as he created us to live. His love achieves that goal when we come to faith in Christ and, consequently, learn to love others. These are not onetime events, even though John stresses elsewhere the need to be born again (John 3:3). Furthermore, the use of the perfect tense where he refers to the new birth indicates that he assumes a Christian has been born again sometime in the past, but that fact has continuing meaning in the present and throughout life (1 John 2:29; 3:9; 4:7; 5:1, 4, 18).

Every day Christians must decide to live with faith in Christ in everything they do and say. Every word and act offer the opportunity to express love for another or not. Thus, Christianity is not only a matter of cognitive assent to the right doctrines, even though statements of faith are an important part of identifying ourselves with biblical truth. If we say we have been born again and have come to know God in Christ, we must either live in accordance with God's revealed will or reveal ourselves as liars. If we say we are followers of Jesus Christ, we must live as Jesus did, with total commitment to obedience to God every day of our lives.

CHAPTER 4

1 John 2:7 – 11

Literary Context

This unit begins to transition into the exhortations that begin in 2:15 by switching from the more general "we" and "the one who says" to the more direct and personal second person subject ("you"), though still in the indicative mood (vv. 7 – 8). The previous verses (2:3 – 6) spoke to the issue of love for God; this section shifts to love for others. It is a preface to the highly structured rhetoric that follows in vv. 12 – 14.

III. Dealing with Sin (2:1 – 6)
→ **IV. Love, Light, and Darkness (2:7 – 11)**
  A. The Continuity of John's Teaching with Jesus' Teaching (2:7 – 8)
  B. The Relationship of Love and Hate to the Light and Darkness Duality (2:9 – 11)
V. Children, Fathers, and Young Men (2:12 – 14)

Main Idea

John extends the light and darkness duality to include the concepts of love and hate. He will continue to build a conceptual universe that leaves no neutral ground. Those who actively love others live in the light and do nothing that will lead others into acts or decisions contrary to the revealed will of God in Jesus Christ.

Translation

(See next page.)

1 John 2:7 – 11

7a	address	Dear friends,
b	assertion	**I am not writing to you a new command** but
c	contrast	an old command,
d	description	which you have had from the beginning.
e	assertion	**The old command is the message that you have heard.**
8a	concession	**Yet I am writing to you a new command,**
b	expansion	something that is realized in him and in you,
c	basis	because the darkness is passing away and
d	contrast	the true light is already shining.
9a	assertion	**The one who says, "I am in the light," and**
b	expansion	**hates their brother or sister**
c	assertion	**is still in the darkness.**
10a	assertion	**The one who loves their brother or sister remains in the light and**
b	assertion	**does not entice them.**
11a	assertion	**The one who hates their brother or sister is in the darkness and**
b	series	**walks in the darkness and**
c	series	**does not know where they are going,**
d	cause	because the darkness has blinded their eyes.

Structure

This unit is part of the larger discourse unit 2:1–17. It is introduced by the vocative "dear friends" (ἀγαπητοί), which expresses the author's love for those to whom he writes, even as he will exhort them to love others. Verse 7 claims continuity with the old command his readers have already heard, forming a contrast with v. 8, which introduces a new aspect to this old command he wishes to explain. Verses 9–11 expand on the light-darkness duality that was introduced in 1:5 with the statement that "God is light" by defining the antithesis between love and hate, or indifference, in relation to light and darkness.

Exegetical Outline

→ **IV. Love, Light, and Darkness (2:7–11)**

    A. The continuity of John's teaching with Jesus' teaching (2:7–8)

        1. He reminds his readers that he loves them (2:7a).

        2. He brings not a new command, but one that his readers have had "from the beginning" (2:7b)

        3. But the coming of Christ, the true light, into the world's darkness is such a monumental event that he gives the command new meaning (2:8)

    B. The relationship of love and hate to the light and darkness duality (2:9–11)

        1. It is impossible to hate a fellow believer and walk in the light (2:9)

        2. Love for the fellow believer shows that one remains in the light (2:10)

        3. The true nature of one who hates a fellow believer (2:11)

Explanation of the Text

2:7 Dear friends, I am not writing to you a new command but an old command, which you have had from the beginning. The old command is the message that you have heard (Ἀγαπητοί, οὐκ ἐντολὴν καινὴν γράφω ὑμῖν ἀλλ᾽ ἐντολὴν παλαιὰν ἣν εἴχετε ἀπ᾽ ἀρχῆς· ἡ ἐντολὴ ἡ παλαιά ἐστιν ὁ λόγος ὃν ἠκούσατε). The vocative "dear friends" (ἀγαπητοί) starts a new unit that explains both the continuity and discontinuity of Christian moral life with previous tradition. The author expresses love for his readers in the context of his exhortation that they must love one another in obedience to Jesus' command.

Modern English Bibles are right to translate this term (ἀγαπητοί) as "dear friends" because the English word "beloved" carries connotations today that might confuse modern readers. But we must not forget that the use of this vocative connects to the major theme of love throughout the letter. The author uses ἀγαπητοί several times in the letter, usually in the context of discussions about God's love as expressed by active love for one another. The author's love for his readers in light of v. 10 (see comments) implies that there is nothing in his teaching that will cause them to stumble or lead them astray.

The author reminds them that what he has just written — that the one who knows God must keep his command and the one who abides in God must live as Jesus lived — is not a new and novel idea, but is an old command. The idea that love for God and obedience to his commands is expressed by love for others was central even to the old covenant, and John's definition of the old command as the "message" (λόγος) may be an allusion to "the ten words" (Exod 34:28; Deut 10:4), or as we know them in English, the Ten Commandments. For the heart of the old covenant was love for God and love for others:

> "Love the LORD your God with all your heart and with all your soul and with all your strength." (Deut 6:5)
> "Do not seek revenge or bear a grudge against anyone among your people, *but love your neighbor as yourself.* I am the LORD." (Lev 19:18, italics added)

In fact, all of Jesus' teaching is squarely centered on this statement that summarizes the old covenant:

> "Love the Lord your God with all your heart and with all your soul and with all your mind." This is the first and greatest commandment. And the second is like it: "Love your neighbor as yourself." All the Law and the Prophets hang on these two commandments. (Matt 22:37 – 40)

In 2:3 – 6, John first addresses how love for the Lord God is expressed, while 2:7 – 11 addresses the second greatest commandment of love for others. There is a circularity to love that flows first from God to the believer, and then back to God as the believer loves others.

Recognizing the centrality of the love command in the Old Testament as well as in Jesus' teaching helps us to understand what it means that John's readers have had this command "from the beginning" (ἀπ᾽ ἀρχῆς). Although the primary reference is no doubt to their first awareness of the gospel message at the beginning of their Christian life, John's point is that the command goes back to Jesus, and then further back to the covenant that God revealed to ancient Israel. John's apostolic teaching is nothing new and novel, but is the culmination of, and consistent with, what God has been saying all along.

2:8 Yet I am writing to you a new command, something that is realized in him and in you, because the darkness is passing away and the true light is already shining (πάλιν ἐντολὴν καινὴν γράφω ὑμῖν, ὅ ἐστιν ἀληθὲς ἐν αὐτῷ καὶ ἐν ὑμῖν, ὅτι ἡ σκοτία παράγεται καὶ τὸ φῶς τὸ ἀληθινὸν ἤδη φαίνει). John makes the point that the coming of Jesus transforms even the old covenant into something new. On the one hand, John highlights the continuity of the command with what God has previously revealed, but on the other he also shows that the circumstances in which that command must be applied are indeed new, for Jesus has come and the light is now shining. That change in redemptive history from old to new covenant justifies calling this apostolic teaching *new*.

The relative clause "something that is realized in him and in you" (ὅ ἐστιν ἀληθὲς ἐν αὐτῷ καὶ ἐν ὑμῖν) is difficult, for the neuter relative pronoun "[something] that" (ὅ) is unexpected; it does not agree grammatically with the feminine noun "command" (ἐντολήν), the expected antecedent. Such a grammatical surprise needs to be considered carefully. As Smalley sees it,

> the allusion here is not just to the law itself, but more widely to the newness (the new quality) of the law of love, and its realization in Christ and in the believer.... Had the writer intended to refer exclusively to the law, rather than to its truth or "realization," a relative pronoun in the feminine would presumably have been required.[1]

---

1. Smalley, *1, 2, 3 John*, 56 – 57.

Andrew Persson also takes the neuter relative pronoun as a reference to the previous statement of the claim of newness. He paraphrases, "I claim that this command is new and you can see that my claim is true both in him and in you."[2]

This interpretation also takes the prepositional phrase "in him" (ἐν αὐτῷ) to be a reference to Christ, construing the pronoun to be masculine rather than the identical neuter form (contra Cully, who translates, "and this claim (that I am writing a new command) is true in and of itself and with respect to you").[3] The basis given, "because the darkness is passing away and the true light is already shining," is an allusion to Jesus, the light of the world (John 1:9; 8:12; 9:5). God is light (1 John 1:5), and he has come into the world in the person of Jesus. That epoch-changing event gives such new meaning to the old command that John can speak of it as a new command.

The light that Jesus brought into the world shines not only in him, but "in you" (ἐν ὑμῖν), those who walk in the light. Darkness is being extinguished as more and more people come to faith in Christ and live out God's love in the world. As God moves history toward its final culmination, darkness and all that is associated with it is passing away. The coming of the light is "already" (ἤδη) here, rather than something that is merely promised for the eschatological future, and John's readers need to align themselves with it, for it is "the true light" (τὸ φῶς τὸ ἀληθινόν). Any alleged light that is not centered in Christ is false, not the genuine light that God is (1:5).

2:9 The one who says, "I am in the light," and hates their brother or sister is still in the darkness (ὁ λέγων ἐν τῷ φωτὶ εἶναι καὶ τὸν ἀδελφὸν αὐτοῦ μισῶν ἐν τῇ σκοτίᾳ ἐστὶν ἕως ἄρτι). There is no better analogy than light and darkness to form a conceptual dualism that defines and separates categories that are antithetical and unmixed. Here John applies the sharp polarity between light and darkness to the moral categories of love and its opposite.

Again John mentions "the one who says…." There may have been people actually saying such things, or this may be purely hypothetical to warn his readers against even thinking such things. Hate for others is not of the light and therefore is not of God, regardless of what the hater may claim — a point that should be taken to heart by those who wrongly think that evil done in God's name is a legitimate means to an end. As Marshall points out, "It is significant that he does not write: 'Whoever *says* that he loves his brother lives in the light.' He is concerned with action, not with words which may not correspond to reality."[4]

How narrowly circumscribed is the Johannine command to love? Does John want his readers to love only other Christians? New Testament writers consistently use the Greek word *adelphos* (ἀδελφός) to refer to fellow believers, whether male or female. John uses the word in this sense to refer to fellow believers, focusing in this letter on relationships between Christians. John's point is not to contradict Jesus' teaching that we are to love our neighbor (πλήσιον) as ourselves (Matt 22:39), or that we love our enemies (Matt 5:44; Luke 6:27, 35), but his focus for the purposes of this letter are on the ethical demands of the gospel toward others in the Christian communities.[5] This restriction is circumstantial because John is writing in the wake of a disruption in the unity of the

---

2. Andrew Persson, "Some Exegetical Problems in 1 John," *Notes on Translation* 4, no. 4 (1990): 19.

3. Cully, *I, II, III John*, 31, 33.

4. Marshall, *Epistles of John*, 132.

5. For a fuller discussion of the sectarian character of John's writings see Robert H. Gundry, *Jesus the Word according to John the Sectarian* (Grand Rapids: Eerdmans, 2002), 57 – 64.

church, where relationships between believers are his primary concern.

John does not define hate here, expressions of which were probably self-evident, though the duality suggests that failure to love actively constitutes hate. His later remark about ignoring the needs of others suggests that even indifference is a failure to love (3:17). These are not terms of emotion but of attitude and behavior toward others. John presses the point that anyone who hates a fellow believer is in darkness, regardless of what they may say, and therefore is not of God. Again, the quality of interpersonal relationship speaks louder than verbal witness.

2:10 The one who loves their brother or sister remains in the light and does not entice them (ὁ ἀγαπῶν τὸν ἀδελφὸν αὐτοῦ ἐν τῷ φωτὶ μένει καὶ σκάνδαλον ἐν αὐτῷ οὐκ ἔστιν). To remain in the light means to remain in God, who is light. Two predicate nominative statements are made about God in 1 John: God is light (1:5) and God is love (4:8). John brings the ethical and moral implications of these two theological statements to bear on the lives of his readers. To remain in the light demands that one loves their brother or sister in Christ. Just as John did not define acts of hate in 2:9, so he does not define acts of love here, though more specific examples are mentioned later (e.g., 3:11 – 12, 17 – 18).

The second clause of this verse, (lit.) "and there is no cause of stumbling in him/it" (καὶ σκάνδαλον ἐν αὐτῷ οὐκ ἔστιν), presents two related problems: (1) how to best translate σκάνδαλον; and (2) what is the referent of the pronoun in the prepositional phrase (ἐν αὐτῷ). Grammatically, the term αὐτῷ could be neuter and understood as "in it," referring back to the light. If it is a generic masculine

("in him"), it refers back to the one who loves. The noun *skandalon* (σκάνδαλον) refers to "an action or circumstance that leads one to act contrary to a proper course of action or set of beliefs."[6] The question is whether it is the one who loves who is not being enticed or those who are being loved. Thus, the clause may be understood to mean:

1. There is nothing in the light that would entice a Christian to act in a way contrary to God's will and call it love.[7] Or,
2. There is nothing in a Christian who is walking in the light that would cause himself or others to act in a way contrary to God's revealed will.[8]

Elsewhere in the New Testament, *skandalon* refers to something that causes someone else to stumble (e.g., Matt 13:41; 16:23; 18:7; Rom 9:33; 11:9; 1 Cor 1:23). Because the context here is the command to love others, that is the likely sense here as well. If so, John is saying that genuine love for another means not putting anything before them that would entice them to act in a way contrary to God's will. This was likely just what the secessionists were doing with their false teaching.

2:11 The one who hates their brother or sister is in the darkness and walks in the darkness and does not know where they are going, because the darkness has blinded their eyes (ὁ δὲ μισῶν τὸν ἀδελφὸν αὐτοῦ ἐν τῇ σκοτίᾳ ἐστὶν καὶ ἐν τῇ σκοτίᾳ περιπατεῖ, καὶ οὐκ οἶδεν ποῦ ὑπάγει, ὅτι ἡ σκοτία ἐτύφλωσεν τοὺς ὀφθαλμοὺς αὐτοῦ). Hate for others is moral darkness that is inconsistent with a God who is light. John has already stated that hating a brother or sister constitutes walking in darkness, regardless if one thinks otherwise (v. 9). He has said that it is love for a fellow believer that demonstrates that one is remaining in the light (v. 10a). If

---

6. BDAG, *s.v.* σκάνδαλον.

7. Dodd, *Johannine Epistles*, 34.

8. Burge, *Letters of John*, 102; Kruse, *Letters of John*, 86; Mar-

shall, *Epistles of John*, 132; Smalley, *1, 2, 3, John*, 62; Schuchard, *1 – 3 John*, 194; Strecker, *Johannine Letters*, 53; Thompson, *1 – 3 John*, 60 – 61.

God is light (1:5) and God is love (4:8, 16), walking in the light cannot be separated from love for others.

John defines love as doing nothing that would entice a brother or sister to act contrary to God's revealed will (v. 10b). Just as darkness is the absence of light, hate is the absence of love. To hate a fellow believer need not involve animosity or violence toward them; in John's thought, it means the failure to love, and by implication behaving in a way that entices a fellow believer to sin. John will relate this polarity between love and hate to false teaching later in the chapter. False teaching is not a loving act because, no matter how well intentioned, it misleads people away from the truth (2:26).

The one who hates by virtue of not loving "is in the darkness" and "walks in the darkness" and "does not know where they are going" because the darkness has blinded them. This indicates a progression. The one who hates by not loving is not on God's side of the duality, even if they claim to be. Furthermore, they "walk in the darkness" by having their decisions and actions motivated and informed by impulses that are not from God. They don't see where this is leading them, because the darkness has blinded them.

Darkness is not neutral; it causes spiritual and moral blindness. Darkness, the absence of light, is the absence of God in one's life. The picture here is of someone who claims to be enlightened, claims to know God, and perhaps hangs out in the church. Nevertheless, it is someone who needs Jesus to touch the eyes of their spirit and dispel the darkness of blindness, as he did to the man born blind physically who exclaimed, "One thing I do know. I was blind but now I see!" (John 9:25).

Theology in Application

Living in the Light

Because "God is light" (1 John 1:5) and Jesus has come as light into a world covered in darkness (John 1:5), John challenges us to consider our own lives in view of this duality. If we are in fellowship with God in Christ, we will walk in the light and do the truth. That is, we will let the revelation of God that Jesus Christ brought inform our every act and decision throughout life. To *remain* in the light means to continue to be motivated by God's will throughout all the challenges and temptations we face. We will keep his commands to believe in his Son and to love one another through every season of our lives. Only in this way do we remain in God.

Love Is Living in the Light

John teaches here that the one who is in the light and loves others does not present them with any enticement that would lead them away from the will of God. What a vast and all-encompassing view of love! Love is not an emotion, nor is it a sentimental abstraction. It is living with others as God intends us to. What a convicting message in a society where so many feel entitled to live for themselves alone and believe that how they live is no one's business but their own. Modern society seems to have lost the ideal of living for the common good (cf. 1 Cor 10:24) and has replaced it with a self-centered philosophy of looking out for number one. To live a Christ-centered life that strives to do right by others is increasingly countercultural.

How much thought do we give to how our example, our words, and our behavior influence those around us, particularly other Christians? The apostle Paul applied this principle to the issue of eating certain foods: "It is wrong for a person to eat anything that causes someone else to stumble" (Rom 14:20), and "Do not cause anyone to stumble, whether Jews, Greeks or the church of God" (1 Cor 10:32). It is not loving to encourage anyone to do something against their conscience, but especially against a conscience that has been formed by obedience to God.

When we do not love, John says, we sin. Although there may, and should, be specific, recognizable acts of love for others, John presents the challenge of loving constantly and consistently in every relationship and interaction. In our every act either we are loving others or we are sinning against them. We are either relating to them rightly as God would want us to or we are not. When we do not love others by doing right by them, we become a stumbling block to their relationship with God. When our example or our words influence others away from obedience to God in Christ, we are in that moment part of the darkness that Christ came to dispel. To habitually live in such a way is to walk in darkness, to be in a place where God is absent from one's life. And because light is needed to sustain life, to live in word and deed contrary to God's revealed will can mean only death. Each time we fail to love there is something that dies a little, whether it be a relationship, our own integrity and wholeness, or our fellowship with God.

1 John 2:12 – 14

Literary Context

The highly structured rhetoric of this section brings John's foundational statements in 1:5 – 2:11 to bear on the specific community(-ities) of believers to whom he is writing. John summarizes his teaching in the first part of this letter in a way that affirms his confidence in his readers as part of reassuring them that they do, indeed, have eternal life. He switches from hypothetical examples in the third person (e.g., "the one who says …," 2:4, 6, 9) to affirming statements in the second person (e.g., "your sins are forgiven," 2:12c, cf. vv. 13, 14) in order to emphasize their own experience of the truths he has been discussing. His readers *have* been living out their faith in Christ, and these verses (2:12 – 14) commend them for that.

But these verses also serve as a janus passage that anticipates the exhortations that follow, given in the second person plural imperative (e.g., 2:15, "Do not love the world …"). John summarizes statements about Christian identity that he has previously explained in greater detail and introduces the topic of overcoming the evil one, which provides the transition into his exhortations about what his readers must do to continue living in Christ with the assurance of eternal life.

Main Idea

The author explains his motivation for writing by describing his original readers in three categories that roughly correspond to different stages in life (children, fathers, young men). Through every stage of a Christian's life, confession for forgiveness of sins, knowledge of the Father and Son, the indwelling of God's Word, and victory over the evil one are necessary aspects of walking in the light. These elements allude to the promises of the new covenant prophesied in the OT.

Translation

1 John 2:12 – 14

12a	address	Children,
b	assertion	**I am writing to you**
c	content	because your sins are forgiven
d	cause	because of his name.
13a	address	Fathers,
b	assertion	**I am writing to you**
c	content	because you do know the One who is from the beginning.
d	address	Young men,
e	assertion	**I am writing to you**
f	content	because you have overcome the evil one.
14a	address	Little children,
b	assertion	**yes, I write to you**
c	explanation	because you have known the Father.
d	address	Fathers,
e	assertion	**yes, I write to you**
f	explanation	because you have known the One who is from the beginning.
g	address	Young men,
h	assertion	**yes, I write to you**
i	explanation	because you are strong and
j	expansion	the word of God remains in you and
k	expansion	you have overcome the evil one.

Structure

This passage is the most rhetorically structured in the letter. Each statement begins with a form of "I write" (γράφω), with the first three statements in the present tense, and the second three, in the aorist (ἔγραψα). The shift in tense should not be pressed beyond recognizing its rhetorical effect, which is to divide the section in two. The division is reinforced by the repetition of words for "children" (τεκνία, παιδία), grouping the passage into two "stanzas" of three statements each. The second triplet both reinforces and advances the statements in the first triplet in a manner similar to Hebrew parallelism. The suggestion that the object of "I write" is 1 John and that "I wrote" refers to another document, maybe the gospel or 2 John, or even to two sections of 1 John, has no grounding in Greek usage or in the immediate context.[1]

Each stanza is further structured by the vocatives: "children" (τεκνία), "fathers" (πατέρες), "young men" (νεανίσκοι). This sequence is repeated (with the slight variation, παιδία) in the second triplet. The syntax of each statement is also identical: a form of γράφω, a vocative, and a *hoti* clause:

A (12a-b)	I am writing	to you,	children,	*hoti*	. . .
B (13a-b)	I am writing	to you,	fathers,	*hoti*	. . .
C (13d-e)	I am writing	to you,	young men,	*hoti*	. . .
A´ (14a-b)	I write	to you,	little children,	*hoti*	. . .
B´ (14d-e)	I write	to you,	fathers,	*hoti*	. . .
C´ (14g-h)	I write	to you,	young men,	*hoti*	. . .

This highly structured rhetoric is effective for making the passage memorable and, therefore, marks it as a (the?) high point of the letter. The needs of remembering material in a largely oral culture necessitate such schemes, which may seem trivial or be missed altogether in our own visual, text-based culture. Ong explains:[2]

> In a primary oral culture, to solve effectively the problem of retaining and retrieving carefully articulated thought, you have to do your thinking in mnemonic patterns shaped for ready oral recurrence. Your thoughts must come into being in heavily rhythmic, balanced patterns, in repetitions or antitheses, in alliterations and assonances, in epithetic and other formulary expressions, in standard thematic settings … in proverbs which are constantly heard by everyone so that they come to mind readily and which themselves are patterned for rhythm and ready recall, or in other

---

1. Brooke Foss Westcott, *The Epistles of St. John* (Grand Rapids: Eerdmans, 1966), 57 – 58; Brooke, *Johannine Epistles,* 41 – 43.

2. Walter J. Ong, *Orality and Literacy: The Technologizing of the Word* (London: Methuen, 1982), 34.

mnemonic form. Serious thought is intertwined with memory systems. *Mnemonic needs determine even syntax.*" (italics added)

The need to remember important material without reference to written text through the use of rhetorical conventions is reflected throughout the NT, and largely escapes those of us who are not native to such a culture.[3] The effect of the rhetorical repetition might be captured in translation by something like "I am writing to you … yes, I write to you" (2:12, 14). After his foundational discussion in 1:1 – 2:11 about sin, light, and love, John is now ready to bring his message to bear specifically and directly on his readers, especially as he is about to pronounce the first exhortation of the letter in 2:15, using his first imperative verb. This highly rhetorical summary of what has been said in 1:5 – 2:11 reassures the readers of John's confidence in them and prepares them for the further teaching that follows, exhorting them to *continue* to be faithful by remaining in the teaching about Jesus.

Exegetical Outline

    V. Children, Fathers, and Young Men (2:12 – 14)

    ➡   **A. Children, your sins are forgiven (2:12)**

        B. Fathers, you know him who is from the beginning (2:13a – c)

        C. Young men, you have overcome the evil one (2:13d – f)

        D. Children, you know the Father (2:14a – c)

        E. Fathers, you know him who is from the beginning (2:14d – f)

        F. Young men (2:14g – k)

            1. You are strong (2:14g – i)

            2. The word of God remains in you (2:14j)

            3. You have overcome the evil one (2:14k)

---

3. For another example, see Karen H. Jobes, "Rhetorical Achievement in the Hebrews 10 'Misquote' of Psalm 40," *Bib* 72 (1991): 387 – 96.

Explanation of the Text

2:12 – 14 Children, I am writing to you because your sins are forgiven because of his name.

Fathers, I am writing to you because you do know the One who is from the beginning.

Young men, I am writing to you because you have overcome the evil one.

Little children, yes, I write to you because you have known the Father.

Fathers, yes, I write to you because you have known the One who is from the beginning.

Young men, yes, I write to you because you are strong and the word of God remains in you and you have overcome the evil one.

(Γράφω ὑμῖν, τεκνία, ὅτι ἀφέωνται ὑμῖν αἱ ἁμαρτίαι διὰ τὸ ὄνομα αὐτοῦ.

γράφω ὑμῖν, πατέρες, ὅτι ἐγνώκατε τὸν ἀπ᾽ ἀρχῆς.

γράφω ὑμῖν, νεανίσκοι, ὅτι νενικήκατε τὸν πονηρόν.

ἔγραψα ὑμῖν, παιδία, ὅτι ἐγνώκατε τὸν πατέρα.

ἔγραψα ὑμῖν, πατέρες, ὅτι ἐγνώκατε τὸν ἀπ᾽ ἀρχῆς.

ἔγραψα ὑμῖν, νεανίσκοι, ὅτι ἰσχυροί ἐστε καὶ ὁ λόγος τοῦ θεοῦ ἐν ὑμῖν μένει καὶ νενικήκατε τὸν πονηρόν.)

The unique rhetorical structure of these three verses requires that they be considered together, as John brings his message to bear on his readers. Although the overall message of this passage clearly affirms the good standing of the readers in John's mind, the details present three exegetical puzzles: (1) how to identify the referents of the three vocatives, "children" (τεκνία, παιδία), "fathers" (πατέρες), "young men" (νεανίσκοι), and their relationship to each other; (2) the shift of tense of the verb "I write" (γράφω) from present to aorist (already discussed in Structure); and (3) how to construe the repeated *hoti* (ὅτι) clause in each statement.

The term "little children" (τεκνία) is used six other times in 1 John (2:1, 28; 3:7, 18; 4:4; 5:21)

in statements that clearly refer to all the original readers collectively and probably echoes Jesus' use of the same term when addressing his disciples in John 13:33 in the opening statement of what is often called the Upper Room Discourse. If "little children" refers to all readers, the other two vocatives ("fathers" and "young men") is most likely a metaphorical or figurative term, unless John was addressing these verses to men only.

The term "fathers" (πατέρες) does not occur elsewhere in John's letters or gospel, but it is found in the NT as a term addressing the presumably older men of a group of people (e.g., Acts 7:2). In the context of 1 John 2:13a, 14b, it would likely be understood as addressing those who are older in the Christian faith.

Although there is a tendency to translate "young men" (νεανίσκοι) with the gender-inclusive "young people," as in many English Bibles, there is no evidence in biblical Greek, where the word occurs almost a hundred times, that the term was ever used inclusively (cf. LXX Ezra 10:1; Ps 77:63; 1 Esd 1:50; Jdt 7:22, 23; Acts 2:17; 5:10 for its use *in distinction from* women). While it may be correct to *apply* this verse to Christian women, and especially because John uses the gender-inclusive term "little children" (τεκνία) to describe all his readers elsewhere, he seems to have chosen to use an exclusively male term here.

The puzzle deepens with the question of the relationship between these three distinct terms. Is it that the entire original audience is being addressed first as "children" and then addressed as divided into two more specific categories, "fathers" and "young men"? If so, would female members of the Johannine church(es) be included in these male metaphors, or was John addressing men only? Or are three groups being addressed? The "little children" (τεκνία) are perhaps those new to the Christian faith, regardless of their age, and despite the term being used elsewhere to refer to all (2:1, 12, 28; 3:7, 18; 4:4; 5:21). But if the "children" are further defined as two groups, "fathers" and "young men," then arguably John would be addressing only men, perhaps not only in 2:12 – 14, but throughout the entire letter. If only men are being addressed, then John is writing either to an all male Christian community or to only the men within a community of both men and women.

To explain this male-specific language, some interpreters offer the possibility that John writes only to the church officers, on the presumption that all such officers were men in the early church, whom he refers to collectively as "children." This theory is weakened by the fact that nowhere in the New Testament are church officers called either "children" or "fathers," though in 1 Pet 5:5 "younger men" (νεώτεροι) are instructed to submit to the elders (πρεσβύτεροι), and Paul instructs Timothy to treat an elder "as if he were your father" (ὡς πατέρα; 1 Tim 5:1).

Trebilco offers an extensive analysis of this question and concludes, "Although we cannot say that women are definitely excluded in 1 John 2:12 – 14, this seems the most likely explanation."[4] His conclusion that in Greco-Roman society only men were public agents, and therefore only men were addressed in public discourse, assumes a literal interpretation of the vocatives. But in an obviously rhetorical structure, the distinction between sense and referent must be observed. The sense of the words "fathers" (πατέρες) and "young men" (νεανίσκοι) is clearly gender specific and does not include women. However, it appears that John is using these words with a rhetorical force to describe *all* of his readers in reference to stages of life.

The idea that John is alluding to stages in life,

whether physical or spiritual, is suggested by the use of νεανίσκος in Greek literature to describe the stage of a man's life when his growth was completed and he was in his prime strength, from twenty-two to twenty-eight years old (e.g., Philo, *Opif.* 105). In that culture, the stages of a man's life (in distinction from that of a woman) were relevant as the male child grew up to assume his role and responsibilities in the civic life of the city.

Given the highly rhetorical character of this passage, it is likely that John does not intend to limit the vocatives to male believers alone. His opening vocative in 2:12, "little children" (τεκνία), brings all his original readers into view and perhaps serves double duty by alluding to the early stage of Christian conversion and growth, which is then represented by his switch to a different word for "children" (παιδία) in v. 14. His address to "fathers" reflects a call to those who are mature enough to be training others in Christian living, and "young men" refers those in the stage of completing their full maturity in spiritual understanding.

This interpretation seems to be confirmed by 5:1, 4, which state that *everyone* who believes that Jesus is the Christ has been reborn as a child of God (5:1) and that such faith overcomes the world (5:4). If so, the full gamut of believers is addressed, though the sequence does not neatly move from oldest to youngest or vice versa. Because there is something said to each of the three groups that has already been said to all readers previously in the letter, the three categories are a rhetorical structure probably not intended to differentiate sharply between the three groups. As Lieu points out, "The characteristics ascribed to each [group] are elsewhere applied to the whole community, and the author would probably not have been too anxious with which any of his readers identified themselves."[5]

---

4. Paul Trebilco, *The Early Christians in Ephesus from Paul to Ignatius* (Grand Rapids: Eerdmans, 2004), 537.

5. Lieu, *I, II, & III John*, 87.

All considered, either John writes with only the male members of the community in mind or he is using these terms metaphorically. If he wrote originally to only men, by extension the same points can be said of Christian women. Regardless of whether male or female, young or old, Christians must remain faithful to the teachings about Christ for their entire lives and avoid being led astray by heresy. Therefore, they must be ready to receive the apostle's teaching, which likely involved rejecting the teaching of those who had left the community (2:19).

The repeated *hoti* clauses in each of the six statements also need exegetical consideration. Are they to be understood as causal ("I write to you … because …")? Or as declaratives that specify content ("I write to you … that …")? Since either is grammatically possible, the answer involves looking at the context of what is said in each statement:

12a, c … children, *hoti* your sins are forgiven because of his name.

13a, c … fathers, *hoti* you do know the One who is from the beginning.

13d, f … young men, *hoti* you have overcome the evil one.

14a, c … little children, *hoti* you have known the Father.

14d, f … fathers, *hoti* you have known the One who is from the beginning.

14g, i … young men, *hoti* you are strong,

14j and the word of God remains in you,

14k and you have overcome the evil one.

On the one hand, although the majority of English Bible translations render *hoti* with "because," a strictly cause-effect relationship is hard to press in these verses. What is said to the children (both τεκνία and παιδία), that their sins have been forgiven (perfect tense), has already been said of all who confess their sin in 1:9. What is said to the fathers (πατέρες), that they have come to know (again, perfect tense) the Father and the One who

is from the beginning, has been already said earlier in the letter (2:3, 4, 5). What is said to the "young men" in v. 14j, that the word of God remains "in them" (ἐν ὑμῖν), is the positive statement of what was said negatively in 1:10 about those who claim to have no sin, implying that the young men do not make this claim.

In other words, the statements that "I am writing to you … *that* your sins have been forgiven … *that* you know God … *that* his word remains in you" would be John's recognition and affirmation that his original readers *have* been living their Christian lives well in light of all that he has just said in 1:5 – 2:11. This affirmation contributes to John's stated purpose of assuring his readers that they do have eternal life (5:13). Furthermore, John introduces the idea that the young men "have overcome" (another perfect) the evil one, a new thought in the letter, but one that will receive more attention in 4:4 and 5:4 – 5. Perhaps John is suggesting that all those who aspire to be strong in the faith — understanding "young men" as a rhetorical analogy — will be called on to overcome the evil one and the world, a topic introduced in the verse that follows immediately (2:15). This, therefore, suggests that the *hoti* is declarative. He is writing *that* these statements are already true of his readers.

On the other hand, taking *hoti* as causal means that he is writing *because* these statements are already true. He is not writing because their sins aren't forgiven, as if to evangelize them. And he isn't writing because they don't know the Father, as if to tell them about God. Nor is he writing because they haven't overcome the evil one, but because they have. This is exactly what he goes on to say in 2:21: "I do not write to you *because* you do not know the truth, but *because* you do know it." In other words, he is writing *because* their current understanding of the gospel of Jesus Christ qualifies them to receive his exhortation about continuing in the truth in light of potential confusion from false teaching.

And his subsequent exhortations can then be heard in the context of this affirmation. Either a declarative or causal sense for *hoti* comes out at about the same place. Furthermore, the original readers may not have pressed any sharp distinction between the two uses of the conjunction, a distinction that is forced on us by having to choose one of two different English words.[6] Jintae Kim observes:

> Even a cursory reading of 1 John 2:12 – 14 brings the new covenant categories of Jer 31:31 – 34 to mind. "Your sins are forgiven" (v. 12) and "you have known the Father" (v. 14) clearly echo Jer 31:34, "They shall all know me, from the least of them to the greatest, says the Lord; for I will forgive their iniquity, and remember their sin no more."[7]

Because the forgiveness of sin is the basis of the new covenant in Jeremiah, the echo of that in 1 John shows that the writer considers the death of Jesus Christ to be the basis of this new relationship with God. This reminder that John's readers are the new covenant people is memorably presented in the highly rhetorical form of 2:12 – 14.

Theology in Application

Early in my life as a young Christian adult, I attended a church where the pastor felt it necessary to give an exuberant altar call every Sunday. I understood this came from a heart that was passionately concerned for the lost. But most Sundays as I looked around, I saw only the faces of those who faithfully attended services three times a week and who were actively involved in the life and ministry of the church. I myself had gone forward multiple times to commit my life Christ, even though it felt redundant and unnecessary. Eventually I got the feeling that through these repeated altar calls the pastor was implicitly accusing all of us of not being faithful enough, of somehow not measuring up to his expectations of our spiritual growth and maturity. No matter how involved we were, no matter what we did, it never seemed enough. I grew discouraged, began to resent his incessant altar calls, and eventually left to attend another church.

John lays down some hard teaching in 1:5 – 2:11: "If we say, 'We have fellowship with him,' and walk in the darkness, we lie" (1:6). "If we say, 'We have no sin,' then we deceive ourselves" (1:8). "The one who says, 'I know him,' and does not keep his commands is a liar" (2:4). "The one who hates his brother or sister is in the darkness" (2:11). I can almost hear the original readers thinking, "Is this what John thinks we are? Who is he talking to?" John well might answer, "If the shoe fits, wear it." But in 2:12 – 14, the apostle affirms those who have in fact been living out their faith well. He wants to reassure them that he *does* know that their sins have been forgiven, that they do know the Father, and that they have overcome the evil one.

For those in positions of spiritual leadership, this is a glimpse of John's pastoral ministry. He is writing in the aftermath of a serious situation that split the church ("they have gone out from us, but they were not of us," 2:19). He is going to make

---

6. Marshall, *Epistles of John*, 136.

7. Kim, "Concept of Atonement in 1 John," 104.

some strong exhortations that implicitly will demand the community's loyalty to his apostolic authority. But first, he wants to affirm them. He reassures them of their fellowship with God and the eternal life they have in Jesus Christ. He affirms that he knows that they do know the truth.

The message here primarily concerns spiritual endurance and growth for readers both then and now. Perhaps not everyone in John's audience had, in fact, experienced the forgiveness of sins by confession and repentance, and so his affirmation of those who have is implicitly a call to confession for all who have this need. Perhaps there were those who did not know God in Christ, and he points to their need to come into the light. Perhaps the word of God was not influencing every area of their lives, and John reminds us that to be at our spiritual prime, *all* areas of life must be brought under the lordship of Christ throughout *all* of our lives. The apostle's affirmation of who his readers are in Christ should motivate them, and us, to continue to overcome the evil one. The next verses spell out what that will mean.

1 John 2:15 – 17

Literary Context

After affirming his confidence in his original readers as living rightly in the light, John begins to exhort his readers directly. Here his apostolic authority asserts its prerogative to express God's will to his people, that they must not love the world or the things of the world. This passage lays the foundation for the theme of overcoming the world that will be developed in the body of the letter that follows, culminating in 5:4 – 5. The impermanence of the world is the framework in which all subsequent topics will be developed and provides the immediate context in which John will discuss the antichrists who have gone out.

> IV. Love, Light, and Darkness (2:7 – 11)
> V. Children, Fathers, and Young Men (2:12 – 14)
> ➡ **VI. Love for World Is Contrary to Love for Father (2:15 – 17)**
>   **A. Command Not to Love the World (2:15)**
>   **B. About the World (2:16 – 17a)**
>   **C. Obedience to the Will of God Means Eternal Life (2:17b)**
> VII. Schism in the Church (2:18 – 28)

Main Idea

The first command that the apostle issues in this letter is found here: "Do not love the world." In light of eternity, all the world has to offer is temporary at best and in rebellion against God at worst. Only a life motivated by obedience to God and his eternal values will survive the passing of the world and all its desires.

Translation

> ### 1 John 2:15–17
>
> | | | |
> |---|---|---|
> | 15a | exhortation | **Do not love the world or** |
> | b | expansion | **the things in the world.** |
> | | | |
> | c | condition | If anyone loves the world, |
> | d | inference | **love for the Father is not in them;** |
> | 16a | explanation | Because everything in the world — |
> | b | list/apposition | the desire of the flesh, |
> | c | list/apposition | the desire of the eyes, |
> | d | list | the pride of life, |
> | e | assertion | —is not of the Father but |
> | f | contrast | is of the world. |
> | 17a | assertion | And **the world and its desires are passing away,** |
> | b | contrast | but **the one who does the will of God remains forever**. |

Structure

This brief paragraph moves from the initial imperative to a causal (*hoti*) clause that explains the reason for the imperative, and then ends with an indicative statement asserting a theological truth that will be built upon later in the letter. It provides the reason why "the world" is aligned with the side of darkness in John's dualistic structure.

Exegetical Outline

→ **VI. Love for World Is Contrary to Love for Father (2:15 – 17)**

    A. Command not to love the world (2:15)

    B. About the world (2:16 – 17a)

        1. What is in the world is not of God (2:16)

        2. The world is passing away (2:17a)

    C. Obedience to the will of God means eternal life (2:17b)

Explanation of the Text

2:15 Do not love the world or the things in the world. If anyone loves the world, love for the Father is not in them (Μὴ ἀγαπᾶτε τὸν κόσμον μηδὲ τὰ ἐν τῷ κόσμῳ. ἐάν τις ἀγαπᾷ τὸν κόσμον, οὐκ ἔστιν ἡ ἀγάπη τοῦ πατρὸς ἐν αὐτῷ). After affirming his confidence in the genuine Christian faith of his readers, John here issues the first of ten imperatives in the letter (also in 2:24, 27, 28; 3:1, 7, 13; 4:1 [2x]; 5:21). He has previously said that the one who loves a brother or sister abides in the light (2:10), so this command stands in sharp contrast, creating a new category in the Johannine duality, the "world" (κόσμος). Living in the light means a life of love for God and for fellow believers; love for the world is excluded from living in the light. In fact, love for the world as John defines it is mutually exclusive with love for the Father (see "In Depth: The 'World' in John's Letters" at 2:16).

Because love for the world is syntactically parallel with "love for the Father" (ἡ ἀγάπη τοῦ πατρός), the genitive is most likely objective, referring primarily to the believer's love for the Father, which is expressed by loving others according to the will of God. This expression of love for God achieves the goal of God's redemptive love for his people (see comments on 2:5a-b). Therefore, those who love God must not love "the world," for by John's definition the world is all that is in rebellion against God. Clearly "love" for the world is of a qualitatively different kind than the love one is to have for a brother or sister, which is an expression of care and concern. Here, "love" refers to an attraction to something that one wishes to enjoy, an indulgence in things that are not in the light. It is to want to participate in what is set in rebellion against God.

IN DEPTH: Being of God (ἐκ) in John's Letters

Elementary Greek grammar books often give the English equivalent of the Greek preposition *ek* (ἐκ) as "out of" or "from." It carries the sense of place of origin, i.e., "I am *from* New Jersey." In John's writings this preposition is used to construct the duality between God and the world, truth and falsehood, righteousness and sin. Reflecting a usage similar to that in the gospel, the author of 1 John repeatedly speaks of being "of [ἐκ] the Father/God/Spirit" or "of [ἐκ] the world/devil" (1 John 2:16; 3:8, 9, 10, 12, 19; 4:1, 2, 3, 4, 5, 6, 7, 13; 5:1, 4, 18, 19; 3 John 11).

To be "of" God or "of" the world specifies the origin of one's impulses, motivations, and spiritual identity. Often the English preposition "from" does not suggest anything more than having come from somewhere. When John writes, "Because everything in the world — the desire of the flesh, the desire of the eyes, the pride of life — is not of [*ek*] the Father but is of [*ek*] the world" (2:16), he means that these things characterize the person who is of the world. The NIV translation of *ek* as "comes from" doesn't capture that sense well. It is not as if such things fly out of the world and into the church; rather, those who love the world and the things of the world are themselves "of" the world. Their basic desires and impulses do not originate with God.

One either is *of* the world/devil or is *of* God, and the only way to be of God is to be reborn as his child (3:1, 2, 10; 5:2). Jesus explains in John 3:5 – 6, "Truly, truly, I say to you, unless one is born of [*ek*] water and the Spirit, he cannot enter the kingdom of God. That which is born of [*ek*] the flesh is flesh, and that which is born of [*ek*] the Spirit is spirit" (ESV). Lieu observes that this use of the preposition *ek* is unusual and characteristic of John's writings, and finds it "striking" that both the gospel and 1 John share this distinctive marker.[1]

Therefore the expression "to be of God" or "to be of the world" is a Johannine way of saying either that one is a child of God who has been delivered from sin, or that one has been born only of the world and remains under God's wrath (John 3:36).

2:16 Because everything in the world — the desire of the flesh, the desire of the eyes, the pride of life — is not of the Father but is of the world (ὅτι πᾶν τὸ ἐν τῷ κόσμῳ, ἡ ἐπιθυμία τῆς σαρκὸς καὶ ἡ ἐπιθυμία τῶν ὀφθαλμῶν καὶ ἡ ἀλαζονεία τοῦ βίου, οὐκ ἔστιν ἐκ τοῦ πατρὸς ἀλλ᾽ ἐκ τοῦ κόσμου ἐστίν). John continues to build a dualistic structure as a moral principle. Having defined "the world" as the comprehensive sphere of human life that is under the control of the evil one, John now names more specifically the things in the world: "the desire of the flesh, the desire of the eyes, the pride of life." "Everything in the world" does not refer to its physical makeup, such as seas and mountains and animals, but to the moral and spiritual impulses that determine how people live.

"The desire of the flesh" (ἡ ἐπιθυμία τῆς σαρκός) is a subjective genitive, i.e., what the flesh desires. In other words, it is the impulse of human behavior that arises from the natural, even God-given, physical needs. The term "flesh" (σάρξ) is used in almost exclusively negative ways in the apostle Paul's writings, but that understanding should not auto-

matically be brought into John's thought. In John's writings, "flesh" is that which is merely human as opposed to divine (John 3:6; 6:63; 8:15). It was John who said that the Word became flesh (John 1:14), and so in John the concept of "flesh" does not denote innate sinfulness as it does, for instance, in Paul. The desires of the flesh may be natural, but our fallen nature drives people to satisfy them in ways that are not of God, leading to things like gluttony, alcoholism, and sexual immorality.

The desire of the flesh is simply the desire for those things that pertain merely to this life, which, in light of eternity, count for nothing (John 6:63). At best, it is shortsighted to allow one's physical needs to become the driving force in life, and in many people it leads to addictions of various kinds. Such a self-centered life is spent on things that have no lasting, eternal value. As John goes on to say in v. 17, "the world and its desires are passing away." Only those who order their lives by God's revealed Word have crossed over from the merely mortal to the eternal.

Because human impulses now operate under

---

1. Lieu, *I, II, & III John*, 95, 121.

the power of the evil one, they are cast here with a negative connotation as being "of the world" (ἐκ τοῦ κόσμου), putting "flesh" in John's writings in antithesis with the Spirit. It is the Spirit that gives birth to spirit (John 3:6) and the Spirit gives life; the flesh counts for nothing (6:63). In the Johannine duality, therefore, life and Spirit align with truth and light; flesh aligns with this fallen order, the world, and is under the power of the evil one. The desires of the flesh are criticized because they are not of the realm of the Spirit, and consequently, of life.

Although the "desire of the eyes" may suggest lust or pride to modern readers, in this statement it stands in distinction from both the desires of the flesh and the pride of life. Given the context of the world's temporary status (cf. v. 17), Brown is probably right that this phrase refers to the shortsighted desire for only what the eyes see physically.[2] He follows Dodd, who defines it as "the tendency to be captivated by the outward show of things without enquiring into their real values."[3] As Brown explains, the eyes in John's gospel are used twelve times in the story of the healing of the blind man (John 9), a sign that makes the point that Jesus must heal spiritual blindness, allowing us to see what is not merely physical but the reality that has been revealed from above. A similar distinction is made in 1 John 1:1, where the author has not only "seen with our eyes" (ὃ ἑωράκαμεν τοῖς ὀφθαλμοῖς) but has also perceived the significance of "what was from the beginning" (see comments on 1:1). Do not love the things of the world that you can see but that have no eternal value. Jesus has healed our spiritual blindness so that we can see the significance and scope of the salvation he has brought into the world.

The Greek word translated "pride" (ἀλαζονεία) is in the semantic domain of pride, arrogance, and boastfulness, and is often used in contexts that express overconfidence in one's own resources and wealth (2 Macc 9:8; 15:6; 4 Macc 8:19; Wisd 5:8; 17:7). The word *bios* (βίος) occurs only twice in John's writings, both in 1 John (2:16; 3:17). Although it is often translated with the same English word "life," it is sharply distinguished from the more common term for "life" (ζωή) that occurs frequently in John's writings to refer to the Life that was revealed, and through whom we are given eternal life.

In the Johannine conceptual framework, *bios* refers to physical life. In both of its occurrences in 1 John, it has the sense of "the means of subsistence,"[4] that is, the resources needed to maintain one's livelihood. While pride in one's occupation and the material goods it provides or pride about one's social status is common enough in every society, in context with the previous two phrases, John is more pointing to those whose security in their worldly things and wealth makes them so prideful as to overlook their need for and dependence on God (cf. Prov 18:11; 30:8). They do not realize that all they have that is not of God will pass away and be of no eternal value.

The list of three negative qualities that specify "everything in the world" follows the convention of using the number three for referring to evil in the ancient world. Philo, for instance, attributes all wars to "the desire for money, or glory, or pleasure."[5] This argues against seeing subordination of the second two to the first or reading them as entirely independent qualities. Furthermore, "all the" (πᾶν τό, the singular article rather than the plural "things") tends to unite these three impulses into

---

2. Brown, *Epistles of John*, 311.

3. Dodd, *Johannine Epistles*, 41, quoted in Brown, *Epistles of John*, 311.

4. BDAG, *s.v.* βίος 2.

5. Philo, *Decal.* 28.153; cf. Lucian's *Hermot.* 7.22 and Justin's *Dial.* 82.4.

one triad in grammatical apposition to "everything in the world." It is meant to refer not to three randomly chosen evils, but to the source of all the evil in the world's way of life lived where the light of Christ has not yet shone, a way of life that will not survive into eternity.

Here John uses, for the first of many times in his letter, the preposition *ek* (ἐκ τοῦ πατρός, "of the Father," and ἐκ τοῦ κόσμου, "of the world"; see "In Depth; Being of God (ἐκ) in John's Letters," above). This construction typically characterizes what is on which side of the duality of light and darkness by conveying its source of origin. Notably, even while Christ's followers are *in* (ἐν) the world, "they are not *of* the world" (ἐκ τοῦ κόσμου οὐκ εἰσίν, John 17:16). While once "of the world," Christ's followers have been called out of the world (John 15:19; 17:6). Therefore, although they still must live in the sphere where the evil one has power, their impulses for how to live come from the Father, who has given them new birth, and not from the world.

IN DEPTH: The "World" in John's Letters

John defines "the world" as that sphere of things that are not the proper object for a Christian's love, but what does that mean? Human cultures? The people who are not believers? Should Christians not love the natural creation? Is love of the sea or the mountains some form of idolatry?

"The world" has already been mentioned in 2:2, where its sin stands in need of Christ's cleansing blood. Elsewhere John says that the world is under the control of the evil one (5:19; John 14:30), which the strong are described as having overcome (1 John 2:13, 14). In John's gospel, the world is under God's judgment (John 9:39; 12:31), and it lies in darkness and sin (1:5; 12:46). Yet John 3:16 tells us, "For God so loved the world that he gave his one and only Son." If God loves the world, why shouldn't his children? John uses the word "world" (κόσμος) to refer, not to the natural creation, nor to human beings as human beings, but to the whole way of life resulting from the fall of humanity under the power of evil, whether organized into social institutions and power structures or practiced by individuals. As Lieu comments:

> Insofar as the world is capable of response (4:5), it is personalized if not embodied in actual men and women; but it is more than the sum total of people, or even of those people who reject the message. In its totality it represents that sphere which is under the sway of the evil one (5:9), and it has its own inherent character and power, which come close to setting it in antithesis to God.[6]

In John's duality, "the world" is all that is not of God, Christ, truth, and light. Therefore, "everything in the world" (πᾶν τὸ ἐκ τῷ κόσμῳ), as John specifies in 2:16, is by definition not in the sphere of God's light. Nothing that is in "the

---

6. Lieu, *I, II, & III John*, 92.

world" originates with God; rather, what is in view is everything that is antithetical to God and his revealed will. God's love for the world is redemptive; when John prohibits believers from loving the world, he means not participating in its ways and values.

The Christian is in a position of tension with respect to the world as John defines it. We are in the world but not "of" (ἐκ) the world. Jesus does not pray for the world, but for those whom God has given him out of it (John 17:9). He prays not that his followers be taken out of the world (17:15), for the only way out is death (17:11, 13); rather, he prays that they might be protected while in the world. This shows the comprehensive scope of "the world." There is nowhere one can go to leave its sphere and remain in this life. Instead of taking them out of the world, Jesus prays that God will protect his followers from the evil one for as long as they must live in the world but not be of the world (17:11, 15).

2:17 And the world and its desires are passing away, but the one who does the will of God remains forever (καὶ ὁ κόσμος παράγεται καὶ ἡ ἐπιθυμία αὐτοῦ, ὁ δὲ ποιῶν τὸ θέλημα τοῦ θεοῦ μένει εἰς τὸν αἰῶνα). John shifts the emphasis to a second quality of the world: its temporary nature. What the world has to offer is temporary; what God has to offer is eternal.

Because John's original readers have been cleansed from sin by Christ's blood (1:7), have come to know God (2:3), and have overcome the evil one (2:14), he affirms that they have been doing the will of God and can claim the reassurance of eternal life (see The Theology of John's Letters). In contrast, the world and all that it desires — food, drink, sex, money, the things always before our eyes, and its overweening pride that rejects any need for God — all of that is passing away. Even the most permanent things of this life that are not of God have no eternal value.

John reminds his readers that only the one who has been called out of the world into the light and who does the will of God will remain when the world and everything in it is gone. Because John writes under divine inspiration with apostolic authority, God is revealing his will through John's words. And his will is that those who know him do not love the world or the things in the world. The one who heeds this call to separate from the ways and attractions of the world is the one who will abide forever.

Theology in Application

Preachers have the reputation of railing against society's evils by identifying specific behaviors that are destructive and sinful — things such as drunkenness, addictions, or sexual immorality. While it is true those behaviors are not of God, John's thinking in this passage strikes at a much deeper level. The three evils he lists are not to be narrowed to three specific vices — as if "the desire of the flesh" was all about illicit sex and pornography — but John insists instead that we question the reigning value system of all of contemporary life at its roots. It is not enough to say that sexual immorality is wrong, or that pride is wrong, or that we must not covet material possessions. While all that is true, they are only symptoms of the much deeper problem of "the world's" alienation from God. All human values, ethics, and morality that are defined by fallen people are fatally flawed because they are built on false premises about reality.

People who reject the knowledge that "God is light" reject God's sovereign prerogative to define the standard of human values and morality. Even if not an atheist at the philosophical level, anyone who rejects God's rule of life in some aspect of their behavior is to that extent an atheist in practice. The underlying problem is a radical autonomy of the human spirit that insists on being its own god. And the result is each person "doing what is right in their own eyes" (cf. Judg 21:25) in a world that no longer has a uniform basis for law and morality. That is the way of "the world" as John uses the term.

His first imperative is, therefore, foundational for all others that will follow: do not love the world. Do not adopt the world's attitudes and ways of life with respect to God. For the attraction to human autonomy is a rejection of and, therefore, a failure to love God. There is no love for God in the one who loves the unbridled desires of the flesh for food, drink, and sex. There is no love for God in one who places the highest value on material things of this life that can be bought and sold but who undervalues the invisible things like love, faithfulness, and goodness. There is no love for God in the one who feels so self-satisfied and secure in the life they have built on their own accomplishments and wealth that they have no need for God.

It is only by allowing God to assume his rightful place in our lives as the sovereign Lord that we can rightfully satisfy physical needs, enjoy material blessings, and have true security to live comfortable and tranquil lives. When John commands us not to love the world or the things in the world, he is speaking of one's most basic life orientation. If our lives are not directed toward God in our every decision of each day, then even our most passionate efforts and causes amount to polishing brass on the *Titanic*. Day by day this world with its values and attitudes and autonomy is passing away. The famous poem "Only One Life" by Charles T. Studd (1860 – 1931) captures John's point well:

> Two little lines I heard one day, Traveling along life's busy way;
> Bringing conviction to my heart, And from my mind would not depart;
> Only one life, 'twill soon be past, Only what's done for Christ will last.

> Only one life, yes only one, Soon will its fleeting hours be done;
> Then, in "that day" my Lord to meet, And stand before His Judgment seat;
> Only one life, 'twill soon be past, Only what's done for Christ will last.

> Only one life, the still small voice, Gently pleads for a better choice
> Bidding me selfish aims to leave, And to God's holy will to cleave;
> Only one life, 'twill soon be past, Only what's done for Christ will last.

Only one life, a few brief years, Each with its burdens, hopes, and fears;
Each with its clays I must fulfill, living for self or in His will;
Only one life, 'twill soon be past, Only what's done for Christ will last.

When this bright world would tempt me sore, When Satan would a victory score;
When self would seek to have its way, Then help me Lord with joy to say;
Only one life, 'twill soon be past, Only what's done for Christ will last.

Give me Father, a purpose deep, In joy or sorrow Thy word to keep;
Faithful and true what e'er the strife, Pleasing Thee in my daily life;
Only one life, 'twill soon be past, Only what's done for Christ will last.

Oh let my love with fervor burn, And from the world now let me turn;
Living for Thee, and Thee alone, Bringing Thee pleasure on Thy throne;
Only one life, 'twill soon be past, Only what's done for Christ will last.

Only one life, yes only one, Now let me say, "Thy will be done";
And when at last I'll hear the call, I know I'll say "'Twas worth it all";
Only one life, 'twill soon be past, Only what's done for Christ will last.[7]

---

7. Widely available on the internet. See, e.g., www.paul
stefanort.com/2009/05/31/only-one-life-ct-studd.

1 John 2:18 – 28

Literary Context

This passage stands at the heart of John's message to his church(es). It brings all that he has said previously about his authority (1:1 – 4), about sin (1:6 – 2:2), and about God's command to believe in Jesus and to love others (2:3 – 17) to bear on the pressing reason for his letter, that some people in the church who have been known as Christians have left, apparently rejecting, for whatever reason, the truth that Jesus is the Christ. Here we find John's plea to his readers that they remain in Christ by continuing to adhere to the apostolic teaching about him. This passage leads from the idea of remaining in Christ to necessary ethical implications for those who are children of God — a topic taken up in 1 John.

Main Idea

John argues that not every idea about Jesus Christ is simply a different perspective on the truth, but there are limits beyond which the truth does not extend. He declares the teaching of "those who went out" to be a lie that has no share in the truth about Jesus Christ taught by John and the apostolic tradition. He exhorts his readers to "remain" in Jesus Christ by not being misled to embrace ideas that lie outside the truth of the apostolic witness to the significance of Christ's life, death, and resurrection.

Translation

---

1 John 2:18 – 28

18a	address	Children,
b	assertion	**it is the last hour,**
c	basis	and just as you heard that antichrist is coming,
d	assertion	even now
e	assertion	**many have become antichrists,**
f	inference	and **so we know**
g	content	that it is the last hour.
19a	concession	**They have gone out from us,**
b	contra-expectation	but **they were not of us;**
c	explanation	for if they were of us,
d	inference	**they would have remained with us;**
e	event	but [they went out from us]
f	result	so that they might be revealed
g	content	that none of them is of us.
20a	assertion	And **you have an anointing from the holy One,**
b	assertion	and **you all are in the know.**
21a	assertion	**I do not write to you**
b	basis	because you do not know the truth, but
c	contra-expectation	because you do know it, and
d	expansion	because no lie is of the truth.
22a	rhetorical question	**Who is the liar** but the one who denies
b	content	that Jesus is the Christ?
c	identification	**This one is the antichrist,**
	apposition	the one who denies the Father and the Son.
23a	assertion	**No one who denies the Son has the Father either.**
b	assertion	**The one who acknowledges the Son has the Father also.**
24a	apposition/ identification	You — what you have heard from the beginning,
b	exhortation	**let it remain in you.**

Continued on next page.

Continued from previous page.

c	condition		If what you have heard from the beginning remains in you,
d	result		**you also will remain in the Son and in the Father.**
25a	identification	And	this is the promise that he himself promised to us —
b	apposition		eternal life.
26	assertion		**I write these things to you about those who are leading you astray.**
27a	reference	But	as for you —
	assertion		**the anointing . . .**
b	identification		that you received from him
c	assertion		**. . . remains in you,**
d	result	and	**you have no need**
e	content		that anyone teach you [about these things]. Rather,
f	contrast		as his anointing teaches you
			about everything [you need to know about this],
g	assertion	and	**it is true**
h	assertion	and	**is not a lie,**
i	exhortation	and	just it has been teaching you,
			remain in him.
28a	address		And now, children,
b	exhortation		**remain in him,**
c	condition		so that when he appears,
d	consequence		we might have confidence and
e	expansion		not be shamed away from him whenever he comes.

Structure

The shocking announcement that "many have become antichrists" confirms that it is "the last hour." This introduces a discussion that arose in the wake of the departure of some members of the community (vv. 18 – 19). John's eschatological perspective on this situation, which opens in v. 18, comes to a close in v. 28, where believers hope to stand unashamed at the return of Christ.

Verses 20 and 27 form an inclusio that refers to the anointing by which John's readers have recognized the apostolic teaching as the truth and which enables them to exercise discernment. John's affirmation that his readers have indeed known the truth (2:21) is matched by his concern that they not be led astray from it by the false teaching to which they have apparently been exposed (2:26). The identification of the belief that Jesus is not the Christ (2:22), as the antichrists taught, lines up with John's exhortation that his readers continue to let the truth they first received to remain in them (2:24a). At the center of this chiastic structure is the pairing of 2:23a and 2:23b, contrasting those who deny the Son, and who consequently don't know the Father, with those who do acknowledge the Son and have the Father also:

2:18 – 19 eschatological context for the discussion
> 2:20 the anointing
>> 2:21 affirmation that readers have the truth
>>> 2:22 the lie: "Jesus is not the Christ"
>>>> 2:23a the one who denies the Son does not have the Father
>>>> 2:23b the one who confesses the Son also has the Father
>>> 2:24a let the truth first received remain
>> 2:26 concern that readers not be led astray
> 2:27 the anointing

2:28 eschatological context for the discussion

This structure argues that one cannot know God the Father and have eternal life apart from the confession that "Jesus is the Christ."

Exegetical Outline

➡ **VII. Schism in the Church (2:18 – 28)**

> **A. John announces the "last hour" (2:18)**
>> 1. It is the last hour (2:18a – b)
>> 2. His readers have heard that antichrist is coming (2:18c)
>> 3. Many have become antichrists (2:18d-e)
>> 4. The "last hour" is confirmed (2:18f-g)

> **B. A group has left the Johannine church(es) (2:19)**
>> 1. They have gone out from us (2:19a)
>> 2. They were not really of us, even though they started with us (2:19b)
>> 3. If they had been of us, they would have stayed (2:19c-d)
>> 4. Their true nature of being not of us has been revealed (2:19e – g)

> **C. The nature of the truth about Christ (2:20 – 21)**
>> 1. John affirms his readers' "anointing" (2:20)
>> 2. John writes to explain the nature of the truth (2:21)
>>> a. John writes not to tell them the truth, but because they already know the truth (2:21a – c)
>>> b. John writes to explain that no lie can be part of the truth (2:21d)

> **D. The false teacher characterized (2:22 – 23)**
>> 1. The false teacher is a liar (2:22a-b)
>> 2. The false teacher is an antichrist who denies both Father and Son (2:22c)
>> 3. The one who denies the Son cannot be in fellowship with the Father (2:23a)
>> 4. The one who confesses that Jesus is the Christ has fellowship with both the Son and the Father (2:23b)

E. Exhortation and promise (2:24 – 27)
1. Don't depart from the orthodox teaching (2:24)
2. You will have eternal life (2:25a-b)
3. Let this letter prevent you from being led astray (2:26)
4. The anointing remains in you (2:27a – h)
    a. so that you have no need for any of these false teachers (2:27d)
    b. The anointing teaches you to discern truth from error (2:27f-h)
5. Remain in him (2:27i)

F. Summarizing John's point in eschatological context (2:28)
1. Remain in him (2:28a-b)
2. Have confidence when he returns (2:28c – e)

Explanation of the Text

2:18 Children, it is the last hour, and just as you heard that antichrist is coming, even now many have become antichrists, and so we know that it is the last hour (Παιδία, ἐσχάτη ὥρα ἐστίν, καὶ καθὼς ἠκούσατε ὅτι ἀντίχριστος ἔρχεται, καὶ νῦν ἀντίχριστοι πολλοὶ γεγόνασιν, ὅθεν γινώσκομεν ὅτι ἐσχάτη ὥρα ἐστίν). This verse introduces the concept of antichrists, which appears to raise a subject that at first glance seems completely disconnected from all that has been previously said. But vv. 18 – 19 bring us to what likely were the circumstances that motivated the letter.

"Antichrists" had emerged from the Johannine group ("us") and had left the community. Their rise and departure led John to conclude that it was "the last hour." Although it may seem that John is introducing a topic disconnected from what he has previously written, the original readers would have known about the split in their church and would have heard all the apostle's words in that context. Something dangerous had happened. The fact that it isn't mentioned explicitly until v. 18 does not imply that it was not of primary concern to John,

because it would have been part of the shared knowledge that John could assume.

Two important exegetical questions arise in this verse. What does John mean by the "last hour"? How are we to understand what he means by "antichrists"? John begins this new unit of discourse with the vocative "children" (παιδία). He is either informing them of something that they did not know or reminding them: "it is the last hour." The "last hour" is characterized primarily by the rise of antichrists.

John is distinctive among the NT writers for his use of "hour" (ὥρα), and he uses it to refer to several different, but related, points in time that have eschatological nuances.[1] In John's gospel, John refers several times to the culmination of Jesus' life as "the hour"; for example, in John 12:23, "Jesus replied, 'The hour has come for the Son of Man to be glorified'" (see also 2:4; 7:30; 8:20; 12:27; 13:1; 17:1). Again in John's gospel, Jesus also uses the Greek word to refer to an indefinite future time that is closely related to, and results from, the culmination of his life; note 4:21, "'Woman,' Jesus re-

---

1. For one recent work see Stefanos Mihalios, *The Danielic Eschatological Hour in the Johannine Literature* (LNTS 436; London: T&T Clark, 2011).

plied, 'believe me, a time [ὥρα] is coming when you will worship the Father neither on this mountain nor in Jerusalem'" (also, 16:2, 4). Finally, the Johannine Jesus uses the word to refer to an eschatological time that, in some sense, has already begun, such as in 5:25, "Very truly I tell you, a time [ὥρα] is coming and has now come when the dead will hear the voice of the Son of God and those who hear will live" (also 4:23; 5:28).

The use of "hour" invokes the eschatological concept of the final stage of God's dealings with the world, a stage inaugurated with the death of Jesus, extending through a period of the world's hostility toward followers of Jesus, and to be consummated on the day of resurrection and judgment at the end of history as we know it (cf. Dan 8:19; 11:40, 41; 12:1). The "last hour" in John is closely related to his phrase "the last day," which seems to refer only to the day of resurrection and judgment; see, for instance, John 6:39, "And this is the will of him who sent me, that I shall lose none of all those he has given me, but raise them up at the last day" (see also 6:40, 44; 12:48).

Many people who have heard the term "antichrist" (ἀντίχριστος) are probably surprised to learn that this term occurs in the NT only in John's letters (1 John 2:18, 22; 4:3; 2 John 7). The antichrist in popular religious culture has strong connections with the book of Revelation, based on identifying the apocalyptic image of the beast with the antichrist, who is often portrayed by modern preachers as a future world ruler who will set himself against Christ and his people in hostile and violent acts and is associated with the number 666.

But John, the only biblical writer to use the term, defines it quite differently. First, there are "many" (πολλοί) antichrists. Second, they are not in the future but have been among, and may have emerged out of, the very community(-ities) to whom John writes, even two thousand years ago. The phrase usually translated "even now many antichrists have come" (καὶ νῦν ἀντίχριστοι πολλοὶ γεγόνασιν) renders the perfect tense of the verb (γίνομαι) as "have come" under the influence of the immediately preceding phrase, where antichrist is said to be "coming." But the syntax also permits the translation suggested here, that "even now many have become antichrists," with the two nominative-words preceding the verb for emphasis ("and now *antichrists many* have become!"[2] This suggests the shocking announcement that while John's original readers (as many readers today) may have been expecting a larger-than-life evil person to arise, the kind of heretical teaching going around was actually an evil of similar proportion that could also effectively destroy the church.[3]

While not requiring it, this rendering may also suggest that the antichrists actually arose from the people of the Johannine congregation(s), making the best sense of "they went out from us but were not of us." And it would heighten the tension that created the need for reassurance if people known well to the original readers, and perhaps even well-thought-of by them, left the fellowship, as opposed to false teachers from outside coming in, spreading their heresy, and departing. As one ancient writer comments, not every false teacher is called an antichrist, "but only of those who join a false sect after they have heard the truth. It is because

---

2. For a similar word order of the predicate nominative construction see Jas 3:1; Josephus, *C. Ap.* 2.282; Philo, *Leg.* 1.89; Plato, *Prot.* 326e; Thucydides, *Hist.* 4.106.1; Isocrates 15 (*Antid.*) 98; Xenophon, *De vectigalibus* 4.22.

3. See L. J. Lietaert Peerbolte, *The Antecedents of the Antichrist: A Traditio-Historical Study of the Earliest Christian*

Views on Eschatological Opponents (Leiden: Brill, 1996); Geert Wouter Lorein, *The Antichrist Theme in the Intertestamental Period* (London: T&T Clark, 2003); Jörg Frey, "Eschatology in the Johannine Circle," in *Theology and Christology in the Fourth Gospel* (ed. G. Van Belle, J. G. Van Der Watt, and P. Maritz; Leuven: Peeters, 2005), esp. 59.

they were once Christians that they are now called antichrists."[4]

Finally, John defines what he means by an antichrist as (1) "the one who denies that Jesus is the Christ [Messiah]" (2:22); (2) "every spirit that does not acknowledge Jesus [come in flesh]" (4:3); and (3) any "who do not confess Jesus Christ coming in the flesh" (2 John 7). Whatever these statements might specifically mean (see comments on each passage), the antichrists are those who have and teach a distorted understanding of Jesus Christ, and so with this passage John raises the important topic of Christology.

For some reason that we may never fully know, in the wake of the schism John feels the need to teach or to remind his readers of the truth about Jesus Christ. All that he has written thus far is preparation for persuading them to continue to have confidence in his authority (1:1 – 4) and to embrace his teaching about Jesus rather than go the way of the antichrists (2:24). He has affirmed the genuineness of his readers' Christian faith (1:5 – 2:17; also 2:21) but apparently senses that they are in jeopardy of being led astray. He writes to reassure them that they do indeed have eternal life through the faith that they have embraced and urgently desires that they continue in that apostolic tradition. This is in light of the fact that many in the community "have become [γεγόνασιν] antichrists," and John writes to prevent such further damage.

The inferential conjunction "and so" (ὅθεν) introduces the deduction from the fact that many have become antichrists, that such a circumstance confirms that it is indeed the last hour. In its most banal sense, there cannot, of course, be antichrists until Christ has come, and so John's statement is a further statement that Jesus Christ has ushered in a new era. By John's definition, anyone who professes to be a follower of Christ but teaches a Christology not in keeping with the apostolic tradition is, indeed, an antichrist, someone who opposes the truth of God in Christ.

2:19 They have gone out from us, but they were not of us; for if they were of us, they would have remained with us; but [they went out from us] so that they might be revealed that none of them is of us (ἐξ ἡμῶν ἐξῆλθαν, ἀλλ' οὐκ ἦσαν ἐξ ἡμῶν· εἰ γὰρ ἐξ ἡμῶν ἦσαν, μεμενήκεισαν ἂν μεθ' ἡμῶν· ἀλλ' ἵνα φανερωθῶσιν ὅτι οὐκ εἰσὶν πάντες ἐξ ἡμῶν). This verse gives a glimpse into the situation that was causing a need in the church for the author's pastoral care. It bears a lot of weight not only in the interpretation of 1 John but also in the reconstruction of the historical situation surrounding John's letters.

For the first time in his letter, John mentions "they," a group of people other than "we" and "you." Furthermore, in v. 18 he has identified "them" with the highly inflammatory term "antichrists." Now he informs or reminds his original readers about those who have gone out from them. But to be sure, "they" were not really "of" us. The negative particle (οὐκ) modifies the verb, not "all" (πάντες), so literally, "All of them were not of us" or, in smoother English, "None of them is of us" (see similar construction in 2:23). Clearly John needs to distance "them" from "us" to avoid lending his approval to them. Why? Who were these people? And was their departure from the Johannine church(es) what motivated John to write?

For the last thirty years or more, the departure of the "secessionists," as they've been called, has not only driven a reconstruction of the historical scenario but also influenced how the rest of 1 John

---

4. Didymus the Blind, *Commentary on 1 John* (ACCS NT 11; ed. Gerald Bray; Downers Grove, IL: InterVarsity Press, 2000), 186 – 87.

has been read. The "if we say" verses in 1:6 – 10 have been read as if they were the points of false teaching about sin that were actually being spread by the secessionists; 2:3 – 11 is often read as an allusion to the refusal of the secessionists to keep God's commands, with the result that they are living in darkness. The christological statements in 2:18 – 27 and 4:1 – 6 are understood as corrections to the anti-Christology of these false teachers, who were negatively affecting the congregation whether or not they were teachers in any formal role.

Daniel Streett nicely summarizes the various theories about who the secessionists were and what they believed:[5]

1. Gnostic Christians, who believed they held mystical knowledge that went beyond the teachings of Jesus, believed matter was evil and, consequently, lived either licentious or ascetic lives. Bultmann (1973) most famously taught this view, but Robert Law (1909) and C. H. Dodd (1946) also held to it, though with some variation among them.[6]

2. Docetist Christians, who believed that Jesus only appeared to be fully human but was not. D. Moody Smith (1991) and George MacRae (1986) have taken this view.[7]

3. Christians who believed that the man Jesus was a completely different being than the Christ-spirit, which descended on Jesus at his baptism and left him prior to his crucifixion. Perhaps they were associated with Cerinthus, who is often identified as a Docetist. Irenaeus documents and refutes this view (*Haer.* 1.26.1; 3.3.4; 3.11.1).

4. Christians who exalted the role of the Holy Spirit as a source of spiritual knowledge to the point of devaluing Jesus' human ministry and atoning death. This view has been proposed by Raymond Brown (1982), Von Walde (1990), and Hans-Josef Klauck (1991).[8]

5. Jewish Christians who departed the Christian community and renounced faith in Christ to return to the synagogue. They are "antichrist" in relation to Jesus in the sense that they are anti-Messiah; that is, they reject Jesus as the Messiah. This view has been most recently defended by Streett (2011) but has been held by earlier interpreters such as Wurm (1903) and O'Neil (1966) and has other recent supporters in Griffith (2002) and Witherington (2006).[9]

A key aspect of such reconstructions is that those who departed were members of the Johannne community who developed an aberrant theology from the original Johannine teachings as found in some redactional layer of John's gospel. Under the assumption that various situations arose from different redactional stages of the gospel, a number of problems and issues were identified. In other words, the reconstruction of the historical situation that prompted 1 John to be written has been closely bound up with theories of the redaction of John's gospel, which in turn have been closely aligned with reconstructions of the Johnnine community and its relationship to mainstream (i.e., Pauline) Christianity of the time. Clearly, acceptance of those reconstructions will depend a lot on whether one subscribes to an extensive redactional history of John's gospel.

More recently, some interpreters are skeptical whether the slim evidence offered by the Johannine texts can continue to bear the weight of such large historical reconstructions, and appeals are being made to scale back the assumptions that have been the mainstay of Johannine scholarship for the last thirty or forty years. The title of Griffith's article, "A Non-polemical Reading of 1 John: Sin, Christology and the Limits of Johannine Christianity," argues for interpretation "that does not require

---

5. Streett, *They Went Out from Us*, 7 – 8.
6. Ibid., 19 – 20.
7. Ibid., 36 – 37.

8. Ibid., 77.
9. Ibid., 90 – 100.

gnosticising or docetic-like opponents" and "without reference to what the group that has left … believes."[10] Streett's doctoral dissertation provides the most recent in-depth treatment of this issue and takes an approach not unlike Griffith's by extensively critiquing the methodology of "mirror reading" (though he himself must depend on it to some extent for his own conclusions).

Mirror-reading involves using the explicit statements and commands of a New Testament writer to construct a plausible situation that may have given rise to those statements and commands. While everyone must mirror-read to some extent, and in fact such inferences are an important part of how language works, it is unwise when interpreting ancient texts to put all one's weight on hypothetical scenarios that may or may not be correct. Streett points out that the polemical material in 1 John is limited to 2:18 – 27 and 4:1 – 6, and that secessionists are not mentioned elsewhere.[11] Therefore, passages that have been traditionally interpreted as part of the polemic against the false teaching of those who went out, such as the "if we say …" statements in 1:6 – 10, should not be read against that background because the secessionists have not yet been introduced in the letter.

While the caution seems warranted, we do know from explicit statements in the text that some who were members of the community have left (2:19), and the author writes to reassure those who remain of their eternal life (5:13). Given that 2 and 3 John are also on the topic of a harmful disruption in the Johannine churches, it seems clear that a rather large event, already well known to the original readers, lies behind all three letters. *Anything* John would have written to them at that moment would have most naturally been read by the original readers in the context of that departure, even if John did not explicitly bring it up in the first sentence of the letter.

Nevertheless, Streett poses some astute questions that go to the heart of the traditional reconstructions:

> Who was the "us" from which the "antichrist" secessionists went out (2:19)? Does it refer to the author's group of "eyewitnesses" in 1 John 1:1 – 3, or to the Johannine community? Why could it not refer more broadly to the early Christian movement as a whole? How do we know that the "antichrists" were a unified group? How do we know that they all left at one time, or even for the same reason?[12]

The theories of the Johannine community and its redactions of the Johannine material probably have overreached the data and can no longer be used as sound interpretive assumptions. It is probably not possible, or necessary, to so specifically accuse the secessionists of even incipient Gnosticism or Docetism. But it is clear that some disruption of the Johannine fellowship has occurred that has potentially dangerous and long-reaching implications such that the author feels compelled to write to those most affected by it. The positive teaching that John offers on the topics of sin, Christology, and love effectively argue to some extent against the foundational principles of both of those ancient heresies and several varieties of modern heresy as well. It is upon John's statements of positive theology that orthodox belief can be established even if the intriguing specifics of the original historical situation are lost to us.

At least two important points are made in v. 19. First, because the false teachers originated in John's own church(es), he does not want anyone to think that he approves of the false teaching. Second, the fact of their departure reveals that those who de-

---

10. Griffith, "Non-polemical Reading of 1 John," 28.
11. Streett, *They Went Out from Us*, 118.

12. Ibid., 119.

parted did not remain in the fellowship with the Father and with his Son, Jesus Christ (1:3), that was based on John's authoritative testimony about "the Word of Life" (1:1 – 3). Although physically participating in the Christian community under John's influence, they had not embraced the truth about Jesus Christ that was the uniting bond of the community. They were among us but "were not of [ἐξ] us."

Could John be criticized for not exercising the same love for his departed brothers and sisters that he commends in 2:10 of those who walk in the light? "So, it's either John's way or the highway!" someone might say. But this is fundamentally to misunderstand love as the NT presents it. Love does not mean getting along with everyone regardless of what they believe in an exercise of tolerance that ignores truth. Love does not trump truth, but insists that there is a truth apart from which people will perish — and his name is Jesus Christ. John does not say, "If you don't agree with me, you must leave," but rather, "If you do not agree with me, you are not embracing the truth that God has revealed in Jesus Christ and therefore have no fellowship with God or us." Had the secessionists known and remained in the truth, they "would have remained" (μεμενήκεισαν) within the Johannine fellowship.

2:20 And you have an anointing from the holy One, and you all are in the know (καὶ ὑμεῖς χρῖσμα ἔχετε ἀπὸ τοῦ ἁγίου καὶ οἴδατε πάντες). John affirms that his readers do not need to follow the teaching of the antichrists because they already know the truth. The Greek word translated "anointing" (χρῖσμα) is unique to John's writings in the NT. In the LXX, it occurs in Exodus referring to the anointing oil used ritually for sanctifying the tabernacle and everything in it, and for consecrating the priests. Here it is likely a pun on the title

"Christ" (χριστός), which is the adjectival form of the verb to anoint (χρίω). Later Christian practices of ritually anointing with oil probably found support here, but it is unlikely that John intended it in that sense here in the context of antichrists who may claim to have an anointing but do not.

The anointing is from "the holy One" (ἀπὸ τοῦ ἁγίου), which, based on frequent use of the phrase elsewhere in the NT, is most likely a reference to the Holy Spirit, though grammatically it could refer to Jesus Christ or the Father. If it refers to Jesus Christ, the thought would be that "you have an anointing from the holy One, who is himself anointed." In Johannine theology the resurrected Christ is the giver of the Holy Spirit (John 20:22), and so a sharp distinction should probably not be made.

The result of having the *chrisma* is that (lit.) "you all know," a phrase that seems to hang incomplete without a direct object. This lack of an object no doubt motivated the textual variant "all things" (πάντα) found in the majority of manuscripts. However, the sense of the more difficult reading in context is probably close to the English phrase, "you are in the know," which means that John recognizes his original readers have the knowledge required for them to understand what is going on. Many English translations insert "you all know the truth," borrowing the object from the next verse.

This may imply that those who went out were claiming some special knowledge of Christ and God that conflicted with "what was from the beginning" (1:1 – 4). Dodd argued that the *chrisma* was the Word of God that is the objective testimony to the truth, for John exhorts his readers to allow the *chrisma* to remain in them (2:27), just as he spoke of the Word of God remaining in them (2:14).[13] It is certainly true that the inscripturated Word

---

13. Dodd, *Johannine Epistles*, 62.

of God is the objective standard of truth against which all claims of spiritual knowledge must be measured. However, since the antichrists emerged from the Christian church, it is likely they too used Scripture to support their heretical views, a practice that has persisted throughout the church's history to this very day.

Furthermore, John seems to be speaking of something internal to his readers that allows them to discern the truth against falsehood. Theologically speaking, *both* the objective, external Word of God and the inward, effectual call of the Holy Spirit are needed for genuine spiritual rebirth. Theologians have referred to that initial call of the Spirit that brings one to faith as "effectual calling," and the ongoing work of the Spirit with respect to Scripture as "illumination." John's use of *chrisma* seems to imply both ideas.

By contrast, those antichrists who went out, departing not only physically from the congregation but also from the apostolic truth, had not received the inward work of the Holy Spirit that permitted them to discern error from truth. Despite participating in the church, they were still spiritually blind and walking in darkness. As Marshall puts it, "the antidote to false teaching is the inward reception of the Word of God, administered and confirmed by the work of the Spirit."[14]

2:21 I do not write to you because you do not know the truth, but because you do know it, and because no lie is of the truth (οὐκ ἔγραψα ὑμῖν ὅτι οὐκ οἴδατε τὴν ἀλήθειαν, ἀλλ᾽ ὅτι οἴδατε αὐτὴν καὶ ὅτι πᾶν ψεῦδος ἐκ τῆς ἀληθείας οὐκ ἔστιν). John brings his dualistic framework to bear on the teaching that his readers have apparently been exposed to. He affirms their knowledge of the truth and draws a sharp line between truth and falsehood.

Here again we see that regardless of its oral qualities and despite its lack of the Hellenistic letter opening and closing, this discourse originated in written form. Furthermore, it was clearly not intended to be an evangelistic tract, since it is written to the original readers not because they need the truth but because they already know it. Here again, John is affirming his confidence in their Christian faith and bolstering assurance that they do have eternal life through it.

The second reason John gives for writing advances his argument against listening to those who have gone out. "I am writing to you," he says, "because no lie is of the truth." One of the confusing things in a controversy is when differing viewpoints are put forth as simply different aspects of the truth. By implication, the secessionists were apparently claiming that their teaching was not contrary to the truth of the Christian gospel, but simply a different way of looking at it. Without denying that there may indeed be different facets to any truth, there is also a difference between truth and falsehood. John's point is that whatever the secessionists were believing and teaching was false, not simply a different perspective on the truth of Jesus Christ.

John himself claims the authority to make such a judgment because he knew the Word of Life that had been from the beginning (1:1 – 4). His authority to discern false teaching from true trumps that of the secessionists. Thus, John's purpose is to teach his readers further about the truth they already know by pointing out its necessary implications and entailments.

2:22 Who is the liar but the one who denies that Jesus is the Christ? This one is the antichrist, the one who denies the Father and the Son (Τίς ἐστιν ὁ ψεύστης εἰ μὴ ὁ ἀρνούμενος ὅτι Ἰησοῦς οὐκ ἔστιν ὁ Χριστός; οὗτός ἐστιν ὁ ἀντίχριστος, ὁ ἀρνούμενος

---

14. Marshall, *Epistles of John*, 155.

τὸν πατέρα καὶ τὸν υἱόν). After establishing that there is truth and that no lie can masquerade as an aspect of truth, John brings that general principle to bear on the situation at hand, which apparently regards the identity of Jesus as the Christ. By John's definition, the liar (in the sense of believing and teaching heresy) is the person who does not have a proper understanding of who Jesus is. Not everything one might hear about Jesus Christ is true, in the first century or in ours.

The conjunction (ὅτι) should be read as introducing direct discourse, i.e., "the one who denies, saying 'Jesus is not the Christ,'" or, slightly paraphrased into smoother English as above, "the one who denies that Jesus is the Christ."

Much depends on how the title "Christ" (Χριστός) is understood. Even before Jesus was born, the Hebrew word "Messiah," which means "anointed," had been translated into Greek in the LXX with the word *christos* (χριστός; e.g., LXX 1 Sam 2:20, 35; 12:3, 5; 16:6). Because of this, in the Gospels when Jesus is referred to during his earthly life as the *Christos*, it should probably be understood as identifying Jesus as the promised Messiah (e.g., Matt 22:42; Mark 12:35; Luke 23:39; John 7:41). But Jesus' resurrection and ascension funded his title with new, unprecedented meaning never anticipated by the concept of the Messiah in Second Temple Judaism. Jesus proved to be the Messiah, yes, but the Messiah turned out to be God himself!

Interpreters who see in the title *Christos* only or primarily the sense found in Judaism of an eschatological deliverer or prophet do not give enough consideration to how Jesus' resurrection transformed the meaning of the word.[15] By the time the NT was written, when the majority of Christians were Gentile believers, the sense of the Christ as understood in Second Temple Judaism had been overtaken in the church by its sense as a title for Jesus that expressed his divine nature, enveloping and transforming those previous expectations. (The later passage 1 John 4:2 – 3 seems to reinforce this understanding that the disagreement was over the nature of Jesus' being; see comments there.)

This historical development of the term introduces an ambiguity in how each of the NT writers uses the word. Because all of the NT books were written after this shift in sense had occurred, some English Bible translations (e.g., NIV 2011, NLT 2007) translate this term with "Messiah" in the Gospels and Acts when referring to Jesus during his earthly ministry and shift to "Christ" in those places that point to his fuller identity as the Son of God. Here in 2:22 the difference is whether John means to say the liar is whoever denies that Jesus is the Messiah, in the historical, Jewish sense, or that Jesus is the Christ in the fuller sense of his divine nature.

Of course, how one reads this statement will determine what kind of heresy the secessionists were likely teaching. Is the heresy about introducing elements of thought about divine beings from pagan Greek philosophy? Or is it about Jewish Christians turning away from Jesus by deciding he isn't the promised Messiah after all, and then by retreating to the synagogue? Either is plausible in the setting of first-century Ephesus, for western Asia Minor had had a large Jewish population since the time of the Seleucid kings in the second century BC.

John identifies the "one who denies that Jesus is the Christ" as an "antichrist." This statement makes

---

15. For instance, Streett, *They Went Out from Us*, 157 – 61. He argues that the denial of Jesus' messiahship indicates that those who went out were converts from Judaism returning to the synagogue. Although he rightly critiques reconstructing the specifics of the heresy through mirror-reading, as maximalist Johannine interpreters have done, his own reconstructed scenario is to some extent subject to the same criticism. Every interpreter must adopt some reconstructed scenario as a context in which to read these letters. The goal is to pile inference upon as little speculation as possible, so Streett's point is well taken.

it clear that there could be no antichrists until the Messiah had come and there was a Christ. That is why the appearance of Jesus marks the start of an era, "the last hour" in John's way of speaking, in which false understandings of his identity work against and oppose the truth that he came to reveal. Therefore, those who hold and teach such heresies are *anti*christs. Even if they think they are drawing closer to God, John claims that to deny that Jesus is the Christ is to deny the Father as well.

2:23 No one who denies the Son has the Father either. The one who acknowledges the Son has the Father also (πᾶς ὁ ἀρνούμενος τὸν υἱὸν οὐδὲ τὸν πατέρα ἔχει· ὁ ὁμολογῶν τὸν υἱὸν καὶ τὸν πατέρα ἔχει). "When you take Jesus as your Savior, you get God as your Father. But if you say 'no' to Jesus, you are also saying 'no' to the Father who sent him."[16] John here further explains that one cannot have fellowship with God the Father and deny that Jesus is the Christ. The right understanding of who Jesus is is a necessary element of true fellowship with the Father, which is the only solid basis of assurance of eternal life (see The Theology of John's Letters).

The repeated mention of "the Son" (τὸν υἱόν) in vv. 21 – 24 in inseparable association with the Father informs our understanding of the ambiguous statement in v. 22 that "Jesus is the Christ/Messiah." One could argue that failing to recognize Jesus as the Messiah fails to comprehend the Father's redemptive plan and covenant promise. The rejection of the Messiah by the very people who were expecting him was a great mystery that the apostles pondered (e.g., John 1:11; Rom 10:21 – 11:27). But here John's thoughts transcend the simple identification of Jesus as the Messiah by pointing to the inner-Triune relationship of the Father and the

Son. The gospel demands more than the belief that Jesus is the Jewish Messiah; John is calling for recognition of the truth that the Jewish Messiah is none other than God incarnate. Therefore, the title "Christ" (Χριστός) as found here probably is a reference to the truth about the divine nature of Jesus Christ as both Messiah and Son of God.

2:24 You — what you have heard from the beginning, let it remain in you. If what you have heard from the beginning remains in you, you also will remain in the Son and in the Father (ὑμεῖς ὃ ἠκούσατε ἀπ᾽ ἀρχῆς, ἐν ὑμῖν μενέτω. ἐὰν ἐν ὑμῖν μείνῃ ὃ ἀπ᾽ ἀρχῆς ἠκούσατε, καὶ ὑμεῖς ἐν τῷ υἱῷ καὶ ἐν τῷ πατρὶ μενεῖτε) This verse is a call to remain in the truth, which is the only way to remain in God. "You" (ὑμεῖς) is a pendent nominative, that is, a hanging nominative that has no verb. It serves to switch the focus from the false teaching of those who went out to the exhortation John has for his readers. The relative clause "what you have heard from the beginning" (ὃ ἠκούσατε ἀπ᾽ ἀρχῆς) is the subject of the third person imperative, "let it remain" (μενέτω), not the nominative pronoun ὑμεῖς.

This is a strong appeal for the readers to hold to the Johannine gospel message as they heard it "from the beginning," a reference to the beginning of their Christian lives in this context. The phrase alludes, however, to what Jesus himself taught as the beginning of the distinctively Christian gospel, which further alludes to God's redemptive plan that reaches all the way back to Genesis (see comments on 1 John 1:1).

The repeated use of "remain" or "abide" (μένω) in the Johannine corpus — well over sixty times in the gospel and letters — emphasizes the continuing state of the believer adhering to the apostolic teaching. It is not enough to believe the gospel at

---

16. Daniel L. Akin, "Truth or Consequences: 2 John 1 – 13," *Faith & Mission* 23, no. 1 (2005): 9.

one point and then to develop one's own theology beyond it. Only those who remain within the teaching of the apostles about Jesus Christ can have an assurance of eternal life, because only those who continue to embrace that message will remain in the Son and in the Father. Again, one cannot be in right relationship to the Father and not to the Son, or vice versa. The mutual indwelling central to the concept of "remaining" is characteristic of John's thought (e.g., John 6:56; 14:10, 17; 15:4 – 7, 9, 10; 1 John 4:15).

2:25   And this is the promise that he himself promised to us — eternal life (καὶ αὕτη ἐστὶν ἡ ἐπαγγελία ἣν αὐτὸς ἐπηγγείλατο ἡμῖν, τὴν ζωὴν τὴν αἰώνιον). John sharply highlights what is at stake between the apostolic Christology he represents and that of those who have gone out. Their physical departure from the congregation(s) demonstrates their departure from the Son and, therefore, from the Father as well. This would be especially ironic if the secessionists were Jewish converts who left the church to return to the synagogue, thinking they could worship God more conveniently as Jews than as Christians, who may have been experiencing increasing persecution.

The secessionists did not remain in what was from the beginning. Eternal life is assured for only those who hold to the apostolic teaching. Spiritual security cannot be found in the latest theological trends that move beyond the need for the atoning blood of Jesus Christ, Son of God. For this is what "he himself," Jesus, promised. John is not citing a specific verse; rather, he is summarizing the promise of eternal life Jesus gives in John's gospel in the context of his teaching that remaining in him is necessary. For instance, in John 15:1 – 6 Jesus teaches that his disciples must remain in him as a branch remains in a vine. Those branches that do not remain in him wither and die, and they are gathered at the end and are burned. The promise

of eternal life by continuing in the faith that Jesus taught about himself is necessarily implied (see The Theology of John's Letters).

2:26   I write these things to you about those who are leading you astray (Ταῦτα ἔγραψα ὑμῖν περὶ τῶν πλανώντων ὑμᾶς). John here makes it clear that those who went out, whatever their beliefs may have been, have situated themselves in opposition to Christ ("antichrists") and no longer remain in the truth God has revealed in Christ. These people may or may not have had any official role as teachers or leaders in the church, but by whatever influence they had, John was concerned for the negative impact they could make on those who remained.

It is certainly legitimate, therefore, to read what John writes in 2:18 – 26 as pertaining to false beliefs that were unsettling the assurance of eternal life. John identifies these false beliefs as not just another way of looking at Jesus, but as an error that has no place in the thinking of those who wish to remain in the Son and the Father. The main point of contention was christological, concerning the true identity and nature of Jesus, although that point of contention may have played out in the ethical behavior of the secessionists as well. Surely any distortion in the truth about who Jesus Christ is would also affect one's thinking about sin and how to deal with it, or perhaps even whether sin exists. The topic of sin, introduced by the "if we say …" statements in 1:6 – 10, can reasonably be understood as part of the consequences of an errant Christology, even if the secessionists were not teaching those ideas explicitly.

2:27   But as for you — the anointing that you received from him remains in you, and you have no need that anyone teach you [about these things]. Rather, as his anointing teaches you about everything [you need to know about this], and it is true and is not a lie, and just it has been teaching you, remain in him (καὶ ὑμεῖς τὸ χρῖσμα ὃ ἐλάβετε ἀπ᾽ αὐτοῦ, μένει ἐν ὑμῖν καὶ οὐ χρείαν ἔχετε ἵνα τις διδάσκῃ ὑμᾶς· ἀλλ᾽ ὡς τὸ αὐτοῦ χρῖσμα διδάσκει ὑμᾶς περὶ πάντων καὶ ἀληθές ἐστιν καὶ οὐκ ἔστιν ψεῦδος, καὶ καθὼς ἐδίδαξεν ὑμᾶς, μένετε ἐν αὐτῷ).

Verse 27 forms an inclusio with v. 20, framing the discussion of the nature of truth with respect to Christology in the context of the inward witness of the Spirit that John calls the "anointing" (*chrisma*, χρῖσμα). Since this term is found only here in the NT, it is likely related to the specific false teaching that John is arguing against, and possibly is a term that had been used by the seccessionists. Perhaps the secessionists were justifying their new ideas with a claim that they had a *chrisma* of the Spirit that took them beyond the apostolic teachings about Jesus Christ (cf. 2 John 9). After all, Jesus himself said that when the Spirit came, he would guide "you" (ὑμᾶς) into all truth (John 16:13).

It seems likely that the secessionists were confident that the Spirit had imparted to them some new spiritual truth, perhaps not recognizing that the "you" in Jesus' statement was directed toward his disciples in the upper room, whom he had chosen to be his witnesses. This made it necessary for John to reassert his apostolic authority (1:1 – 4) and to declare any teaching false that was inconsistent with that given by those whom Jesus had commissioned. Those apostolic witnesses were the ones who got to say what was of the truth and what was not (1:1 – 4).

John reminds his readers that they were convinced by the teaching about the person and nature of Jesus Christ and previously embraced that as truth. This John attributes to the genuine working of the Holy Spirit within them. Now they are being confronted with teaching about Jesus that in some way contradicts what they previously embraced, regardless of whether the error ran in the direction of incipient Gnosticism, Docetism, or a retreat into

Jewish tradition. John has labeled that teaching a lie that is incompatible with the truth that has been taught "from the beginning" (2:24). He now reassures his readers that the discernment they have exercised in the past that brought them to faith is the genuine work of the Spirit, and that they have no need for anyone who teaches something new and different, no matter how "spiritual" such new teaching may appear. John is confident that the Spirit will confirm his teaching about Jesus Christ because the Spirit has inspired it (cf. 1 John 5:7 – 8).

It is likely that this also is an allusion to the new covenant promises of Jer 31:33, where God promises that his Torah will be in the hearts and minds of the new covenant people (cf. 1 John 2:14), such that they will not need to be taught (Jer 31:34, "No longer will they teach their neighbor …").[17] That inner working of the Spirit that John's readers have experienced is the genuine work of God, and whatever the secessionists claim is a false "anointing."

John writes to those who already know everything they need to know about the person and work of Jesus, and he exhorts them to continue with it and consequently "remain in him." By necessary inference, to embrace the false teaching is a step that would take one outside of, or "beyond" (2 John 9), the truth of Jesus Christ.

2:28 And now, children, remain in him, so that whenever he appears, we might have confidence and not be shamed away from him whenever he comes (Καὶ νῦν, τεκνία, μένετε ἐν αὐτῷ, ἵνα ἐὰν φανερωθῇ σχῶμεν παρρησίαν καὶ μὴ αἰσχυνθῶμεν ἀπ᾽ αὐτοῦ ἐν τῇ παρουσίᾳ αὐτοῦ). John points out the eschatological consequences of remaining in the truth. The Lord Jesus will return, and that provides the perspective from which to make moral and spiritual decisions about how to live.

"And now, children" (καὶ νῦν, τεκνία), signals

---

17. Kim, "Concept of Atonement in 1 John," 105.

a summary that puts John's exhortation to remain in Jesus Christ in the context of the *parousia* (παρουσία), the return of Christ. This is the first and only mention of Christ's second coming using this term in John's gospel and letters. In John 14:18 Jesus promises that he will come back to his followers, a statement that may have caused some confusion between the Lord's presence with the church through the Spirit and his second coming. John reminds his readers that assurance of eternal life entails being confident to stand before God when Christ returns. This affirms the ongoing existence of Jesus Christ in the postresurrection state and argues against any thought that the Spirit has replaced Jesus. The conditional "if" (ἐάν) does not introduce uncertainty about Christ's return in John's mind but is used in the sense of "whenever."[18]

This reference to Christ's return frames the topic of Christology with an eschatological perspective that was suggested previously with the announcement that it is the "last hour" (2:18). The eschatological perspective is important because what a person believes about the future has great influence on how they think and live today. How ashamed one would feel to stand condemned before Jesus Christ and finally see the truth of who he is after a lifetime of believing wrongly about him and teaching others to do the same — and there are many ways to believe wrongly about Jesus:

- The error of rejecting Jesus as the Jewish Messiah will be revealed when he returns to bring God's redemptive plan begun in covenant with ancient Israel to its final consummation.
- The error of rejecting Jesus' blood as an atoning sacrifice will be revealed when he stands as Judge of all our sin.
- The error of believing that the Spirit leads away from the orthodox teaching about Jesus Christ to some generic spirituality will be revealed when Jesus appears as the only Lord whom the Holy Spirit glorifies.
- The error of rejecting Jesus as the Son of God, believing him to be merely a righteous teacher of religion, will be revealed when he comes again rightfully ruling and reigning over all the cosmos.

The apostolic witness about the person and work of Jesus Christ was given by God to reveal these things now, so that the Lord's people may live their lives in light of them. Therefore, John says, "remain in him." Do not be misled by those who claim to have the Spirit of God but are actually self-deceived. "They went out from us." "They" are not of (ἐξ) us. "They" are in darkness. "They" are apart from God. "They" do not have the promise of eternal life. "Remain in him" (μένετε ἐν αὐτῷ) is a good summary statement of all the Johannine writings concerning how a Christian should live, the topic to which John turns next.

Theology in Application

Who gets to speak for God? What is the role of the Spirit in guiding the understanding of the church? What is the relationship of spiritual truth to the first-century life of Jesus? Not unlike the ancient world in which John wrote, our world today is also full of voices claiming spiritual truth as a way to know God. And the prevailing winds of our time blow in the direction of tolerance of any and all religious beliefs.

---

18. BDAG, *s.v.* ὅταν 2.

The Nature of Spiritual Truth

Perhaps John's major point in this passage addresses the nature of spiritual truth. Not every claim to truth about God is just another form of monotheism. Just because God is invisible does not mean that anything one might imagine about him has a legitimate claim to be the truth. One source of confusion today is that truth is determined by what most people believe, as if by vote. Such a view puts the foundations of truth on shifting sands, as the culture and demographics of a population change over time. This idea of truth by majority opinion leads to the idea that all personal opinions about God are of equal value. This idea has led to a reader-response approach to the Bible, expressed in statements such as, "Well, that might be what it means to you, but to me it means...." If each person is an equal arbiter of truth, especially of religious or moral truth, then majority rule would be the best that human society could achieve.

In the context of a monotheistic culture, differing viewpoints about God and how to know him are put forth as simply different aspects of the truth, even when they are at root incompatible. The idea that there are many paths that lead to the same God may be well intended to keep the peace, but it belies a fundamental misunderstanding of monotheism. Certainly there are in fact many facets of truth when speaking of a complex subject such as God and his relationship to the world. Christian theologians can speak of Christology, soteriology, pneumatology, eschatology, ecclesiology, and theology proper. But not every idea about God in our world today is simply a matter of looking at him from a different perspective; there is a difference between truth and falsehood. And this is perhaps the most difficult claim of John's message, and of the entire NT, to uphold today. Even many professing Christians are more open to accepting spiritual "truth" from other religions without critiquing it against the orthodox apostolic teaching handed down through the ages. As Ben Witherington comments:

> In **1 John 2:21** our author indicates that truth and lies are at polar extremes from one another, or as C. H. Dodd puts it, they are generically different. A lie is not, for example, some aspect of the truth. "To suppose that it *is* may be a false kind of tolerance, or just muddled or lazy thinking. As for tolerance, at least it is clear that no one has any business to tolerate falsehood along with the truth in his own mind."[19]

Thus, the primary application of John's message in this passage must be the recognition that there is such a thing as heresy, and sometimes it can even come from those who profess to be Christian.

---

19. Witherington, *Socio-Rhetorical*, 488 (bold and italics original), quoting Dodd, *Johannine Epistles*, 55.

Truth and the Spirit

Related to the question of discerning truth from heresy is the question of the role of the Spirit in guiding the understanding of the church. This arises in at least two contemporary topics, the charismatic movement and the task of theological exegesis. While debate may go on about whether the charismatic gifts continue to operate today as they did, for instance, when Paul wrote to the church at Corinth (1 Cor 12 – 14), orthodox Christian theology recognizes the essential and ongoing work of the Holy Spirit in believers through every generation. Without his work, no one could genuinely come to know God. As Jesus said, there is truth that the Spirit will reveal because it could not be stated and understood until after Jesus' death and resurrection:

> I have much more to say to you, more than you can now bear. But when he, the Spirit of truth, comes, he will guide you into all the truth. He will not speak on his own; he will speak only what he hears, and he will tell you what is yet to come. He will glorify me because it is from me that he will receive what he will make known to you. (John 16:12 – 14)

The apostles commissioned as Jesus' witnesses, primarily those present in the upper room when Jesus spoke these words, provided this Spirit-inspired interpretation of the significance of the life, death, and resurrection of Jesus when they wrote, or were responsible for the writing of, the books of the NT. Apostolic testimony was completed with the closing of the canon. But orthodox Christian doctrine continued to develop over the first four centuries of the church, and even today issues arise that demand theological inquiry. Furthermore, the task of theological exegesis of Scripture is to infer meaning from the biblical texts that goes beyond their specific historical context to address issues and concerns that the church has not before faced. What is the role of the Spirit today in revealing truth, especially since our only encounter with the living God is through the Holy Spirit?

Jesus himself delimits such claims of Spirit-revealed truth: they must "glorify" Jesus Christ. Any teaching that claims the Spirit's authority must involve the incarnate Son of God who atoned for sin on the cross. The issue at the time John wrote — who is Jesus? — remains the central issue today. The only authorized source that answers that question is the divinely inspired, apostolic teaching preserved in the pages of Scripture. Therefore, the question of the canon of Scripture that has been raised by bringing writings such as the *Gospel of Thomas* and the *Gospel of Judas* to the public's attention is relevant to John's exhortation to "remain in him." Neither Jesus nor John denies the need for the ongoing exposition of Scripture in the church, but John affirms that we already have all the knowledge we need about who Jesus Christ is. John's point is that the truth of apostolic teaching, now preserved in the canon of Scripture, is the full truth; it lacks nothing that the secessionists of his day or the recently discovered so-called gospels have to offer.

John's claim that eternal life is found only by remaining in Jesus Christ and continuing to embrace the apostolic teaching about him is not a popular message in the religiously pluralistic times in which we live. The shift in religious demographics in the United States during the last fifty years puts the church increasingly in the position of having to defend the particularity of Christianity. It is Jesus himself who claimed that he *is* the truth and that there is no way to God the Father except through him (John 14:6). Will the church find the boldness to preach that message in these times? What consequences will result for those who preach this message in a society in which Christians find themselves a minority? That is perhaps the greatest spiritual challenge of our time.

The Diversity within the Unity of Truth

There is also an important corollary to John's teaching about the nature of the truth. Even within orthodox, apostolic teaching about Jesus Christ, there is still much room for discussion and debate. The gospel writers themselves show amazing variety in how they present four different perspectives on Jesus' life. James's emphasis that true faith must be lived out through deeds (Jas 2:17) stands alongside of Paul's insistence that deeds cannot earn anyone salvation (e.g., Rom 3:28; Gal 2:16).

It would be an egregious error to label other Christians as antichrists because they disagree with our interpretation of Scripture on issues such as the mode of baptism, the ordination of women, or the cessation of the spiritual gifts. Certainly leaving one local church to attend another, as one's season of life or situation requires, does not bring one under John's condemnation as those who "went out." There is, however, no reason to look to other religions or trendy theological ideas for new and better truth about how to know God.

1 John 2:29 – 3:10

Literary Context

The discussion of the confidence a believer has in view of Christ's return and the believer's consequent assurance of eternal life extends through 3:22. Within that eschatological context, John presents the heart of his argument of how he wants his readers to live in the wake of the event that has disturbed the congregation(s). This passage extends John's conceptual duality into the realm of ethics, discusses the true nature of Christian believers as children of God, and provides further basis for security concerning eternal life. This passage appears to be pastoral instruction about how to live differently from those who would mislead either by their teaching or by their example (3:7). In the context of the disruption caused by those who went out, this unit is perhaps an implicit argument against them and a further explanation of why "they were not of us" (2:19), even though they had been within John's Christian community.

Main Idea

How one lives expresses whether one is born of God or of the devil. Those born of God cannot sin in the specific way that unbelievers do, but they must nevertheless live rightly as God defines it. Love for others is the hallmark of that righteous life, because those born of God have received the Father's love.

Translation

1 John 2:29 – 3:10

29a	condition	If you know that he is righteous,
b	inference	**you know** also that everyone who lives righteously has been born of him.
3:1a	exclamation	**See such love the Father has given to us**
b	apposition	that we should be called the children of God —
c	assertion	and **we are!**
d	basis	For this reason,
e	assertion	**the world does not know us,**
f	cause	because it did not know him.
2a	address	Dear friends,
b	assertion	**now we are children of God,**
c	assertion	and **what we will be has not yet been revealed.**
d	assertion	**We know** that whenever he [Christ] appears,
e	assertion	**we will be like him,**
f	basis	because we will see him just as he is.
3a	assertion	And **everyone who has this hope in him purifies himself**
b	comparison	just as that One [Jesus Christ] is pure.
4a	assertion	**Everyone who does sin indeed is lawless,**
b	explanation	for **sin is lawlessness.**
5a	assertion	And **we know that that One appeared**
b	purpose	to take away sins,
c	assertion	and **there is no sin in him.**
6a	assertion	**Everyone who remains in him does not sin;**
b	assertion	**everyone who sins has neither seen him nor**
		known him.
7a	address	Children,
b	exhortation	**let no one mislead you;**
c	assertion	**the one who lives rightly is righteous;**
		just as that One is righteous.
8a	assertion	**The one who does sin is of the devil,**
b	basis	because the devil has been sinning from the beginning.
c	purpose	For this reason
d	assertion	**the Son of God appeared,**
e	result	so that he might destroy the works of the devil.
9a	assertion	**No one who has been born of God sins,**
b	explanation	because his [God's] seed remains in them,
c	expansion	and **they are not able to sin**
d	explanation	because they have been born of God.
10a	assertion	In this way **the children of God and the children of the devil are distinguished:**
b	assertion	Everyone who does not do what is right is not of God,
c	expansion	even the one who does not love their brother and sister.

Structure

Two imperative verbs structure the argument of this section. In 3:1 the readers are exhorted to see (ἴδετε) that the new birth offered by God through faith in Jesus Christ is an expression of the Father's love. With that introduction, John makes several assertions having to do with the eschatological hope and, consequently, how that hope must motivate how his readers live now. He then argues that sin is incompatible with living as a child of God, because sin is a rejection of God's authority.

The second imperative (v. 7) exhorts his readers to not "let [anyone] mislead" (πλανάτω) them on this topic of how to live. Those who claim to be children of God but who live like the devil are expressing their true paternity. It is not what one says, but how one lives that distinguishes those truly born of God from those who are not (cf. Jas 2:14 – 26).

The unit transitions back to the topic of love for others previously mentioned in 2:10 by asserting that those who fail to love others are no better than those who commit overt acts of sin.

Exegetical Outline

→ **VIII. Who Are the Children of God? (2:29 – 3:10)**

    A. "Like father, like son" (2:29 – 3:1)

        1. Those who do righteousness have been born of God (2:29)

        2. God's love revealed in his children (3:1)

    B. The hope of our eschatological lives (3:2 – 3)

        1. When Christ appears, God's children will be like him (3:2)

        2. So those with this hope imitate Christ now (3:3)

    C. The nature of sin (3:4 – 6)

        1. Sin is *anomia* (3:4)

        2. Sin frustrates God's purpose in sending Christ (3:5)

        3. Remaining in him means not sinning (3:6a)

        4. Sinning means not knowing God truly (3:6b)

    D. Who's your daddy? (3:7 – 10)

        1. Don't be deceived (3:7a – b)

        2. How you live reveals who you are (3:7c – 9)

            a. The one who does righteousness is righteous (3:7c)

            b. The one who sins is of the devil (3:8a-d)

                i. because the devil is characterized by sin (3:8a-b)

                ii. but the Son of God came to destroy the devil's works (3:8c-e)

            c. The one who is born of God does not sin because God's seed is in them (3:9a-b)

            d. The one who is born of God is not able to sin because they have been born of God (3:9c-d)

        3. Sin divides the children of God from the children of the devil (3:10a-c)

            a. Everyone who does not live rightly is not of God (3:10a-b)

            b. Even the one who does not love their brother and sister (3:10c)

Explanation of the Text

2:29 If you know that he is righteous, you know also that everyone who lives righteously has been born of him (ἐὰν εἰδῆτε ὅτι δίκαιός ἐστιν, γινώσκετε ὅτι καὶ πᾶς ὁ ποιῶν τὴν δικαιοσύνην ἐξ αὐτοῦ γεγέννηται). John transitions from the exhortation to remain in him in 2:28 to explaining that only children of God can live in the way that remaining in him requires, namely, living without sin.

With 2:29 John draws an inference from the assumption that all his readers would agree with, namely, that God is righteous. In fact, God's character and ways define what it is to be righteous. No one can bring some standard against which they evaluate God; God himself defines righteousness (see comments on 1:5). John assumes his readers agree with this and states it as a general condition as he has previously done (see 1:6 – 10). From this assumption he infers that everyone who has been born of God lives righteously, as God defines righteous living.

This is the first occurrence in the letter of the theme of new birth with God as Father, a theme that is foundational in John's gospel (1:3; 3:3 – 8) and now becomes a persistent and important theme in this letter (1 John 3:9; 4:7; 5:1, 4, 18). With this assertion, John defines what he meant in 2:28 by remaining in God and Christ so that his readers will have confidence and not be driven from Christ by shame. He reintroduces the theme of sin and right living through love that he previously discussed (1:6 – 10; 2:1 – 11), but now he links it to the idea of a nature that is like God's because he is the Father. "Like father, like son," as the saying goes.

The phrase "has been born of him" (ἐξ αὐτοῦ γεγέννηται) helps explain the more than thirty occurrences of the preposition *ek* (ἐκ) used throughout the letter (see "In Depth: Being of God (ἐκ) in John's Letters" at 2:15). For example (italics added):

2:16: " … is not *of* the Father but is *of* the world" (οὐκ ἔστιν ἐκ τοῦ πατρὸς ἀλλ' ἐκ τοῦ κόσμου ἐστίν)

2:19: "They have gone out from us, but they were not *of* us" (ἐξ ἡμῶν ἐξῆλθαν, ἀλλ' οὐκ ἦσαν ἐξ ἡμῶν)

2:21: " … no lie is *of* the truth" (πᾶν ψεῦδος ἐκ τῆς ἀληθείας οὐκ ἔστιν)

3:8: "the one who does sin is *of* the devil" (ὁ ποιῶν τὴν ἁμαρτίαν ἐκ τοῦ διαβόλου ἐστίν)

4:1: "test the spirits, if they are *of* God" (δοκιμάζετε τὰ πνεύματα εἰ ἐκ τοῦ θεοῦ ἐστιν)

This use of *ek* is also an expression common in John's gospel, such as in John 1:13, "children born not of natural descent, nor of human decision or a husband's will, but born of God [ἀλλ' ἐκ θεοῦ ἐγεννήθησαν]." In such uses, *ek* expresses the concept of "issues from" or "originates with"; and when used with the verb γεννάω ("to conceive a child"), it implies fatherhood (cf. John 8:41). There is perhaps no more sweeping an expression of the newness of a life redeemed by Christ than that of the birth metaphor. One's birth defines identity in fundamental and in some sense unchangeable categories. Note that the verb γεγέννηται ("has been begotten") is in the perfect tense, denoting that the new birth precedes the ability to live righteously.

The new birth metaphor is found also in the apostle Peter's writings (1 Pet 1:3), where it explains the radical transformation necessary to enter the kingdom of God. One cannot get there on a passport or on a visa; it takes nothing less than new birth with God as Father to bring a person into the kingdom (John 3:5). And the benefits of the new birth are all-encompassing. Because God is by nature eternal, those reborn as his children have eternal life. The merely mortal cannot enjoy eternal life, which John insists can only happen through the new birth from above (3:6). But God is not only eternal; he is righteous, and so those who are his children are righteous also.

3:1 See such love the Father has given to us that we should be called the children of God — and we are! For this reason, the world does not know us, because it did not know him (ἴδετε ποταπὴν ἀγάπην δέδωκεν ἡμῖν ὁ πατὴρ ἵνα τέκνα θεοῦ κληθῶμεν· καὶ ἐσμέν. διὰ τοῦτο ὁ κόσμος οὐ γινώσκει ἡμᾶς ὅτι οὐκ ἔγνω αὐτόν). The world is alienated from God, and God's love creates people who are his children and who then also become alienated from the world. Although the chapter division may lead readers to see this as the beginning of a new unit of discourse about the Father's love, it is organically connected to 2:29. John is still concerned with the topic of God's children living righteously, but he now brings love into discussion again. Because God is eternal, his children have eternal life. Because God is righteous, his children live righteously. Because God loves, his children must love (3:10).

The *hina* clause ("that we should be called") is in apposition with "such love" (ποταπὴν ἀγάπην). It expresses the content of God's love, not its purpose. God's love for people is expressed in allowing us to become his children and in providing a way for that to happen through Jesus' death and resurrection, even though we have repeatedly rejected him and sinned against him.

But because Christians have been born *of* God, they are no longer *of* the world. Their new nature originates not with the desires and impulses of the world, but with the righteousness of God. The world doesn't recognize this, because by John's definition the world is those who do not know God and, therefore, do not recognize his ways and his character. They are not *of* God. Therefore, they do not know those who have been born of God.

This reality, of course, doesn't mean that suddenly a new Christian has undergone some kind of

face transplant that makes them unrecognizable to family and friends (although the transformation of physical facial expression and mannerisms in those forgiven by God can be dramatic). John is saying that the world cannot appreciate or understand Christians because what makes them tick is something the world cannot understand. Just as the world did not recognize and appreciate Jesus since he was so unlike the people's expectations for the Messiah (John 1:11), the world will misunderstand and reject those born of God as well. The world is another sphere of existence (a parallel universe, so to speak) that John has labeled "darkness." Because the world does not originate with God and has not been born of God, it is not in covenant with God and will pass away. Only what is *of* God, what is in the light, will last forever.

3:2 Dear friends, now we are children of God, and what we will be has not yet been revealed. We know that whenever he [Christ] appears, we will be like him, because we will see him just as he is (ἀγαπητοί, νῦν τέκνα θεοῦ ἐσμεν, καὶ οὔπω ἐφανερώθη τί ἐσόμεθα. οἴδαμεν ὅτι ἐὰν φανερωθῇ ὅμοιοι αὐτῷ ἐσόμεθα, ὅτι ὀψόμεθα αὐτὸν καθώς ἐστιν). God's love is expressed by giving believers new birth as his children. John immediately addresses his readers as "dear friends" (lit., "beloved ones") and again turns their attention to the eschatological future when Jesus will return. Using the same language as in 2:28, "when he appears" (ἐὰν φανερωθῇ) is a conditional in syntax, in which ἐάν overlaps meaning with ὅταν ("whenever").

John's point, that God's children are a work in progress, is suggested by the emphatic fronting of "now" (νῦν). We are *now* children of the Father, even with all our faults and flaws and, yes, sins. But it is not God's purpose to allow his children to be as we are now, for the full benefit of our status cannot be even imagined in this world (cf. 1 Cor 2:9). It has to be revealed, and that revelation lies still in the future. Jesus' apostles could not fully understand the truth about him until after his death and resurrection, for they had no categories in which to comprehend something that God had never before done (John 16:12). Similarly, the full effect of being a child of the Father with eternal life is not something anyone can comprehend now.

But having seen a glimpse of the eternal future in his encounters with the resurrected Jesus, John can say with confidence that when Jesus returns, "we will be like him." Jesus himself said, "Because I live, you also will live" (John 14:19). Because Jesus shared in our humanity fully, whatever he became as a resurrected human being, we also will become. But John's concern here is not about metaphysical speculation on the afterlife; it is about ethical living and reflecting the character of our Father. It is about the children bearing a family resemblance to the Father. As Calvin has commented on this verse:

> For as to our body we are dust and a shadow, and death is always before our eyes; we are also subject to a thousand miseries, and the soul is exposed to innumerable evils; so that we find always a hell within us. The more necessary it is that all our thoughts should be withdrawn from the present view of things, lest the miseries by which we are on every side surrounded and almost overwhelmed, should shake our faith in that felicity which as yet lies hid.[1]

The culmination of this transformation into being fully like Christ, both "physically" and morally, is "because we will see him as he is" (ὅτι ὀψόμεθα αὐτὸν καθώς ἐστιν).[2] Exactly how seeing Christ is the cause of the transformation is left unspecified. But surely when he returns, the full impact of his identity, of which humanity can now

have only a feeble glimpse, will transform every desire, every motivation, every impulse. Therefore, that beatific vision of Christ and how we will be like him motivates the lives of God's children *now*.

3:3 And everyone who has this hope in him purifies himself, just as that One [Jesus Christ] is pure (καὶ πᾶς ὁ ἔχων τὴν ἐλπίδα ταύτην ἐπ᾽ αὐτῷ ἁγνίζει ἑαυτόν, καθὼς ἐκεῖνος ἁγνός ἐστιν). Because what we believe about the future influences how we live today, John appeals to the future as the basis for encouraging his readers to purify themselves today.

The Greek word translated "hope" (ἐλπίδα) has a somewhat stronger sense of certainty than does the English word. One might say, "I hope it rains today; we really need it." There the word "hope" expresses a strong wish or desire, which may or may not have any basis in the meteorological conditions. Or one might say, "I invest in my retirement account in the hope of a secure future." There "hope" is more than a wish; it is a confidence that the action taken is the actual basis for realizing the desire, though wild fluctuations in the market may introduce less certainty into that hope. But when John speaks of the Christian's eschatological future, there is no uncertainty because it is based on what Jesus Christ has *already* done. The only reason that this attitude is referred to as a "hope" is that it is still future. It is a certain hope that is merely awaited.

That certain future, with all the benefits and blessings of being like Jesus when he returns, provides the motivation for a believer to become more like Jesus in the way of life now. John doesn't say a believer "will purify" or "should purify." He uses the present active indicative, "purifies." The Greek verb translated "purifies" (ἁγνίζω) is used a few times in the NT to refer to religious rituals that a person

---

1. John Calvin, *The Gospel according to St. John 11 – 21 and the First Epistle of John*, accessed from Accordance Calvin's Commentaries (complete), formatted and hypertexted by OakTree Software, version 1.7.

2. Urban C. von Wahlde (*The Gospel and Letters of John*

[Grand Rapids: Eerdmans, 2010], 3:101) stands alone in taking this ὅτι clause as a second part of the content of what "we will know," i.e., "we know *that* we will be like him and *that* we will see him as he is." He must also supply a καί, for which there is no textual evidence.

performed according to the OT purity laws (John 11:55; Acts 21:24, 26; 24:18). But Peter, James, and John take that idea and apply it internally to moral character:

Jas 4:8: "Come near to God and he will come near to you. Wash your hands, you sinners, and purify your hearts, you double-minded."

1 Pet 1:22: "Now that you have purified yourselves by obeying the truth so that you have sincere love for each other, love one another deeply, from the heart."

John uses the word similarly to refer to the moral transformation of the believer that takes the place of external religious rituals in the life of the Christian. Just as OT rituals set one apart for a special time of service to God or to enter his presence, all of the Christian's life is to be set apart by a moral consecration in one's way of life. This is to be in imitation of the example of Jesus Christ, whom Christians will be like when he returns. Just as Jesus Christ set himself apart in an obedience to God that qualified him to achieve the purpose for which he came, Christians are to set themselves apart in obedience to God's revealed will. The one whose future is to be like Jesus embraces this exhortation, but those who have no interest in being like Jesus must question their eschatological future, even if they profess to be Christian.

3:4 Everyone who does sin indeed is lawless, for sin is lawlessness (Πᾶς ὁ ποιῶν τὴν ἁμαρτίαν καὶ τὴν ἀνομίαν ποιεῖ, καὶ ἡ ἁμαρτία ἐστὶν ἡ ἀνομία). John now turns to those who do *not* live as if they wish to become like Jesus, exposing the true nature of their behavior. Anytime such a person sins, he or she acts in a way that is not like Jesus. But here John reveals the true nature of sin — not as individual, unrelated random acts, but as originating from an

attitude that resents God's moral demands on their lives, an attitude that John refers to as "lawlessness" (ἀνομία, *anomia*). This word is formed by the alpha privative (ἀ-), which functions much as the prefix "un-" does in English words, and a cognate of the word *nomos*, the noun for "law," yielding "un-lawness," or in better English, "lawlessness."

When John says that sin is *anomia*, he is saying more than that every sin is in some sense an infraction of the Mosaic law. That would be a rather banal and tautologous statement. The word *anomia* is used more than two hundred times in the LXX. In a passage in which the Lord describes the penalty for covenant disobedience, Lev 26:43 displays the sense of *anomia* well: "They themselves shall accept their lawlessness [*anomia*] on account of which *they disdained my judgments and were vexed in their soul by my ordinances* (NETS, italics added). To be "lawless" does not mean simply to break the law; it means to disdain the very idea of a law to which one must submit. Many atheists have this root problem of rejecting the idea of the existence of God because their hearts are lawless and they reject the thought of a Being to whom they must submit. *Anomia* is the rejection of God's authority and the exaltation of the autonomy of the self. As one of my colleagues said, "The Rule of Law is about all people being equally subject to the law. Some people love law. Others consider themselves above the law. They may use the laws to control others. They may consider the freedom to do what they want the greatest law."[3]

There is something innate in human nature that causes each of us to resent the idea of submitting to a higher authority than ourselves. Any parent of a two-year-old can attest to that. But a necessary part of maturing into a productive member of a family or society is learning the appropriate respect for

---

3. With thanks to Prof. John Zimmermann for this conversation.

law and authority. The OT book of Judges shows how a society descended into moral anarchy when "everyone did as they saw fit" (Judg 21:25). The human heart became lawless in the garden of Eden when Adam and Eve thought their opinion that the fruit was good overruled God's authority when he forbade them to eat from a certain tree. It is from the lawless heart that acts of sin flow.

The foundation of a right relationship with God is acknowledging that he himself defines the standard of right and wrong, and that we must be willing to submit ourselves to his authority. The psalmist rejoices for those willing to bring themselves under God's covenant, for he does not deal with us as our *anomia* deserves (Ps 102:10 LXX; 103:10 Heb. and Eng.). And in the ancient Greek translation of his message the prophet Isaiah explained that the Suffering Servant would be pierced for our *anomia* (Isa 53:5 LXX).

In the NT, *anomia* is never used to refer to transgression of the Mosaic law, but Jesus does use it to refer to eschatological judgment:

> Not everyone who says to me, "Lord, Lord," will enter the kingdom of heaven, but *only the one who does the will of my Father* who is in heaven. Many will say to me on that day, "Lord, Lord...." Then I will tell them plainly, "I never knew you. Away from me, you [who do *anomia*!]." (Matt 7:21 – 23, italics added; see also Matt 13:41; 23:28; 24:12)

It is striking that John uses similar language in 3:4, pointing out that whoever sins is really doing *anomia*. His point is to shock his readers into seeing the true nature of what they may think of as individual, unrelated acts; such acts arise from a heart of lawlessness. As Yarbrough points out, the word *anomia* "always refers to those who have resolutely turned away from God, to the point that they can no longer be regarded as his people but are in fact his enemies."[4] It was used in Jewish and

Christian apocalyptic literature to describe the activity of Satan against God immediately before the end.[5]

The apostle Paul uses this word to describe the "man of lawlessness [ἀνομία]," who is otherwise known in Christian eschatology as the antichrist (2 Thess 2:3; cf. Rom 6:19; 2 Cor 6:14; 2 Thess 2:7). How shocking it is to see the true nature of sin — that it is of the same nature as the antichrists, the world, and darkness. Anyone who expects to stand in confidence and to be like Jesus Christ when he returns must deliberately and vigorously reject sin, for not to do so reveals a heart that rejects God's authority.

3:5 And we know that that One appeared to take away sins, and there is no sin in him (καὶ οἴδατε ὅτι ἐκεῖνος ἐφανερώθη ἵνα τὰς ἁμαρτίας ἄρῃ, καὶ ἁμαρτία ἐν αὐτῷ οὐκ ἔστιν). John further presses the point that sin has no place in the Christian's life, for Jesus came into this world for the very purpose of taking away sins.

How can one who claims to be a follower of Jesus and who is becoming like him find any rationalization for sin? The statement that there is no sin in Jesus Christ says more than that Jesus never committed a sin during his life on earth. It says that one cannot remain in him and sin, for there is no sin in Jesus. John is building a case against the person who wishes to be known as a Christian and yet who defends those practices and attitudes that God has defined as sin. To do such a thing is to be lawless and reject God's authority.

3:6 Everyone who remains in him does not sin; everyone who sins has neither seen him nor known him (πᾶς ὁ ἐν αὐτῷ μένων οὐχ ἁμαρτάνει· πᾶς ὁ ἁμαρτάνων οὐχ ἑώρακεν αὐτὸν οὐδὲ ἔγνωκεν αὐτόν). John now defines more explicitly what remaining in God means: refraining from sin. There

---

4. Yarbrough, *1 – 3 John*, 182.   5. Culy, *I, II, III John*, 71.

is an association between seeing God in Christ and knowing God (cf. John 1:18). The one who has not seen him is still blind and in the dark. Even those who think they see and know God have not truly seen and known him if they continue to live with sin in their lives. They lack the vision and knowledge of Jesus, who he is, and what he came to do.

The statement that everyone who remains in him "does not sin" is difficult. The NIV represents the common way of reading the continuous aspect of the present tense "do not sin" (οὐχ ἁμαρτάνει) as "No one who lives in him *keeps on* sinning."[6] However, the present tense is also found in 5:16, but there it refers to individual acts of sins rather than habitual sin, and this would introduce a further tension. Furthermore, it seems that a subtle connotation in verbal aspect would not be suitable to bear such an important point. Marshall reads the present tense as an implicit imperative, stating what Christians *ought* to be, yielding a statement of the ideal, "anyone who lives in him ought not to sin."[7] However, there are no clear parallels of this volitive use of the present tense elsewhere.

Wallace rejects taking the present tense here as "continually" and suggests it may be a proleptic gnomic present that will be true when the eschatological hope is realized.[8] The conditional implicit in the statement can be paraphrased as, "*if* someone remains in him, they do not sin"; this suggests that sinning is mutually exclusive with remaining in Christ. This does not mean that a Christian who sins hops in and out of Christ, but as Bede put it, "in so far as he abides in him, he does not sin."[9] Therefore, when tempted to sin, a Christian must decide whether they wish to live in Christ, recognizing that there is no way to justify sin as compatible with life in Christ.

The original readers no doubt began to feel the same discomfort that modern readers feel when getting to this verse. Since sin is in fact a present reality in every life, and even in the lives of those who are followers of Christ, how can anyone remain in him? There is a distinct tension in 3:6 – 9.[10] The tension that begins here comes to its fullest press with John's statement in 3:9 that the one born of God "is not able to sin." John is beginning to separate the sheep from the goats (see comments on 3:9).

3:7 – 8 Children, let no one mislead you; the one who lives rightly is righteous, just as that One is righteous. The one who does sin is of the devil, because the devil has been sinning from the beginning. For this reason the Son of God appeared, so that he might destroy the works of the devil (Τεκνία, μηδεὶς πλανάτω ὑμᾶς· ὁ ποιῶν τὴν δικαιοσύνην δίκαιός ἐστιν, καθὼς ἐκεῖνος δίκαιός ἐστιν· ὁ ποιῶν τὴν ἁμαρτίαν ἐκ τοῦ διαβόλου ἐστίν, ὅτι ἀπ᾽ ἀρχῆς ὁ διάβολος ἁμαρτάνει. εἰς τοῦτο ἐφανερώθη ὁ υἱὸς τοῦ θεοῦ, ἵνα λύσῃ τὰ ἔργα τοῦ διαβόλου).

John first referred to Satan in 2:13 as "the evil one," but here he brings the devil and his "works" (τὰ ἔργα) into his dualistic framework as an opponent of God and the target of Jesus' saving incarnation. The devil is mentioned by the name "Satan" only once in the Johannine corpus (John 13:27), but "devil" occurs also in John's gospel (6:70; 8:44; 13:2), and Jesus refers to him as "the prince of this world" (12:31; 14:30; 16:11). First John prefers the term "the evil one" (1 John 2:13, 14; 3:12; 5:18, 19), which is found only once in the gospel (John 17:15). The references are to the one who exercises a cosmic power over human beings

---

6. Burge, *Letters of John,* 150; Thompson, *1 – 3 John,* 94 – 95; Westcott, *Epistles of John,* 104.

7. Marshall, *Epistles of John,* 181.

8. Wallace, *Greek Grammar,* 524 – 25.

9. Cited by Marshall, *Epistles of John,* 181 n20.

10. See Colin G. Kruse, "Sin and Perfection in 1 John," *ABR* 51 (2003): 60 – 70.

that is expressed in the rejection of the revelation of God's redemptive plan in Christ, for to embody Christ's message constitutes the destruction of the devil's works.

By addressing his readers once again as "children" (τεκνία), John recalls to mind the question of whose children they are. The reference to the devil implies the question of whom they resemble, the Father or the evil one. Do they embody the gospel message, or are they opposed to the true significance of Jesus? His opening exhortation, "let no one mislead you," certainly suggests that there was an opportunity to be misled on the topic of sin and righteousness, whether presented by those who departed the community or by others. This perhaps provides a further explanation of how those who went out from John's Christian community(-ies) were, in fact, not truly one with them (2:19).

John begins to draw a line that applies his conceptual dualism to the question of whose spiritual child a person is. John fears his readers may be misled about the relationship between what one does and who one is. The one who does what is right according to God's standard and who, therefore, acknowledges and accepts God's authority is righteous in the same way that Jesus was. The phrase "the one who lives righteously" (ὁ ποιῶν τὴν δικαιοσύνην) is repeated from 2:29, where it forms the subject of the passive form of the verb "has been born [γεγέννηται] of him [God]." Any claim to be a child of God while living in ways that contradict God's revealed standards is a false claim.

In fact, the one who does sin is "of the devil" (ἐκ τοῦ διαβόλου; cf. John 8:44). There is no neutral ground; either one is a child of God or one is a child of the devil! The practice of sin characterizes the devil, who has been at it "from the beginning." Those who sin are therefore like the devil, in contrast to those who live righteously and are like

Jesus, the Son of God. What we *do* reveals who we are, regardless of who we *say* we are. The implicit question confronting John's readers is "Who's your daddy?" Are you of God? Or are you of the devil?

To sin is to be like the devil because from the beginning, in Eden, the devil encouraged disobedience to God and, ironically, justified it as the way of being like God (Gen 3:5). Being like God in the sense of conforming one's character to his is a good thing, but Satan twisted the idea into the impulse to sin. Adam and Eve, and all human beings after them, grasped at becoming like God through rejecting God's authority over them. Thus, the one who is truly like God, Jesus Christ the Son, appeared so that he could destroy that deceitful work of the devil and restore people to their eschataological destiny of being like Jesus, that is, like God in human form (1 John 3:2). But it is only through the rejection of disobedience (i.e., sin) that the children of God can assume that family likeness. To persist in sin reveals the presence of *anomia* (3:4) and contradicts any claim to have been born of God. This thought leads into 3:9, one of the most startling verses in the Bible.

3:9 No one who has been born of God sins, because his [God's] seed remains in them, and they are not able to sin, because they have been born of God (Πᾶς ὁ γεγεννημένος ἐκ τοῦ θεοῦ ἁμαρτίαν οὐ ποιεῖ, ὅτι σπέρμα αὐτοῦ ἐν αὐτῷ μένει, καὶ οὐ δύναται ἁμαρτάνειν, ὅτι ἐκ τοῦ θεοῦ γεγέννηται). References to the new birth are found ten times in 1 John (2:29; 3:9 [2x]; 4:7; 5:1 [3x], 4, 18 [2x]; cf. John 3:3 – 8). Here the *hoti* clause defines what it means to have been born of God (notice the perfect tense of the participle): God's seed remains in the one who has been born of God. As Kruse points out, it might at first glance seem that Christ is God's seed that remains in the believer.[11] How-

---

11. Kruse, *Letters of John*, 125.

ever, he is likely right that the metaphor is more "bold," in that it refers to the regenerative impulse, the Holy Spirit, who effects the new birth and who remains in and with the believer. This seems to say that those who have been regenerated by the Spirit are indwelt by the Spirit and therefore will not sin.

The statement that "no one who who has been born of God sins" immediately raises the existential question, "Who, then, is born of God?" And it seems to make John contradict himself in light of 1 John 1:7 and 2:1, verses that offer to believers the blood of Jesus as a remedy for acknowledged sin. And why does John exhort his readers in 5:16 to pray for the brother or sister who sins if a Christian is not able to sin?

One unacceptable approach is to just write off John as internally self-contradictory. But Brown, who thinks "we should never assume that ancient authors were stupid or illogical and could not see the difficulties, especially within the same brief piece of writing," suggests that the problem indicates we must go deeper for the solution.[12] He recognizes the contradiction, but suggests that it points to two different kinds of perfectionism — one a heretical teaching based on a distortion of John's gospel and the other the orthodox perfectionism that John expresses here.[13] Swadling has suggested that 3:6 and 9 are actually heretical statements made by the secessionists, who had also made the claim that they were without sin (1:8, 10).[14] But there is no hypothetical "if we say ..." in this passage, and the assertion that no one who has been born of God sins functions as an integral part of John's argument that distinguishes children of God from those of the devil (3:10).

The most common way of explaining what John means in order to resolve both the existential angst of Christians who nevertheless sin and John's apparent contradiction of himself is to press the durative aspect of the present tense of the verb in 3:9, "does not do sin" (ἁμαρτίαν οὐ ποιεῖ), to mean that those born of God do not and cannot sin *habitually*, even while recognizing that they do sin occasionally. Pressing the present tense to serve this purpose is appealing because it not only quickly diminishes the tension between John's statements in 1:10 and 3:6, 9, but also reduces the psychological tension readers feel. However, this interpretation does not do justice to the vigor of John's argument, and to explain it away quickly may cause us to miss the point. Furthermore, as Kruse astutely points out:

> The use of the present tense says nothing about the habitual or nonhabitual character of the sinning, but only shows that the author has chosen to depict the sinning as something in progress, rather than as a complete action. And, in any case, the present tense is also used in 1:8 where such a distinction between occasional and habitual does not fit the argument.[15]

Kruse is almost certainly on target to suggest that *anomia* is the key to understanding these difficult statements.[16] When "sin" (ἁμαρτία) is first mentioned in this passage in 3:4, it is identified there with *anomia*, and both Greek words have the definite article. Because neither article is anaphoric, referring back to a specific previously mentioned sin in the immediate context, the article functions to designate a category of sin that is identified with lawlessness ("and sin is lawlessness," ἡ ἁμαρτία ἐστὶν ἡ ἀνομία). This suggests that John is not referring to every sin as *anomia*, but is concerned with the sin that leads to eschatological judgment

---

12. Brown, *Epistles of John*, 413.

13. Ibid., 81 – 83, 413.

14. H. C. Swadling, "Sin and Sinlessness in 1 John," *SJT* 35 (1982): 205 – 11, cited by Smalley, *1, 2, 3 John*, 162.

15. Kruse, "Sin and Perfection in 1 John," 66.

16. Ibid., 69 – 70.

(i.e., apostasy). John will later say in 5:16 – 17 that there is sin that does not lead to death.

But what sin is not *anomia*? It is sin that has been confessed and cleansed by the blood of Jesus Christ (1:9; 2:1 – 2). The sin of a believer who acknowledges and confesses it is of a different type than the sin of those who refuse to confess and submit to God's authority. It is the *anomia* sin that leads to death that the one born of God is not able to commit because God's seed remains in them (σπέρμα αὐτοῦ ἐν αὐτῷ μένει) and they have been born of God (ἐκ τοῦ θεοῦ γεγέννηται).

The Christian may sin, but if they are truly of God, they will agree with him that their sin *is* sin, will confess it, and turn from it. They will, as Marshall puts it, become what they are.[17] This is quite different from those who refuse to define sin as God defines it, who rationalize their behavior as not being sin, or who otherwise defy God's authority in their lives. In John's thought, the one who lives righteously, though perhaps not sinlessly, is a child of the Father and contrasts with the one who does *anomia* and has not been born of God, at least not yet.

Having been born of God and having his seed within is given as the reason why a genuine child of God cannot commit *anomia* sin. It is in the very nature of conversion that one comes both to believe in God's existence and authority and to acknowledge one's own sin that made the cross of Jesus necessary.

The question of what "his seed" (σπέρμα αὐτοῦ) denotes is debatable. There is a basic ambiguity about the referent. It could be some indwelling regenerative agent from God — taking "in him" (ἐν αὐτῷ) to refer to the believer. In that case, it is still unspecified if that agent is the Holy Spirit, the word of God, the *chrisma* mentioned in 2:27, or something else. Or "his seed" could refer to God's offspring, semantically equivalent to τέκνα — which would require taking "in him" (ἐν αὐτῷ) to refer to God and would then mean that the offspring of God does not commit *anomia* sin because he/they remain in God. In this interpretation, God's seed could be a reference to his Son, mentioned in the previous verse, whose indwelling presence keeps the believer from sin.

On the one hand, this interpretation jibes with 1 John 5:18, if "the One begotten of God" (ὁ γεννηθεὶς ἐκ τοῦ θεοῦ) there is understood to be Jesus, who keeps "everyone born of God" (πᾶς ὁ γεγεννημένος ἐκ τοῦ θεοῦ) from the sin that leads to death (see comments on 5:18). On the other hand, every other occurrence of "seed" (σπέρμα) in John's writings refers to descendants (John 7:42; 8:33, 37), but never to Jesus, which suggests that 3:9 may be another statement that those born of God do not sin because they remain in God.[18]

Other interpreters take "seed" (σπέρμα) in the context of the birth metaphor to be a regenerative agent analogous to human sperm that begets children. Some interpreters further specify the referent of the *sperma* and agent of spiritual regeneration to be the word of God or the gospel,[19] or to be the Holy Spirit.[20] On this train of thought, the point is perhaps "the transference of character traits — spiritual DNA, as it were — through spiritual descent from the Father."[21] Because those born of God share his character, they are incapable of committing the sin of which John speaks. Regardless of how this difficult expression is understood, it is clear that, as Lieu notes, "being born from God

---

17. Marshall, *Epistles of John*, 183.
18. As Yarbrough, *1 – 3 John*, 193.
19. Dodd, *Johannine Epistles*, 77 – 78.
20. Kruse, *Letters of John*, 125.

21. Culy, *I, II, III John*, 77; also the CEB translation, "Those born from God don't practice sin because God's DNA remains in them."

means to continue to be vivified by God's creative power; such birth cannot be lost or abrogated."[22]

3:10 In this way the children of God and the children of the devil are distinguished: Everyone who does not do what is right is not of God, even the one who does not love their brother and sister (ἐν τούτῳ φανερά ἐστιν τὰ τέκνα τοῦ θεοῦ καὶ τὰ τέκνα τοῦ διαβόλου· πᾶς ὁ μὴ ποιῶν δικαιοσύνην οὐκ ἔστιν ἐκ τοῦ θεοῦ, καὶ ὁ μὴ ἀγαπῶν τὸν ἀδελφὸν αὐτοῦ). John brings this unit to a summary statement in 3:10 that gives his purpose for writing as he does, and he invites his readers to ask who their spiritual father is. He is not concerned with the topic of the effectual call or regeneration, as 3:9 may suggest to minds of a theological bent. He is not interested in discussing various degrees of sin, such as whether sexual immorality is better or worse than theft. The author's main interest is to extend his conceptual dualism into the ethical world of his readers, showing them that how they live expresses their true paternity. It brings an im-

plicit challenge: Are you a child of the light or a child of the devil?

The phrase "in this way" (ἐν τούτῳ) is probably cataphoric (i.e., pointing forward to the next statement), but it joins all that has just been said to the statement that everyone who does not do what is right, as God defines it, is not "of God" and must question whether they have been born of God. No assurance of eternal life is possible (cf. 5:13) for anyone who claims to be a child of God but wants to live like the devil (see The Theology of John's Letters).

John brings the discussion back to the love command that he mentioned in 2:10. Having established there that love for fellow believers characterizes those who are in the light, here he presses the point that the failure to love is sin. To do what is right by God's standard means not simply refraining from *acts* of evil. It also means to maintain a right attitude toward others that motivates acts of love. John will explain in 3:11 – 12 that a failure to love is a sin of commission because it violates God's long-standing command "that we love one another."

Theology in Application

The Wonder of the New Birth

What a wonder it is that God himself is the origin of a person's eternal, spiritual life just as physical life originates with a human father. Saying the sinner's prayer or joining the church doesn't do justice to the wonder of the reality such acts reflect, even though confession and church membership are good in themselves. The necessity of being born again to the Father shows the depths of sin's destruction. Nothing less than a new birth can restore the life that was lost to sin. Nothing less than a new life can remedy the brokenness of a person's relationship with God and destroy the works of the devil — both his work in Eden and in the ongoing effect of the evil that Satan has unleashed in the world.

The reconciliation that God offers through new birth comes from his love. Such love, John says, took wretched, sinful, rebellious, ungrateful people and gave to them

---

22. Lieu, *I, II, & III John*, 138.

the new identity of being a child of God, with all the wonders that entails. Being born of God is as irreversible as having been born physically. Just as one cannot be unborn physically, the concept of the new birth suggests that once one has been born of the Father, it is a permanent and eternal relationship that forms the firm foundation of the assurance of eternal life. As Lieu observes, the life that issues from the new birth cannot be lost or abrogated.[23]

Those who turn away from God by not acknowledging and confessing sin have not been born of him, even if they claim they are. That is because just as a child bears a genetic similarity to his father, those who have been born of God have a changed disposition toward him and his authority. The destruction of the work of the devil entails the destruction of that radical autonomy that put Adam and Eve in the place of God and that infects every person born physically. Those who refuse to call sin what God has called sin and who refuse to confess and repent of it are still exercising a willful autonomy that by definition is not of God.

There is no neutral ground in John's duality; one is either a child of God or a child of the devil. This is because one is either born of God or not. The practice of sin characterizes the devil, who has been at it "from the beginning," and those who sin bear a resemblance to him. In contrast, those who live rightly bear a resemblance to Jesus, the perfect example of what a human child of God is to be.

Sin and the New Life

John builds a case against the person who wishes to be known as a Christian and yet defends practices and attitudes that God has defined as sin. To do such a thing is to be lawless and to reject God's authority, and this should rightfully call into question one's assurance of eternal life, because it calls into question one's identity as someone born of God.

But John also acknowledges that even those who have been born of God do sin, and he calls his readers to acknowledge and confess their sin because God is faithful and just and will forgive confessed sin based on the cleansing power of Jesus' blood (1:7 – 2:2). Yet at the same time he speaks of the inability of someone born of God to sin (3:9), making a qualitative difference between the sins committed by a believer that are confessed and cleansed and the sin that a believer is not able to commit. As Köstenberger explains this apparent contradiction:

> In all this, John makes clear that it is not spiritual perfection that is expected; such perfection awaits the second coming of Christ. Yet regeneration will inexorably produce a heart that confesses sin and continues in righteousness. Continuing in sin is an impossibility for those who are truly God's children (1 John 3:9: "cannot").[24]

---

23. Ibid.

24. Köstenberger, *Theology of John's Gospel and Letters*, 268.

The sin that a born-again child of God is not able to commit is *anomia*, that radical autonomy that rejects God's authority to define how people are to live. Those truly born of God will not deny their sin or reject God's authority to name it, but will confess their sin and be cleansed by Christ's blood. In this way the sin of the believer is different from even the same sinful acts that unbelievers commit. But because every sin expresses an implicit rejection of God, John exhorts God's children not to sin but to let the nature of their Father shine through their words and deeds.

1 John 3:11 – 18

Literary Context

This periocope is integrally related to 3:1 – 10 because, despite the paragraphing in the Greek NT, the causal clause (introduced with ὅτι) gives the reason why the believer who does not love a brother and sister (3:10) is counted as someone who does not live rightly. This passage expounds on the third of the three major themes of the letter, which is love. In chapter 1 John introduced the topic of sin and the proper attitude of the believer toward it. Then in chapter 2 he took up the topic of right belief about Jesus as the Christ within the context of the recent departure of the secessionists from the community, whom John considers to be antichrists. Here, the third major topic of love is discussed. These three themes will reappear in chapters 4 and 5.

VIII. Who Are the Children of God? (2:29 – 3:10)

→ IX. Love One Another (3:11 – 18)

    A. The Command to Love One Another (3:11 – 12)

    B. Application to John's Readers (3:13 – 15)

    C. Love Means Laying Down One's Life (3:16 – 18)

X. Children of God Can Be Confident (3:19 – 24)

Main Idea

The distinguishing difference between children of God and children of the devil is love for God and others, defined here to be a compassionate response to the life-sustaining needs of others. Because one's most dire need is eternal life, it is never loving to teach heresy that will lead people away from life in God, as the secessionists were doing. Furthermore, sustaining the physical lives of the vulnerable poor in the church is the proper way to return God's love and to channel it to the benefit of his children.

Translation

1 John 3:11–18

11a	identification	For **this is the instruction that you heard from the beginning,**
b	content	**that we love one another.**
12a	contrast	Do not be like Cain, who was of the evil one and **murdered his brother.**
b	rhetorical question	And **why did he murder his brother?**
c	cause	Because **his works were evil,**
d	contrast	but **the works of his brother were righteous.**
13a	address	[And so] brothers and sisters,
b	inference	**do not marvel if the world hates you.**
14a	assertion	We know
b	content	**that we have crossed over from death into life**
c	basis	**because we love the brothers and sisters.**
d	inference	**The one who does not love remains in death.**
15a	assertion	**Everyone who hates their brother or sister is a killer,**
b	assertion	and **we know that no killer has eternal life abiding in them.**
16a	assertion	In this way **we have known love,**
b	basis	because that One laid down his life on our behalf.
c	exhortation	And [so] **we ought to lay down [our] lives** on behalf of the brothers and sisters.
17a	condition	Whoever has the resources necessary for living and
b	expansion	sees their brother or sister has a need, and
c	expansion	shuts their heart to them,
d	rhetorical question	**how does the love of God remain in them?**
18a	address	Children,
b	exhortation	**let us not love** in word or talk, but
c	contrast	in actions and truth.

Structure

The unit continues the thought of 3:7 – 10 by opening with a causal clause (ὅτι) that makes v. 11 the grounds for the claim in v. 10, that the one who does not love their brother or sister in Christ is not of God. The closing vocative "children" (τεκνία) in v. 18 forms an inclusio with the same word in v. 7, and both allude back to the identity of John's readers as children of the Father (3:1). This structure suggests that distinguishing the children of God from the children of the devil (v. 10) is the main point of the passage. Everything discussed in the pericope — the command to love one another, Cain's murder of his brother, and the issue of the vulnerable poor in the church — is to be understood within this context. Just as God's love motivated his action to bring life to those who would be his children (3:1), God's children return his love by having life-giving compassion for others.

Exegetical Outline

→ **IX. Love One Another (3:11 – 18)**

    A. The command to love one another (3:11 – 12)

        1. Cain as counterexample (3:12a)

        2. Righteous deeds provoked hatred (3:12b – d)

    B. Application to John's readers (3:13 – 15)

        1. So don't be surprised if the world hates believers (3:13)

        2. Love for the brothers, those who do what is right, confirms that one has passed over from death to life (3:14)

        3. Everyone who hates the righteous person is a murderer (3:15a)

        4. No murderer has eternal life (3:15b)

    C. Love means laying down one's life (3:16 – 18)

        1. Christ's example defines love (3:16a – b)

        2. Believers ought to follow Christ's example (3:16c)

        3. Compassion for the needs of others is a way of laying down one's life (3:17)

        4. Love must be expressed not only in word, but also in deeds (3:18)

Explanation of the Text

3:11 For this is the instruction that you heard from the beginning, that we love one another (Ὅτι αὕτη ἐστὶν ἡ ἀγγελία ἣν ἠκούσατε ἀπ᾽ ἀρχῆς, ἵνα ἀγαπῶμεν ἀλλήλους). John circles back to one of the major exhortations of the letter: love for one another. The initial *hoti* ("for") subordinates this statement to the preceding thought that those who do not love their brother or sister are not of God, because they are directly disobeying the instruction that Jesus himself gave to the embryonic church (John 13:34; 15:12, 17), that his followers love one another. Moreover, this command echoes and develops the OT command of love for one's neighbor (Lev 19:18). John is about to explain a motive that clearly shows that the failure to love others is symptomatic of a failure to love God.

3:12 Do not be like Cain, who was of the evil one and murdered his brother. And why did he murder his brother? Because his works were evil, but the works of his brother were righteous (οὐ καθὼς Κάϊν ἐκ τοῦ πονηροῦ ἦν καὶ ἔσφαξεν τὸν ἀδελφὸν αὐτοῦ· καὶ χάριν τίνος ἔσφαξεν αὐτόν; ὅτι τὰ ἔργα αὐτοῦ πονηρὰ ἦν, τὰ δὲ τοῦ ἀδελφοῦ αὐτοῦ δίκαια). John gives the counterexample of Cain, the world's first murderer, who killed his own brother. Cain's motive for killing his brother reveals a foundational spiritual principle about life in this world: those who do not do what is right hate those who do.

Because Cain was the first murderer in the biblical story of humankind, in later tradition he was known as the archetype sinner. For instance, Philo identifies Cain's sin as stemming from self-love that leads to eternal death (*Sacr.* 1.3; *Det.* 10.32; 27.103; *Post.* 6.21).[1] The targums on Gen 4:8 quote Cain as expressing the attitude, "There is no judgment, there is no judge, there is no other world, there is no gift of good reward for the righteous, and no punishment for the wicked."[2] This tradition about Cain would have been familiar to NT writers and readers in the first century. Cain is also mentioned in Jude 11 to refer to false teachers, because they "have taken the way of Cain." In commenting on Jude, Michael Green explains that Cain "stands for the cynical, materialistic character who defies God and despises man. He is devoid of faith and love."[3] Cain is, therefore, the personification of *anomia*.

The traditional identification with Cain of those who oppose God powerfully explains John's reference to him in v. 12 and gives further insight into the situation into which John was writing. Cain and Abel were brothers, just as those in the Christian churches to which John is writing considered themselves brothers and sisters in the faith, including those who had gone out from those communities (2:19). But even though Cain and Abel were brothers, they did not have the same character; Cain was of the evil one, for his behavior toward his brother revealed that. Fratricide was the result of a motive that lay deep in Cain's heart: he knew that what Abel had offered to God was right, but his own offerings were not. Cain resented Abel for his brother's righteousness and acted on that hateful impulse.

Apparently there were those brothers and sisters in the Johannine churches who were living rightly in the Lord and walking in the light. But others were not; instead, these were attempting to justify and rationalize their beliefs and practices (1:6 – 10). Such negative, and potentially lethal, influence on a fellow believer is, in effect, hate. It is not loving to sway someone to disobey God or to believe false things about him, for that puts someone in spiritual jeopardy. Someone who does that is not of God, and in the Johannine discourse, that means they are of the world and the evil one.

3:13 [And so] brothers and sisters, do not marvel if the world hates you ([καὶ] μὴ θαυμάζετε, ἀδελφοί, εἰ μισεῖ ὑμᾶς ὁ κόσμος). John reminds his readers of Cain to explain the true relationship between Christian believers and the world. The world, which is self-deceived in its rejection

---

1. *The Works of Philo* (trans. C. D. Yonge; Peabody, MA: Hendrickson, 1993).

2. *Targum Pseudo-Jonathan: Genesis* (vol. 1B of *The Aramaic Bible: The Targum*; ed. Kevin Cathcart et. al.; trans. Mi-

chael Maher; Collegeville, MN: Glazier, 1992), 33.

3. Michael Green, *The Second Epistle of Peter and the Epistle of Jude* (TNTC; Grand Rapids: Eerdmans, 1968), 186.

of God (cf. John 1:8 – 10), resents those who try to obey God through their living by biblical values and principles. Elsewhere John gives the verdict on the world:

> Light has come into the world, but people loved darkness instead of light because their deeds were evil. Everyone who does evil hates the light, and will not come into the light for fear that their deeds will be exposed. (John 3:19 – 20)

In other words, in John's mind, Cain represents the world's attitude toward the light and toward all who intend to live their lives in the light. A similar dynamic is found in the story of Noah, who obeyed God by building the ark, but in that same act implicitly "condemned the world" (Heb 11:7).

The world hates righteousness, so it should be no surprise that it hates "you," John says to those who are living out their faith in Christ. But Jesus also taught that the world *cannot* hate those who don't live in him, "but it hates me because I testify that its works are evil" (John 7:7). Is 1 John 3:13 contradicting John 7:7? Not at all. The world would not hate the believer except when it sees Christ in him or her. To the extent that the believer agrees with Jesus' testimony about evil and changes their life to do right, those who are of the world hate them for it (John 15:18 – 19; cf. 17:14).

3:14 We know that we have crossed over from death into life because we love the brothers and sisters. The one who does not love remains in death (ἡμεῖς οἴδαμεν ὅτι μεταβεβήκαμεν ἐκ τοῦ θανάτου εἰς τὴν ζωήν, ὅτι ἀγαπῶμεν τοὺς ἀδελφούς· ὁ μὴ ἀγαπῶν μένει ἐν τῷ θανάτῳ). John has constructed a dualism between life and death, and he now states explicitly what was formerly implied, that Christian believers have crossed over to life when they came to faith in Christ. Love for others is characteristic of walking in the light and of remaining in Christ; therefore, the person who

does not love demonstrates that they have not yet crossed over that divide.

"We know" is here the inclusive we, making an emphatic distinction in comparison to the world. In John's thinking, those who follow Christ and walk in the light are in fellowship with the life-giving God, but those who don't do so remain in the realm of darkness and death. The person who lives rightly in Christ is characterized by love, not resentment. That transformation of one's attitude toward the Lord and his people marks those who have already crossed over from death to life (John 5:24). Genuine human love is the expression of salvation, not its cause.

If someone doesn't love righteousness, that person remains in death. Death here is not a future event but refers to the realm into which the fall in the garden of Eden has put us all. The failure to love characterizes the realm of death and is equivalent to being in the darkness (2:9, 11). This is likely why John's gospel says of Judas that as soon as his betraying hand had taken the bread from Jesus, he went out, "and it was night" (John 13:30). Judas left Jesus and went out in the darkness. John includes that small ironic detail to show that Judas was leaving the light, the source of light, and choosing instead to go out into the darkness and the realm of death. Having been known as a "brother" to the disciples, Judas nevertheless showed himself to be not of them, just as some from the Johannine church(es) "went out" (1 John 2:19). Judas did not love Jesus by embracing the way of life Jesus taught. Even if Judas didn't intend Jesus' death and felt he could force Jesus' hand to rise to the political power, Judas rejected Jesus' way.

The perfect tense of the verb, "we have passed over [μεταβεβήκαμεν] from death into life," expresses what scholars refer to as John's realized eschatology. While most NT writers speak of salvation and the deliverance from God's judgment as something that is yet future (future eschatology),

John considers it something that believers have already experienced. This should not be taken to mean that John did not believe in a future judgment or a consummation of God's redemptive plan that would bring eschatological blessing in the future after time as we know it ends. John speaks as he does because of the conceptual dualism he is using to explain his theology.

Conversion to faith in Jesus Christ is by definition a renunciation of the past ways that alienated us from God and an admission that our sin needs to be forgiven and cleansed. To embrace Jesus Christ in faith means to have come into the light where the darkness of spiritual blindness has been cured. There is fellowship and joy not only over one's own conversion, but over the conversions of others who in like-mindedness have also come to faith in Christ and desire to live their lives in the light. This is the sign that one is no longer under the coming judgment of the world, but has passed over from darkness into light.

3:15 Everyone who hates their brother or sister is a killer, and we know that no killer has eternal life abiding in them (πᾶς ὁ μισῶν τὸν ἀδελφὸν αὐτοῦ ἀνθρωποκτόνος ἐστίν, καὶ οἴδατε ὅτι πᾶς ἀνθρωποκτόνος οὐκ ἔχει ζωὴν αἰώνιον ἐν αὐτῷ μένουσαν). John makes the stunning association of hate with killing. Since those who have passed over from darkness into light love the light and love living in the light, they will love their brothers and sisters who also desire to live their lives rightly before God. In this context, everyone who hates their brother is like Cain, who hated his brother for living rightly before God. Such an attitude led to physical murder. But to hate someone because they are living rightly, and consequently pressuring them by example or teaching to live like the world, is a wish for their spiritual death and is, in effect, spiritual murder.

The word translated "killer" (ἀνθρωποκτόνος)

occurs in the NT only in John's writings, though it is also found in secular Greek writers. Etymologically it is formed from the two Greek words "person" (ἀνθρωπο-) and "kill" (κτείνω) — so more literally a "person killer." Jesus used the same word to identify the devil, and his words in John 8:44 help to explain why those who teach heresy by example or words can be described as a killer:

> You belong to your father, the devil, and you want to carry out your father's desires. He was a murderer [ἀνθρωποκτόνος] from the beginning, not holding to the truth, for there is no truth in him. When he lies, he speaks his native language, for he is a liar and the father of lies.

Consider how the devil brought death to Adam and Eve, and through them to all human beings. God said in Gen 2:17, "when you eat from it you will certainly die." In Gen 3:4 – 5, the devil contradicts God and even impugns God's character by saying that God knew Adam and Eve wouldn't die but would become like God. Adam and Eve believed the lie and brought death into the world. Heresy is by nature a lie that pulls a person away from God and has the same kind of death-inducing power. Because God is the source of life, there is no place to go but death if one turns away from God.

Because of the fall, every human being is born already turned away from God and in the state of death. Christ came to reconcile people to God and restore them to eternal life, but that is impossible while one is under the hold of the death-inducing lie that what God has said is wrong and that God cannot be trusted (see The Theology of John's Letters). Neither genuine life nor love exists outside the sphere of existence that has its origin in the new birth that God offers in Jesus.

3:16 In this way we have known love, because that One laid down his life on our behalf. And [so] we ought to lay down [our] lives on behalf of the brothers and sisters (ἐν τούτῳ ἐγνώκαμεν τὴν ἀγάπην, ὅτι ἐκεῖνος ὑπὲρ ἡμῶν τὴν ψυχὴν αὐτοῦ ἔθηκεν καὶ ἡμεῖς ὀφείλομεν ὑπὲρ τῶν ἀδελφῶν τὰς ψυχὰς θεῖναι). The apostle wants his readers to love others in the way that the Lord defines love, not in the way the world does. He points to Jesus ("that One"), who laid down his life on our behalf, as the true expression of genuine love.

To press the point home, he explicitly states that "we" also should lay down our lives on behalf of others. This immediately gives pause, for Jesus actually died on behalf of those he came to save. Does John really expect his readers to die for others? Jesus' death was a once-for-all-time event in God's redemptive plan, so how could anyone imitate that? The phrase to "lay down one's life" occurs in the NT only in John's gospel and letters, and particularly in the teaching of Jesus in John 15:12 – 17 (italics added):

> My command is this: *Love each other as I have loved you. Greater love has no one than this: to lay down one's life for one's friends.* You are my friends if you do what I command. I no longer call you servants, because a servant does not know his master's business. Instead, I have called you friends, for everything that I learned from my Father I have made known to you. You did not choose me, but I chose you and appointed you so that you might go and bear fruit — fruit that will last — and so that whatever you ask in my name the Father will give you. *This is my command: Love each other.*

Clearly here in 1 John 3:16 John is alluding to this teaching. Jesus connects the command to love by laying down one's life for one's friends with his calling of his followers to bear lasting fruit. John implicitly defines Jesus as a friend who has laid down his life in the most literal, physical way possible for those he will call his friends — those he has chosen and appointed to bear fruit. The im-

plication is that fruit bearers are those who will in turn lay down their lives for Jesus, and by extension, for other believers, whom Jesus calls "friends." But what did Jesus mean by saying that his followers should lay down their lives for others?

Jesus taught in John 10:11 that he is the good shepherd who lays down his life for his sheep. Although not unheard of, it is unusual for a shepherd to die for his sheep. More routinely shepherds spent their lives caring for the needs of the sheep to keep them alive. This is how the phrase to "lay down life" is used elsewhere in Greek, where it refers to taking a risk for another, even hazarding one's life for another, but not to a sacrificial death.[4] In the next verse, John goes on to indicate that this too is what he has in mind: love is expressed by providing for the life-sustaining needs of others.

3:17 Whoever has the resources necessary for living and sees their brother or sister has a need, and shuts their heart to them, how does the love of God remain in them? (ὃς δ' ἂν ἔχῃ τὸν βίον τοῦ κόσμου καὶ θεωρῇ τὸν ἀδελφὸν αὐτοῦ χρείαν ἔχοντα καὶ κλείσῃ τὰ σπλάγχνα αὐτοῦ ἀπ' αὐτοῦ, πῶς ἡ ἀγάπη τοῦ θεοῦ μένει ἐν αὐτῷ;). In John's exhortation, laying down one's life as the proper expression of love involves meeting the need of others for the basic necessities needed to sustain life.

In 2:16, John cautioned against becoming so secure and prideful in one's worldly things and wealth as to overlook one's need for and dependence on God (see comments on 2:16). Now he cautions against seeing fellow believers in dire need for life's sustenance and taking no action to provide for that need. God is the ultimate source of all provision, but most often he distributes it through people helping people. Everything we have is by the grace of God, and to withhold life resources from those in need blocks his channel of provision

---

4. Lieu, *I, II, & III John*, 149.

for them. This circularity of God's love for believers and the believer's love for God mitigates the need to determine whether the genitive "love of God" (ἡ ἀγάπη τοῦ θεοῦ) expresses love from God or love for God in this statement.

If the greatest commandments are to love God and to love others as oneself (Matt 22:37, 39; Mark 12:30 – 31; Luke 10:27), love is the fulfillment of God's purposes for us. Jesus defines the love of neighbor in the parable of the good Samaritan as providing life-sustaining resources (Luke 10:25 – 37). In this familiar story, the Samaritan takes extraordinary measures to see to the well-being of the Jewish man who has been beaten by robbers, providing shelter, food, and medical care at his own personal expense. In Luke's context, the parable answers the question, "Who is my neighbor whom I must love?" The parable not only defines neighbor, but also defines what love for others looks like.

In this case, the Jewish expert in the law was no doubt stunned to hear that he must love the one he loved to hate, the unclean Samaritan! But it also implies that one need not *like* one's neighbor; instead, one must respond in compassion to the dire need for what will sustain life, a concern expressed throughout Scripture (cf. Deut 15:7 – 8, 10). The entire episode in Luke's gospel is set in the context of the question: "What must I do to inherit eternal life?" This is also a major theme of 1 John in its purpose to reassure its readers that they do in fact have eternal life.

Understanding love in this way provides further insight into how hate, which John defines as the failure to provide for the life-sustaining needs of another, amounts to murder (3:15). It also makes good sense of the exhortation to lay down one's life as not something to be achieved by those heroic few who rush into burning buildings to save others, but as something that everyone can do. Those who work for a living spend their time (i.e., their lives) earning a livelihood. Sharing those earned resources with the vulnerable poor means that one is laying down one's life for the benefit of others. And depending on one's situation, spending resources to sustain another's life may involve some risk, as the phrase in its original cultural use indicated.

3:18 Children, let us not love in word or talk, but in actions and truth (Τεκνία, μὴ ἀγαπῶμεν λόγῳ μηδὲ τῇ γλώσσῃ ἀλλὰ ἐν ἔργῳ καὶ ἀληθείᾳ). With this, John closes his discourse on love that began in 3:1, when he marveled over the Father's love that we should be his children. Children of God must live out the family resemblance by doing what is right, including loving their brothers and sisters in the church by not teaching heresy that will lead them astray and by providing resources of sustenance for those in need. Love is the most basic expression of Johannine ethics, the kind of love that goes deeper than mere words and platitudes and becomes a willingness to act on the behalf of the best interests of others. This means first of all that love is expressed not in feelings and sentiments, but in actions.

Of equal importance is that those deeds are done "in truth" (ἐν … ἀληθείᾳ). John uses "truth" throughout his writings to refer to the gospel message, and so to act in truth means more than to act truly, i.e., sincerely (see "In Depth: 'Truth' in John's Letters" at 1:6). The words and acts of the believer must be consistent with the spiritual truths God has revealed in Christ (e.g., that sin is serious enough for Jesus to have died for it). Loving others in acts consistent with the gospel is how the believer returns the love they have received from God in Christ (cf. John 3:16).

Theology in Application

Love: Not Just an Affair of the Heart

Love is the hallmark characteristic of God's children who are walking in the light. But if you asked the person on the street what love is, you might get answers such as, "Love is a feeling." Or, "Love is a commitment." Or, "Love is sacrifice." And almost certainly someone would say, "Love is sex." The ancient Greeks thought love was a madness of the mind. As theologian Jonathan Wilson has said, "Love is a terribly debased term today, almost beyond rescue as a description of the good news of the kingdom come in Jesus Christ."[5] And to make matters worse, as I. Howard Marshall observes, "Most people associate Christianity with the command to love, and so they think that they know all about Christianity when they have understood its teaching in terms of *their own concept of love*" (italics added).[6] No wonder John's readers then and now need a lesson on what love is and why it's important.

When Jesus laid down his life on the cross, it was not an arbitrary or irrelevant act of love. One of the questions one could ask about the crucifixion is how the death of one man two thousand years ago could have any relevance for others today. This perception of its irrelevance may be why some might see Jesus' teachings as being of greater relevance for others than his death. The nature of Jesus' death reveals the deep, deep need of humanity for redemption. James Denney explains by analogy:

> If I were sitting on the end of the pier on a summer day enjoying the sunshine and the air, and some one came along and jumped into the water and got [*sic*] drowned "to prove his love for me," I should find it quite unintelligible. I might be much in need of love, but an act in no rational relation to any of my necessities could not prove it. But if I had fallen over the pier and were drowning, and some one sprang into the water, and at the cost of making my peril, or what but for him would be my fate, his own, saved me from death, then I should say, "Greater love hath no man than this." I should say it intelligibly, because there would be an intelligent relation between the sacrifice which love had made and the necessity from which it redeemed.[7]

The NT explains how the death of one man two thousand years ago does have relevance for the lives of others. John insists that God's love is most clearly expressed on the cross, because it provided for humanity's deepest need. Jesus' death substitutes for our own. By his death, Jesus saves us from our own.

Similarly, love as the Bible defines it is doing what is needed to care for the needs of others. This doesn't exclude warm feelings or commitments, but it means that Christians should live in a way that considerately responds to the needs of those

---

5. Jonathan R. Wilson, *For God So Loved the World: A Christology for Disciples* (Grand Rapids: Baker Academic, 2001), 131.

6. Marshall, *Epistles of John*, 192.

7. James Denney, *The Death of Christ* (London: n.p., 1951), 103, quoted in Marshall, *Epistles of John*, 193.

around them. It means making life-sustaining resources available to meet the needs of those in dire circumstances — providing clean water, food, clothing, shelter, and of greatest importance, the true gospel of Jesus Christ.

The World Cannot Love

But it does seem in this fallen world that no good deed goes unpunished, and John expected the world to "hate" Christian believers (3:13), even as it hated Jesus. Should this statement make Christians paranoid? Should it motivate the perception of religious persecution at every slight insult? Does such an expectation foster a bad attitude that tends toward cynicism? Believers must be thoughtful about how they understand what John is saying and how they apply that to the specific circumstances of their lives.

John explains the attitude of the world by reminding us of the story of Cain and Abel. Cain hated Abel for no reason other than that he was bitter and resentful that Abel did the right thing, which revealed his own deeds as unrighteous. Cain could have observed Abel, repented of what he was doing, and joined his brother in doing what was right. Instead, Cain found Abel's righteousness to be such an offense that he murdered him to try to be rid of the conviction he felt, but instead was permanently marked by it.

Thus, no matter how nice Christians may be to others, those of the world will feel implicitly accused and condemned by the Christian's faith in a Savior who died for sin because the world does not want to believe in sin. To the unbelieving world, morality can appropriately be based on education to correct ignorance and on some sense of social fairness, but not on the existence of a holy God who is entitled to define right from wrong and expect us to live by it.

There is the great divide between those who are willing to acknowledge their sin and step into the light through faith in Christ and those who stubbornly hold to moral standards of their own making and reject God's love. Clergy and others in Christian professions probably feel this acutely, because identifying oneself as a minister or Bible profesor at a party among unbelievers is almost certainly going to make for a lonely evening. People known to be "religious" make others who do not share a belief in the Lord feel uncomfortable.

When I was a child, before coming to faith in Christ, there was a young girl at school who was the daughter of Christian missionary parents. Her clothes were clean but quite worn and far from the fashions of the day. She seemed different from other children in undefinable ways, and in ways that made her a target of the mean taunts of her classmates. After I became a Christian, I looked back on that school year with shame that I didn't befriend that poor, lonely child. I don't remember teasing her as some did, but I also didn't risk my own social standing in the class to stand beside her. I participated in the world's hate for that child of God, that daughter of missionary parents, who now could likely be a good friend. There is something in fallen human nature that wants to avoid people who believe in such a thing as God's truth and who attempt to live by it.

Given that this divide is reflected in the Johannine duality constructed on the opposites of light and darkness, it is not surprising that the apostle's concern in this letter is for how Christians treat each other. While one's effort to live rightly might be misunderstood and indicted by the world, that shouldn't be the way it is in the church. It appears that those who left the Johannine church(es) perhaps felt that they had moved beyond the need for Jesus' atonement (see comments on 5:6a-c). They were perhaps critical of those who continued to hold to the apostolic teachings.

Is there not such a divide in the church today, especially in Europe and North America, where, for instance, Christians who hold to a standard of biblical morality that defines marriage as a lifelong commitment between one man and one woman are being criticized and attacked by professing Christians who support the redefinition of family involving same-sex marriage? Since the most basic spiritual need is for the truth that leads to eternal life, John shows us that one cannot claim to love others while teaching heresy, for to teach by word or example anything that leads someone away from God is to lead them away from spiritual life.

Love for Others

Even though the specific cirumstances of John's letter made him focus on Christian love for other believers, the letter is set within the larger context of Jesus' teaching about love for others. God brings people into the world with the intent that they will have what they need to sustain life — water, food, clothing, shelter. God's love for them is channeled through his children who are willing to share of their own more abundant resources. But does God feel the love of his children when wealthy churches are building luxurious new buildings and a child starves to death somewhere every four seconds?[8] As Jesus said, from everyone to whom much is given, much is expected (Luke 12:48), for those to whom much is given are expected to be channels of God's love into the lives of others. The causes of poverty around the world are complex, and often the resources given are hijacked by evil and corrupt people before they reach their intended destinations. In spite of such things, the church needs to be ever vigilant about its own stewardship of resources, to prevent the tragedy that there be entire churches that are not "of God."

---

8. UNICEF statistic, see www.unicef.org/mdg/poverty.html (accessed 2 Sept. 2011).

1 John 3:19–24

Literary Context

After discussing the nature of loving others as God would have it and having modeled this love on God's love for his children (3:1 – 18), John addresses the psychological/spiritual feelings of inadequacy and failure that believers face when sincerely trying to live rightly (3:19 – 22). He reassures his readers that even when their inner voice of conscience nags, God knows that the hearts of his children are in the right place, and they can trust God's mercy and grace and approach him in confidence. The very acts of believing in Christ and providing for the needs of others are evidence that God's Spirit dwells within them, for the type of love that God defines is not characteristic of fallen and unredeemed people.

The introduction of the Spirit's role in the life of the believer in v. 24 marks a major transition to chapter 4, where the relationship between love empowered by the Spirit and truth revealed by the Spirit is discussed.

IX. Love One Another (3:11 – 18)

➡ **X. Children of God Can Be Confident (3:19 – 24)**

　　A. Having Confidence in God's Grace (3:19 – 22)

　　B. Doing What God Wants (3:23 – 24)

XI. The Spirit of Truth Must Be Discerned from the Spirit of Error (4:1 – 6)

Main Idea

John reassures his readers that even though the demands of love for others may stir feelings of being inadequate and incapable, the understanding that God knows the Spirit-empowered impulses of his children's hearts better than they know themselves will silence that accusing inner voice.

Translation

1 John 3:19 – 24

19a	assertion	And	**this is how we will know that we are of the truth,**
b	expansion	and	how **we will put our heart at rest before him:**
20a	condition		whenever our heart convicts us. For
b	assertion		**God is greater than our hearts, and**
c			**he knows everything.**
21a	address		Dear friends,
b	condition		when our heart does not convict us,
c	inference		**we have confidence before God,**
22a	assertion		and **we receive whatever we ask from him,**
b	basis		because we keep his commands and
c	expansion		do what is pleasing before him.
23a	identification	And	**this is his command:**
b	content		to believe in the name of his Son,
c	apposition		Jesus Christ, and
d	expansion		to love one another,
e	comparison		just as he gave the command to us.
24a	assertion	And	**the one who keeps his commands remains in him [God],** and
b	assertion		he himself in them;
c	identification		and in this way **we know that he remains in us:**
d	basis		from the Spirit, whom he gave to us.

Structure

This pericope bridges the topics of love and truth that are so central to the Johannine message. Verse 19 points back to the discussion of what it means to truly love others as God defines it by showing that one's obedience to that command indicates that one is "of the truth." The last verse of the section (v. 24) points forward to the discussion of the role of the Holy Spirit in bringing truth and love together.

Exegetical Outline

→ **X. Children of God Can Be Confident (3:19 – 24).**

    A. Having confidence in God's grace (3:19 – 22)

      1. Loving in deed and truth is how we know we are "of the truth" (3:19a)

      2. But one's inner voice of the heart accuses and convicts (3:19b – 20)

        a. We need to put our heart at ease (3:19b)

        b. For God knows us better than we know ourselves (3:20)

      3. Confidence before God (3:21 – 22)

        a. Requires a heart at ease before him (3:21)

        b. Results in prayer that God answers (3:22)

    B. Doing what God wants (3:23 – 24)

      1. Believe in his Son, Jesus Christ (3:23a-c)

      2. Love one another (3:23d-e)

      3. Remain in him (3:24a-b)

      4. We know we remain in him because faith and love show that we have been given the Spirit (3:24c – d)

Explanation of the Text

The Greek syntax of vv. 19 – 20 allows for a number of ways of reading these verses. The number of textual variants in them indicates that readers throughout the history of the church have offered various ways to make the best sense of these statements. Despite the difficulties, it is clear that the apostle is addressing one of his major purposes for writing, the assurance of the good standing with God he wishes his readers to have.

John addresses the problem of Christian conscience here, that inner voice ("heart") that accuses one of failing to live up to God's expectations. Despite believing correctly about Jesus Christ, and even while striving to live out the gospel in our relationships, every Christian still has a conscience that reminds us of our failed intentions, our laziness that has motivated sins of omission, the unkindnesses we've done to others in a rash or impatient moment. The apostle has been laying out a tall order of what it means to love one another. But

he does not wish to lay a guilt trip on his readers by suggesting that God requires some unattainable perfect obedience for good standing with him. Despite the difficulties in the passage, the main point is that the path to assurance in times of self-doubt is trust in God.

3:19 – 20a And this is how we will know that we are of the truth, and how we will put our heart at rest before him: whenever our heart convicts us (Καὶ ἐν τούτῳ γνωσόμεθα ὅτι ἐκ τῆς ἀληθείας ἐσμέν, καὶ ἔμπροσθεν αὐτοῦ πείσομεν τὴν καρδίαν ἡμῶν ὅ τι ἐὰν καταγινώσκῃ ἡμῶν ἡ καρδία). John now addresses the problem of a Christian's conscience in light of the great demands of love.

"And this is how" (καὶ ἐν τούτῳ) links the previous exhortation to love one another in both deeds and truth to the important topic of inner assurance. Although formally the phrase could point forward, that reading would sever these verses from the immediate context and makes less sense than reading the phrase as pointing back (anaphoric reference). Larsen also finds this to be anaphoric, the only one of the twelve occurrences of "in this" (ἐν τούτῳ) in 1 John.[1]

Assurance requires knowledge that one is "of the truth" (ἐκ τῆς ἀληθείας), and to be of the truth (i.e., to be of God) entails both outward deeds on behalf of others and right beliefs. Just as James claims that "faith by itself, if it is not accompanied by action, is dead" (Jas 2:17), John teaches that those who are of the truth must live out that truth through deeds that respond appropriately to the needs of others. The future tense of "we will know" (γνωσόμεθα) is gnomic, meaning that it is a general truth that can be applied at any time. In other words, living rightly in relationship with others is the fruit of being right with God, and whenever that is true, it makes visible the inner reality of who one is. Conversely, if one stops living in right relationship with others, one will eventually have reason to doubt one's future with God, because we know that we will be judged before him.

Although one could question whether "we will put our heart at ease" (πείσομεν τὴν καρδίαν ἡμῶν) continues the content clause (ὅτι) of what we know ("we know that we are of the truth and … [that] we will put our hearts at ease"), the future tense of both "know" and "put at ease" suggests these two verbs are to be read in parallel ("In this way we will know that we are of the truth and [in this way also] we will put our heart at ease"), as in NIV, ESV, NRSV.

The first two words at the beginning of v. 20 (ὅ τι) are difficult to construe, regardless of how we read v. 19, and the problem is compounded by the second *hoti* (ὅτι) later in the verse. Were they originally intended as two words (ὅ τι) or as one (ὅτι)? If we read that the result of obeying this exhortation to act in loving deeds and truth is twofold (i.e.,

"we will know" *and* "we will put our heart at ease"), then the start of v. 20 may be read either as "because [ὅτι] if our heart convicts us" or "whenever [ὅ τι] our heart convicts us." This latter reading is derived by reading the ὅτι as two words, ὅ τι (as in Mark 6:23; 1 Cor 16:2; Col 3:17), "whatever our heart convicts us about," i.e., "whenever" it convicts us about anything (as in NASB).

The second *hoti* clause, in v. 20b, would then be read as giving further support for why John's readers can put their hearts at ease before God, "for God is greater than our heart and he knows all things" (also NIV 1984, NRSV).

This confusing array of exegetical options is represented by the major translations:

NIV (1984): This then is how we know that we belong to the truth, and how we set our hearts at rest in his presence whenever our hearts condemn us. For God is greater than our hearts, and he knows everything.

NIV (2011): This is how we know that we belong to the truth and how we set our hearts at rest in his presence: If our hearts condemn us, we know that God is greater than our hearts, and he knows everything.

ESV: By this we shall know that we are of the truth and reassure our heart before him; for whenever our heart condemns us, God is greater than our heart, and he knows everything.

NRSV: And by this we will know that we are from the truth and will reassure our hearts before him whenever our hearts condemn us; for God is greater than our hearts, and he knows everything.

NKJV: And by this we know that we are of the truth, and shall assure our hearts before Him. For if our heart condemns us, God is greater than our heart, and knows all things.

Any way of construing these two verses leaves some part of the syntax unsatisfied. Despite the

---

1. Larsen, "The Phrase ἐν τούτῳ in 1 John," 27 – 38.

exegetical ambiguities, the major gist of John's thought is clear. The NLT nicely captures it: "It is by our actions that we know we are living in the truth, so we will be confident when we stand before the Lord, even if our hearts condemn us. For God is greater than our hearts, and he knows everything."

3:20b-c For God is greater than our hearts, and he knows everything (ὅτι μείζων ἐστὶν ὁ θεὸς τῆς καρδίας ἡμῶν καὶ γινώσκει πάντα). John continues to reassure his readers' conscience. Evidently the statement "God is greater than our hearts, and he knows everything" is supposed to put one's heart at ease when combined with the deeds obedient to the love command. But how is this so? Someone might accuse me of one thing, but in my heart I could add a hundred more to their list. The fact that God knows *everything* is more likely to drive us into further despair about our shortcomings. And how are we to understand the statement that "God is greater than our hearts"?

John's primary point is that Christian believers can have confidence before God even when their inner voice accuses them. In the first place, if someone feels legitimate guilt over sin, John has already made the foundational point that cleansing is available by the blood of Christ upon confession (1:7; 2:1 – 2). But for a believer who *is* sensitive to the needs of others, there is an almost ever-present sense of not doing enough to meet those needs.

First, there is "illegitimate guilt" that can be generated when a person's internal moral compass has been shaped, for instance, by unrealistic expectations, a distorted understanding of moral truth, a perfectionistic attitude toward self-behavior, and so forth. Second, since the needs around us far exceed our ability to respond, how should Christians deal with feeling inadequate in the face of

great need? At what point, if any, should we not feel guilty about the unmet needs of others? John's reference to the heart that accuses may be illustrated by the uncomfortable feeling many people get when viewing images of starving children in Africa. People could give until they themselves were starving, and yet they would make little dent in such overwhelming need.

But God transcends our hearts in his omniscience, and this makes him the ultimate judge. The inner voice of our conscience is not always a reliable indicator, as the apostle Paul explains in 1 Cor 4:3 – 5:

> What about me? *Have I been faithful?* Well, it matters very little what you or anyone else thinks. *I don't even trust my own judgment on this point.* My conscience is clear, but that isn't what matters. It is the Lord himself who will examine me and decide. So be careful not to jump to conclusions before the Lord returns as to whether or not someone is faithful. When the Lord comes, he will bring our deepest secrets to light and will reveal our private motives. And then God will give to everyone whatever praise is due. (NLT, italics added)

God calls us to do what we can and leave the rest to him. We must do our best to love others, and then we need to trust God, not only for our further provision, but also for our own peace of mind about it before him. I. Howard Marshall states it well:

> John says that we can set our hearts at rest whenever they condemn us.... For God understands us better than our own hearts know us, and in his omniscience he knows that our often weak attempts to obey his command spring from a true allegiance to him.[2]

In other words, reassurance cannot come from within us, but must come from the objective truth

---

2. Marshall, *Epistles of John,* 197 – 98.

about God and his gracious mercy that sent Jesus to the cross. And because God already knows everything we've done or failed to do, we can confess to him both our legitimate guilt for failing to love others as fully as we ought and what may be illegitimate guilt, resting in God's just and merciful judgment alone. As Lieu summarizes it, "The primary intention is to trust in God in the face of anxiety."[3] That is the only way to have assurance of salvation and peace of mind.

3:21 Dear friends, when our heart does not convict us, we have confidence before God (ἀγαπητοί, ἐὰν ἡ καρδία [ἡμῶν] μὴ καταγινώσκῃ, παρρησίαν ἔχομεν πρὸς τὸν θεόν). Having confidence with God depends on putting our heart at ease. It is hard to approach someone we feel we have wronged, much less ask them for something. Whether a wrong is justified or merely imagined, it introduces a negative tension into a relationship. Perhaps this is why Jesus teaches that if a Christian realizes a brother or sister has something against them, they are the one who is to go and seek to make things right (Matt 5:23–24). This pattern of interpersonal dynamics began back in the garden, when Adam and Eve realized they had wronged God, and they hid from him (Gen 3:8). But God, who knew he had been truly wronged, took the initiative to seek them out, a gracious act that he has been extending to wayward human beings ever since.

John realizes that there are many ways every Christian falls short of God's standards, and he has just presented a tough one: our inability to rightly and fully love others. How can anyone feel that they have done that as well as possible? And so self-doubt and a feeling of disappointing God can often result when believers sincerely seek to serve

and obey him. But those feelings must be put to rest (vv. 19–20) before God can be enjoyed. Only when that accusing inner voice has been silenced can a believer have confidence before God.[4]

3:22 And we receive whatever we ask from him, because we keep his commands and do what is pleasing before him (καὶ ὃ ἐὰν αἰτῶμεν λαμβάνομεν ἀπ᾽ αὐτοῦ, ὅτι τὰς ἐντολὰς αὐτοῦ τηροῦμεν καὶ τὰ ἀρεστὰ ἐνώπιον αὐτοῦ ποιοῦμεν). The obedient response of loving others and the realization that any self-doubt can be silenced by trusting God, who knows us better than we know ourselves, lead to greater spiritual maturity and understanding of God's will. With the accusing inner voice silenced, a believer is free to approach God in prayer with the confidence that God will respond in a positive manner to the requests we lay before him.

Jesus himself invited his followers to ask "anything" in his name, with the promise that he will do it (John 14:14; 15:16; 16:23; also Matt 21:22; Mark 11:24). Later in this letter John repeats the thought with the qualification "whatever we ask according to his will" (1 John 5:14–15), a qualification that was no doubt understood in the Christian tradition. This idea is conveyed here by the *hoti* clause, "because we keep his commands and do what is pleasing before him." Although this may sound like a quid pro quo deal — we do something for God and he repays us by granting something we ask for — it is nothing of the kind. It is another way of saying that people who keep God's command and do what pleases him *know* God's will. As a result, they will ask only what is consistent with what they know of God, for they are his children.

Jesus taught that following him requires us to trust and depend on the Father and to ask as an acknowledgment of that dependence. On his

---

3. Lieu, *I, II, & III John*, 156.
4. Note that the conditional "if" (ἐάν) can come close to

the sense of "when," and John uses it in that sense here and elsewhere in the letter (e.g., 2:28); see BDAG, *s.v.* ἐάν 2.

last night with his disciples he told them, "And I will do whatever you ask in my name, so that the Father may be glorified in the Son. You may ask me for anything in my name, and I will do it" (John 14:13 – 14). God is pleased to grant such requests to his children because it reveals his glory through Jesus and shows that God's power is at work in the world when his children invoke it by their prayers.

3:23 And this is his command: to believe in the name of his Son, Jesus Christ, and to love one another, just as he gave the command to us (καὶ αὕτη ἐστὶν ἡ ἐντολὴ αὐτοῦ, ἵνα πιστεύσωμεν τῷ ὀνόματι τοῦ υἱοῦ αὐτοῦ Ἰησοῦ Χριστοῦ καὶ ἀγαπῶμεν ἀλλήλους, καθὼς ἔδωκεν ἐντολὴν ἡμῖν). John explains that faith in Jesus constitutes obedience to God. God sent his Son into the world and is pleased when people believe in Jesus Christ, for that is the only way to be reconciled to God and to others. The question of whether the subjunctive verb translated "we believe" should be present (πιστεύωμεν) or aorist (πιστεύσωμεν) arises in the Johannine corpus elsewhere (e.g., John 20:31), and while of interest to textual critics, the form of the verb does not radically alter the meaning of the statement. The verbal sense of "believe," especially when used in the context of "remaining," a concept so distinctive of the Johannine corpus, implies continuing in that faith throughout life (a durative idea) and not a onetime "sinner's prayer" moment, regardless of whether the verbal form is present or aorist.

Jesus himself taught that "the work of God is this: to believe in the one he has sent" (John 6:29). As Lieu points out, "God's command is directed toward the authority of God's Son," whose task it is to render void the works of the devil.[5] "Just as he gave the command to us" is likely a reference to Jesus' teaching on the two greatest commands, to love God and to love others (Matt 22:37 – 40; Mark

12:30 – 31; Luke 10:27). Here John brings Christology and ethics together: love God (by believing in Jesus) and love one another.

3:24 And the one who keeps his commands remains in him [God], and he himself in them; and in this way we know that he remains in us: from the Spirit, whom he gave to us (καὶ ὁ τηρῶν τὰς ἐντολὰς αὐτοῦ ἐν αὐτῷ μένει καὶ αὐτὸς ἐν αὐτῷ· καὶ ἐν τούτῳ γινώσκομεν ὅτι μένει ἐν ἡμῖν, ἐκ τοῦ πνεύματος οὗ ἡμῖν ἔδωκεν. One of the distinctive concepts of the Johannine corpus is that genuine children of God remain, or abide (μένω), in Christ and the Father. This Greek word occurs more than thirty times in John's gospel and more than twenty-five times in his letters. Abiding or remaining in him has been described as:

- loving one's brother and sister (2:10)
- doing the will of God (2:17)
- honoring what was heard from the beginning (2:24)
- receiving God's anointing (2:27)
- keeping "his commands" (3:24).

The mutual abiding of the believer in God/Christ and of God in the believer is for the "one who keeps his commands," which likely refers to the greatest and second greatest commands of love for God and love for others (v. 23). Verse 23 involves both God the Father and his Son Jesus Christ, and so the antecedent of the masculine singular pronouns of v. 24 is ambiguous. Are "his" commands God the Father's? Or Jesus Christ's? Although the command to believe in Jesus Christ originates with God the Father, the exposition of the two greatest commands — love for God and love for others — was given by Jesus during his earthly ministry. Clearly John is not concerned to distinguish between them when he refers to "his commands," for another Johannine distinctive in the protection of

5. Lieu, *I, II & III John*, 158.

monotheism is that what the Father says and does, Jesus says and does (John 3:34; 5:19; 10:30; 14:10).

Moreover, the mutual abiding in God and God in the believer is also a distinctive Johannine teaching (John 14:10 – 11, 20). Jesus says, "Before long, the world will not see me anymore, but you will see me.... On that day you will realize that I am in my Father, and you are in me, and I am in you" (14:19 – 20). Jesus teaches that this mutual abiding extends also to the Spirit, which results in the full participation of the Trinity within the believer:

> And I will ask the Father, and he will give you another advocate [*paraclete*] to help you and be with you forever — the Spirit of truth. The world cannot accept him, because it neither sees him nor knows him. But you know him, for he lives with you and *will be in you.* (14:16 – 17, italics added)

The same thought underlies 1 John 3:24, where the apostle claims that the one who keeps God's commands remains in God and that we can know we remain in God because of the presence of the Holy Spirit in us. Because the Spirit is the mark of divine indwelling, given to those who belong to the community of faith and obedience, the important question arises about the person who claims to have faith in Christ and may claim to be living obediently as the "Spirit" leads them, but who has begun to live in unorthodox ways. That leads to the topic of how to discern the spirits that the apostle takes up in chapter 4.

This is the first of twelve references to "spirit" (πνεῦμα) in the letter. Two exegetical questions arise: (1) What is the significance of the prepositional phrase ἐκ τοῦ πνεύματος (also in 4:13)? (2) Is this a reference to the Holy Spirit or to the human spirit of the believer transformed by his or her conversion to faith in Christ? John's writings are known for their use of double entendre,[6] and his use of πνεῦμα here allows for a double meaning

in the Greek that English capitalization (s/Spirit) will not permit.

The human spirit is that which motivates and animates one's behavior, and a person can find that motivation in the darkness of this world or in the light of Jesus Christ. The human spirit that expresses love toward God and others has been transformed by the Spirit of God, the Holy Spirit. John consistently uses the prepositional phrase "of the ..." (ἐκ τοῦ ...) to indicate origin within his conceptual dualism. It is not that we know that God remains in the believer because he has given us a portion of his Spirit, as if the phrase were partitive in sense, but that the spirit of the believer is motivated and animated by the Holy Spirit because of their new birth. A believer has God's Holy Spirit because God is their Father (cf. Rom 8:16).

The role of the Holy Spirit is a major theme of John's gospel. John the Baptist predicts that the One coming will baptize with the Spirit (John 1:33). Jesus is identified as the one on whom the Spirit descends and remains (1:32 – 33; 3:34). The new birth, which figures so prominently in John's gospel, is accomplished by the Spirit (3:5 – 8), who is referred to metaphorically as wind (3:8) and living water (4:13 – 14; 7:37 – 39), and as the Spirit of truth, which "the world" cannot accept (14:17; 16:13). Jesus speaks extensively of the Holy Spirit as "another Advocate [*paraclete*]" in 16:7 – 14 as he details the Spirit's work. In John's gospel not only is the coming of the Spirit dependent on and following the death of Jesus (16:7), but also he is given by the resurrected Christ (20:22).

Given the major role the Holy Spirit plays in John's gospel, John's letters are relatively muted, with only six references (1 John 3:24; 4:2, 6, 13; 5:6, 8). Furthermore, those references are always in the context of discerning the truth and the Spirit's role as a witness to the truth about the significance of

---

6. Köstenberger, *Theology of John's Gospel and Letters*, 132.

Jesus' death (4:2, 6; 5:6, 8). This suggests that the situation into which John writes the first letter is one where claims to the Spirit may have been used by the antichrist secessionists to authorize their teaching, which John considers false. He specifically instructs his readers on how the Spirit of God is recognized (4:2), which is inseparably bound to the truth that Christ has come in the flesh (4:2), by both water and blood (5:6).

The one who keeps the commands to believe in the Christ of the apostolic witness and consequently to love others is the one who knows the mutual indwelling, because that faith and love expressed by the believer's spirit have their origin in the Holy Spirit. Only through the power and work of the Holy Spirit can a person love God through faith in Christ and love others rightly. As Bultmann observed, "love is not a general human possibility, but a gift [from God]."[7] He goes to explain:

> In referring here, surprisingly for the first time, to the spirit as the effective power of God, the author has created the transition to 4:1ff, which indicates, however, that the effect of the spirit consists not only in the keeping of the commandments and in mutual love, and therefore not only in a new self-understanding, but also in faith in the revelation in Jesus Christ, which serves as their basis; *the effect of the spirit thus also consists in right confession, just as "anointing," according to 2:20, 27, also bestows right knowledge.*"[8]

With this introduction of the Spirit as the One who empowers a love for God and others, John will begin to unpack the relationship between love and truth, a topic that comprises much of the rest of the letter and was apparently important in the original historical context of pastoral care in the wake of the secessionists. The passage began with the statement that obedience to the love command (3:19) is the indicator that one is "of the truth." The relationship between truth and love is also important to the church today, as biblical truth comes under increasing attack as being unloving, exclusivist, and narrow-minded.

Theology in Application

We know we are "of the truth," and therefore we know we are children of God, when we don't just claim to love others, but love them through our actions in accordance with the gospel ("let us … love … in actions and truth," 3:18). John and other NT writers define love as the considerate response to the needs of others (3:17), which is something we can do even if we don't particularly *like* the person in need.

But the nature of the response appropriately varies, depending on who is in need. How one responds to the needs of family and intimate friends would be appropriately different from how one responds to the needs of those in the neighborhood or in the church or around the globe. But an appropriate response to the needs of others is expected of God's children. Such love, depending on the circumstances and the people involved, might mean providing money or other resources to assist someone in need, spending time to assist such a person, or even possibly offering something as radical as an organ donation to keep someone alive. God expects us to do what we can, not what we can't. But love is not limited to these occasional dire situations.

---

7. Bultmann, *Johannine Epistles*, 59.   8. Ibid., 60 (italics added).

Love as Keeping God's Commands

Love for others should characterize the daily life of the Christian by keeping the moral commands that God has instituted to protect human relationships, commands such as "you shall not murder," "you shall not commit adultery," "you shall not steal," and "you shall not give false testimony" (Exod 20:13 – 16). These sins are the very opposite of love for others.

Nevertheless, even while we intend to love others rightly and fully, the needs around us are so great, and we are so limited and flawed, that one might still be plagued by an accusing inner voice. We all know that many of our good intentions have gone wrong or been left undone, or have fallen short in some way. Furthermore, loving others can also be complicated by the emotions evoked by the response we get from them.

The feeling that we have disappointed God despite our best efforts can destroy our intimacy with the heavenly Father, which should be characteristic of his children. The feeling that well-intended acts have somehow backfired and caused hurt and misunderstanding may actually undermine our motivation to continue to love others in action by breeding frustration, resentment, and the desire to withdraw from others. Sometimes it seems that the saying is true: "No good deed goes unpunished!"

A Heart at Rest

In this passage John relates the divine and human aspects of reassurance that will put our hearts at rest so we can have a right relationship with God and with those he brings into our lives. He explains that faith in Christ and the impulse to love others by responding to their needs are evidence of the Holy Spirit within a believer (v. 24). While the believer must exhibit both faith and loving acts, both are gifts that originate with God's Spirit and not with us. Thus, our obedience is itself evidence that we have been reconciled to God and are his children. John teaches that we can still our inner voice that accuses and berates by remembering that God is greater than our hearts and he knows everything, especially those things we cannot know.

God recognizes that our flawed, inadequate attempts to love others are genuine acts of faith and love. He knows all about the people we attempt to love and the situations that have given rise to their needs. Our attempt to respond to another's need may be misguided or miscalculated. The person we try to love may rebuff our good intent. Our loving act may actually flow from motives that are not unmixed with selfishness or our own needs. There are many reasons why even our best acts may leave us feeling unsettled, unsure, and confused inside. Love can be complicated, and God knows that; his own love for the world has been misunderstood, rebuffed, and rejected. Still, he continues to love his creation by providing what we need to sustain life physically and spiritually.

The apostle knows that his readers need to quiet their hearts in order to continue in their faith in Christ and in their love for others. For a heart that constantly accuses us of disappointing God will erode our resolve to love, and it will keep us from enjoying our relationship with our heavenly Father. Feelings of inadequacy or failure will impede our prayer life by making us shy away from God. John's remedy for quieting a restless heart is surprisingly simple to state, but possibly difficult to achieve: trust God, who knows all things and who knows us better than we know ourselves. Trust God's regenerative power working within. Trust God's knowledge of how his Spirit has transformed you and continues to do so throughout your life, even when your own spirit grows weak. Don't turn away from faith in Christ or from loving others. Remain in him.

CHAPTER 11

1 John 4:1 – 6

Literary Context

John has rephrased the first and second greatest commandments, love God and love your neighbor, in 3:23 as "to trust/believe in the name of [God's] Son, Jesus Christ, and to love one another." He elaborates on each of these commands, first in this pericope (4:1 – 6) by discussing a fuller understanding of Jesus Christ as having "come in flesh" (4:2). Next, he will return to the subject of loving one another in 4:7 – 21.

> X. Children of God Can Be Confident (3:19 – 24)
> ➡ **XI. The Spirit of Truth Must Be Discerned from the Spirit of Error (4:1 – 6)**
>   **A. Test If the Spirits Are from God (4:1 – 3)**
>   **B. Those Who Are of God Understand Each Other (4:4 – 6c)**
>   **C. This Is How to Discern the Spirit of Truth from the Spirit of Error (4:6d)**
> XII. God's Love Expressed (4:7 – 16)

Main Idea

Not every claim for spiritual truth is valid, and the primary test is whether the claim is consistent with orthodox Christology that centers on the incarnation of Jesus Christ, Son of God. Many false prophets who are in "the world" are causing confusion and schism. John warns his readers not to be gullible, but to test the teachings they hear against the message of the author.

Translation

(See next page.)

1 John 4:1–6

1a	address	Dear friends,
b	exhortation	**do not believe every spirit,**
c	expansion	but **test the spirits,** if they are of God,
d	basis	because many false prophets have gone out into the world.
2a	basis	In this way **you know the Spirit of God:**
b		every spirit that acknowledges Jesus Christ has come in flesh is
	source	from God; and
3a	contrast	every spirit that does not acknowledge Jesus [come in flesh] is
	source	not from God.
b	expansion	And **this is the [spirit] of the antichrist,**
		which you have heard
	content	is coming, and
	assertion	now is already in the world.
4a	address	Children,
b	assertion	**you are of God,**
c	assertion	and **you have overcome them,**
d	basis	because greater is the one in you than
e	comparison	the one in the world.
5a	assertion	**They are of the world;**
b	result	because of this
		they speak from the world's viewpoint,
c	assertion	and **the world listens to them.**
6a	contrast/assertion	**We are of God;**
b	assertion	**the one who knows God hears us,**
c	contrast	[but] **whoever is not of God does not hear us.**
d	conclusion	**This is how we know the spirit of truth and the spirit of deception.**

Structure

This passage forms one of the major exhortations in the letter. The vocative "dear friends" (ἀγαπητοί) and a shift to the second person plural verb form "do not believe" (μὴ ... πιστεύετε) signal a shift in the discourse that brings the discussion back to the readers' own situation. This segment extends to v. 7, where another vocative "dear friends" (ἀγαπητοί) both closes this exhortation and begins a new one. The reason for the exhortation in v. 1a-c is presented through v. 3 with criteria for making the discernment commanded in v. 1.

Reassurance of the recipients' spiritual state is offered with v. 4, using the emphatic, explicit pronoun "you" (ὑμεῖς) and an embedded vocative, "children" (τεκνία). The shift to the first person plural "we" in v. 6 underscores the author's desire for and assumption of unity between him and the readers, which distinguishes them from the false prophets and the world (v. 1d).

Exegetical Outline

→ **XI. The Spirit of Truth Must Be Discerned from the Spirit of Error (4:1 – 6)**

    A. Test if the spirits are from God (4:1 – 3)

        1. Many false prophets have gone out (4:1b)

        2. The Spirit of God, who acknowledges Jesus Christ has come in flesh, is from God (4:2)

        3. Any spirit that does not acknowledge Jesus Christ has come in flesh in not from God (4:3a)

        4. Such a spirit is the spirit of the antichrist, which is already in the world (4:3b)

    B. Those who are of God understand each other (4:4 – 6c)

        1. You are of God and have overcome the spirits of antichrist (4:4)

        2. The spirits of antichrist speak (4:5)

           a. from the world's perspective (4:5a-b)

           b. are heard by the world (4:5c)

        3. We are of God (4:6a-c)

           a. The one who knows God listens to us (4:6b)

           b. The one who is not of God does not listen to us (4:6c)

    C. This is how to discern the Spirit of truth from the spirit of error (4:6d)

Explanation of the Text

4:1 Dear friends, do not believe every spirit, but test the spirits, if they are of God, because many false prophets have gone out into the world (Ἀγαπητοί, μὴ παντὶ πνεύματι πιστεύετε, ἀλλὰ δοκιμάζετε τὰ πνεύματα εἰ ἐκ τοῦ θεοῦ ἐστιν, ὅτι πολλοὶ ψευδοπροφῆται ἐξεληλύθασιν εἰς τὸν κόσμον). John now turns to the topic of discerning sources of spiritual truth. This unit of the letter is set off with the vocative "dear friends" (ἀγαπητοί). John follows that vocative up with two imperatives (imperatives are also in 2:24, 27, 28; 3:1, 7, 13; 5:21), commanding those whom God loves, and John loves, to test the spirits.

After pointing to the Holy Spirit in 3:24 as the evidence that one remains in God and God in them, John immediately feels it necessary to raise the problem of discerning the spirits, for not every "spirit" is from God. This move suggests that one of the issues with which he is dealing in this letter is the problem of professing Christians who claim to

have the Spirit, but who speak and act in ways that John knows are not of God.

One of the exegetical issues that needs attention here is how to understand the referent of "spirits" (πνεύματα), the only occurrence of the plural form in John's gospel and letters. The Greek word *pneuma* (πνεῦμα) has a large semantic range; it can be used to refer to physical wind (Matt 11:7; 14:30, 32), breath (Acts 17:25; 2 Thess 2:8), angels (Heb 1:7, 14), demons (Matt 8:16; 12:45), other noncorporeal beings (Num 27:16 LXX), the incorporeal part of the human person (2 Cor 7:1; Col 2:5), and the third member of the Trinity (Matt 28:19). Of these possible referents, demons are most often assumed to be the spirits mentioned here.

But the meaning should be controlled by John's use of the same term in 3:24, where it was used to refer to the manifestation of God's Spirit in the life of a believer. This is consistent with Jesus' teaching in John's gospel (John 3:8): "The wind [πνεῦμα] blows wherever it pleases. You hear its sound, but you cannot tell where it comes from or where it is going. So it is with everyone born of the Spirit [πνεῦμα]." This usage is also consistent with Paul's teaching on the manifestations of the Spirit (1 Cor 14:12). This use of the word can be defined as "the Spirit of God as exhibited in the character or activity of God's people or selected agents."[1] Similarly, the word *pneuma* can also refer to activating impulses that are not of God (2 Cor 11:4) but that are expressed in human words and actions, which is likely the sense to be understood here in 4:1.

Within the context of the situation into which John writes, there were apparently professing Christians who were teaching false things by appealing to the authority of the Holy Spirit. By instructing to "test the spirits," John is saying more than "Do not believe every person who claims to have the Spirit." In the Johannine dualism, the human spirit is motivated and energized by impulses that come either from God's Spirit or from the diabolical spirit of deception (4:6d). In that sense, the demonic is involved here, but not in the sense that the "spirits" are individual demons possessing or influencing those who have gone out from the Johannine churches. John is concerned to instruct his readers to be aware of and discern between two opposing spiritual forces at work that can be manifested in human behavior apart from demonic possession. In the context of the Johannine churches, these two forces were being manifested by true and false confessions of faith in Christ.

John wants his readers to recognize that even for professing Christians, there are other forces at work than the Holy Spirit, and he refers to those forces as "spirits" that must be tested. They must be tested by the gold standard, not of human ex-

perience or opinion, but of sound Christology. The association of Jesus, the Spirit, and the gospel message is very much Paul's point as well: "For if someone comes to you and preaches a Jesus other than the Jesus we preached, or if you receive a different spirit [πνεῦμα] from the Spirit [πνεῦμα] you received, or a different gospel from the one you accepted, you put up with it easily enough" (2 Cor 11:4; cf. 1 Cor 12:3).

John's readers need to understand that not everything said or done by someone who professes to have the Holy Spirit is of God, because many false prophets have gone out into the world. The reason John gives for the necessity of testing the spirits confirms that he uses the word *pneuma* to refer to the activating impulse of human behavior, which may be of the Spirit or of the world. False prophets speak falsely because, regardless of what they think, they are not speaking the truth about God and his work (cf. 1 Tim 4:1; Rev 16:13 – 14).

The false prophets John has in mind, whose teaching is energized by impulses not of God, "have gone out into the world" (ἐξεληλύθασιν εἰς τὸν κόσμον). In John's conceptual universe, the world is the place that is without God. To speak falsely in God's name is to locate oneself in the world. The verb "have gone out" likely refers back to 2:19, where John mentions people who were once part of the Johannine church(es) but who had literally left the community. His point there is that even though they were once a part of the community, that does not mean that they were "of" those who knew the truth.

4:2 – 3a In this way you know the Spirit of God: every spirit that acknowledges Jesus Christ has come in flesh is from God; and every spirit that does not acknowledge Jesus [come in flesh] is not from God (ἐν τούτῳ γινώσκετε τὸ πνεῦμα τοῦ

---

1. BDAG, *s.v.* πνεῦμα 6.

θεοῦ· πᾶν πνεῦμα ὃ ὁμολογεῖ Ἰησοῦν Χριστὸν ἐν σαρκὶ ἐληλυθότα ἐκ τοῦ θεοῦ ἐστιν, καὶ πᾶν πνεῦμα ὃ μὴ ὁμολογεῖ τὸν Ἰησοῦν ἐκ τοῦ θεοῦ οὐκ ἔστιν).

John is concerned throughout his letter with the epistemological issue of how a person can have genuine knowledge of the invisible God. Indeed, knowing God is a major theme of both the Fourth Gospel, where knowing God is identified as having eternal life (John 17:3), and this letter. As Moberly points out, "John's concern is intrinsic to any form of Christian faith. For where notions of divine self-revelation and corresponding human knowledge of God play a crucial role, possibilities of error and the deception of either self or others abound."[2]

Evidently, John's readers find themselves in a confusing situation, where discernment of the truth is needed, and the apostle reminds them here of the necessity of the recognition of the incarnation of Jesus Christ for true knowledge of God, because the Word became flesh specifically to reveal the otherwise invisible God (John 1:14, 18). Therefore, everyone who has a true knowledge of God acknowledges that "Jesus Christ has come in flesh" — that is, that the Son of God became a human being.

The incarnation is the heart of Christian epistemology. Consequently, the converse is also true, that anyone who does not acknowledge Jesus as come in flesh is not of God; that is, they have not acquired the true knowledge of God through the revelation of himself in Jesus Christ. Martinus De Boer has pointed out:

> The "coming" into the world of Jesus Christ, the Son of God, does not merely denote his visible appearance on the worldly stage. His "coming" *as such* includes saving action (the performance of signs, the giving of light, etc.). The coming is … a "salvific mission." In short, the verb "to come" in

Johannine christological contexts not only means (denotes) "to appear on the scene" but also signifies (connotes) "to act salvifically," "to accomplish a saving mission," "to effect salvation," or some equivalent expression.[3]

In other words, the statements of Jesus that use the perfect tense "I have come" (ἐλήλυθα) refer directly to his saving mission (John 5:43; 7:28; 8:42; 12:46; 16:28; 18:37). Therefore, the confession that Jesus Christ "has come" in flesh does not simply acknowledge that Jesus was a historical person, but expresses the redeeming significance of his incarnate life, death, and resurrection on behalf of the human race.

Notice that the first occurrence of "Jesus Christ" (Ἰησοῦν Χριστόν) in v. 2 is anarthrous, but that the second reference in v. 3a omits "Christ" and is articular (by the best judgment of textual criticism). This anaphoric article in v. 3a implies that John means, "every spirit that does not acknowledge this Jesus that I just mentioned, that is, the Jesus Christ who has come in flesh, is not of God." In other words, not just any acknowledgment of Jesus will pass as true knowledge of God. As Moberly writes:

> If faith in God in and through Jesus is in some way the key to human existence — as the Prologue to John's Gospel puts it — then there is a need for criteria not only to specify the content of this faith but also to determine when it is, and is not, truly present.[4]

Here, John specifies the necessary content of faith, apart from which there is no true knowledge of God. He will again refer to the "coming" of Jesus Christ in 5:6 with the phrase "in water and in blood" (see comments). But here his emphasis seems to be on the significance of the salvific mission of the Christ as a human being. The criterion

---

2. Moberly, "'Test the Spirits,'" 297.
3. De Boer, "The Death of Jesus Christ," 336 – 37.

4. Moberly, "'Test the Spirits,'" 297.

of determining when this content of faith is present in a person's life is the love for others who believe the same (the brothers and sisters), mentioned in 3:23 as the second command of God (see comments). John will immediately return to the topic of love in 4:7 – 14, and then back to the truth that Jesus Christ is the Son of God in 4:15 – 17, and back to love in 4:18 – 21, and yet again back to orthodox Christology in 5:1 – 6!

The understanding that Jesus Christ, the Son of God, became a human being to reveal God the Father is at the heart of John's orthodoxy. This was implied in the opening verses of the letter (1:1 – 4) with their emphasis on the historical reality of the eternal life that had been revealed in the person of Jesus Christ. As Jesus himself said, "Anyone who has seen me has seen the Father" (John 14:9). And the thought was restated in 1 John 2:22 with the definition of the antichrist as one who "denies that Jesus is the Christ."

Because John links his insistence that Jesus Christ "has come in flesh" also to the antichrists, who reject this truth in some way (4:3), and because the antichrists were previously implicated with those who had gone out (2:19 – 23), apparently some type of christological dispute among professing Christians had arisen in the Johannine church(es). In the tradition of Johannine interpretation, the emphasis on "the flesh" has led scholars to understanding the nature of that dispute as involving a form of Gnosticism, perhaps an incipient Docetism, which claimed that Jesus Christ only appeared to be human. More recently, scholars have rightly moved away from so specifically identifying the nature of the dispute (and indeed a few question whether there was a dispute at all). As Moberly astutely observes, "the concern is not that Jesus' mission on earth is *real* as opposed to *apparent*, but rather that it is *definitive* for knowledge of God."[5]

By viewing this christological argument in the context of the nexus of love for others (3:23) and the possession of the Holy Spirit (3:24), we gain insight into the situation into which John writes. There were people in the Johannine community who had professed faith in Christ and claimed to possess the Spirit but whose beliefs in some way deviated from orthodox Christology. Their views apparently disputed the claim that the locus of true knowledge about God, and thus possession of eternal life, is centered in the historical incarnation of the Son of God in Jesus Christ. The need for discernment arose because of the confusion their departure had caused, since not everything said and done by professing Christians is of the Spirit. It may be of the world.

4:3b And this is the [spirit] of the antichrist, which you have heard is coming, and now is already in the world (καὶ τοῦτό ἐστιν τὸ τοῦ ἀντιχρίστου, ὃ ἀκηκόατε ὅτι ἔρχεται, καὶ νῦν ἐν τῷ κόσμῳ ἐστὶν ἤδη). John associates a rejection of Christ having come in flesh with the antichrist. The statement that Jesus Christ has come in flesh would certainly argue against a docetic impulse (and perhaps more strongly when 1 John 5:6 is also considered). But there are several other kinds of heretical views that this statement refutes. Because all of them strike at the heart of truth about Jesus Christ, they can be identified as being of the spirit of the antichrist rather than the Spirit of Christ. The spirit of antichrist does not acknowledge that Jesus Christ has come in flesh.

The Greek construction that reads literally, "the of the antichrist" (τὸ τοῦ ἀντιχρίστου), with the double article (τὸ τοῦ), indicates the elision of the neuter noun for spirit (πνεῦμα). The spirit of antichrist was already in the world when John wrote, and it was energizing the many false

---

5. Ibid., 300 (italics original).

prophets who had gone out (4:1). As discussed under 4:1, the word *pneuma* here refers to activating impulses that are not of God. The spirit of antichrist is "of the world," the order of human life that has developed in rejecting God and his redemptive plan for humanity. The spirit of antichrist may be demonic, though John does not speak of the spirits in that way here. They may be well-intended but self-deceived human impulses that did not take God into account. In that sense, the spirit of antichrist has been in the world ever since the opportunity to reject or misunderstand the true Christ of God arose with Jesus.

Scholars have identified several ways that the denial that Jesus Christ "has come in flesh" would be an antiorthodox understanding of the identity and mission of Jesus Christ. There are two elements in the claim; the meaning of "has come" and that of a coming "in flesh." Notably "flesh" in John's writings is not as negative as in Paul's, for the Word has become flesh (John 1:14).

Smalley follows Marshall in understanding "has come" to refer to the "coming" of the preexistent Son of God into the world permanently united with human flesh (rather than merely inhabiting a human body temporarily, as an adoptionist view held by Cerinthius suggested).[6] This view that the "coming" is a reference to the incarnation is supported when the perfect tense participle translated in v. 2 as "has come" (ἐληλυθότα) is read against the background of John's gospel, where same tense of the verb "to come" (ἔρχομαι) is found eleven times in statements such as John 18:37, "the reason I [Jesus] was born and came [ἐλήλυθα] into the world is to testify to the truth." The incarnation argues against both a view that Jesus Christ

was merely human and a view that he was a divine being who could not be human (e.g., Docetism).

Taking a different view, Brown argues that the issue at stake is soteriology, not Christology:

> There is no suggestion of such a radical docetism in the adversary views criticized by I and II John. The epistolary author seems concerned with the salvific importance of the flesh and the death of Jesus, not with a defense of the reality of Jesus' humanity ... the issue is not that the secessionists are denying the incarnation or the physical reality of Jesus' humanity; they are denying that what Jesus was or did in the flesh was related to his being the Christ, i.e., was salvific.[7]

In other words, the antichrists were not necessarily docetists who disputed the full human nature of Jesus Christ; they simply did not recognize the death of Jesus as atonement for sin.

As noted above in the discussion on 4:2 – 3a, Martinus De Boer argues that in Johannine writings, Jesus' coming includes his saving action and mission. For him, the secessionists *did* ascribe salvific importance to the life of Jesus, but the dispute centered on what aspect of Jesus' life provided cleansing from sin. He argues that they believed it was not the blood of Christ but the waters of baptism, which Jesus himself instituted; the cross itself played no role in the soteriology of the antichrists.[8]

Lieu suggests a third way of viewing the dispute between the antichrists and John when she writes:

> It might have been easy to ask, "Do we still need that initial story [of Jesus' life]; does it matter?" Indeed, 1 John's own pattern of thought, with its strong emphasis on what God has done in identifying them as God's children, could lead to precisely such questions about the continuing relevance of Jesus.[9]

---

6. Smalley, *1, 2, 3 John*, xxiii, 223; so also Dodd, *Johannine Epistles*, 96; Yarbrough, *1 – 3 John*, 223; Marshall, *Epistles of John*, 205.

7. Brown, *Epistles of John*, 58, 505.
8. De Boer, "Death of Jesus Christ," 339.
9. Lieu, *I, II, & III John*, 170.

Why would professing Christians think that the life and death of Jesus would have diminished relevance? Perhaps because, as John himself has just reassured them (3:24), they possess the Spirit. Their encounter with God in Christ is mediated through the Holy Spirit and was not directly with the historical Jesus. Moreover, Jesus himself promised that the Father would send "another *paraclete*," the Holy Spirit, who would be with them forever (John 14:16). The "Spirit of truth" mediates the teachings of Jesus (14:26) and testifies about him (15:26). Therefore, the dispute may have involved the role of the Spirit in relation to the role of Jesus.

Tom Thatcher develops this aspect of the dispute when he writes on 1 John 5:6:

> John and the "AntiChrists" appealed to the same Jesus tradition but interpreted that tradition in radically different ways. While the AntiChrists emphasized the believer's *continuing revelatory experience via the Spirit*, John insisted that the new revelations must be consistent with the community's teaching about the historical Jesus.[10]

On this view, the dispute was over where the locus of revelation lay and what role the apostolic tradition about the bearers of the eyewitnesses of Jesus' life should play. The antichrists may have argued that all access to Jesus should be through the ongoing revelation of the Holy Spirit, with John insisting that the locus of revelation was in the apostolic witness of the historical Jesus, such that all claims must square with the facts of his life, death, and resurrection.

There is simply not enough information in the text to allow a specific reconstruction of the antichrists' beliefs that put them at odds with John. We may never know which of these various readings of 4:2 – 3, often in light of 5:6 – 7, come closest to characterizing the dispute in the Johannine church(es). But there are some points that can be noted with greater certainty.

First, the perfect tense of the verb "has come" (ἐληλυθότα) in 4:2 indicates that the point being made about Jesus Christ has a present significance resulting from the past action of his coming (i.e., his earthly life). The difference between understanding the "coming" as a reference to the incarnation and understanding it as referring to Christ's salvific mission is slight, since both focus on the earthly life of Christ. Furthermore, both the incarnation of the preexistent Christ and the redemptive purpose of the incarnation are taught not only elsewhere in John's writings but throughout the NT.

Yes, there is a clear distinction between a view that is docetic and a view that locates atonement in the baptism or another aspect of Jesus' life, such as his teachings, as classic liberal Protestantism was prone to do. But John's teaching here, and the teaching of the NT more broadly, would argue against both. To understand John's point, we don't need to know specifically which issue was prominent in the heretical teaching of the secessionists that led him to call them antichrists. What both of these views have in common is the necessity of the full humanity of Jesus Christ, a point that sits well with the opening verses of the letter (1:1 – 4). The significance of the human life of Jesus Christ is what is largely at stake, and that significance can be used to counter a whole range of unorthodox teachings about Jesus.

Second, John presents this statement about Jesus Christ having come in flesh as the criterion for testing whether a teaching ("spirit") is of God or not. The need for that testing is presented in light of the fact that God has given his children his Spirit, but that raises the possibility of someone making a claim in the name of the Spirit that is

---

10. Tom Thatcher, "'Water and Blood' in AntiChrist Christianity (1 John 5:6)," *SCJ* 4 (2001): 235.

not of God. And so the role of the Spirit in revelation specifically in relationship to Jesus is also an important aspect of the dispute that John must address. Again, it is the earthly life of Jesus Christ that John claims is the locus of such revelation, and any teaching ("spirit") that does not square with the historical life of Christ, including his death and resurrection, cannot be of God.

Included in this Johannine dispute is the debate over who gets to interpret the significance of the life of Christ. The fact that Jesus died on a cross in Jerusalem is a historically verifiable statement attested outside the NT by even Roman historians. But the interpretation of that historical event is not self-evident. That Jesus *Christ* died in Jerusalem *for our sins* is an interpretive statement.

Another aspect of John's dispute with the secessionists is about who has the authority to interpret the significance of Jesus. Jesus commissioned men who personally knew him to be his witnesses. Even his teaching in John 14:26 and 15:26 can be understood as primarily addressed to his close circle of disciples, who would bear authoritative testimony to the gospel, and not to any and every subsequent Christian. The completed NT was not available to John's original readers as it is to us today. To believe the NT is to believe not only the historical facts about Jesus, but the divinely inspired NT writers' interpretation of the significance of those facts.

John argues here that to know God truly is to find the source of that knowledge in the earthly life, death, and resurrection of Jesus Christ as John and other apostolic witnesses attest to it. The ongoing work of the Holy Spirit coheres with that testimony, and claims to his authority cannot justify "[going] beyond … the teaching of Christ" (2 John 9).

4:4 Children, you are of God, and you have overcome them, because greater is the one in you than the one in the world (ὑμεῖς ἐκ τοῦ θεοῦ ἐστε, τεκνία, καὶ νενικήκατε αὐτούς, ὅτι μείζων ἐστιν ὁ ἐν ὑμῖν ἢ ὁ ἐν τῷ κόσμῳ). John now affirms and reassures his readers that, despite any confusion, they are of God. The discernment of who is of God and who is not does not depend on any mystical experience. It concretely rests on a cognitive statement about Jesus Christ. The Christians to whom John writes are those who have remained with him in the wake of the departure of those who went out into the world. He writes to assure them that their choice to stay, and what this says about what they believe, is true and right. Again John uses the perfect tense in "you have overcome [νενικήκατε] them." Those who were not "of us" went out (2:19), showing they were not of God. By not being swayed by those who left, those who remain in the Johannine church(es) have overcome whatever appeal the false teaching may have had.

John then gives a reason for his readers' persistence in the truth: "because greater is the one in you than the one in the world." Who is this one? The masculine, not neuter, articles do not allow a referent to the neuter noun "spirit" (πνεῦμα) here, though that would have followed nicely ("the Spirit in you is greater than the spirit that is in the world"). The one who has overcome the world is Jesus Christ (John 16:33), and it is his presence by the Spirit in and among the true children of God that enables them to understand his identity and remain in the truth. The opposition to Christ (i.e., the antichrist) is the one who is in the world. If John's gospel is allowed to inform the question, there we find reference to the "prince of this world" (John 12:31; 14:30; 16:11) who stands judged by Christ. Those who left the truth and went out into the world were those who, despite what they may have thought, were not born of God but were drawn into the darkness.

This verse reinforces the conceptual dualism around which John frames his letter and further helps to define his use of "world" (κόσμος). God's children are separated in this dualism from those "of the world." The world is that part of humanity that prefers to walk in darkness, that rejects the gospel Jesus Christ offers, sometimes by perverting it.

4:5 They are of the world; because of this they speak from the world's viewpoint, and the world listens to them (αὐτοὶ ἐκ τοῦ κόσμου εἰσίν, διὰ τοῦτο ἐκ τοῦ κόσμου λαλοῦσιν καὶ ὁ κόσμος αὐτῶν ἀκούει). The Johannine duality is defined between the poles of being "of God" (ἐκ τοῦ θεοῦ) and being "of the world" (ἐκ τοῦ κόσμου). While John affirms that his original readers are "of God," those who do not acknowledge that Jesus Christ "has come in flesh" are "of the world."

John does not allow that such people may claim the name of Christ, for their rejection of his truth has put them outside the bounds of Christianity. Even while they teach about Christ, their thoughts are shaped not by the gospel but by worldly categories of religion and philosophy. Such professing "Christians" listen to the world, and speak back to the world its own message, varnished in Christian terms. Therefore, the world receives their message, even though it is a distortion of the gospel.

4:6 We are of God; the one who knows God hears us, [but] whoever is not of God does not hear us. This is how we know the spirit of truth and the spirit of deception (ἡμεῖς ἐκ τοῦ θεοῦ ἐσμεν· ὁ γινώσκων τὸν θεὸν ἀκούει ἡμῶν, ὃς οὐκ ἔστιν ἐκ τοῦ θεοῦ οὐκ ἀκούει ἡμῶν. ἐκ τούτου γινώσκομεν τὸ πνεῦμα τῆς ἀληθείας καὶ τὸ πνεῦμα τῆς πλάνης). In the terms of the Johannine duality, John and his church(es) are "of God" (ἐκ τοῦ θεοῦ). The "we" here is almost certainly associative (see comments on "we" at 1:1), where John includes those believers who receive his teaching as being also "of God." Therefore, those who know God truly will recognize God's truth in what John teaches. Those who reject John's teaching about the gospel of Jesus Christ, who do not "hear" him and those who are like-minded, are not of God. But those who listen

to God as he is revealed in Jesus Christ, and who speak God's message of sin, repentence, and atonement, are not received by the world.

What else could be expected when the One who created the world was not recognized by the people of the world (John 1:10)? When the Word of God who came to redeem the world was rejected (John 1:11)? With 1 John 4:6, John draws the boundary of the duality — between truth and error, between God and the world, between those of God and those of the world — at the divide between the acceptance and rejection of the apostolic teaching that he offers. The issue implicitly is about who gets to say what is true about God and Christ and the salvation offered to the world. Who gets to speak for God in this world?

With v. 6b John draws to a close the unit of the letter he began in 4:1 with his exhortation to test the spirits to see if they are of God. How does one conduct such a test? Those who are of God acknowledge that Jesus Christ has come in flesh. They adhere to the orthodox teaching about Christ that was proclaimed by the apostles he chose to be his witnesses. Those who embrace that teaching represented by John show by that act of faith that they too are of God. Those who teach otherwise about Jesus Christ are not of God; they are johnnies-come-lately who do not truly know God. They may be sincerely self-deceived, thinking they are speaking from the Holy Spirit, but actually they speak from the spirit of the world.

The apostolic teaching is the only arbiter. Some may feel that John is being arrogant to hold up his own beliefs as the only truth about God. Don't the opinions and beliefs of others count equally? But he is not being arrogant; he is taking a stand for truth as he contends for his readers to remain with him in the safety of the apostolic teaching of those who were commissioned as witnesses of Christ, who have seen and heard and touched the Life that was revealed (1:1 – 4).

Theology in Application

John is concerned in this letter about his readers being led astray by professing believers who, though perhaps well intentioned, are in the final analysis self-deceived about how to know God and about the significance of Jesus' earthly life, death, and resurrection (2:26). We today are in somewhat less jeopardy in the sense that we have the completed and closed canon of the NT, which is the repository of all apostolic teaching about Jesus Christ. When we hear teaching about the gospel of Jesus Christ, we can measure it against that canon of Scripture.

In John's day, before the NT had come into existence, claims about revelation from the Holy Spirit were harder to discern, but they were judged on essentially the same basis: apostolic teaching as it was embodied in the men who had been chosen by Jesus to be his witnesses, and those in close association with them. We see in John's letters a situation in the early church where professing Christians claimed to have truth about God in Christ from the Spirit but where that supposed truth in serious and substantial ways did not line up with the apostolic truth known to John.

This problem was not limited to the Johannine church(es) in Ephesus or wherever they were located, for we see a similar situation troubling the apostle Paul in Corinth, where he taught the churches to distinguish between the Spirit of God and the spirit of the world (1 Cor 2:12 – 3:1). In fact, he teaches there is a spiritual gift of distinguishing between spirits (12:10). For wherever there is divine revelation mediated by the Spirit, there is the possibility of error and the consequent deception of self and others.

The Spirit Is Not Divided

Today as in John's time there is the problem of professing Christians who speak and act in ways that contradict other professing Christians, sometimes in terms that are mutually exclusive. John's point in the first century is still valid today, that not everything done and said by a professing Christian is necessarily of the Holy Spirit; they may be speaking from the spirit of the world that has distorted their understanding of the truth of Jesus Christ and his significance. The adjudicator of truth about God now is the same as it was for John — the apostolic witness, but now it has been inscripturated in the NT. No teaching that contradicts or is inconsistent with those of the NT can be accepted as truth about or from God, regardless of who says it.

John argues here that to know God truly is to find the source of that knowledge in the earthly life, death, and resurrection of Jesus Christ as John and other apostolic witnesses attest to it. The ongoing work of the Holy Spirit coheres with that testimony, as Jesus himself promised (John 14:26; 15:26), and claims to the authority of the Spirit do not justify "[going] beyond … the teaching of Christ" (2 John 9). No believer can claim to outgrow the need of atonement and think they are being led to do so by the Holy Spirit. A claim that human religion has evolved beyond the need for blood atonement cannot be received as from God's Spirit. Claims for a socially constructed morality that shuns biblical instruction in favor of relativism are of the world and are not of God.

John's concerns in this passage are still at issue today, for the apostolic teaching that John used to separate truth from error has been inscripturated in the NT. Those who embrace its teaching are "of God." Those who reject or distort its message are sadly self-deceived. If such people find a voice of leadership in the church, they will lead others, not to sound Christian theology, but to what John called antichrist teaching.

1 John 4:7 – 16

Literary Context

John has restated in distinctive Christian form the first and second greatest commandments, love for God and love for neighbor (cf. Matt 22:37 – 40; Mark 12:30 – 31; Luke 10:27). In 3:23 he writes, "And this is [God's] command: to believe in the name of his Son, Jesus Christ, and to love one another." In 4:1 – 6 he has further discussed what it means to believe in Jesus Christ as the one who "has come in flesh." Now John turns the reader's attention to the second restated commandment, the command to love one another. Notice the repetition of "love one another" (ἀγαπῶμεν ἀλλήλους) in 3:23 and 4:7, and note that the Spirit is given as the basis of assurance of remaining in him in both 3:24 and 4:13. This extended discussion about love spans 4:1 – 21 and elaborates on the relationship between love for one another and the love of God, both his for us and ours for him.

XI. The Spirit of Truth Must Be Discerned from the Spirit of Error (4:1 – 6)

➡ **XII. God's Love Expressed (4:7 – 16)**

    A. The Command to Love One Another (4:7 – 10)

    B. The Command to Love One Another Restated (4:11 – 14)

    C. Confession That "Jesus Is the Son" Is Necessary for One to Remain in God (4:15 – 16)

XIII. God's Love Perfected in the Believer (4:17 – 5:3)

Main Idea

John here identifies both the source and definition of love as God himself. God's love is most supremely expressed in the sending of the Son as an atoning sacrifice for our sin so that we might live eternally through him.

Translation

(See next page.)

1 John 4:7 –16

7a	address	Dear friends,
b	exhortation	**let us love one another,**
c	basis	because love is of God,
d	series	and **everyone who loves has been begotten of God** and
e	series	[the one who loves] knows God.
8a	assertion	**The one who does not love does not know God,**
b	basis	because God is love.
9a	assertion	**In this way God's love has been expressed among us:**
b	basis	that God has sent his one and only Son
		into the world
c	purpose	so that we might live through him.
10a	assertion	**In this way is love [defined]:**
b	contra-expectation	not that we have loved God, but
c	assertion	that he loved us and
		sent his Son [to be] an atoning sacrifice for our sins.
11a	address	Dear friends,
b	condition	if God loved us like this,
c	exhortation	**we also ought to love one another.**
12a	assertion	**No one has ever seen God.**
b	condition	If we love one another,
c	assertion	**God lives in us,**
d	assertion	and **his love is completed in us.**
13a	assertion	**In this way we know**
b	content	that in him we live and
c	content	he in us:
d	basis	because he has given to us of his Spirit.
14a	assertion	And we have beheld and
		testify
b	content	that the Father sent his Son [to be] the Savior of the world.
15a	description	Whoever acknowledges
b	content	that Jesus is the Son of God —
c	result	**God lives in them**
d		and **they live in God.**
16a	assertion	And **we have known and**
		have trusted the love that God has for us.
b	assertion	**God is love**
c	assertion	and **the one who lives in that love lives in God,**
d	assertion	and **God lives in them.**

Structure

This passage continues the discussion begun in 4:1 ("Dear friends, do not believe every spirit, but test the spirits …"), a discussion that will continue through to 4:21 ("the one who loves God must also love their brother or sister"). This passage contributes to the larger discussion by providing a visible criterion by which those who are of God may be identified. John here resumes the question of discernment raised in 4:1 – 2 by pointing out that those who have been given the Spirit of God (4:13) are those who have received God's love through faith in Jesus Christ, who has come in the flesh (4:2). Because the sending of God's Son in the flesh as an atoning sacrifice (4:10) is the definitive expression of God's love, those who have received and benefited from the Father's love will, by virtue of their spiritual relationship to the Father, manifest that love for others in their lives.

John's continued argument here has two parts, 4:7 – 10 and 4:11 – 14, each prefaced by the vocative "dear friends" (ἀγαπητοί). The major exhortation of this passage is expressed twice; first in 4:7 with the hortatory subjunctive, "dear friends, let us love one another," and second in 4:11, "dear friends … we also ought to love one another," considering how God has loved us. The first part explains love as the hallmark characteristic of those who have been born of God, who have been given life through the Son whom God sent into the world. It moves from the exhortation to love one another, to the statement that God is love (i.e., defines love), to a discussion of the nature of love that God has defined by sending his Son as an atoning sacrifice.

Verses 9 and 10 are nearly parallel:

Verse 9

A In this way God's love has been expressed among us:
  B that God sent his one and only Son into the world
    C so that we might live through him.

Verse 10

A′ In this way is love [defined]: …
  (not that we loved God, but that he loved us)
  B′ and sent his Son
    C′ to be an atoning sacrifice for our sins.

The second part of the passage explains that only as Christians express love for one another as God defines it, is God's love made evident and visible and only then is it in fact perfected among his people. Such expression of love for one another is therefore the evidence of remaining in him and of having been given God's Spirit. Only those who exhibit this love are qualified to testify to the supreme act of God's love, the sending of his Son as Savior of the world. Therefore, the testimony of those who do not exhibit such love for fellow believers should not be received (cf. 2:19). As

Moberly points out, "This love enables critical discernment to take place."[1] A similar role of love in spiritual discernment is found with Paul's famous love chapter (1 Cor 13) located within the discussion of the discernment of spiritual gifts (1 Cor 12).

These two segments of the argument are sandwiched between the repeated statement that "God is love" (vv. 8b, 16b), which forms the theological foundation of the command to love.

Exegetical Outline

→ **XII. God's Love Expressed (4:7 – 16)**

    A. The command to love one another (4:7 – 10)

        1. Love is of God (4:7a-c)

        2. The one who loves (4:7d-e)

            a. has been born of God (4:7d)

            b. knows God (4:7e)

        3. The one who does not love (4:8)

            a. does not know God (4:8a)

            b. because God is love (4:8b)

        4. God's love revealed (4:9 – 10)

            a. God sent his Son so we might live (4:9)

            b. God's love defines love (4:10)

    B. The command to love one another restated (4:11 – 14)

        1. God's love is made visible in Christian love for each other (4:11 – 12c)

        2. God's love reaches its intended goal (4:12d)

        3. God's Spirit assures us of right relationship with him (4:13)

        4. The Spirit's testimony is that the Son is Savior of the world (4:14)

    C. Confession that Jesus is the Son is necessary for one to remain in God (4:15 – 16)

        1. The mutual indwelling of the believer and God rests on belief in Jesus as Son of God (4:15)

        2. "We" who make that confession have known and have believed God's love expressed in the Son (4:16a)

        3. God is love (4:16b)

        4. Remaining in God requires remaining in his love expressed in Christ (4:16c-d)

---

1. Moberly, " 'Test the Spirits,' " 303.

Explanation of the Text

4:7 Dear friends, let us love one another, because love is of God, and everyone who loves has been begotten of God and [the one who loves] knows God (Ἀγαπητοί, ἀγαπῶμεν ἀλλήλους, ὅτι ἡ ἀγάπη ἐκ τοῦ θεοῦ ἐστιν, καὶ πᾶς ὁ ἀγαπῶν ἐκ τοῦ θεοῦ γεγέννηται καὶ γινώσκει τὸν θεόν). John returns yet again to his major exhortation of love for one another. He begins a new unit of exhortation, again addressing his readers as "dear friends" (ἀγαπητοί), the term he uses several times in the context of his remarks about love. Occurring with equal frequency is the term "children" (τεκνία), which most often occurs in discussions involving the fatherhood of God.

The rationale given for the love command is that love is a defining characteristic of God. Therefore, those who have been born of God are also defined by their love for others — like father, like son, as the saying goes. In fact, exhibiting the love characteristic of the Father evidences a personal knowledge of God. In this way, "everyone who loves" is circumscribed. It is not everyone who loves in whatever way pleases him or her who has been born of God, but everyone who loves as *God defines love* (see comments on 4:8). Note that the verb "has been begotten" (γεγέννηται) is in the perfect tense, denoting that the new birth precedes love and knowledge.

John may be presenting this teaching not only to motivate right relationships within the community, but also to provide a criterion of discernment concerning those who are not truly members of it. Moberly points out that John is concerned to articulate a "critical theological epistemology," that is, how one can know that they know God, and also

to identify those who are not truly a part of the believing community.[2] The demonstration of love by those who have received God's love in Christ continues the discussion of the discernment of spirits begun in 4:1.

4:8 The one who does not love does not know God, because God is love (ὁ μὴ ἀγαπῶν οὐκ ἔγνω τὸν θεόν, ὅτι ὁ θεὸς ἀγάπη ἐστίν). John underscores the relationship between love and knowledge of God, who is love. If everyone who loves has been begotten of God and knows God, the converse is also true: the one who does not love does not know God.

This is the third time John has mentioned the one who does not love (ὁ μὴ ἀγαπῶν). Such a person is not of God (3:10), remains in death (3:14), and here, does not know God. Therefore, such a one does not have eternal life, for the essence of that life is knowledge of God and the one whom he has sent (cf. John 17:3). The failure to love is not simply an ethical failing, but means that one remains in the darkness of sin, apart from salvation. Those who fail to love are outside the Christian community and have no truthful testimony of God, for they have no true knowledge of God. Personal knowledge of God and love for others as God defines it are inseparable. John's exhortation therefore implicitly demands self-examination.

The statement that "God is love" is one of the best-known verses even among people who are not Bible readers. In John's letter, it stands alongside the similar statement, "God is light" (1:5). Neither of these statements is an absolute metaphysical maxim about the essence of God's being,[3] but these statements point to God's authority to define sin in

---

2. Ibid., 297.
3. See Kruse, *Letters of John*, 157; Rick Williamson, *1, 2, &*

3 John: A Commentary in the Wesleyan Tradition (Kansas City: Beacon Hill, 2010), 142.

the first instance, and his authority to define sin's opposite, love, in the second. God's defining love is best revealed in his salvation of humanity on the cross, for it was love that sent God's Son into the world to suffer and die (4:10; cf. John 3:16; see "In Depth: 'Love' in John's Letters" at 4:16).

Although this biblical statement is so well known by those outside the Christian church, it is also largely, and sometimes grossly, misunderstood, for love is distorted and misunderstood in our society. Ask someone on the street what love is, and you're likely to get a variety of answers. "Love is a feeling," some may say. "Love is a commitment." "Love is a sexual relationship." "Love is sharing." "Love is an orientation." Or perhaps, "Love is an abstraction that is hard to define, but you'll know it when you see it." Proper interpretation requires allowing John to define what he means by love. Proper theology means rooting the definition in God's authority.

If all the Law and Prophets can be summed up by two commands, to love God and love others as you love yourself, then a biblical definition has to do with right behavior in relationships. How does one express love for God? John tells us that love for God means keeping his commands (5:2; 2 John 6), which involves how we treat one another (1 John 4:20–21). How we treat one another rightly is defined by Jesus' interpretation of the OT moral law, as given in Matt 5 and his self-giving demonstration of love on the cross. Thus, John presupposes that his message will be read, not using the world's definitions, but within the context of the greater biblical discussions that define love.

Note that the syntax of the Greek does not permit the terms of the statement to be reversed, as Yarbrough points out:

John does not say that love is God, a statement found nowhere in Scripture. "There have always been some who wished to apotheosize human love, but it cannot be done."... To do so would be to replace a living, personal, and active God with an intellectual, ethical, volitional, or emotional abstraction. This is the last thing that the language of 1 John, or the graphic portrayal of God incarnate in the Gospels, would permit.[4]

Furthermore, as Moberly points out,

a theoretical definition of deity in terms of a supreme human quality ... can give rise to Feuerbach's potent critique that the quality is more ultimate than the deity, and that to keep the quality, while disposing of the deity, is to hold firm to the one thing needful.[5]

This tendency to define God by human concepts of love leads directly to self-serving heresy, such as is often presented by popular spirituality. While being interviewed, a religious talk-show host mentioned a spiritual experience he once had of "what is defined by love, or oneness, or God."[6] He went on, "Ultimately, our faith and deeds give us an experience of love and connectedness. The more good we do, the more experience we have with God, or love." When asked what was his message to the audience, he replied, "We are all made of love, God is love, and *we are God*" (emphasis added).[7] This is clearly an aberrant understanding of John's teaching (cf. 4:10).

4:9 In this way God's love has been expressed among us: that God has sent his one and only Son into the world so that we might live through him (ἐν τούτῳ ἐφανερώθη ἡ ἀγάπη τοῦ θεοῦ ἐν ἡμῖν, ὅτι τὸν υἱὸν αὐτοῦ τὸν μονογενῆ ἀπέσταλκεν ὁ θεὸς εἰς τὸν κόσμον ἵνα ζήσωμεν δι᾽ αὐτοῦ). John

---

4. Yarbrough, *1–3 John*, 237, quoting Gerard S. Sloyan, *Walking in the Truth: Perseverers and Deserters: The First, Second, and Third Letters of John* (NTC; Valley Forge, PA: Trinity Press International, 1995), 45.

5. Moberly, "'Test the Spirits,'" 305–6.

6. Bob Barber, "Show Bridges Heaven and Earth," *Profiles in Faith*, *Santa Barbara News-Press*, January 3, 1998.

7. Ibid.

is the NT writer who most clearly explains how God has shown his love for humanity. Both here and in the most famous gospel verse, John 3:16, the sending of his Son to be lifted up on the cross is the supreme expression of God's love for his fallen creation. God was not obligated to seek and to save any human being, but this was the purpose of the incarnation of Christ. The wonder of God's grace is that any of us, in our willful, rebellious nature, have received the eternal life that Christ offers because of God's love (see The Theology of John's Letters).

The Son is again called the *monogenēs* (μονογενής) Son (John 1:14, 18; 3:16, 18; cf. Heb 11:17), the unique Son of God (μόνος + γένος). The traditional translation "only begotten" is a theological interpretation introduced by Jerome's Latin translation. But the original language emphasizes the uniqueness of Christ, not his begottenness. God has many children, both sons and daughters throughout history, but Jesus is not just one of them. He is unique, the *monogenēs* Son, who was with God and was God (John 1:1). And the good that came from his death was also unique, for his is the only death through which we have been given life (cf. John 17:3).

The uniqueness of Jesus Christ is foundational in Christian theology. Christianity is not based on human sacrifice, for God did not choose one of his human children to be sacrificed on behalf of the others. God's love in that case could be questioned. But God himself stepped into humanity in the person of Jesus, making Jesus a unique human being, uniquely qualified to pay the penalty for the fallen human race. God himself was willing to be sacrificed on the cross, to experience human life and death; such is his love for us. Therefore, God's love is not contingent on the circumstances of our lives. Good things may happen; bad things may

happen; but God's constant, eternal love remains unchanged because of the cross, which stands unchangeable throughout all of human history.

4:10 In this way is love [defined]: not that we have loved God, but that he loved us and sent his Son [to be] an atoning sacrifice for our sins (ἐν τούτῳ ἐστὶν ἡ ἀγάπη, οὐχ ὅτι ἡμεῖς ἠγαπήκαμεν τὸν θεόν, ἀλλ' ὅτι αὐτὸς ἠγάπησεν ἡμᾶς καὶ ἀπέστειλεν τὸν υἱὸν αὐτοῦ ἱλασμὸν περὶ τῶν ἁμαρτιῶν ἡμῶν). John must define love as it originates with God and not with human thoughts and emotions. Just as in our times, love was a word in the first century with many different definitions and connotations, so to be sure his readers don't misunderstand, John defines the love he is talking about. (Note the anaphoric article, referring to love as it was mentioned in vv. 7 – 9.) Here, John says, is the true origin of love: God himself.

Human history has witnessed many things motivated by love for God, some of them horrendous acts of evil. Even the most pure and well-intentioned "love" for God that has its origin in only human emotions and sentiments is not the kind of love of which John speaks. In 4:8, John has already stated that "God is love," and in 4:9 that God's love motivated the incarnation of Jesus Christ, so that "we might live through him." Here, he restates that true love is the love that originates with God himself, not whatever might pass for love by human origin and definition. The kind of love of which John speaks does *not* have its origin within the human being but is from God's Spirit.

In the double accusative "his Son an atoning sacrifice" (τὸν υἱὸν αὐτοῦ ἱλασμόν), *hilasmon* functions as a predicate nominative.[8] God's love for the human race focuses on the problem of sin and our need for redemption. Although the word translated "atoning sacrifice" (*hilasmos*) is found in the NT

---

8. Wallace, *Greek Grammar*, 185 n33.

only here and in 1 John 2:2 (see comments there), the cognate verb *hilaskomai* is found in the LXX, where it means to forgive people their sins (Exod 32:14; Deut 21:8; 2 Kgs 5:18; 24:4; 2 Chr 6:30; Pss 25:11; 65:3; 78:38; 79:9; Lam 3:42). In the NT this verb occurs but twice — in Luke 18:13 and Heb 2:17. In the first case, it is in an appeal to God for forgiveness (ἱλάσθητί μοι); in the second it is in a description of the work of Jesus the high priest, to make atonement for sin.

Forgiveness of sin is at the heart of atonement and is the clearest expression of God's love. We cannot truly love God or others until we have received God's redemptive love offered in Christ, the forgiveness of our sin based on the atoning sacrifice of Jesus Christ himself (see "In Depth: 'Love' in John's Letters" at 4:16).

Verses 9 and 10 exhibit a parallelism centered on the topic of God's love (see Structure, above). Commenting on redemption in 1 John, Lyonnet writes:

> It can be seen at once, not only how intimately the notion of Christ-*hilasmos* is connected with the love of God the Father, but also how strictly parallel the statements in v. 9b and v. 10b are, so that the phrase "*hilasmos* for our sins" accurately corresponds to the phrase "that we may live through him...."[9]

This is consistent with the use of this word in 2:2. The sending of God's Son is stated in each verse to be the expression of God's love. In 4:9, the purpose/result of the sending (*hina* clause) is that we may live through Christ. In v. 10, the sending of the Son is to be the atoning sacrifice for our sins. The parallel indicates that it is the atonement for sins that achieves God's loving purpose of eternal life for his people. Genuine, pure human love derives from God's love, a love that sent the Son to be

an atoning sacrifice for our sins. Having received *that* love from God, a person can then love God and love others truly (see The Theology of John's Letters).

4:11 Dear friends, if God loved us like this, we also ought to love one another (Ἀγαπητοί, εἰ οὕτως ὁ θεὸς ἠγάπησεν ἡμᾶς, καὶ ἡμεῖς ὀφείλομεν ἀλλήλους ἀγαπᾶν). God's love for his people forms the basis of our love for one another.

Verse 11 forms a nearly chiastic inclusio with v. 7:

A Dear friends,
 B let us love one another,
  C because love is of God.

A′ Dear friends,
  C′ if God loved us like this,
 B′ we also ought to love one another.

The first class condition of fact assumes God's love for his people as the basis of our love for one another. But if the definition of love is revealed in Christ's atoning sacrifice of himself on the cross, how can we love one another in any similar way? To answer this question, note that God's love focused its action on our greatest need, and the achievement of such love secured the reconciliation of our relationship with him. Similarly, our love for others should recognize their needs, and we should seek to maintain a right relationship with them.

Recall Jesus' discussion of the command to love one's neighbor as oneself in the parable of the good Samaritan (Luke 10:25 – 37), in which he defines both "neighbor" and "love." The command to love is not a demand for forced intimacy or shallow sentimentality. It is a command to meet the needs of others when we encounter them. To act with redemptive love toward others means to forgive

---

9. Lyonnet, *Sin, Redemption, and Sacrifice*, 154.

those who need our forgiveness, just as God forgave us in Christ. It means to spend our time and money (i.e., lay down our lives) meeting the needs of others. In certain rare and extreme instances, it may mean actually giving our lives so that others may live (see comments on 3:16 – 18).

4:12 No one has ever seen God. If we love one another, God lives in us, and his love is completed in us (θεὸν οὐδεὶς πώποτε τεθέαται. ἐὰν ἀγαπῶμεν ἀλλήλους, ὁ θεὸς ἐν ἡμῖν μένει καὶ ἡ ἀγάπη αὐτοῦ ἐν ἡμῖν τετελειωμένη ἐστίν). John now reminds his readers of the theme of God's revelation of himself in Christ by repeating almost verbatim a statement found in John 1:18. In that text, the unique God, the Son Jesus Christ, who is closest to the Father, has made God known. And the center of that revelation of God is his love for fallen human beings that on the cross provided the cure for our fatal sinfulness.

Here in 1 John 4:12, it is the Christians' love for one another, derived from God's love for us, that is revelatory. As Lieu points out, "If God is love, it follows that love is a, perhaps *the*, mode of divine presence."[10] The invisibility of God is a major premise of the Johannine books (cf. John 1:18), but God is revealed in human expression, first and most supremely in Jesus (1:18; 5:37; 6:46), and second in the quality of Christians' relationships with others.

One might expect the statement "if we love God, then God remains in us," so it is somewhat surprising to read instead, "if we love *one another*, God lives in us." A similar surprise was found in 1:6, where John explains that the one who walks in darkness cannot have fellowship with God. He then states the converse, "But if we walk in the light … we have fellowship with *one another* …" (italics added), exactly where we would expect to find "fellowship with God" instead.

Because God is invisible in the material world we inhabit, how does one express love for God and have fellowship with him? We can't hug him or send him a nice Valentine on February 14. Consistently the NT speaks of love for God in terms of relationship with his people, as we gather *together* for worship, as we pray *for one another*, as we take Holy Communion *together*. Although Christianity in North America has a very "Jesus-and-me" quality, the NT writers did not conceive of an independent, maverick Christian (cf. 1 Pet 2:4 – 5). Even the OT commands that stipulated obedience to God were largely commands concerning how to treat others (Exod 20:12 – 17; Deut 5:16 – 21). Biblically defined love for others is our appropriate expression of love for God. When Christians love others as God defines love, God remains in us making his presence known, and his love is completed in us (ἡ ἀγάπη αὐτοῦ ἐν ἡμῖν τετελειωμένη ἐστίν).

Three questions arise here. (1) Does "in us" mean collectively as God's people (i.e., "among us") or in each believer individually? (2) Is "his love" (ἡ ἀγάπη αὐτοῦ) objective (i.e., one's love for God) or subjective (i.e., God's love for us)? (3) What does it mean that such love "is completed" (τετελειωμένη ἐστίν)? (See further discussion of this verb in comments on 2:5 and 4:17.)

(1) All throughout the NT, the prepositional phrase "in us" (ἐν ἡμῖν) presents a certain ambiguity when it refers to Christian believers. But in many (most? all?) instances, the difference between the collective sense and the individual is not great or significant. Collectively, the Christian church is made up of individual believers, those who have come to like-minded faith in Christ and have been born anew by the Spirit who dwells within them individually. Therefore, because the collective is composed only and exhaustively of the individual

---

10. Lieu, *I, II, & III John*, 185 (italics original).

believers, there is arguably little difference between "in us" and "among us."

(2) The answer to the question of whether "his love" is objective[11] or subjective[12] is found in the way John defines love between God and his people as reciprocal in nature. Some interpreters consider a third sense, taking the genitive as one of quality that refers to God's kind of love, and then conclude that all three senses are present in this verse.[13] That is, we love because God first loved us (4:19, see below). But God has deemed it necessary that we express our love for him in the act of loving other human beings with a love that derives from the kind of love he has shown for us in Christ.

(3) Such love "is completed" (τετελειωμένη ἐστίν), or has been brought to its intended goal and fullest form (note perfect tense), when we love others. It is through human beings that God's love "finds its fulfilment on earth."[14] If we note that the same verb is used in 2:5 with reference to the love of God, these two verses are mutually interpretive, suggesting a subjective genitive as the answer to the second question. Therefore, John is saying that God's love for us reaches its intended completion or goal when we in turn express love for others, completing the reciprocity between God and his people.[15]

4:13 In this way we know that in him we live and he in us: because he has given to us of his Spirit (Ἐν τούτῳ γινώσκομεν ὅτι ἐν αὐτῷ μένομεν καὶ αὐτὸς ἐν ἡμῖν, ὅτι ἐκ τοῦ πνεύματος αὐτοῦ δέδωκεν ἡμῖν). John introduces the role of the Holy Spirit as evidence of God's presence in the believer's life. The invocation of the Spirit here is the basis on which a Christian knows that he or she is right with God and shows that Christian love is motivated by the Spirit, not by sentimental human emotion. The

next verse concerns the Christian testimony that God sent his Son to be the Savior of the world. This flow of thought closely follows John 17:18 – 26 (italics added):

> John 17:18: "As *you sent me* into the world, *I have sent them* into the world."
>
> John 17:21: "… that all of them may be one, Father, just as you are in me and I am in you. May they also *be in us* so that the world may believe that you have sent me."
>
> John 17:26: "I have made you known to them … in order that *the love you have for me may be in them*."

Christian love is the expression of us being in God (who is love) and him in us. That unity also has an evangelistic and revelatory purpose so that the world might see the presence of God's love in Christ. The Spirit is the assurance of God's presence in us and us in him. As Kruse asks:

> When the author introduces the giving of the Spirit as the ground of assurance in 4:13, is he implying: (a) that the Spirit motivates love for fellow believers and the objective practice of love is the basis of their assurance; or (b) that the Spirit teaches the truth about God's sending Jesus as the Saviour of the world and knowing this provides believers with the basis of assurance; or (c) that the very presence of the Spirit himself in believers creates the sense of assurance?[16]

While there may be truth to all three options, the third can be a matter of dispute and is likely to have been involved in the schism mentioned in 2:19. People may sincerely claim to have the Spirit, but what is the objective basis of such a claim, especially when serious differences between professing Christians with the same claim arise?

The first option may be the tangible expression

---

11. E.g., Dodd, *Johannine Epistles*, 113.
12. E.g., Strecker, *Johannine Letters*, 157.
13. Marshall, *Epistles of John*, 217; Smalley, *1, 2, 3 John*, 49.
14. Westcott, *Epistles of St. John*, 152.
15. Smalley, *1, 2, 3 John*, 248.
16. Kruse, *Letters of John*, 163.

of the Spirit's presence, but many good people who are not believers can do loving things quite apart from the Spirit's presence in them.

The second option is likely John's point, when compared with the similar statement in 3:24, "And the one who keeps his commands remains in him [God], and he himself in them; and in this way we know that he remains in us: from the Spirit, whom he gave to us." "The one who keeps his commands" corresponds to the exhortation to love one another (see 4:11 – 12), and both are followed by similar statements, "in this way we know that he remains in us" (3:24; cf. 4:13). The next verse after 3:24 (i.e., 4:1) concerns revelation and the discerning of spirits that led into this discussion about love. How is the Spirit of truth discerned from the spirit of error? The Spirit of truth acknowledges that Jesus Christ has come in the flesh, which is the objective ground of salvation and the basis for reassurance. Therefore, 3:24 and 4:13 form an inclusio and indicate, as Kruse points out,

> that the Spirit teaches the truth about God's sending Jesus as the Saviour of the world and knowing this provides believers with the basis of assurance.... It is neither the very presence of the Spirit nor the activity of the Spirit producing love for fellow believers that the author has in mind here, but rather the Spirit as witness to the truth about Jesus proclaimed by the eyewitnesses.[17]

The Spirit provides inner testimony of the truth that God's love is not expressed in some generic spiritual truth, as seems likely the secessionists were teaching, but in the sending of the Son to be the Savior of the world because he is the atoning sacrifice for our sins. Belief in that testimony provides the assurance that one remains in God and he in them.

4:14 And we have beheld and testify that the Father sent his Son [to be] the Savior of the world (καὶ ἡμεῖς τεθεάμεθα καὶ μαρτυροῦμεν ὅτι ὁ πατὴρ ἀπέσταλκεν τὸν υἱὸν σωτῆρα τοῦ κόσμου). With this verse the author returns to his role as a witness by echoing 1:1 – 4, with which he opened the letter with the topic of the source of authoritative truth about eternal life. This statement affirms that the author considers himself the bearer of spiritual truth, a truth that is not relativized by one's nationality, ethnicity, or philosophy. Because the Son is the only Savior for *all* the people of the world (2:1 – 2), any claim to spiritual truth not based on Christ's atoning death is false and cannot form the basis of assurance about eternal life.

4:15 Whoever acknowledges that Jesus is the Son of God — God lives in them and they live in God (ὃς ἐὰν ὁμολογήσῃ ὅτι Ἰησοῦς ἐστιν ὁ υἱὸς τοῦ θεοῦ, ὁ θεὸς ἐν αὐτῷ μένει καὶ αὐτὸς ἐν τῷ θεῷ). The subjective presence of love and the Spirit in the believer's life is brought back to the objective basis of the incarnation of God in Christ. Because love for one another is based on the revelation of God's love expressed on the cross of Jesus Christ, it is the one who acknowledges that revealed truth who has been reconciled to God. Fellowship with God would not be possible without the historical fact of the incarnation.

However, it is not sufficient to believe in the historical Jesus; one must also believe that the man Jesus was the Son of God whom the Father sent to atone for sin. Mutual indwelling of God in the believer and the believer in God echoes John's gospel, where the verb "remain" (μένω) occurs dozens of times in reference to the intimate relationship between the three members of the Trinity (e.g., John 1:32, 33; 14:10; 15:10). Believers in Christ have the privilege of entering into a fellowship with God

---

17. Ibid.

(1 John 1:3; cf. John 12:46; 14:17; 15:4–7). The idea of living or abiding with God stands behind the promise of having a place in the Father's house, which is a reference to eternal life (John 14:2, 23; see The Theology of John's Letters).

The chiastic structure gives a memorable quality to the promise:

ὁ θεὸς ἐν αὐτῷ μένει *God* in them [sing.] abides
καὶ αὐτὸς ἐν τῷ θεῷ and they [sing.] abide in *God*

4:16 And we have known and have trusted the love that God has for us. God is love and the one who lives in that love lives in God, and God lives in them (καὶ ἡμεῖς ἐγνώκαμεν καὶ πεπιστεύκαμεν τὴν ἀγάπην ἣν ἔχει ὁ θεὸς ἐν ἡμῖν. Ὁ θεὸς ἀγάπη ἐστίν, καὶ ὁ μένων ἐν τῇ ἀγάπῃ ἐν τῷ θεῷ μένει καὶ ὁ θεὸς ἐν αὐτῷ μένει). Faith in the atoning death of Jesus Christ is faith in God's love for us. The one who lives in that atoning love is alive in God. In this statement John brings love, faith, and atonement for sin together in his readers' thoughts.

Verses 14 and 16 have parallel structures:

v. 14	καὶ ἡμεῖς τεθεάμεθα καὶ μαρτυροῦμεν
	A And we have beheld and testify
	ὅτι ὁ πατὴρ ἀπέσταλκεν τὸν υἱὸν σωτῆρα τοῦ κόσμου
	B that the Father sent his Son [to be] the Savior of the world.
v. 16	καὶ ἡμεῖς ἐγνώκαμεν καὶ πεπιστεύκαμεν
	A′ And we have known and have trusted
	τὴν ἀγάπην ἣν ἔχει ὁ θεὸς ἐν ἡμῖν
	B′ the love that God has for us.

This parallel reinforces the thought that the sending of the Son as Savior is the expression of God's love for us. Seeing that truth leads to testifying to it; knowing that truth calls us to trust in it. Only by trusting in God's atoning love do we have assurance of eternal life in fellowship with God.

John repeats the statement that "God is love," first mentioned in 4:8b in reference to the one who does not love and therefore does not know God. As Brown observes, the first statement that "God is love" in 4:8 reveals the motive for the sending of the Son, and this second occurrence "stresses the result (divine abiding) in the Christian."[18] Here the statement is the ground for one to remain in that love (note anaphoric article pointing back to 4:8b), and by doing so, remain in God. The one who remains in God's love, expressed on the cross of Jesus, stands in contrast to "the one who does not love" and thereby demonstrates that they do not know God (4:8a), and that they have not been born of God (4:7). A person's love — for God and for others — is anchored in the cross of Jesus.

IN DEPTH: "Love" in John's Letters

John's definition of love is anchored in God's nature ("God is love," 4:8, 16), just as his definition of morality is similarly grounded in the statement that "God is light" (see comments on 1:5). These statements imply an essential theological

18. Brown, *Epistles of John*, 560.

point, that God is God and human beings are not. Definitions of human love and morality cannot originate from human thinking apart from God, for it is only God himself who by his nature is qualified to define such foundational truth.

As Brown observes, the statement that "God is love" is not equivalent to the statement "God loves," for "loving is not just another action of God, like ruling. Rather, all God's activity is loving activity."[19] Therefore, even God's judgment and punitive actions are subsumed by his loving nature. This is why the atoning sacrifice of Jesus Christ on the cross is where God's love for humanity is most clearly expressed, for it is where love unites the demands of both God's justice and his mercy (3:16). John teaches that anyone who refuses God's love as expressed in the atoning sacrifice of Jesus cannot possibly know God truly (4:16).

Therefore, the statement that "God is love" also argues against many of the concepts of God's nature popular in religious thought today, for "God is not pictured as a wrathful judge, a nitpicking accountant, or an avenger lying in wait. Rather, God is represented as generous, self-giving, and compassionate."[20] This depiction of God in John's letters requires an understanding of God as a personal being, not merely a "higher power" or an apotheosis of a humanly defined abstraction called "love." Moreover, as Luther wrote, "These are simple words, but they are words that require faith in the highest degree — faith against which everything that is not of the Spirit of God fights. Conscience, the devil, hell, the judgment of God, and everything resist, in order that we may not believe that God is love."[21]

Yarbrough points out, "No trait is more inherent to God as depicted in 1 John than the active will to love."[22] And in this second occurrence of the statement "God is love," John is stressing God's nature as the reason Christians must love others if they are to "remain in God." As a communicable attribute of God, God's indwelling love in the life of the believer causes him or her to love others, that is, to live with others by the moral standard of God's light, for the opposite of love is sin. When a person is born again as a child of the Father, the Father's traits become increasingly apparent in that person's life. If God is generous, self-giving, and compassionate, those who claim to know him as their Father must also be. The children of God must love as God loves.

---

19. Ibid., 515.
20. Schuchard, *1–3 John*, 445–46.

21. *Luther's Works* (American edition; St. Louis: Concordia, 1955–), 30:301, quoted in Schuchard, *1–3 John*, 485.
22. Yarbrough, *1–3 John*, 237.

Theology in Application

God, Love, and Sacrifice

Three major points are clear in this passage: (1) God is the only one who has the authority to define what "love" is. (2) God's love for us is supremely expressed on the cross of Jesus Christ. (3) There can be no genuine love for God or for others that is not anchored in one's faith in the atoning cross of Jesus. As Jonathan Wilson observes:

> As we enter that kingdom [of God], we enter into a salvation that is also the way *of love*. Love is a terribly debased term today, almost beyond rescue as a description of the good news of the kingdom come in Jesus Christ. However, the New Testament is full of the language of love, particularly as Christ exemplifies God's love and enables that same love in us. Therefore, we must work to recover an understanding and practice of love.[23]

Poets write about it, singers sing about, greeting cards convey the sentiment of love. But our world is full of whacky, irresponsible, and even perverse definitions of love that are used to rationalize selfishness, manipulate others, and even give evil free rein in the name of love. Because of our sinful, fallen human nature, we have lost the ability to define, much less practice, love as we were created to do. And so the NT closely associates love for God with morality. As both creator and judge, God gets to define love and to stipulate how it is to be practiced. But his definition is so unlike the world's that those who prefer their own, more self-serving definition often reject it.

When taken without God's definition of love, John's statement that "everyone who loves has been begotten of God and ... knows God" (4:7) is inevitably misused to justify just about anything the human heart can imagine, because the world is full of counterfeit love. People attempt to justify illicit romantic relationships and homosexual relationships in the name of a "love" that is defined by merely human emotions and ideas, even as powerful as those may be. Parents and spouses may confuse a need to control with love. Some may attempt to justify euthanasia or abortion by some false definition of love. But love is the opposite of sin, and anything practiced that the Bible defines as sin cannot be authentic love.

The violent death of a man executed as a seditious criminal would be the last place one would expect to see a demonstration of love, but that is exactly where the NT locates it. Such love is not based on human motives or emotions, but finds its impetus in the merciful heart of the creator God, who would rather submit to earthly horrors himself than condemn his beloved human race to perish. The cross of Jesus Christ is God's love extended across the chasm that stranded us on hell's side, separated from God and trapped in our sin. There is no other bridge by which we can

---

23. Wilson, *For God So Loved the World*, 131 (italics original).

cross over from death into life (John 5:24). It is only being cleansed from our sin that allows us to be reconciled to God and relate rightly to one another. The word God uses to describe relating rightly to others is "love."

Is God Loving?

People can experience many horrible things in life, leading both Christians and unbelievers to question God's love. How could a loving God let such horrible things happen as we see continually in the daily news? Without diminishing the reality of pain and suffering, John's answer would be that God has already loved each of us to the fullest extent by providing that crossover from death to life. For death is the worst this life can bring against us, but when this life has been swallowed up by eternal life, even the worst is not our defeat. Because God's fullest love has already been given in Christ more than two thousand years ago, it is not based on what we do or what others do to us. What greater gift of love could God give than freedom from death? (See The Theology of John's Letters.)

When someone has experienced freedom from sin and freedom from death, they are able to love God and others as God intended. This is because love will not allow us to sin against others, for love is the opposite of sin. And when sinned against, we are enabled to forgive others because our Lord Jesus has atoned for that sin. We can reveal God's forgiveness and love to the offender through our forgiveness.

1 John 4:17 – 5:3

Literary Context

This pericope continues the discussion that began in 4:7 on how love for others expresses love for God. It provides a theological basis for this argument and ties the topic to eschatology by (1) pointing to the believer's confidence to face the coming day of judgment without fear (4:17 – 18), (2) explaining that it is impossible to love God without loving fellow believers (4:19 – 21), and (3) showing how having been born of God through faith in Christ entails the command to love others who have also been reborn (5:1 – 2).

XII. God's Love Expressed (4:7 – 16)

→ **XIII. God's Love Perfected in the Believer (4:17 – 5:3)**
   A. God's Love Perfected in the Believer Produces Confidence to Face the Coming Day of Judgment (4:17 – 18)
   B. The Believer's Love for God Is Demonstrated through Love for One Another (4:19 – 21)
   C. What the New Birth through Faith in Christ Produces (5:1 – 3)
XIV. The Blood, Eternal Life, and Assurance (5:4 – 13)

Main Idea

John presents the theological basis for the command that Christians are to love one another by building on his argument in 4:9 – 10 that God's love for us is best displayed in the atonement of the cross of his Son, Jesus Christ. When God's atoning love has fully reached its goal in a believer's life, it produces two results: (1) they will rest in the assurance that they have nothing to fear in the coming judgment; (2) God's transforming love enables believers to love others, which fulfills the command to love God. Being reborn through faith in Christ entails loving others who share such faith.

Translation

1 John 4:17 – 5:3

17a assertion — **In this way God's love has been perfected with us,**
b result — with the result that we may have confidence in the day of judgment,
c basis — because just as that One is,
d expansion — we also are in this world.

18a assertion — **There is no fear in God's love;**
b contrast — rather, **his love that has been perfected [in us] casts out fear,**
c basis of 18b — because fear implies punishment,

d inference — and **the one who fears has not reached the goal of God's love.**

19 assertion — **We love** because he first loved us.

20a condition — If anyone says, "I love God" and hates his brother or sister,

b inference — **they are a liar.**
c basis — For **the one**
         who does not love the brother or sister whom they have seen

d inference — **. . . is not able to love** the God whom they have not seen.

21a assertion — **And this is the command from him:**
b content — that the one who loves God must also love their brother or sister.

5:1a assertion — **Everyone who believes**
b content — that Jesus is the Christ
         . . . has been born of God.

c assertion — And **everyone who loves the Father loves his child as well.**

2a identification — **So this is how we know that we love the children of God:**
b explanation — when we love God and
c — do his commands.

3a basis — For **this is the love of God:**
b explanation — that we keep his commands,

c expansion — and **his commands are not burdensome.**

Structure

This passage is composed of three parts, 4:17 – 18; 4:19 – 21; and 5:1 – 3. John first explains the goal of God's ongoing love in the believer's life with respect to the future judgment; he then goes on to explain that love for God entails love for others. The prepositional phrase in 4:17, "in this way" (ἐν τούτῳ), links this pericope to the previous statement in 4:16, that the one who remains in God's love remains in God and therefore has eternal life. "In this way," by remaining in God's love, which is centered on the atoning death of Jesus, "we" have confidence to face the coming day of judgment without fear.

The second part of the passage shows that Christian love for others is derived from God's love, and that it is impossible to love God genuinely without loving other believers.

At first glance it may seem that John has moved to a new topic of faith and new birth in 5:1, especially since the discussion of faith continues in 5:3 and following. But the second part of 5:1 concerns love for those born of God and brings the discussion of love begun in 4:7 to its conclusion. This is a good example of how tightly braided John's topics are, such that janus verses like this stand between two related topics.

Exegetical Outline

→ **XIII. God's Love Perfected in the Believer (4:17 – 5:3)**

    A. God's love perfected in the believer produces confidence to face the coming day of judgment (4:17 – 18)

        1. Only by the believer's remaining in God's love can God's love for the believer reach its culmination (4:17a-d)

           a. When God's love is perfected in the believer, confidence results (4:17a-b)

           b. When God's love is perfected in the believer, he or she is like Jesus (4:17c-d)

        2. Perfected love casts out the fear of punishment (4:18)

    B. The believer's love for God is demonstrated through love for one another (4:19 – 21)

        1. Christian love derives from God's love (4:19)

        2. One cannot love God and not love others (4:20)

        3. Love for God entails love for others (4:21)

    C. What the new birth through faith in Christ produces (5:1 – 3)

        1. Love for others who have been reborn (5:1)

        2. Love for God by keeping his commands (5:2)

        3. Love for God defined: keep his commands (5:3)

Explanation of the Text

4:17 In this way God's love has been perfected with us, with the result that we may have confidence in the day of judgment, because just as that One is, we also are in this world (Ἐν τούτῳ τετελείωται ἡ ἀγάπη μεθ’ ἡμῶν, ἵνα παρρησίαν ἔχωμεν ἐν τῇ ἡμέρᾳ τῆς κρίσεως, ὅτι καθὼς ἐκεῖνός ἐστιν καὶ ἡμεῖς ἐσμεν ἐν τῷ κόσμῳ τούτῳ). John explains that God's love has a transforming purpose in the life of the believer that allows Christians to face God's judgment with confidence.

Some interpreters take the phrase "in this way" (ἐν τούτῳ) to point forward to the *hina* clause,[1] but it is preferable to understand it as pointing backward to the statement just made, because it then mirrors the thought in v. 12.[2] The anaphoric article, "the love" (ἡ ἀγάπη), points backward and indicates that the love in view is that just previously mentioned in v. 16. Mutual love — God's for the believer and the believer's for God — comes to its fullest realization when a believer looks toward the day of judgment with confidence. This coheres with John's purpose to reassure his readers that they do in fact have eternal life because of their right belief in Jesus.

The preposition "with" (μεθ’), where one might expect "in" (ἐν), emphasizes the communal nature of this love and reminds readers of John's desire that they remain in God's love in Christ to enjoy fellowship with "us" (1:3).[3] The perfect passive verb (τετελείωται) is a divine passive; "God's direct and transformative presence" in the community brings his love to its goal (see comments on this verb at 2:5 and 4:12).[4] God loves us by sending his Son as an atoning sacrifice for our sin so that we might

not perish but have eternal life (John 3:16). When that love has completed its work in our lives, we are freed from fear of death and can stand confidently before God's judgment, washed clean in Jesus' blood (cf. Heb 2:14 – 18). John has previously stated the same thought in 2:28, "And now, children, remain in him, so that when he appears, we might have confidence and not be shamed away from him whenever he comes."

It is difficult to see at first how the remainder of the verse, "just as that One is, we also are in this world," logically functions. The demonstrative pronoun translated "that One" (ἐκεῖνος) is used often in John's writings where one might expect a personal pronoun, and it often refers to God or Jesus. Here it almost certainly refers to Jesus because the phrase "in the world" suggests the human presence of the Son (cf. 2:6; 3:5, 16; John 1:18). Clearly John is presenting an analogy between "we are in this world" and "that One is," perhaps with the prepositional phrase "in the world" to be understood. The variant reading here in NA 27 (but omitted from NA28) reflects an interpolation that takes this to be an analogy between how Jesus "was in the world blameless and pure" and how "we" are to be in this world. By this understanding, the analogy is to the mode of being. Ben Witherington understands the analogy to be showing "no fear in the face of judgment or punishment." He observes, "If there was ever a person who walked this earth in whom love was perfected and fear was banished, it was Jesus."[5] Kruse lists three representative interpretations:[6]

(1) Christ has retained in heaven the characteristic he had on earth and is

---

1. E.g., NIV 2011; Bultmann, *Johannine Epistles*, 72; Culy, *I, II, III John*, 115 – 16; Smalley, *1, 2, 3 John*, 233.

2. As Lieu, *I, II, & III John*, 193; Marshall, *Epistles of John*, 223; Yarbrough, *1 – 3 John*, 257; Burge, *Letters of John*, 189; Westcott, *Epistles of St. John*, 157.

3. Lieu, *I, II, & III John*, 193.

4. Yarbrough, *1 – 3 John*, 259.

5. Witherington, *Socio-Rhetorical*, 536.

6. Kruse, *Letters of John*, 167 – 68.

still a pattern for his followers on earth (Schnackenburg).

(2) Believers are children of God just as Christ is the Son of God, and because Christ is the Judge, believers need not fear (Brown).

(3) Believers in this world who love as Christ loved his disciples show that they live in God and need not fear judgment (Kruse).

Brown points out that the various interpretations of this statement fall into three categories: Christ's incarnate human status, his moral life, and his love for others; but he rejects all such analogies with the "terrestrial" Christ because he takes "in this world" to describe us but not Christ: "The logic of the statement is that since we are already like Christ, we shall not be judged harshly."[7] Smalley offers perhaps the best understanding by linking this text with the Farewell Discourse in John's gospel, which does seem to underlie the letter.[8] He understands John to be saying that "the relationship of believers to God in the world can and should reflect that of Jesus to God (as it was on earth, and as it still *is* in heaven: this includes the Son's own 'confidence' before God)" (italics original). He paraphrases v. 17, "As he [Jesus] is (in the Father's love), so we are (in him, and therefore in the Father's love) in the world (obediently making God's love known)."[9]

4:18 There is no fear in God's love; rather, his love that has been perfected [in us] casts out fear, because fear implies punishment, and the one who fears has not reached the goal of God's love (φόβος οὐκ ἔστιν ἐν τῇ ἀγάπῃ, ἀλλ᾽ ἡ τελεία ἀγάπη ἔξω βάλλει τὸν φόβον, ὅτι ὁ φόβος κόλασιν ἔχει, ὁ δὲ φοβούμενος οὐ τετελείωται ἐν τῇ ἀγάπῃ). If God's love for us is most clearly expressed in the atoning death of Jesus to cleanse us from our sins and free

us from fear of God's judgment, then there is nothing left for us to fear once we have fully comprehended God's love for us. (Note that the anaphoric article "in *the* love" [ἐν τῇ ἀγάπῃ] indicates the love in view is the same love mentioned in vv. 16 – 17; see comments on 2:5 and 4:12 for discussion of the perfect tense verb.)

John points out that fear implicitly entails a fear of punishment or suffering related to the object of fear. A fear of water implies a fear of drowning. A fear of fire implies a fear of being burned. A fear of God's judgment implies a fear of punishment. Note that the only other occurrence of "punishment" (κόλασιν) is found in the eschatological context of Matt 25:46, where the Master condemns the goats to "eternal punishment [κόλασιν]." But if God so loved the world that he sent his unique Son to deliver the world from perishing (cf. John 3:16), the punishment has already been meted out to Jesus Christ on our behalf. The mission of God's redeeming love is completed in a believer's life only when they realize fully that there is nothing of eternal condemnation left to fear. As Yarbrough puts it, "There is no fear of estrangement from God in the love that by definition establishes intimacy with God."[10]

4:19 We love because he first loved us (ἡμεῖς ἀγαπῶμεν, ὅτι αὐτὸς πρῶτος ἠγάπησεν ἡμᾶς). God's love for us is the source of all genuine human love for God and others. Both as Creator and Redeemer, God has taken the initiative.

Some people are quick to condemn God for all the evil in the world, doubting either his goodness or his ability to do anything about evil. But the greater question is perhaps where do love, beauty, and joy come from? Theologians may debate whether love is an attribute of the character of God

---

7. Brown, *Epistles of John*, 529.

8. Smalley, *1, 2, 3 John*, 258 – 59. See also Yarid, "Reflections of the Upper Room Discourse," 65 – 76.

9. Smalley, *1, 2, 3 John*, 259.

10. Yarbrough, *1 – 3 John*, 262.

in distinction from his other attributes, or whether love is actually the sum of God's attributes, but John is clear that God's love precedes human love. To whatever extent the world's counterfeit "loves" intersect true love as God defines it, it is because of God's common grace at work.

All human love is distorted by our fallen nature, such that no one can truly love God or others as we ought. It is only when a person comes to Christ and begins to realize the extent and nature of God's love that their ability to love rightly can be transformed by the work of the Spirit. To whatever extent the Christian community achieves and enjoys genuine love, it is only because God first extended his cross-shaped love to the human race.

4:20 If anyone says, "I love God" and hates his brother or sister, they are a liar. For the one who does not love the brother or sister whom they have seen is not able to love the God whom they have not seen (ἐάν τις εἴπη ὅτι ἀγαπῶ τὸν θεόν, καὶ τὸν ἀδελφὸν αὐτοῦ μισῇ, ψεύστης ἐστίν· ὁ γὰρ μὴ ἀγαπῶν τὸν ἀδελφὸν αὐτοῦ ὃν ἑώρακεν, τὸν θεὸν ὃν οὐχ ἑώρακεν οὐ δύναται ἀγαπᾶν). Here John comes full circle in his discussion of love, especially for fellow believers ("brother or sister"), that he introduced back in chapter 2 and picked up again in chapter 3:

> 2:9 – 11: The one who says, "I am in the light" and hates their brother or sister is still in the darkness. The one who loves their brother or sister remains in the light and does not entice them. The one who hates their brother or sister is in the darkness and walks in the darkness.

> 3:10: In this way the children of God and the children of the devil are distinguished: Everyone who does not do what is right is not of God, even the one who does not love their brother and sister.

> 3:14 – 17: We know that we have crossed over from death into life because we love the brothers and sisters. The one who does not love remains in death. Everyone who hates their brother or sister is a killer, and we know that no killer has eternal life abiding in them. In this way we have known love, because that One laid down his life on our behalf. And [so] we ought to lay down [our] lives on behalf of the brothers and sisters. Whoever has the resources necessary for living and sees his brother or sister has a need, and shuts their heart to them, how does the love of God remain in them?

The command to love God was long-standing in the Jewish faith from which Christianity emerged. Ancient Israel's foremost command was the Shema, "Love the Lord your God with all your heart and with all your soul and with all your strength" (Deut 6:5). Such love for God was coupled with obedience to the covenant, which included treating others rightly, both fellow Israelites and foreigners. John's argument is similar: love for God must be constituted by love for others, particularly fellow believers.

The premise that God is unseen is part of John's argument that the failure to love the brother or sister who is in front of our eyes prevents our ability to love God. Some interpreters take this as an argument from the easier to the harder case on the premise that it is easier to love another person who is present than to love God, who is intangible and invisible.[11] After all, one can send a Valentine to or hug a person, but not even FTD delivers flowers to God. Or, as Calvin explains, "It is a false boast when anyone says that he loves God but neglects his image which is before his eyes."[12] So how are human beings to express love for God? What can we give him? Anyone who has lived within the

---

11. E.g., John Stott, *The Epistles of John* (TNTC; Grand Rapids: Eerdmans, 1964), 171.

12. Calvin, *St. John 11 – 21 and the First Epistle of John.*

church for any length of time could dispute the premise of how much easier it is to love people than God, but that is probably not John's point.

Others understand the argument to mean that since God is invisible, there is no way to know if someone loves him or not, but a relationship with another person can be easily observed and evaluated.[13] This argument also seems vulnerable, since there *is* observable behavior that can express love for God, such as not taking his name in vain, attending worship, praying, and the like. Furthermore, even outward behavior both toward others and toward God can be equally tainted by impure motives.

Perhaps there is another thread to John's thought related to the revelation of God in Christ. The unseenness of God is overcome by the incarnation of Christ, who has come for the very purpose of revealing God (John 1:18). Perhaps the idea in the present verse is that the one who does not love their Christian brother or sister is not able to love God apart from his visible manifestation in Jesus Christ; that is, only a believing Christian can genuinely love the one true God. Therefore, love for the unseen God must be defined by the Christian gospel, which, as John will say in v. 21, means that one must love others.

John has argued sufficiently about the origin of love in God's redemptive purposes, the self-sacrificing nature of God's love in Christ, and the transformation of the believer's love by the Spirit to now conclude in v. 20 that a profession of love for God is an empty lie if love for fellow believers is absent. In other words, a failure to love others means that a person has failed to see the God who is revealed in Jesus Christ and therefore is unable to love God at all. In this way, love for God is identified with the knowledge of Christ.

Conversely, love for others is empty if not derived from love for God in Christ. Because human love derives from God's love, the two are inextricably joined. As D. Smith puts it, "The gospel cannot be reduced to a kind of benign humanism with a horizontal, but no vertical, direction. Our love for each other is beautiful, ennobling, but ringed with sadness and ultimately tragic apart from love of God."[14]

If genuine love for others is supremely based in God's redeeming love, then in addition to caring for the needs of the community (3:14 – 17), no word or deed is loving that puts an obstacle in the way of others knowing the true value of the cross of Jesus (2:10). Although John may not be directly addressing the "antichrists," who left the congregation (2:19), his explanation of genuine love condemns anyone who would profess to know and love God but then teaches something other than the atoning cross of Jesus as its basis.

4:21 And this is the command from him: that the one who loves God must also love their brother or sister (καὶ ταύτην τὴν ἐντολὴν ἔχομεν ἀπ' αὐτοῦ, ἵνα ὁ ἀγαπῶν τὸν θεὸν ἀγαπᾷ καὶ τὸν ἀδελφὸν αὐτοῦ). John here disallows any argument that one can truly love God but be indifferent or hateful toward others in the community. Although the discussion has referred to "God" (θεός), John's discussion of love clearly alludes to Jesus' teaching in the gospel just after he washed the feet of his disciples:

> John 13:34: "A new command I give you: Love one another. As I have loved you, so you must love one another."
>
> John 14:15: "If you love me, keep my commands."
> John 15:17: "This is my command: Love each other."

Thus, John is saying that there is no love for

---

13. E.g., Smalley, *1, 2, 3 John*, 263 – 64; Marshall, *Epistles of John*, 225 – 26; Dodd, *Johannine Epistles*, 123.

14. Smith, *First, Second, and Third John*, 120.

God that is not focused on Jesus Christ. Kruse points out that this passage accomplishes two ends: first, John reassures his readers that they really do know God; second, he wants to show them that the claims of religious people to know and love apart from Christ (the secessionists?) are false.

5:1 Everyone who believes that Jesus is the Christ has been born of God. And everyone who loves the Father loves his child as well (Πᾶς ὁ πιστεύων ὅτι Ἰησοῦς ἐστιν ὁ Χριστὸς, ἐκ τοῦ θεοῦ γεγέννηται, καὶ πᾶς ὁ ἀγαπῶν τὸν γεννήσαντα ἀγαπᾷ [καὶ] τὸν γεγεννημένον ἐξ αὐτοῦ). John bases his final point in the argument that Christians must love fellow believers by pointing again to their faith in Jesus Christ, who is the Father's expression of love for his children. As Yarbrough pithily says, "The road to love … is paved with faith" in Christ.[15] John does not suggest that belief in Jesus as the Jewish Messiah is an adequate basis for Christian faith, but that "Christ" (Χριστός) should be understood in its later sense as a title referring to the Son of God (see "In Depth: Messiah or Christ?" at 1:3). Calvin commented on the nature of this faith of which John speaks:

> The only true way of believing is when we direct our minds to him. Besides, to believe that he is the Christ, is to hope from him all those things which have been promised as to the Messiah.
>
> Nor is the title, *Christ*, given him here without reason, for it designates the office to which he was appointed by the Father. As, under the Law, the full restoration of all things, righteousness and happiness, were promised through the Messiah; so at this day the whole of this is more clearly set forth in the gospel. Then Jesus cannot be received as Christ, except salvation be sought from him, since for this end he was sent by the Father, and is daily offered to us.[16]

If someone has come to such faith in Christ, that person has been born again as a child of God into the Father's family (cf. 2:29; 3:9). This faith in Christ presumably produces love for God the Father, that is, "the begetter" (τὸν γεννήσαντα). A person who loves the Father also loves the Father's child, "the one who has been begotten from him" (τὸν γεγεννημένον ἐξ αὐτοῦ). This statement builds on the idea that Jesus Christ, Son of God, whom believers love, is the begotten of the Father (5:18; cf. Nicene Creed, "begotten not made"). But here John uses that christological point to argue that all who have come to faith in Christ are also children of the Father to be likewise loved.

It is striking that Christian believers are brought into a relationship with the Father that is described in the same terms as the Son's relationship with the Father, though certainly not identical with it.[17] This distinction is made in 1 John, which refers to Jesus as God's Son (υἱός) but to all believers as his children (τεκνία). Therefore, "anyone who loves God necessarily loves a God who begets offspring; love of those others who like oneself are begotten by God follows inescapably."[18] In fact, not to love fellow believers is evidence that one has not truly been born of God (2:9 – 11; 3:9 – 10, 14 – 17; 4:20).

5:2 So this is how we know that we love the children of God: when we love God and do his commands (ἐν τούτῳ γινώσκομεν ὅτι ἀγαπῶμεν τὰ τέκνα τοῦ θεοῦ, ὅταν τὸν θεὸν ἀγαπῶμεν καὶ τὰς ἐντολὰς αὐτοῦ ποιῶμεν). John restates the relationship between love for God and obedience to his commands.

Although this Greek sentence looks simple, there are some exegetical questions that need to be considered before concluding John's meaning here. First, which way does the prepositional phrase "in this way" (ἐν τούτῳ) point, forward to

---

15. Yarbrough, *1 – 3 John*, 269.
16. Calvin, *Commentaries on the Catholic Epistles*, 250.
17. Lieu, *I, II, & III John*, 200.
18. Ibid. Similarly Kruse, *Letters of John*, 171.

the next clause (cataphoric) or backward to what was just stated (anaphoric)? Second, while the second occurrence of "we love" (ἀγαπῶμεν) is clearly subjunctive, following after "when" (ὅταν), could the first also be subjunctive? And is there a way of understanding what John says here that is not viciously circular or tautologous? For as Brown points out, "One tests love for God by love for brothers (4:20 – 21) and then tests love for brothers by love for God."[19]

In the common view that takes the prepositional phrase "in this way" (ἐν τούτῳ) as pointing forward (as in NIV, NLT, and most English translations), it points to the ὅταν clause: "This is how we know we love ... when we love God and carry out his commands."[20] On this reading, loving God and carrying out his commands is how we know that we love the children of God, which seems to be the reverse of what John has just previously argued in 4:20. But rather than a contradiction or convolution, it is another way of saying that we cannot define love for others until we obediently love God. In other words, "love is not defined instinctively but is rather revealed (3:16; 4:19), so that the knowledge that we love is grounded in the love of God and the keeping of his commandments."[21]

But some interpreters have seen the prepositional phrase "in this way" (ἐν τούτῳ) to refer to the preceding statement. As Dodd explains it:

The words "by this" now refer to what precedes (cf. iv. 6, iii. 19), and we have a perfectly logical argument, which may be thus stated in syllogistic form:

He who loves the parent loves the child:

Every Christian is a child of God:

Therefore, when we love God we love our fellow Christians.[22]

Howard Marshall agrees that up to this point in the letter John has been arguing that it is love for the brothers and sisters that shows one truly loves God (3:14 – 18; 4:20), not the other way around. Thus, he argues that the prepositional phrase points back to the preceding statement, but also that the verb is "a virtual statement of obligation," yielding, "by this principle, namely that we must love our father's [other] children, we know that we *ought* to love the children of God" (italics added).[23] Verse 1 then is read as the theological principle on which our love for brothers and sisters is commanded, because they too are God's children. However, there are no clear parallels of this use of the present indicative (but see discussion of 3:6).

A similar problem arises with taking the first "we love" (ἀγαπῶμεν) as a subjunctive, since in form it could be either indicative or subjunctive. As Wallace explains the relationship of the subjunctive to the imperative (which lacks a first plural form), *"the subjunctive is also used for volitional notions ... an acceptable gloss is often should."*[24] If the volitive sense of the subjunctive can be allowed here, the thought expressed is that because of the principle in 5:1 (ἐν τούτῳ), we *should* or *ought to* love the children of God.

Nevertheless, without clear parallels for this use of the present subjunctive, the volitive sense of the first occurence of "we love" (ἀγαπῶμεν) probably comes more from the context of John's exhortation than from the mood of the verb. The volitive

---

19. Brown, *Epistles of John*, 566.

20. As also Culy, *I, II, III John*, 121; Kruse, *Letters of John*, 171; Smalley, *1, 2, 3 John*, 268.

21. With thanks to Jon Laansma for personal conversation about this.

22. Dodd, *Johannine Epistles*, 125.

23. Marshall, *Epistles of John*, 227; so also C. Haas, M. de

Jonge, and J. L. Swellengrebel, *A Handbook on the Letters of John* (New York: United Bible Societies, 1972), 133.

24. Wallace, *Greek Grammar*, 463 (italics original); also A. T. Robertson, *Grammar of the Greek New Testament in Light of Historical Research* (New York: Hodder & Stoughton, 1914), 930; cf. D. B. Munro, *A Grammar of the Homeric Dialect* (Oxford: Clarendon, 1891), 287 – 90.

sense of the verb is necessary for taking "in this way" (ἐν τούτῳ) as pointing back to 5:1. But taking "we love" (ἀγαπῶμεν) as indicative and the prepositional phrase as pointing at the *hotan* (ὅταν) clause *is* consistent with the logical flow of John's argument that love for others is defined only by first loving God and doing his commands:

4:20: One cannot love God and hate their brother or sister.
5:1:   Everyone born of God loves others also born of God.
5:2:   Only by loving God by keeping his commands is love for others defined.
5:3:   Love for God means keeping his commands.

Calvin's thoughts on this are worth quoting at length:

> He briefly shows in these words what true love is, even that which is towards God. He has hitherto taught us that there is never a true love to God, except when our brethren are also loved; for this is ever its effect. But he now teaches us that men are rightly and duly loved, when God holds the primacy. And it is a necessary definition; for it often happens, that we love men apart from God, as unholy and carnal friendships regard only private advantages or some other vanishing objects. As, then, he had referred first to the effect, so he now refers to the cause; for his purpose is to shew that mutual love ought to be in such a way cultivated that God may be honored.[25]

John's logic is also consistent with the OT moral code of the covenant, where covenant obedience to God was expressed in keeping the Ten Commandments, some of which regulated behavior toward others, such as "You shall not murder," "You shall not steal," and "You shall not give false testimony" (Exod 20:1 – 17; Deut 5:6 – 21). Love for others is not a sentimental emotion or merely getting along; it is living in right relationships with others by not murdering, not stealing, not giving false testimony, and the like, and by meeting the need of others for life's sustaining provisions. Moreover, the work that God commands is "to believe in the one he has sent" (John 6:29).

The apparent circularity of the argument that Brown points out may be seen, as Smalley explains, as inherent in the inextricability of love for others and love for God, "for the fact is that each kind of love (for God, and for others) demonstrates the genuineness of the other, and reinforces it."[26] Von Wahlde sees this rhetoric as "intended to show the unity of these obligations."[27] Therefore, as John argues, it is impossible to love God and treat others in ways that violate God's revealed will.

5:3 For this is the love of God: that we keep his commands, and his commands are not burdensome (αὕτη γάρ ἐστιν ἡ ἀγάπη τοῦ θεοῦ, ἵνα τὰς ἐντολὰς αὐτοῦ τηρῶμεν, καὶ αἱ ἐντολαὶ αὐτοῦ βαρεῖαι οὐκ εἰσίν). John clearly and explicitly defines love for God as obedience. One cannot claim to love God and be indifferent to his commands. Because one loves God, his commands are not burdensome but liberating. The word translated "burdensome" (βαρύς) does not occur frequently in the NT (Matt 23:4, 23; Acts 20:29; 25:7; 2 Cor 10:10). John's statement recalls that of Jesus in Matt 11:30, "My yoke is easy and my burden is light." When we are set free by Christ to love God, we are set free to live rightly with one another as God has defined "rightly." That freedom is light compared to the weight and heaviness of sin.

---

25. Calvin, *Commentaries on the Catholic Epistles.*
26. Smalley, *1, 2, 3 John*, 268.
27. Von Wahlde, *Gospel and Letters*, 3:174.

Theology in Application

Free from Fear

Reassurance of eternal life is based on God's love, which is most clearly expressed on the cross, and that love when properly understood frees us from fear of God's coming day of judgment (vv. 17 – 18). Perhaps a primary reason that so many people have a difficult time trusting God's love is that society at large, and even the church to some extent, has let go of the idea that we will be judged by a holy and righteous God after this life. Consequently, the gracious atonement for our sin is not viewed as the greatest gift of love but as an irrelevant and outdated belief of primitive religion.

Instead of pondering the cross of Jesus Christ, fallen creatures seek God's love and goodness elsewhere in a fallen creation. Horrible things such as the untimely death of innocents, gruesome violence, cataclysmic natural calamities, and "man's inhumanity to man" seem to weigh heavily against God's goodness (or his omnipotence), all of which cause many to doubt God's love for us. If there is no sin and no judgment of sin, then Jesus' death was a horrible farce.

But John and all the other NT writers argue that there is no greater expression of God's love than the cross of Jesus, and to accept God's love and continue in it means embracing the gospel of Jesus Christ by acknowledging our sin, repenting of it, and living in Christ. John underscores that apart from this gospel, there is no assurance of eternal life. John further teaches that there is no genuine love for God apart from embracing the gospel of Jesus Christ and continuing in it (see The Theology of John's Letters).

The cross of Jesus delivers us from the coming judgment and frees us to live and love as God created us to do. The NT is full of ethical and moral principles, but John's writings are strangely void of anything other than the command to love one another. In fact, John says, a person is self-deceived who claims to love God but is indifferent toward his church. So many in our modern society see themselves as spiritual, but have disdain for the church and organized religion. While churches and denominations certainly have their flaws and problems, it is an oxymoron to think that one can love and worship God in splendid isolation from the gospel of Jesus Christ. It is only in community with others who have received God's atoning love in the cross of Christ that one can truly love God. It is only in the ups and downs of relationships with other believers that one has the opportunities to love.

Love Takes a Community

John repeatedly points to Jesus' new command that his followers must love one another. But is this really a useful principle of Christian ethics since the command is so broad and vague and depends so much on how "love" is defined? Andreas Köstenberger asks, "What is John's moral vision? Some have difficulty identifying John's ethics or allege a limited interest in moral conduct on John's part."[28] Wayne Meeks points out that the Fourth Gospel "offers no explicit moral instruction"; John's "only rule is 'love one another,' and that rule is 'both vague in application and narrowly circumscribed, being limited solely to those who are firmly within the Johannine circle.' "[29] Richard Hays observes the same issue: "The strongly sectarian character of the Johannine vision stands at the opposite pole within the New Testament from Luke's optimistic affirmation of the world and its culture."[30] If John's writings were all we had, these points would be well taken. The command to love one another seems too broad to be of practical value in guiding specific behavior, and it seems focused on the Johannine community to the exclusion of those outside.

Hays points out that immediately before Jesus gave the new command to his disciples to love one another (John 13:34), he washed their feet, demonstrating that love means "humble service of others."[31] The fact that John reflects Jesus' teaching that focused special attention on his followers' relationships with one another does not deny the fact that Jesus also taught about loving one's neighbor, even the neighbor one is most likely to hate (Luke 10:25 – 37). He expounded on the Ten Commandments, reinforcing their ongoing relevance to his followers (Matt 5:17 – 6:4), and he preached an ethical foundation for life in the Beatitudes (5:3 – 11). Although John exhorts his readers not to love the world (1 John 2:15), he also acknowledges that God so loved the world that he sent his Son to die for its sins (John 3:16). "Thus, Jesus' death is depicted by John ... as an act of self-sacrificial love that establishes the cruciform life as the norm for discipleship."[32]

Beyond the Gospels we have the NT letters, full of ethical and moral instruction for a variety of life and cultural situations. John clearly believed there is an ethical and moral standard for Christians that involves principles revealed by God (1 John 2:15; 3:6, 7, 10, 24; 5:3, 18; 3 John 11). But he subsumes the ethical and moral codes of Judaism under the authority of Jesus, who sums them all up as "love your neighbor" and defines his disciples as a particular group of "neighbors" to love (John 13:34).

Johannine Ethics

So John *does* present an ethical grounding for Christian life, which, as Köstenberger points out, "is a call to evangelistic mission that is grounded in God's love for the world and undergirded by communal love and unity."[33] In fact, one could argue that without John's moral vision centered in the cross, all ethical behavior would be just going through the motions. It is good to feed hungry people, but if those same

---

28. Köstenberger, *Theology of John's Gospel and Letters*, 510.

29. Wayne A. Meeks, "The Ethics of the Fourth Evangelist," in *Exploring the Gospel of John: In Honor of D. Moody Smith* (ed. R. Alan Culpepper and C. Clifton Black; Louisville: Westminster John Knox, 1996), 318.

30. Hays, *Moral Vision*, 139.

31. Ibid., 144.

32. Ibid., 145.

33. Köstenberger, *Theology of John's Gospel and Letters*, 514.

people are heading toward their judgment without Christ, is it loving to give them bread but not the Bread of Life? Is it loving to affirm Christian brothers and sisters in their sin rather than call them to live as God has revealed in Scripture?

John does expect his readers to care for others in need (3:17 – 18), but the real and present danger of that moment was that his readers might be led astray and not continue in genuine faith in Jesus Christ (2:19; 3:7; 4:1 – 3; 2 John 7 – 11). As Kösten-berger concludes:

> John's moral vision is simple yet profound. Knowing the world's spiritual and moral darkness apart from the light, Jesus Christ, John holds out no hope for those without Christ. He does not discuss keeping the law; he does not explicitly address the issue of righteousness other than to urge rejection of sin (1 John 3:6; cf. 3:4 – 10); he does not engage the isssue of works, other than to report Jesus' answer to those who asked him what they must do to perform the works required by God: "The work of God is this: to believe in the one he has sent" (John 6:29).[34]

In a religiously pluralistic society (as we live in today), the greatest act of love — the sharing of God's love in Christ — is increasingly perceived as a self-righteous power play that is taboo in polite company. Jesus was sent into such a world, and as he was returning to the Father he said, "Peace be with you! As the Father has sent me, I am sending you" (John 20:21). This call to continue to proclaim the gospel of Jesus Christ in a pluralistic society increasingly hostile to the idea of exclusive spiritual truth will be the church's greatest challenge in the years to come.

---

34. Ibid., 523.

CHAPTER 14

1 John 5:4 – 13

Literary Context

This passage advances and concludes the argument begun in 4:1 concerning the need to discern the origin of spiritual truth, for not every teaching about God has its origin with him (4:1 – 3). That argument progressed from the need for discernment of the truth to the challenge of overcoming wrong teaching (4:4 – 6) by listening to the Spirit of truth. Those born of God, who have been given the Spirit of truth, must love one another, for love for God is expressed through love for others (4:7 – 16). When God's love reaches its goal, fear of judgment will be gone (4:17 – 18), because God's own testimony confirms a "water and blood" gospel as the truth through which eternal life is given.

Main Idea

John argues that a "water only" gospel rejects God's own witness about his Son, Jesus Christ, whose atoning death is necessary for any true spiritual knowledge and assurance of eternal life.

Translation

(See next page.)

1 John 5:4 – 13

4a	assertion	For **everything born of God overcomes the world.**
b	identification	And **this is the triumph that overcomes the world —**
c	apposition	our faith.
5a	rhetorical question	**Who is** the one who overcomes the world,
b	identification	except the one who believes
c	content	that Jesus is the Son of God?
6a	assertion	**He is the one who came** through **water and blood —**
b	identification	not in water alone — but
c	contrast	in water and in blood.
d	assertion	And **the Spirit is the one who bears witness,**
e	basis	because the Spirit is the truth.
7	expansion	For **there are** **three who bear witness:**
8a	list	the Spirit, and
b	list	the water, and
c	list	the blood,
d	assertion	and **the** **three** **agree as one.**
9a	condition	Since we receive human testimony,
b	comparison	**the testimony of God is greater,**
c	explanation	because this is God's testimony
d	content	that he has testified about his Son.
10a	assertion	**The one** **who** **believes in the Son of** God **has this testimony within them.**
b	assertion	**The one** **who does not** **believe** God **has made God a liar,**
c	explanation	because they have not believed the testimony that God has testified about his Son.
11a	identification	And **this is the testimony:**
b	identification	that God has given eternal life to us and
c	assertion	this life is in his Son.
12a	assertion	**The one who has** **the Son** **has life;**
b	assertion	the one who does not have **the Son of God does not** **have life.**
13a	assertion	**These things I write to you who believe in the name of the Son of God**
b	purpose	so that you might know that you have eternal life.

Structure

John's circular, or braided, thought patterns, in which he returns to topics again and again, has allowed interpreters to see a number of apparently overlapping chiasms.[1] Smalley sees in 5:1 – 4 "a nearly chiastic" structure:[2]

A faith and love (v. 1)
  B love and obedience (v. 2)
  B′ love and obedience (v. 3)
A′ victory and faith (v. 4)

But because 5:3 mentions love for the last time in the letter, this commentary has grouped it with the substantial discussion of that topic in the previous section (4:7 – 5:3).

Exegetical Outline

→ **XIV. The Blood, Eternal Life, and Assurance (5:4 – 13)**
   A. Faith in the Son of God overcomes the world (5:4 – 5)
   B. The testimony (5:6 – 13)
       1. Jesus Christ has come through water and blood (5:6a-c)
       2. The Spirit is the witness to the truth (5:6d-e)
       3. Three witnesses (5:7 – 8)
       4. Receiving God's testimony (5:9 – 13)
           a. God's testimony is greater than human testimony (5:9)
           b. Faith is the necessary response (5:10)
           c. God promises eternal life (5:11 – 13)
               i. The Son is essential to life (5:11 – 12)
               ii. Confidence for life is possible (5:13)

Explanation of the Text

5:4 For everything born of God overcomes the world. And this is the triumph that overcomes the world — our faith (ὅτι πᾶν τὸ γεγεννημένον ἐκ τοῦ θεοῦ νικᾷ τὸν κόσμον, καὶ αὕτη ἐστὶν ἡ νίκη ἡ νικήσασα τὸν κόσμον, ἡ πίστις ἡμῶν). Because Jesus destroyed the works of the devil (3:8) and has overcome the world, those who have been born of God (note the perfect tense) also overcome the world by their faith in Christ.

The extensive discussion in 4:7 – 5:3 has already argued that love for God is inseparably joined to love for others, and the love of both God and others is closely connected to faith in Christ and obedience to God's commands. The present verse paral-

---

1. Cf. von Wahlde, *Gospel and Letters*, 3:175 – 77.

2. See Smalley, *1, 2, 3 John*, 265 – 66.

lels the thought of 5:1 (see the chiastic structure in Structure, above). Verse 1 states that everyone who believes that Jesus is the Christ has been born of God; v. 4a, that everything born of God overcomes the world. Therefore, everyone who believes that Jesus is the Christ overcomes the world.

The use of the neuter (πᾶν) where one would expect the personal generic masculine (πᾶς) occurs elsewhere in John's writings (John 6:37, 39; 17:2, 24; 1 John 1:1, 3). Translating it as "everyone," Marshall wonders if the use of the neuter shows the influence of the neuter gender of the Greek words for "child" (τέκνον or παιδίον).[3] Or perhaps the elided neuter noun is "spirit" (πνεῦμα). Smalley suggests that its deliberate use here generalizes the reference to "the power of the new birth … not only its possession by each individual."[4] Here it seems to suggest that everything that has its origin in God — the one born of God, perhaps God's providential working in history, and even faith itself — has happened in order to resist and ultimately triumph over the fallen, sinful, and rebellious tendencies of the world's order. At the time John wrote, that world included those who had gone out (2:19), and therefore right belief in Christ would overcome even the antichrists' false teaching.

John does not teach here some enthusiastic triumphalism, but points to faith in the true gospel of Jesus Christ that is "ours," that is, that held by the author and those who share like faith. In John 16:33 Jesus said that he has "overcome" the world (Gk. perfect, νενίκηκα). Therefore, those who have faith in Christ have faith that this is so, and likewise that faith overcomes all that is of the world (cf. 2:13 – 14; 4:4; 5:5). The statement here that everything/everyone born of God overcomes the world informs the interpretation of 2:14 – 15, where the "young men" (νεανίσκοι) are said to be overcomers.

5:5 Who is the one who overcomes the world, except the one who believes that Jesus is the Son of God? (τίς δέ ἐστιν ὁ νικῶν τὸν κόσμον εἰ μὴ ὁ πιστεύων ὅτι Ἰησοῦς ἐστιν ὁ υἱὸς τοῦ θεοῦ;) The answer to this rhetorical question is "no one!" No one can overcome the world except those whose trust is in Jesus Christ. The only one who has overcome the world is Jesus (John 16:33), the Son of God, who came into the world, and he shares his triumph with those who put their trust in him.

John presses the identity of Jesus not simply as a great teacher, prophet, or even the Messiah. He consistently identifies Jesus with God the Father, as God's Son who shares the divine nature (1:3, 7; 2:22 – 24; 3:8, 23; 4:9 – 10, 14, 15; 5:5, 9 – 13, 20). Without faith in Christ, no one is able to face down the evil, the hopelessness, and the self-defeat that this world presses against us day by day. There may be many self-help gurus who write and speak about how to live a better life, and some of what they say may be helpful and worthwhile. But what is of the world cannot give us victory over the world. Without trust in Christ, who came into the world from God, even the most successful life is swallowed up in the defeat of death.

5:6a-c He is the one who came through water and blood — not in water alone — but in water and in blood (οὗτός ἐστιν ὁ ἐλθὼν δι' ὕδατος καὶ αἵματος, Ἰησοῦς Χριστός, οὐκ ἐν τῷ ὕδατι μόνον ἀλλ' ἐν τῷ ὕδατι καὶ ἐν τῷ αἵματι). John further elaborates on the true gospel, that Jesus Christ, the Son of God, "came" through water *and* blood (5:6a).

How should these two elements, water and blood, be understood? Are they to be taken literally or as symbols of spiritual concepts? Are they a hendiadys or two separate elements?[5] Is it exegetically significant that in the first instance John uses

---

3. Marshall, *Epistles of John*, 228 n37.
4. Smalley, *1, 2, 3 John*, 270.

5. "Hendiadys" is a term from Greek rhetoric that specifies one referent although using two words. In English the phrase "black and blue" to refer to bruising would be a hendiadys.

the preposition "through" (διά), but in the second clauses uses "in" (ἐν, 5:6b, c), though both can indicate manner (BDF §198[4])? And whether or not John is addressing the teaching of the secessionists (cf. 2:19), it sounds as if there was a real danger of the claim that Jesus Christ came by water alone, and John is emphatically correcting thinking that moves in that direction.

In the first occurrence of "water and blood" (ὕδατος καὶ αἵματος in 5:6a), the two words are joined by the single preposition *dia* (διά), which has led some interpreters, such as John Calvin, to take it as a hendiadys referring to the cleansing and life-giving effects of Jesus' death, when blood and water are said to have flowed from Jesus' side (John 19:34 – 35; cf. Ezek 36:25 – 27).[6] Michaels follows Calvin in this, explaining that the author of 1 John "interprets the blood and water from Jesus' side at the crucifixion as a kind of 'testimony' (μαρτυρία), comparable to the well-known 'testimony that God testified about his Son' at Jesus' baptism."[7]

Although Michaels is almost certainly right that 1 John intends to reassert the significance of Jesus' death against false teaching, against this interpretation is the second reference to water and blood (5:6c), which clearly separates them by repeating the preposition ἐν and, more importantly, distinguishes the coming in water alone (5:6b) from the coming in water and blood. The fact that 1 John refers to "water and blood" where the gospel has "blood and water" suggests that this was not a conventional hendiadys in use to refer to Jesus' death. But perhaps most decisively, 5:8 counts *three* witnesses, not just two — as would be expected if

water and blood were a hendiadys referring to Jesus' death — by separating each of the three with the conjunction "and" (καί) and including a definite article with each.

If the two words are taken as two distinct, literal references, interpreters have suggested that the phrase "water and blood" refers to Jesus' physical birth and death, respectively, since birth involves the water (amniotic fluid) breaking (but also involves blood).[8] Or perhaps the water refers to Jesus' baptism that inaugurated his public ministry.[9] Either way, John's emphasis on not in water *alone* might then suggest that the significance of Jesus Christ is not in just his earthly life as a teacher and religious leader, but that his death is also significant and relevant.

In the tradition of Tertullian, Augustine, and Ambrose, some have suggested that "water and blood" might refer to the two sacraments of water baptism and the Eucharist as modes in which Christ comes into a believer's life, but some modern interpreters, such as Schnackenburg, see sacraments in v. 7 but a historical reference to Jesus' life in v. 6.[10] This reading is similar to that of the debate in studies of John's gospel whether the bread-from-heaven discourse in John 6, written some decades after Jesus' lifetime, was intended to refer to the Eucharist, especially John 6:54, "Whoever eats my flesh and drinks my blood has eternal life." But rather than a direct reference to the Eucharist, eating and drinking in John 6 is a metaphor for believing in the atoning value of Jesus' death, the event to which the Eucharist also points.

A eucharistic reading of 1 John 5:6 would mean

6. Calvin, *Commentaries on the Catholic Epistles*.

7. J. Ramsey Michaels, "By Water and Blood: Sin and Purification in John and First John," in *Dimensions of Baptism: Biblical and Theological Studies* (ed. Stanley Porter and Anthony R. Cross; London: Sheffield Academic, 2002), 159.

8. E.g., Witherington, *Letters and Homilies*, 1:545.

9. E.g., Kruse, *Letters of John*, 177; also D. A. Carson, "The

Three Witnesses and the Eschatology of 1 John," in *To Tell the Mystery: Essays on New Testament Eschatology in Honor of Robert H. Gundry* (ed. Thomas E. Schmidt and Moisés Silva; JSNTSup 100; Sheffield: Sheffield Academic, 1994), 216 – 32.

10. E.g., Rudolf Schnackenburg, *The Johannine Epistles: Introduction and Commentary* (trans. R. Fuller and I. Fuller; New York: Crossroad, 1992), 233, esp. n108; 236.

taking "water" literally as the element of the sacrament of baptism, but the blood comes into a believer's life figuratively through the wine or juice drunk at Holy Communion. Moreover, "blood" would be an unprecedented way of referring to the Eucharist. Furthermore, there is no other reference to the Eucharist in John's letters that would suggest this was part of the controversy. Also against this reading is the aspect of the substantival aorist participle "the one who came" (ὁ ἐλθών), which Witherington argues is decisively against a sacramental reading, since the verb is not "in the present tense indicating an ongoing coming," presumably into the life of the believer through the sacraments.[11]

Tom Thatcher proposes that "water" is a symbol of the Holy Spirit and "blood" a symbol of the physical nature of Jesus culminating in the atonement on the cross.[12] He argues that the secessionists were pushing Jesus' *paraclete* statements in John 13 – 17 beyond the limits of orthodoxy. Misunderstanding might arise from Jesus' statements that he would come to his disciples by the Spirit of truth whom he would send (John 14:16 – 18), that the Spirit would be the disciples' guide into all truth (16:13 – 15), and that the Spirit would teach them "all things" (14:26). Some may have used such statements to argue against the return of Christ after the Spirit came at Pentecost. Or perhaps some rejected the teaching of the apostles on the mistaken belief that the Spirit was the only teacher they needed. Perhaps the secessionists claimed that the Spirit had given them the teaching that John found heretical.

Thatcher's interpretation recognizes the frequent use of water in John's gospel to symbolize the Holy Spirit — for example in John 4, where Jesus promises "living water" for those who would believe in him. John 7:37 – 39 explicitly identifies "living water" as the Spirit who would be given to believers after Jesus was glorified. This symbolic use of water is a metaphor for the Spirit and also the constellation of associations that John makes with the Spirit, such as the impartation of truth and eternal life (see The Theology of John's Letters). Thatcher suggests that when the antichrists argued that Jesus came through water only, they meant that "everything significant about Jesus has been revealed to the Church through the Spirit," which led to diminishing the significance of Jesus' life and death, perhaps leading to claims of new revelations that were not consistent with apostolic teaching.[13]

This view coheres with John's emphasis on apostolic authority that opens the letter (1:1 – 4) and the fact that something had happened that led people to leave the Christian community where John's apostolic authority was present (2:19). Thatcher's theory also provides a context to understand John's statement in 2 John 9, "Everyone who goes beyond and does not remain in the teaching of Christ does not have God." The biggest argument against Thatcher's interpretation is 5:8, where both the Spirit *and* the water are listed separately as two of the three witnesses.

If the use of the verb "come" (ἔρχομαι) here carries the connotation of Christ's salvific mission, as argued in our comments on 4:2, then the prepositional phrases "in the water" and "in the blood" in 5:6c (ἐν τῷ ὕδατι and ἐν τῷ αἵματι) are instrumental datives adverbially modifying the elided verb "come" (ἐλθών), which suggests that the salvific mission of Jesus was achieved *both* by water and by blood, not by water alone. The discussion of 4:2, where the similar phrase "Jesus Christ has come in

11. Witherington, *Letters and Homilies*, 1:543.

12. Tom Thatcher, "'Water and Blood,'" 205 – 34. For a previous interpretation that moved in the same direction, see

K. Grayston, *The Johannine Epistles* (NCBC; Grand Rapids; Eerdmans, 1984).

13. Ibid., 247.

flesh" was first mentioned, does occur in the context of discerning spiritual truth and recognition that not every teaching is from the Holy Spirit.

The reason 1 John 5:6 is such a conundrum for us no doubt has to do with the fact that "1 John is written to people who know what the secessionist crisis is about firsthand. These readers of 1 John thus frequently need only a brief, allusive phrase to know what the author is referring to."[14] For those in the Johannine church(es) the phrases "Jesus Christ has come in flesh" (4:2) and "came through water and blood" (5:6) probably called to mind teaching and context that subsequent readers lack. That historical factor is further complicated for subsequent readers by the multiple connotations of the "water" symbol we observe in John's gospel. So how is water to be understood here in 5:6?

Thatcher is likely right that John's correction of false teaching is needed because of a misconstrual of the water symbol in the gospel. As Thatcher explains:

> John and the "AntiChrists" appealed to the same Jesus tradition, but interpreted that tradition in radically different ways. While the AntiChrists emphasized the believer's continuing revelatory experience via the Spirit, John insisted that new revelations must be "consistent with" the apostolic teaching about the historical Jesus.[15]

Close attention to the syntax suggests that John refers to "water alone" to allude to the false teaching he is about to correct, but then uses it as part of a reference to Jesus' earthly life ("water and blood"). The first mention of "water and blood" in 5:6a (ὁ ἐλθὼν δι' ὕδατος καὶ αἵματος) probably is a hendiadys referring to the atoning humanity of Jesus, with water likely a reference to his baptism,

in which the Spirit's testimony plays a central role (John 3:32 – 34). "Water and blood" refers to the earthly life of Jesus in its efficacy for atonement.

The separation of the terms "water" and "blood" in their second occurrence in 5:6c by the repetition of the preposition and article (ἐν τῷ ὕδατι καὶ ἐν τῷ αἵματι) is the clue that John is breaking up the hendiadys because he needs to correct a misconstrual of the "water" symbol. John mentions water first because he *does* want to affirm the salvific connotation represented by "water" as a metaphor for the Spirit, but he also wants to add to it the essential element of "blood." The Spirit is essential because he applies atonement to the believer's life. But the blood is essential as the objective basis of that atonement. John *does* need to affirm the role of the Spirit in salvation, so he cannot say simply "not by water" and leave it at that. As a corrective statement it makes sense that John uses "water" in a double sense — first in reference to the way the false teaching about the Spirit is employing it, and then in a correction that refers to the water *and* the blood as symbols of the atoning life of Jesus.

If so, the thought needing correction probably *is* that some were identifying "water" with the Spirit (as per Thatcher).[16] But he then offers the correction that salvation is achieved not by the water (Spirit) *alone* (5:6b) but by the water *and* by the blood (5:6c), that is, by Jesus' atoning humanity. So understood, John is tying the presence of the Spirit, who is the witness to the truth in the church after the resurrection, to the Spirit's witness of both the baptism of Jesus and his death. It was the Spirit who descended on Jesus at his baptism, providing a witness of Jesus' true identity (John 1:32 – 34). And when Jesus "gives up" his spirit on the cross, his

---

14. De Boer, "Death of Jesus Christ," 331.

15. Thatcher, "'Water and Blood,'" 235; see also idem, "1 John," in *The Expositor's Bible Commentary* (ed. Tremper

Longman III and David E. Garland; rev. ed.; Grand Rapids: Zondervan, 2006), 13:493.

16. Thatcher, "'Water and Blood,'" 247.

death releases the Spirit to come (19:30; 20:22; cf. his teaching in 16:7 about the necessity of his going away for the Spirit to come). In other words, John argues that there is no testimony from the Spirit that ignores or contradicts the atoning death of Jesus, which was likely involved in what the false teachers were suggesting.

While we may never know the exact problem with the thinking of the secessionists, the correction presented in 5:6, 8 addresses at least two false ideas: (1) that the significance of Jesus was focused only in his teachings and miracles, as opposed to his death and resurrection, which suggests that Jesus was nothing more than a prophet or a religious teacher; (2) that everything significant about Jesus is revealed to the church by the Spirit as an ongoing source of revelation, perhaps with claims to truth not organically related to and consistent with the atonement of Jesus' death (cf. 2 John 9).

John does not deny the role of the Spirit, but he anchors it in the historical life of Jesus, of whose significance the Spirit reminds the church. Either of these two false directions opposes the redemptive mission of Jesus Christ and is therefore "antichrist" in nature (cf. 2:18 – 23). By this understanding, John is opposing *any* teaching that demotes or eliminates the cross, a heresy symbolized by a "water only" gospel; the full significance of the incarnation of Jesus Christ is upheld only by a "water and blood" gospel.

John's correction would thus speak against a docetic Christology, such as Cerinthianism, but it is not necessary to presume that particular heresy. John must uphold the presence and power of the Holy Spirit in the believer's life while also holding the historical Jesus to be essential to the Christian faith. The Spirit *alone* is insufficient because our sin must be atoned for. Jesus' physical life and death as a human being is at the heart of the atonement, without which no true knowledge of or fellowship with God is possible (cf. 1:7, 9).

5:6d-e And the Spirit is the one who bears witness, because the Spirit is the truth (καὶ τὸ πνεῦμά ἐστιν τὸ μαρτυροῦν, ὅτι τὸ πνεῦμά ἐστιν ἡ ἀλήθεια). John continues to affirm the role of the Spirit in the gospel of Jesus Christ. Here we see the necessity of holding together both the objective, historical event of Jesus' atoning crucifixion, which is independent of any individual's opinion about it, and the personal wooing and witness of the Holy Spirit, who applies that atonement to the individual believer. While the Spirit is necessary for salvation, his role is always coupled to and anchored in the earthly life of Jesus Christ, sent by the Father as an atoning sacrifice for sin. Even though the Spirit continues to speak to the church, his witness is in complete harmony with the truth, the orthodox teaching of the atonement of Jesus Christ.

Twice John has stated that God has given "us" the Spirit (3:24; 4:13), and in both occurrences it is the presence of the Spirit that confirms to the believer that God lives in them and they in God. The presence of the Spirit is evidenced when the believer listens to and accepts the apostolic witness as the truth (4:6); any other truth claim not consistent with that witness is deemed not of God and is therefore false. In this way, the genuine presence of God is identified with an objective set of knowledge that originated with Jesus and was codified in the testimony of apostolic witnesses, such as that of the beloved disciple of John's gospel and the elder of the Johannine letters. In this sense the Spirit *is* the truth, and any truth claim apart from the apostolic teaching cannot be of the Spirit of God. Therefore, the Spirit is the one who bears witness to an individual that the apostolic teaching of the gospel is true and trustworthy (note the present tense suggesting the ongoing work of the Spirit).

5:7 – 8 For there are three who bear witness: the Spirit, and the water, and the blood, and the three agree as one (ὅτι τρεῖς εἰσιν οἱ μαρτυροῦντες, τὸ πνεῦμα καὶ τὸ ὕδωρ καὶ τὸ αἷμα, καὶ οἱ τρεῖς εἰς τὸ ἕν εἰσιν). John underscores here the witness of three distinct but inseparable elements of the salvation that expresses the Father's love through the atoning death of Jesus, the Son of God, which has been recognized as the truth by all genuine believers.

John personifies the water and the blood as witnesses that, while referring to the earthly life of Jesus, continue to witness to God's love and offer of redemption throughout all time. The "blood" is unambiguously a reference to the death of Jesus that continues to "witness" throughout time. The specific referent of "water" remains obscure and may be intended to connote multiple connotations alluding to John's gospel (see comments on v. 6). Calvin seems to suggest the Spirit is one witness but mentioned twice.[17] Thatcher wonders if it might not be two aspects of the Spirit's witness: first, his close association with events during Jesus' earthly life, and then his ongoing work in the church after Jesus' death and resurrection.[18]

The witness of the Spirit was prominent in both Jesus' baptism and his death. Jesus' public ministry began when the Spirit descended on him at his water baptism (Matt 3:13 – 17; Mark 1:9 – 13; Luke 3:21 – 23; John 1:29 – 34). Although John's gospel does not include the story of Jesus' baptism, it does highlight the testimony of John the Baptist (John 1:19 – 36), and he was the one who first identified Jesus as Son of God when the Spirit descended as a dove. In John's gospel the death of Jesus is linked to the giving of the Holy Spirit in a scene that evokes God's breathing life into his human creation (John 19:30, 34; 20:22; cf. Gen 2:7 LXX). What is clear

is the unity of the three that bear witness — literally in the Greek "are into one" (note neuter gender, ἕν). This unity of redemptive purpose refutes whatever ideas concerning the Spirit, the water, and the blood were leading people into falsehood, probably distortions of these three elements as they occur in John's gospel.

The mention of *three* witnesses was apparently a convention of that culture (cf. Deut 17:6; 19:15; Matt 18:16; 2 Cor 13:1). The recognition of the involvement of the three persons of Father, Son, and Spirit as trinitarian doctrine developed probably led to the insertion of what is now known as the Johannine comma, which appears in Latin manuscripts but not in any Greek earlier than the fourteenth century. While modern English uses the word "comma" to refer to a punctuation mark, in earlier English usage it referred to a phrase. The Johannine comma is an additional phrase inserted between 5:7 and 5:8 that still appears in Bibles that use the same Greek text from which the King James Version was translated in 1611. It reads (additional phrase in italics):

> For there are three who testify *in heaven:*
> *Father, Word, and Holy Spirit;*
> *and these three are one;*
> *and there are three who testify on earth:*
> the Spirit and the water and the blood;
> and these three agree as one.

While it is virtually certain that John did not write this additional phrase, it represents an interpretation that captures the unity of the Godhead with respect to salvation that is reflected in the earthly life of the incarnate Son and the ongoing work of the Holy Spirit in human lives.

---

17. Calvin, *Commentaries on the Catholic Epistles.*   18. Personal communication, 28 February 2012.

IN DEPTH: How the Johannine Comma Happened

Only Bibles following the King James tradition that venerate the Greek text as it existed in the sixteenth century continue to print the Johannine comma, despite the universal consensus of scholars that it is a late addition to the text and despite the fact that we know the story of how it came to be in texts from the sixteenth century.[19]

The first Greek NT to be printed rather than copied by a scribal hand was produced by Erasmus in 1515, followed by subsequent editions in 1516 and 1519. The first edition was criticized because it did not include the additional testimony of the heavenly witnesses in 1 John 5:7 – 8 that appeared in the Latin versions. Erasmus answered the criticism with the explanation that the additional phrase was not in any of the Greek manuscripts, despite its presence in the Vulgate. In the heat of the moment Erasmus said that if the additional phrases were found in even one Greek manuscript, he would include them in the next printing.

Before his next edition appeared, Erasmus was presented with a Greek manuscript that included the additional material, and he reluctantly included it with a note that he suspected the manuscript had been made to order for the occasion. That manuscript (Greg. 61) was likely written by a Franciscan friar in Oxford in 1520, who translated the disputed words back into Greek from the Latin Vulgate. It does not even appear in manuscripts of the Latin Bible earlier than AD 800. There it appears a margin gloss found its way into the body of the text of subsequent Latin manuscripts, creating the cause of Erasmus's troubles.

5:9 Since we receive human testimony, the testimony of God is greater, because this is God's testimony that he has testified about his Son (εἰ τὴν μαρτυρίαν τῶν ἀνθρώπων λαμβάνομεν, ἡ μαρτυρία τοῦ θεοῦ μείζων ἐστίν, ὅτι αὕτη ἐστὶν ἡ μαρτυρία τοῦ θεοῦ ὅτι μεμαρτύρηκεν περὶ τοῦ υἱοῦ αὐτοῦ). John first establishes that what he is saying is not just of human origin, but has its ultimate origin in God. The first class condition, or condition of fact, states the assumption that human testimony is accepted routinely as one of our epistemological sources. We can know something by direct experience, by logical inference, or by believing what someone else tells us. If one is willing to receive human testimony, how much more should one be willing in principle to accept the testimony of the all-knowing God.

But that is not quite the reason John gives for the superiority of God's testimony. The first *hoti* clause is a causal clause ("because"), and it introduces a christological reason; the second is epexegetical: "this is God's testimony" = what "he has

---

19. Bruce M. Metzger, *The Text of the New Testament: Its Transmission, Corruption, and Restoration* (New York: Oxford University Press, 1980), 62, 101 – 2.

testified about his Son." God's testimony about the Son trumps any merely human ideas such as those John was attempting to correct.

The referent of the demonstrative pronoun "this" (αὕτη) points forward to the *hoti* clause. What is God's testimony? It is the testimony he has given (note perfect tense), and that testimony already given is not about generic spiritual principles but is about his Son, Jesus Christ. God first gave his testimony at the baptism of Jesus when he identified Jesus as his Son (Matt 3:17; Mark 1:11; Luke 3:22; John 1:33). In John's gospel, John the Baptist hears and preaches God's testimony about his Son, accrediting Jesus' words. The Baptist explains, "The one who comes from heaven is above all.... He testifies to what he has seen and heard.... Whoever has accepted it [his testimony] has certified that God is truthful" (John 3:31 – 33).

The beloved disciple of John's gospel is the one "who testifies to these things and who wrote them down. We know that his testimony is true" (John 21:24). Testimony is a central theme of John's gospel, which is itself God's testimony about Jesus. In 1 John, that testimony is "what we have heard, what we have seen with our eyes, what we have perceived, and our hands have touched" (1 John 1:1). Perhaps 1 John 5:9 is an invitation to read John's gospel as a speech act of God's deposition concerning the identity of Jesus.

The author of 1 John assumes that his testimony about the truth stands in unbroken lineage back to God's testimony about Jesus, and he is zealous to protect it from all other, errant claims to truth, such as those apparently offered by the antichrists. The witness of the Spirit, the water, and the blood are all integrally a part of God's testimony. Therefore, 5:9 is making not just a general claim that God's testimony is greater than human testimony,

but the specific claim that the nature of God's testimony is about Jesus, not anything or anyone else.

5:10 The one who believes in the Son of God has this testimony within them. The one who does not believe God has made God a liar, because they have not believed the testimony that God has testified about his Son (ὁ πιστεύων εἰς τὸν υἱὸν τοῦ θεοῦ ἔχει τὴν μαρτυρίαν ἐν αὑτῷ·[20] ὁ μὴ πιστεύων τῷ θεῷ ψεύστην πεποίηκεν αὐτόν, ὅτι οὐ πεπίστευκεν εἰς τὴν μαρτυρίαν ἣν μεμαρτύρηκεν ὁ θεὸς περὶ τοῦ υἱοῦ αὐτοῦ).

The Christian is, by John's definition, one who has heard the NT witness, has recognized it as God's interpretation of the significance of the life and death of Jesus his Son, and has internalized it as their own belief. But the rejection of the gospel of Jesus Christ is not a morally neutral act. John would not look favorably on the pluralistic, culturally centered view of religious belief that is so popular today, that one's belief is what is true for you but has no claim on me. Precisely because the apostolic testimony about Jesus is God's testimony, to hear it and not believe it entails making God a liar.

This is the second time John mentions making God a liar. The first time (in 1:10) involves the denial of personal sin. God says that human beings are sinners who are alienated from him, living in darkness with death their only future. But in his love he sent his Son to atone for that sin, to reconcile people to himself. Note the repetition of the phrase from 5:9, "God has testified about his Son" (μεμαρτύρηκεν ὁ θεὸς περὶ τοῦ υἱοῦ αὐτοῦ). God has given his testimony, and it stands for all time. When someone rejects God's love offered in Christ in favor of some other system of belief (or nonbelief), they implicitly declare that they know better than God, thus "making" him a liar.

---

20. Reflecting the text of the NA 28th edition. See Yarbrough, *1 – 3 John*, 4 – 5.

5:11 And this is the testimony: that God has given eternal life to us and this life is in his Son (καὶ αὕτη ἐστὶν ἡ μαρτυρία, ὅτι ζωὴν αἰώνιον ἔδωκεν ἡμῖν ὁ θεός, καὶ αὕτη ἡ ζωὴ ἐν τῷ υἱῷ αὐτοῦ ἐστιν). The testimony of God is firm, rooted in his character, revealed in his Son, and witnessed by the Spirit, the water, and the blood. John now brings his argument back to address the assurance he wishes his readers to have. God testifies, and he cannot lie, that he offers to all (2:2) what he gave to "us" who have believed his testimony about his Son, namely, the gift of eternal life that is found in no one other than God's Son, Jesus Christ. So closely does John's argument link God's testimony about Jesus to the witness of the Spirit, the water, and the blood that any claim that excludes the Spirit, the water, or the blood is not God's testimony, but merely human ideas devoid of the power to save and assure.

5:12 The one who has the Son has life; the one who does not have the Son of God does not have life (ὁ ἔχων τὸν υἱὸν ἔχει τὴν ζωήν· ὁ μὴ ἔχων τὸν υἱὸν τοῦ θεοῦ τὴν ζωὴν οὐκ ἔχει). This statement summarizes what John has been discussing since 4:1, where he points out that not all "truth" is God's truth, but only that which is of the Spirit in accord with the significance of Jesus' life, death, and resurrection.

The expression "the one who has the Son" is similar to 2:23, where John states that the one who "has" (ἔχει) the Father is "the one who acknowledges the Son," and the one who denies the Son does not have the Father either. This is another way of saying that Jesus Christ is the only way to God (cf. John 14:6), a thought that was just as off-putting to ancient society as it is to many people today.

5:13 These things I write to you who believe in the name of the Son of God so that you might know that you have eternal life (Ταῦτα ἔγραψα ὑμῖν ἵνα εἰδῆτε ὅτι ζωὴν ἔχετε αἰώνιον, τοῖς πιστεύουσιν εἰς τὸ ὄνομα τοῦ υἱοῦ τοῦ θεοῦ). John now begins to bring his letter to a close, forming an inclusio with 1:4. As 1:4 marks a transition between the opening and body of the letter, 5:13 marks a transition between the body and the closing, and it could be grouped either with what precedes or with what follows. It is considered here because it continues the same topic of eternal life mentioned in 5:11 – 12.

John begins to draw his letter to a close by reminding his readers that his purpose is to reassure them that they were right to believe in Christ, and exhorting them to continue to do so even in the wake of whatever disturbance has recently troubled the church (cf. 2:19; 4:1). This is the third assurance John gives his readers after addressing the false ideas about Christ and Christian living to which they were likely exposed (cf. 2:12 – 14, 20 – 21).

The aorist tense of the verb (ἔγραψα) is epistolary and refers not to a previous letter ("I wrote") but to the present letter ("I write"). After opening the letter with the first person plural "we write" (γράφομεν), the author switches to the singular "I write" throughout the rest of the letter, consistently using the present tense in 2:1, 7, 8, 12, 13 and then switching to the aorist in 2:14, 21, 26; 5:13. The demonstrative pronoun (ταῦτα) most likely refers to all that has been previously written, because the theme of eternal life was introduced in the opening of the letter (1:2), and the topics of sin, love, and right thinking about who Christ is have all been linked to it (e.g., 1:7; 2:9; 5:6).

This verse is strikingly similar to the purpose statement of the Fourth Gospel in John 20:31: "These are written that you may believe that Jesus is the Messiah, the Son of God, and that by believing you may have life in his name." The gospel is logically prior in its relevance to believers, since it presents reasons to believe; 1 John exhorts those who have believed to continue in that faith, even in the face of confusing circumstances.

Theology in Application

What We Believe about the Future Determines How We'll Live Today

In the busyness of daily life, it is easy to lose sight of one's eternal future and not even give it a thought until one is confronted with mortality at the grave of a friend or loved one. The priorities of our modern lives probably include working, meals, worship, exercise, shopping, mowing the grass, maintaining our homes and cars, spending time with family and friends, and so on. The importance of life after death seldom comes to mind, even for Christian believers.

Yet nothing seems to have been a greater concern to the author of John's gospel and letters than securing people in the only source of eternal life, Jesus Christ, the Eternal Life sent to earth to die and to open the way through death to life for all who would believe and follow. Jesus' atoning death — the "water and blood" gospel — is the heart of Christian theology. No theology that claims otherwise can be true, for God's testimony confirms *only* a "water and blood" gospel, not a "water only" gospel. Today's theological trend toward a "nonviolent" atonement, while perhaps well intentioned, is a modern expression of the kind of thinking the apostle corrects by reminding his readers that Jesus Christ did not come by water only, but that his blood is essential for the atonement that secures our eternal life after death.

Is What We Believe That Important?

Many in modern society don't seem to think that one's choice of a particular religious belief, or no religious belief, is an important decision. It certainly isn't viewed as a life-or-death matter. But rejecting the offer of eternal life in Jesus Christ is not a morally neutral decision (see The Theology of John's Letters). John says that whoever hears the gospel and refuses to believe it implicitly calls God a liar, for the Christian witness to the gospel has its ultimate origin in God's witnessing revelation that Jesus *is* his Son who was sent to atone for our sins (5:10).

John's teaching corrects a smorgasbord approach to belief in God that is just as popular today as it was in the first century. We live in a world with many religions, and we increasingly rub elbows in our workplaces and neighborhoods with the people who practice them. Many of these religions teach and practice good moral principles, and our colleagues and neighbors may be very fine, upstanding people. In fact, they may be nicer and better people than some of the Christians we know! It may be tempting in today's social climate to "water down" the gospel of Jesus Christ, denying the need for atonement for sin or emphasizing the common moral principles that Christianity shares with other religions. Against the polite, but erroneous, belief that all religions lead to God, Jesus states, "I am the way and the truth and the life. No one comes to the Father except through me" (John 14:6).

It is no accident that these three terms, "way," "truth," and "life," are coupled in this statement. As a religious belief, only Jesus is the *way* to God because only Jesus atoned for sin and then rose victorious from his grave. Only Jesus came from God, as God enfleshed in a human body like ours, and he came to reveal the otherwise unseen and invisible God. Therefore, any spiritual *truth* claims not based on this revelation of God in Christ are just whistling in the dark. Finally, Jesus is the *life*, first because his own eternal life as a member of the Godhead was enfleshed in his human body (1 John 1:2), and second because his human body arose from the grave. It is through his eternal life that we live (cf. John 14:19).

John's purpose in writing the letter we know as 1 John was to bring assurance of eternal life to his readers, who were apparently being exposed to a "water only" gospel. He points out the necessity of a "water and blood" gospel that embraces the cross of Jesus and doesn't preach just the teachings of Jesus, or the blessings of Jesus, or the spirit of Jesus, as many seem inclined to do today. A "water only" gospel might satisfy some for this life, but its value stops at the grave. For it provides no assurance of reconciliation with God, no atonement for our sin, and no promise of life after death.

15

1 John 5:14 – 21

Literary Context

Having begun the transition from the body of the letter to its closing in 5:13, this passage brings the letter to a close by turning once again to the topics of sin (5:14 – 19), first introduced in 1:6, and knowing the truth (5:20). Following an emphatic statement of Christ's deity (5:20), the letter ends with a somewhat abrupt and enigmatic command to keep away from idols (5:21).

Rhetorical criticism argues for the unity of this pericope as part of the original letter.

> All of 5:13 – 21 functions to reiterate major topics of the work. Without this section the work would have been severely truncated by Greco-Roman rhetorical standards.... The thematic symmetry between the opening and closing of 1 John is evidence that the final version was intended to include vv. 13 – 21.[1]

The initial conjunction (καί) suggests that this section is related to the previous statement of John's purpose for writing (5:13), which itself is a summary statement of the letter. Following the purpose statement, this passage implies that assurance of eternal life rests on two major points: (1) handling sin correctly (5:16 – 17), and (2) knowing the true God, who is eternal life (5:20). This closing includes two exhortations: (1) pray for others who sin (5:16), and (2) keep away from idols (5:21). The teaching of the entire letter is likely subsumed by the final command, "Keep yourselves from idols," which may form an inclusio with possible allusions to idols in the opening of the letter (1:1 – 4). The opening verses share with this final passage the topic of eternal life, confirming that this is the overarching topic that most concerns the author.

---

1. Watson, " 'Keep Yourselves from Idols,' " 288.

Main Idea

We can know the one true God because the Son of God has come to give us understanding. Knowledge of the one true God is the basis of eternal life (cf. John 17:3). To follow an errant understanding of Christ is to follow after idols and to commit the sin that leads to death by moving outside the realm of light and eternal life. It is the failure to remain in him.

Translation

(See next page.)

Structure

Six statements of what "we know" form a framework for John's final words ("we know" [οἴδαμεν] in 5:15 [2x], 18, 19, 20; "we know" [γινώσκομεν] in 20):

1. We know God hears those who pray according to his will (v. 15).
2. We know that we have the things we ask of God (v. 15).
3. We know that the one born of God does not sin because Christ protects him or her (v. 18).
4. We know that we are of God and the whole world is under the devil's power (v. 19).
5. We know that the Son of God has come and has given understanding to us (v. 20).
6. We know the true God (v. 20).

These statements lie between two exhortations: (1) to pray with confidence for others who sin (5:16), and (2) to keep away from idols, the seemingly abrupt final statement of the letter in 5:21. John closes his message with a reiteration of its major topics using repetition, emotional appeal, and amplification.[2]

---

2. Ibid., 288 – 89.

1 John 5:14 – 21

14a	identification	And **this is the confidence we have with him,**
b	identification	that whatever we ask according to his will,
c	assertion	he hears us.
15a	condition	And if we know
b	content	that he hears us, whatever we ask,
c	assertion	[then] **we know that we have the things requested** that we have asked from him.
16a	condition	If anyone sees their brother or sister commit sin that does not lead to death,
b	exhortation	**let them ask,**
c	result	and **God will give to that brother or sister life,**
d	expansion	to those whose sin does not lead to death.
e	assertion	**There is sin that leads to death;**
f	explanation	**I am not saying you should pray about that sin.**
17a	assertion	**All unrighteousness is sin,**
b	assertion	but **there is sin that does not lead to death.**
18a	assertion	**We know**
b	content	that everyone who has been born of God does not sin, but
c	basis	**the One begotten of God protects them,** and
d	expansion	**the evil one does not take hold of them.**
19a	assertion	**We know**
b	content	that we are of God, and
c	assertion	[that] the whole world lies under the power of the evil one.
20a	assertion	And **we know**
b	content	that the Son of God has come and
c	assertion	that he has given understanding to us
d	purpose	so that we might know the True One.
e	assertion	And **we are in the True One,**
f	restatement	in his Son,
g	apposition	Jesus Christ.
h	assertion	**This One is the true God and eternal life.**
21a	address	Children, [in light of what we know]
b	command	**keep yourselves from idols.**

Exegetical Outline

➡ **XV. Knowing God (5:14 – 21)**

    A. Prayer for a sinning brother or sister (5:14 – 17)

        1. Confidence to ask God (5:14 – 15)

        2. Intercession on behalf of a brother or sister (5:16 – 17)

    B. What "we know" (5:18 – 20)

        1. We know that everyone who is born of God does not sin (5:18)

        2. We know that we are of God and the world is under the evil one (5:19)

        3. We know that the Son of God has come, bringing understanding of the truth (5:20)

    C. Closing exhortation (5:21)

Explanation of the Text

5:14 And this is the confidence we have with him, that whatever we ask according to his will, he hears us (Καὶ αὕτη ἐστὶν ἡ παρρησία ἣν ἔχομεν πρὸς αὐτόν, ὅτι ἐάν τι αἰτώμεθα κατὰ τὸ θέλημα αὐτοῦ ἀκούει ἡμῶν). Although at first glance John seems to be introducing a new topic (prayer), this verse is a transition into a final discussion about sin and the believer's responsibility toward brothers or sisters who are not living in Christ (cf. 2:11; 3:6; 4:11). John habitually returns to topics previously introduced, and while he has not discussed prayer earlier in the letter, he has repeatedly discussed sin.

The initial conjunction (καί) relates this unit to 5:13, which concerns the reassurance of eternal life. John is concerned for the spiritual state of the people in his church(es), knowing that they have been exposed to false teaching and practices by those who have left (2:19). He has argued extensively throughout the letter for the need to live without sin, the need to discern the origin of teaching about God, and the necessity of the blood of Jesus as part of the true gospel. So what are his readers to do when they see a brother or sister not living according to the apostolic teachings? Before exhorting them to prayer for one another (5:16 – 17), he reminds them that God does hear

the requests of his people that are asked according to his will. This picks up the similar thought previously expressed in 1 John 3:21 – 22.

The demonstrative pronoun in the phrase "this is the confidence" (αὕτη ἐστὶν ἡ παρρησία) likely points forward to the statement, "whatever we ask according to his will, he hears us." The preposition *pros* (πρός) likely carries a similar sense to its use in John 1:1, where the Word is said to be "with God" (πρὸς τὸν θεόν). One might expect the more common preposition *meta* (μετά) with the genitive, but *pros* (πρός) not only suggests a static presence and spatial proximity but connotes personal relationship. Thus, John is stating that believers have confidence in their personal relationship and communication with God. This echoes Jesus' statements in John 16:23 – 26, that his Father will give whatever his followers ask "in [his] name."

While many readers will immediately wonder what is God's will that we might ask for, that is not quite the point here. John will explain what to ask for in vv. 16 – 17. As Yarbrough comments, "There are no explicit limits set to such requests, although it is likely that John assumes that believers will pray in keeping with God's purposes.... John's point is to affirm *that* we know God hears when we request, not that we have unerring discernment as to what we should be requesting."[3] This assurance of personal communion with God is also the context in which seemingly unanswered prayer requests should be understood.

5:15 And if we know that he hears us, whatever we ask, [then] we know that we have the things requested that we have asked from him (καὶ ἐὰν οἴδαμεν ὅτι ἀκούει ἡμῶν ὃ ἐὰν αἰτώμεθα, οἴδαμεν ὅτι ἔχομεν τὰ αἰτήματα ἃ ᾐτήκαμεν ἀπ' αὐτοῦ). John has just reminded his readers that God hears the prayers of those who ask according to his will. He now belabors the point further with a third class, general conditional sentence, "if we know ...," which uses an indicative form of "know" (οἶδα) where one would expect either a subjunctive verb following *ean* (ἐάν) or a first class conditional with *ei* (εἰ) and the indicative.

Culy suggests this may be a mild rebuke of the readers "by portraying something as hypothetical ... that has just been established as true ... the fact that it has just been established as true may have led the writer to weaken the third class condition by using an indicative rather than the expected subjunctive."[4] (Note that this is the third occurrence of an unexpected indicative verb form that raises debated exegetical issues; cf. 5:2.) Had John used the first class condition of fact, the sense would be "since we know that hears us...." But introducing the conditional *ean* (ἐάν) suggests the possibility that his readers have been praying without having that confidence of knowing that God hears. If so, the nuance would be along the lines of Jas 1:6 and Mark 11:24 — that one must ask God without doubting that he hears. Brown, however, translates *ean* (ἐάν) with the indicative here as a first class conditional ("since ..."), but then mentions it as little different from *ean* with the subjunc-

tive in v. 14b.[5] He notes that the exhortation to pray forms a chiasm across 14b and 15a: "ask ... hear ... hear ... ask."

The verb "hear" (ἀκούει) suggests that God understands the request and answers prayer. God answers our requests ... always? Does believing that we are heard magically grant what we ask for? (See Theology in Application below for further discussion.) How does confidence that God hears us amount to our having what we ask? To properly ask of God, one must always submit to his perfect and omniscient will. Even Jesus in the garden of Gethsemane prayed, "not as I will, but as you will" (Matt 26:39; cf. Mark 14:36; Luke 22:42). Since in any given situation we may not know whether what we're asking is in God's will, whenever it seems God has *not* answered, we must receive that in the confidence of knowing we were heard. We *do* have what we ask according to his will even if his will is "No" or "Not yet."

5:16 – 17 If anyone sees their brother or sister commit sin that does not lead death, let them ask, and God will give to that brother or sister life, to those whose sin does not lead to death. There is sin that leads to death; I am not saying you should pray about that sin. All unrighteousness is sin, but there is sin that does not lead to death (Ἐάν τις ἴδῃ τὸν ἀδελφὸν αὐτοῦ ἁμαρτάνοντα ἁμαρτίαν μὴ πρὸς θάνατον, αἰτήσει καὶ δώσει αὐτῷ ζωήν, τοῖς ἁμαρτάνουσιν μὴ πρὸς θάνατον. ἔστιν ἁμαρτία πρὸς θάνατον· οὐ περὶ ἐκείνης λέγω ἵνα ἐρωτήσῃ. πᾶσα ἀδικία ἁμαρτία ἐστίν, καὶ ἔστιν ἁμαρτία οὐ πρὸς θάνατον).

Having explained from several perspectives that sin is incompatible with Christian life, John now addresses the issue of sins that his readers may see others commit. Verse 16 is perhaps the most troubling to new readers of the NT, for it immediately

---

3. Yarbrough, *1 – 3 John*, 300 (italics original).
4. Culy, *I, II, III John*, 134.

5. Brown, *Epistles of John*, 607, 610.

raises the question, "What is the sin that leads to death?" and the second quickly follows, "Have I committed, or could I commit, this sin?"

A search of random blogs shows that various popular ideas have been offered, such as false teaching, blasphemy against the Holy Spirit, and apostasy. Others offer that "brother or sister" refers not to a Christian believer, but to an unbeliever who hangs out at church. Or perhaps the sin that leads to death is a sin that deserves capital punishment. Some point out that God tells Jeremiah (Jer 14:10 – 11) not to intercede for the people of Judah, who listen to false prophets' assurances that God's judgment will never come. It is ironic that the present verse shakes some readers' confidence in their salvation, since John's purpose is to reassure his readers of their eternal life.

This is the fourth and final discussion about sin in a believer's life (see 1:7 – 10; 2:1 – 12; 3:4 – 9). In 1:7 – 10, John made the point that any claim to be without sin is self-deceit and implicitly calls God a liar. In 2:1 – 12, John furthered the discussion by stating that sin has been forgiven by the atoning sacrifice of Jesus Christ, but rather than providing a license to sin, Jesus' death should motivate Christians to live righteously.

In 3:4 – 9, John explained the complete incompatibility of sin with life in Christ by offering this strong statement: "No one who has been born of God sins, because his [God's] seed remains in them, and they are not able to sin because they have been born of God" (3:9). There we concluded that the specific sin in view was "lawlessness" (ἀνομία), the sin of the deliberate rejection of God's authority (see the discussion there).

In the passage before us, John instructs his readers about what they are to do when they see a Christian brother or sister sinning a sin that does not lead to death. They are to pray for that sinner. John recognizes here that some of his readers will sin in various ways, and he puts some responsi-

bility on the members of the congregation for the spiritual health of the church. His exhortation to "anyone" to intercede is remarkable because in the ancient world, mediation between humans and the divine world was limited primarily to priests and prophets. This is perhaps an expression of John's belief in the "priesthood" of all believers (cf. 1 Pet 2:9).

John begins with a general condition, "if" (ἐάν, not a condition of fact), and the indefinite pronoun "anyone" (τις). The exhortation applies to any or all of his readers at any future time who happen to see a brother or sister sinning. He modifies "sinning" (ἁμαρτάνοντα) by adding the cognate noun as the direct object of the participle, "a sin that does not lead to death" (ἁμαρτίαν μὴ πρὸς θάνατον). Note that whatever sins are in view, they are observable to others. These are not hidden sins of the heart, but sins that are committed in ways others can perceive.

The phrase "not leading to death" (μὴ πρὸς θάνατον) is found elsewhere in John's writings in John 11:4, in which Jesus says Lazarus's illness will not end in death, where it was clearly referring to physical death and to Jesus' intention to raise Lazarus to physical life from his grave. But in John's first letter, every mention of "life" (ζωή) has been to eternal life after death (1 John 1:1, 2; 2:25; 3:14, 15; 5:11, 12, 13, 16), which is also its primary referent in John's gospel (e.g., John 3:15, 16, 36; 5:24, 39, 40; 6:40, 53, 54; 14:6; 17:3; 20:31). Furthermore, John has just stated his purpose for the letter in 5:13, that his readers may have assurance of eternal life. So how does John's recognition of sin in a believer's life figure into that?

There is ambiguity about the antecedents of the pronouns in 5:16b-c. Who will give life to whom? The Greek reads (lit.), "If anyone sees … he will ask and he will give to him life" (Ἐάν τις ἴδῃ … αἰτήσει καὶ δώσει αὐτῷ ζωήν). For clarity, let's use "pray-er" to refer to the believer who sees another sinning, and "sinner" to refer to the sinning brother or sister, even while recognizing that pray-ers can and do sin and that sinning believers probably do pray. In the case of seeing a brother or sister sinning, the pray-er should intercede in full confidence that God will give life to the sinner. It is clearly the pray-er who "will ask" (imperatival future), and almost certainly life will be given to the sinner, since John's point is about the relationship between the sin of believers and the assurance of eternal life (cf. Jas 5:20). Although there is nothing in the syntax that suggests a change in the implied subject of "he will give" (δώσει), only God can bestow eternal life, even if the pray-er has functioned as an intermediary.[6]

But if the sinner is a fellow believer, don't they already have eternal life (cf. John 5:24)? Does this mean that they've somehow lost it by sinning? The future tense of "will give" (δώσει) does not mean that the sinner doesn't have eternal life already, but reflects the fact that eternal life is still a future reality. Therefore, it expresses a reassurance that sin that does not lead to death will not disqualify a sinning believer from eternal life when they pass from this life. This is not to say that the eternal life of a sinning believer depends on the prayers of others, but that dealing with sin in the church is a corporate responsibility (see Theology in Application, below).

John also is not diminishing the seriousness of sin. He has already exhorted his readers not to sin (2:1; 3:9), for sin does not reflect their family resemblance to God the Father; rather, it characterizes those who are still in darkness and of the devil (3:5, 6, 8). Yarbrough comments:

> Divine parentage does not generate the breaches of faith, ethics, or love that John warns against.

Christians, accordingly, are not chronically characterized by these fundamental deficiencies or lapses. If they are, they are not Christians, in John's outlook.[7]

But John recognizes that even true Christians do sin, and so he must explain how it is that Christians can have eternal life despite their sins after coming to faith in Christ's atonement. This is necessary because his stark dualism between life and death, and righteousness and sin, would logically imply that no one who sins could have eternal life. He explains this tension in 5:17 by pointing out that although all unrighteousness is sin, there is sin that does not lead to death, and there is sin that does. Because death is separation from God, "death" is in opposition to eternal life here, and so it refers to what happens beyond physical death. As Yarbrough explains:

> This is surely a reference to the benefits of "eternal life" already alluded to frequently in the epistle (1:1–2; 2:25; 3:14–15; 5:11–13). God will keep that person in his fellowship despite his or her (perhaps even grave) transgression. The picture of Jesus saying that he would pray for Peter so that he would return after his denials comes to mind (Luke 22:32).[8]

Furthermore, as Westcott observed, "All sin tends to make the fellowship [with God] less complete. Yet not all equally; nor all in a fixed and unalterable degree."[9]

Interpreters throughout church history have offered various explanations of the sin that does lead to death that involve a distinction either between different kinds of sin or between different kinds of sinners:

1. deliberate vs. unintentional sin (cf. Lev 4:2; 5:1; Num 15:30–31; Num 18:22)[10]

---

6. See Brooke, *Johannine Epistles*, 146; Bultmann, *Johannine Epistles*, 87 n16; Haas, *Letters of John*, 150.

7. Yarbrough, *1–3 John*, 310.

8. Ibid., 307.

9. Westcott, *Epistles of St. John*, 191.

10. Burge, *Letters of John*, 216.

2. "mortal sins," to use Roman Catholic terminology, such as murder, adultery, and idolatry, vs. venial sins[11]

3. blasphemy against the Holy Spirit (cf. Mark 3:28 – 30)

4. apostasy, such as discussed in Heb 6:4 – 6[12]

5. the deliberate and persistent rejection of the truth in Christ

Deliberate, intentional sin will surely destroy a believer's assurance that they have eternal life, and John notes that those who "walk in the darkness" are self-deceived if they think they have fellowship with God (1:6). The one who sins is of the devil and is not living in Christ (3:6 – 9). If a professing Christian deliberately and intentionally chooses to sin, they have every reason to doubt their salvation and need to repent. How much more the danger if the sin is a grave one, such as murder, adultery, or idolatry.

Since the time of Thomas Aquinas, heinous behaviors such as those just noted earned the special term of *mortal sin* in the Roman Catholic Church, as opposed to *venial sin*, of a lesser kind. If this is what John means here, he is saying that "small" sins should be addressed by intercession on behalf of others but not the "big" ones, which have made a person ineligible for eternal life. But against this view is Jesus' teaching that anger is as bad as murder, and lust as bad as adultery (Matt 5:21 – 22, 27 – 28). Furthermore, biblical people such as Moses, David, and Paul would be beyond redemption because Moses committed murder (Exod 2:12), David committed both adultery and murder (2 Sam 11:1 – 21), and Paul, by his former name Saul, was complicit in the deaths of some of the earliest Christians (Acts 8:1, 3). All of these were premeditated and deliberate sins, and yet Moses, David, and Paul found the grace of God's forgive-ness. As Westcott understands it, "The thought is not of specific acts as such, but of acts which have a certain character: There is that which must be described as sin unto death, there is that which wholly separates us from Christ."[13]

The thought of Mark 3:28 – 30 brings us closer to an understanding of the sin that leads to death, for there Jesus states explicitly that blasphemy against the Holy Spirit is an eternal sin that will never be forgiven. In context Jesus said this during his public ministry when people were attributing his power to Satan (Mark 3:22). That basic confusion and mistaken identity of God's work and power in and through Jesus prevented people from being reconciled to God through him. As long as one rejected Jesus, no forgiveness would be possible because Jesus is the only means of forgiveness. Therefore, such blasphemy remains unforgiven.

Although in Mark 3 the context is in reference to unbelievers, the "sin that leads to death" in 1 John 5:16 – 17 is along these same lines, for it refers to sin that is characteristic of those who belong to darkness rather than light. In 1 John 3, John introduced the word "lawlessness" (ἀνομία), which is used throughout the NT to refer to the sin that characterizes those who are perishing (Matt 7:23; 13:41; 23:28; Rom 6:19; 2 Cor 6:14; 2 Thess 2:3, 7; Heb 1:9). It is the word used to refer to the "man of lawlessness [ἀνομία]," who is usually understood to be an antichrist (2 Thess 2:3). So understood, in 1 John 5:16 the sin that leads to death is of that same nature. And yet, even *anomia* can be forgiven by Christ's atonement (Rom 4:7; Titus 2:14; Heb 10:17) — unless one persists in refusing the only means of forgiveness that God offers in Christ.

In the context of 1 John, the sin that leads to death must be related to the statement in 5:12, "The one who has the Son has life; the one who

---

11. Chiefly authored by Aquinas according to Grayston, *Johannine Epistles*, 143.

12. Grayston, *Johannine Epistles*, 144.

13. Westcott, *Epistles of St. John*, 192.

does not have the Son of God does not have life" and is therefore on the path that leads to death. This context is also confirmed by exegesis of 5:21 (see comments below). Sin that leads to death is that which excludes one from the realm of life, sin that prevents one from having the Son. As Thompson suggests, "'sin unto death' is already evidence that one lives in the realm of death, in the world, under the control of the evil one, and not in the sphere of life and righteousness granted by God to those who trust in Christ's work on their behalf."[14] Verses 11 – 12 stand in the context of the claim that to believe a "water only" gospel (5:6) is to reject the testimony of God himself (5:7 – 9). In John's historical context, the professing Christians who argued for a "water only" gospel that diminished or eliminated the need for atonement are being implicated in 5:16 – 17 as those who are committing sin that leads to death. The sin that leads to death, therefore, is the sin of rejecting Christ's atonement, the sin of calling God's testimony a lie (1:10; 2:22; 5:10).

Those whose sins do *not* lead to death commit sins "unwittingly and which do not involve rejection of God and his way of salvation. The sinner is overcome by temptation against his will; he still wants to love God and his neighbor, he still believes in Jesus Christ, he still longs to be freed from sin."[15] The brother or sister who is sinning the sin that leads to death has a heart that has not been transformed by the new birth. Despite their self-identification as a Christian and their presence in the gatherings of the church(es), they have refused to believe in Jesus Christ, to follow God's commands, and to love their brothers and sisters. As

Kruse suggests, "the sin that does not lead to death is the sin of the believer ... the sin that does lead to death is most likely that of the unbeliever."[16] Scholer also emphasizes that "the 'sin not unto death' is one which a believer can and does commit and the 'sin unto death' is one which a believer does not and cannot commit."[17]

John then limits the focus of the prayer that he is exhorting in 5:16e-f. Tan is correct that the prepositional phrase "about that [sin]" (περὶ ἐκείνης) modifies the verb "I am speaking" (λέγω, i.e., "not about that sin [that leads to eternal death] I am speaking").[18] But contra Tan's further inference, the *hina* clause expresses content of "I am speaking" (λέγω).[19] As the NLT translates, "I am not saying you should pray for those who commit it [the sin that leads to death]." As Marshall observes, this "cumbrous rendering" is meant to emphasize what John is *not* saying, namely, that he is not forbidding prayer for such.[20]

Is John being hard-hearted by instructing prayer only for those whose sin does not led to death? At the time John wrote, it is likely he was referring to those who had left his church(es) as committing the sin that leads to death (2:19). They denied that Jesus is the Christ come in the flesh, denied that he came in both water and blood, and thereby denied the significance of his atoning death. They had put themselves beyond the fellowship of apostolic Christian belief, and therefore John is focusing his pastoral attention on strengthening the fellowship of those who remain. There is no point in interceding for the sins of those who persist in beliefs about Jesus that prevent them from receiving God's forgiveness. John simply says, "I am not saying that

---

14. Thompson, *1 – 3 John*, 142.

15. Marshall, *Epistles of John*, 248.

16. Kruse, *Letters of John*, 194.

17. David M. Scholer, "Sins Within and Sins Without: An Interpretation of 1 John 5:16 – 17," in *Current Issues in Biblical and Patristic Interpretation* (ed. Gerald F. Hawthorne; Grand Rapids:

Eerdmans, 1975), 232; see also Thompson, *1 – 3 John*, 142.

18. Randall K. J. Tan, "Should We Pray for Straying Brethren? John's Confidence in 1 John 5:16 – 17," *JETS* 45 (2002): 599 – 609.

19. Wallace, *Greek Grammar*, 475; Culy, *I, II, III John*, 136.

20. Marshall, *Epistles of John*, 246 n19.

you should pray about the sin that leads to death." He does not forbid praying for those who have left the church and are still in need of God's transforming grace in Christ; that is just not the situation he is addressing here.

In a similar way, Jesus focused on his disciples in John 17:9 and did not pray for the world, but this does not mean that he was indifferent or hostile toward the world he came to save (cf. John 3:16). It is therefore going beyond the text to argue that John "does not want prayers for such sins,"[21] or that he has misapplied Jesus' example "under the tension" of the situation.[22]

Marshall raises the interesting question of "why one Christian should intercede for another Christian if his sin is not one that leads to death."[23] The probable answer to this lies in 5:17 (cf. 3:4). All unrighteousness is sin, and even for the believer who has eternal life, sin is is a serious and destructive matter, for "sin is lawlessness [ἀνομία]" (3:4). "Sin remains sin, and sin is dangerous, because it is characteristic of life apart from God."[24] There is the possibility that sin will entice and draw someone away, perhaps first by yielding to temptation, then by a decision to sin deliberately, and finally perhaps by turning away from God and forgiveness altogether.

Furthermore, sin usually involves other people, which erodes the unity and fellowship of the Christian community and blemishes the integrity and reputation of the church. As Christians intercede for others they see are not living consistently in Christ, the one whom the Father has drawn and who has truly come to Christ will not persist in sin (John 6:37), but will be brought to repentence.

5:18 We know that everyone who has been born of God does not sin, but the One begotten of God
protects them, and the evil one does not take hold of them (Οἴδαμεν ὅτι πᾶς ὁ γεγεννημένος ἐκ τοῦ θεοῦ οὐχ ἁμαρτάνει, ἀλλ᾽ ὁ γεννηθεὶς ἐκ τοῦ θεοῦ τηρεῖ αὐτόν, καὶ ὁ πονηρὸς οὐχ ἅπτεται αὐτοῦ). For the second time in the letter, John emphatically states that the person who has been born of God does not sin (cf. 3:9). The parallel phrases in 3:9 (πᾶς ὁ γεγεννημένος ἐκ τοῦ θεοῦ ἁμαρτίαν οὐ ποιεῖ) and 5:8 (πᾶς ὁ γεγεννημένος ἐκ τοῦ θεοῦ οὐχ ἁμαρτάνει) suggest that the same sin or type of sin is in view.[25] As argued above, that sin is the sin of lawlessness (ἀνομία), a rejection of God's authority to define sin and, consequently, a rejection of God's grace.

Having just taught, on the one hand, that sin covered by Christ's atonement does not disqualify a believer from eternal life, John now quickly reminds his readers, on the other hand, that sin is completely incompatible with new life in Christ. While it is true that people genuinely born of God cannot commit sin that leads to death, John does not give license to anyone who thinks they may go on sinning with impunity so that grace might increase (cf. Rom 6:1), because thinking along those lines is characteristic of those who, in fact, have not been born of God. It is the kind of erroneous thinking that John refuted in 1:5 – 10, that sin is not really a serious issue.

A major exegetical issue in this verse is whether the aorist passive participle in the second clause ("the One begotten of God") refers to Jesus or to the believer, and another issue related to that decision, whether the text originally read "protects him" (αὐτόν, as NA27) or "keeps himself" (ἑαυτόν, as the NA28). Even though "the One begotten of God" may sound like it refers to Jesus Christ, especially to our post-Nicene ears, there is

21. Brown, *Epistles of John*, 613.
22. Dodd, *Johannine Epistles*, 137.
23. Marshall, *Epistles of John*, 248 – 49.
24. Ibid., 248.
25. Painter, *1, 2, and 3 John*, 322.

no (other) biblical reference to Jesus that uses this exact expression (though cf. 5:1). Brown therefore translates, "No one who has been begotten of God commits sin; rather the one begotten by God is protected, and so the Evil One cannot touch him,"[26] but then comments, "It does not make much difference" whether the Christian guards himself or God guards him, "for only the Christian's status as a child of God enables him to protect himself."[27]

However, the use of two different forms of the same verb "beget" (γεννάω) may indicate a distinction that allows two referents. It occurs first as a perfect passive participle to refer to the believer and then as an aorist passive, which most interpreters do take as a reference to Jesus Christ.[28] Perhaps John means to suggest the shared nature that reborn Christians have with the sinless man, Jesus Christ. By this reading, John reassures his readers that they are safe because Christ protects them. While the powers of evil may tempt, entice, and otherwise influence the believer, even to the point of lapses into sin, the evil one cannot take hold of a child of God to remove them from the light and life and drag them back into darkness and death.

This verse alludes to Jesus' promise in John 10:28 – 29, "I give them eternal life, and they shall never perish; no one will snatch them out of my hand. My Father, who has given them to me, is greater than all; no one can snatch them out of my Father's hand" (cf. 17:15; Rom 8:39). Despite such dire warnings about sin that leads to death in 1 John 5:16 – 17, John's readers can rest assured in what Christ has done:

- he brought eternal life (1:2)
- he cleanses sin (1:7)
- he intercedes with the Father (2:1)
- his death atones for sin (2:2)
- he destroys the devil's works (3:8)
- he demonstrated God's love (3:16)

All of these are summarized by 5:18 as the protection the Father has given to his children through Jesus Christ.

5:19 We know that we are of God, and [that] the whole world lies under the power of under the evil one (οἴδαμεν ὅτι ἐκ τοῦ θεοῦ ἐσμεν καὶ ὁ κόσμος ὅλος ἐν τῷ πονηρῷ κεῖται). John here returns to the duality between the world and God's children that is so characteristic of his thinking. The inclusive "we" refers to those who have been born of God and therefore are no longer of the world, a world that lies under the power of the evil one, the devil. The reason the devil cannot "touch" or take hold of one of God's children is that they are no longer within the realm of his power.

IN DEPTH: What We Know

The topic of knowledge of God and its source is of primary concern to John. The Son of God entered history in human form to reveal who God is — truth that would otherwise remain unseen and unknown (John 1:18). That revelation of God in Christ is the source of true knowledge about God, which cannot be acquired from any other source. The importance of true knowledge about God is seen in Jesus' statement in John 17:3, which directly relates knowledge

26. Brown, *Epistles of John*, 609.
27. Ibid., 622.

28. See Yarbrough, *1 – 3 John*, 4.

of God with eternal life: "Now this is eternal life: that they *know* you, the only true God, and Jesus Christ, whom you have sent" (italics added). And the attainment of eternal life is paramount to John's gospel, for it is the reason that gospel was written: "But these are written that you may believe that Jesus is the Messiah, the Son of God, and that by believing you may have life in his name" (20:31).

It appears that some of the statements in John's gospel, or the tradition that those statements represent, were being distorted and misunderstood to the point that true knowledge of God was being jeopardized. False teaching and beliefs were apparently the cause of the schism in the church(es) to which 1 John was written, for it was written so that those who believe in the name of the Son of God may *know* that they have eternal life (1 John 5:13). It is only logical, therefore, that 1 John be centrally concerned with the true knowledge of God and its source (see The Theology of John's Letters).

The opening verses of the letter (1:1 – 4) stress that not every spiritual leader who might appear on the scene has the authority and knowledge to speak the truth about Jesus Christ. Only those whose knowledge and authority go back to Jesus himself are qualified to teach the facts about Jesus and the significance of his life. Throughout the letter John refers to what "we know" with the implication that anyone who teaches or believes otherwise is not teaching the truth about Christ.

Using two different verbs for knowing (οἶδα and γινώσκω), John makes remarkable statements throughout his letter that outline the truths of the gospel (italics added):[29]

1 John	Text[30]	Commentary
2:3	This is how we *know* that we *know* him: if we keep his commands.	There is no assurance apart from obedience.
2:4	The one who says, "I *know* him," and does not keep his commands is a liar, and the truth is not in them.	There is no true knowledge of God apart from obedience.
2:5 – 6	This is how we *know* that we are in him: the one who says, "I remain in him," ought also himself to walk just as that One walked.	There is no true knowledge of God apart from discipleship.
2:13	Fathers, I am writing to you because you *do know* the One who is from the beginning.	Christian maturity entails personal knowledge of the eternal God.

Continued on next page.

---

29. For an analysis of these verbs in the structure of 1 John, see B. A. du Toit, "The Role and Meaning of Statements of 'Certainty' in the Structural Composition of 1 John," *Neot* 13 (1979): 84 – 100.

30. Italics are added to the Scripture citations in all cases.

1 John	Text	Commentary
2:14	Little children, yes, I write to you because you *have known* the Father. Fathers, yes, I write to you because you *have known* the One who is from the beginning.	To be a child of God and to become a mature Christian means to know God truly.
2:18	Children . . . even now many have become antichrists, and so we *know* that it is the last hour.	Knowledge of God provides discernment.
2:29	If you *know* that he is righteous, you *know* also that everyone who lives righteously has been born of him.	True knowledge of God is the basis for Christian ethics.
3:1	For this reason, the world does not *know* us, because it did not *know* him.	"The world" is all those who do not know Jesus.
3:6	Everyone who sins has neither seen him nor *known* him.	True knowledge of God requires obedience.
3:16	In this way we have *known* love, because that One laid down his life on our behalf.	True knowledge of God allows true love.
3:19	This is how we will *know* that we are of the truth.	Assurance requires true knowledge of God — that one "belongs to the truth."
3:20	. . . whenever our heart convicts us. For God is greater than our hearts, and he *knows* everything.	True knowlege of God allows us to put our guilt to rest.
3:24	In this way we *know* that he remains in us: from the Spirit, whom he gave to us.	True knowledge of God requires the Spirit.
4:2	In this way you *know* the Spirit of God.	True knowledge of God requires true knowledge of the Spirit.
4:6	We are of God; the one who *knows* God hears us, [but] whoever is not of God does not hear us.	True knowledge of God means accepting the teaching of his apostles.
4:7	Everyone who loves has been begotten of God and . . . *knows* God.	True knowledge of God motivates love.
4:8	The one does not love does not *know* God.	True knowledge of God motivates love.
4:13	In this way we *know* that in him we live and he in us: because he has given to us of his Spirit.	Assurance requires the Spirit.
4:16	And we have *known* and have trusted the love that God has for us.	True knowledge of God means we know God loves us.
5:2	So this is how we *know* that we love the children of God.	Assurance requires love.
5:20	We *know* that the Son of God has come and that he has given understanding to us so that we might *know* the True One.	We cannot know God truly apart from knowing the Son of God.

5:20 And we know that the Son of God has come and that he has given understanding to us so that we might know the True One. And we are in the True One, in his Son, Jesus Christ. This One is the true God and eternal life (οἴδαμεν δὲ ὅτι ὁ υἱὸς τοῦ θεοῦ ἥκει καὶ δέδωκεν ἡμῖν διάνοιαν ἵνα γινώσκομεν τὸν ἀληθινόν, καὶ ἐσμὲν ἐν τῷ ἀληθινῷ, ἐν τῷ υἱῷ αὐτοῦ Ἰησοῦ Χριστῷ. οὗτός ἐστιν ὁ ἀληθινὸς θεὸς καὶ ζωὴ αἰώνιος). We come in 5:20 to a marvelous summary statement about true knowledge of God and its source. What a privilege to know that the Son of God has come!

But Christian knowledge of the truth must be more than the acknowledgment of Jesus' birth and death; it must entail trusting Jesus as the source of understanding about God. Jesus, the incarnate Son of God, has given us "understanding" (διάνοια, *dianoia*) — that facility and disposition to comprehend the significance of his coming. This is the same word Jesus used when he summed up the greatest commandment, "Love the Lord your God with all your heart and with all your soul and with all your mind [*dianoia*]" (Matt 22:37; cf. Mark 12:30; Luke 10:27). The word is also found in the ancient Greek translation of that great promise in Jer 31:33 as the place where God will write his laws of the new covenant:

> "This is the covenant I will make with the people of Israel
> after that time," declares the LORD.
> I will put my law in their minds [*dianoia*]
> and write it on their hearts.
> I will be their God,
> and they will be my people.

The Son of God gives us a new covenant understanding so we might know the True One (τὸν ἀληθινόν). This is the masculine singular form of the adjective meaning "true, genuine." It is less com-

mon in the NT than the noun for "truth" (ἀλήθεια), which occurs more than a hundred times, forty-five of which are in John's gospel and letters. The masculine form of *alēthinon*, as opposed to the neuter, indicates a personal "True One," who in context refers to God. This forms a second connection to John 17:3, "Now this is eternal life: that they know you, the only true [ἀληθινόν] God, and Jesus Christ, whom you have sent." There were many false ideas about gods/God in the Greco-Roman world, just as there are today (see Theology in Application). To know the true God, one must acquire new covenant understanding through Jesus Christ.

To know "the True One" is to be "in" him through his Son, Jesus Christ. This concept is similar to the apostle Paul's idea of union with Christ (Rom 6:5; 1 Cor 6:17; Phil 2:1). To be "in Christ" is to be joined to his eternal life, his destiny; this is the basis for Jesus' statement, "Because I live, you also will live" (John 14:19).

Some may dispute whether the antecedent of the demonstrative pronoun "this" (οὗτός) in 5:20h ("*This One* is the true God and eternal life") is "Jesus Christ," which makes an indisputable statement of Christ's deity, or is a restatement of 5:20d, to make explicit that "the True One" is a reference to God. "Jesus Christ" is the nearest antecedent, and the identity of "this one" as eternal life echoes 1 John 1:2d-e, "the eternal Life, which was with the Father and has appeared to us." Dodd sees a wider reference that gathers together all that John has been saying about God: "how He is light, and love; how He is revealed as the Father through His Son Jesus Christ; how He is faithful and just to forgive our sins; how He remains in us — and **this**, he adds, **is the real God**, the one eternal Reality."[31]

Even if "Christ" is not the explicit antecedent, John's logic requires this to be a statement of Jesus' deity, and all that Dodd sees gathered together is

---

31. Dodd, *Johannine Epistles*, 140 (bold original).

gathered in Jesus Christ. For by John's statement, to be "in the True One" means to be "in Jesus Christ." It is only by being in the True God who is eternal life that anyone can have eternal life (see The Theology of John's Letters).

5:21 Children, [in light of what we know] keep yourselves from idols (Τεκνία, φυλάξατε ἑαυτὰ ἀπὸ τῶν εἰδώλων). John brings us to what seems a rather sudden end to his letter. Some modern readers have wondered if the original ending did not survive, but there is no manuscript evidence to support such a conjecture. But the original recipients would most likely have seen this "punchline" as a rhetorically powerful ending that demanded a response to the implied question, "Whom will you serve? The one true God or idols, who represent only false ideas, darkness, and death?"

John focuses his readers' attention on this statement by introducing it with a vocative, the seventh and final occurrence of "children" (τεκνία), a term of intimacy and endearment. The imperative verb with the reflexive pronoun "keep yourselves" (φυλάξατε ἑαυτά) indicates the personal responsibility and effort that John expects of his readers as they move forward in their Christian lives with the benefit of his teaching in this letter. It is a different verb than in 5:18 ("keep," τηρέω) and has the defensive sense of "guarding" against loss or escape.

The prepositional phrase "from [the] idols" (ἀπὸ τῶν εἰδώλων) indicates separation, which is appropriate with a verb that has the nuance of guarding against (φυλάξατε). But the ambiguity begins with the noun phrase "the idols" (τῶν εἰδώλων), which is perplexing because idols have not been previously mentioned and the definite article suggests that some specific idols are in John's thought. The

article likely is anaphoric, referring back to what has been warned against.

What is clear is that this command stands in the context of what has just been stated that "we know" in vv. 18, 19, and especially 20, that the Son of God has brought knowledge of the one true God, against whom "the idols" stand in opposing contrast. Are these idols to be understood as literal objects of wood and stone that represented the pagan deities in the various temples throughout the city of Ephesus? Some interpreters point out that the critique of idol worship in Isaiah is linked with the concept of witness, so John is exhorting his readers to forsake the rituals of idol worship as a witness to Christ even if it means persecution or martydom (cf. 3:16; 5:6).[32] But neither the topic of idol worship nor persecution has been mentioned, and given that John characteristically returns to previous topics, this interpretation seems unlikely, even though Ephesus and its environs were indeed filled with graven images of the gods.

Most interpreters take the reference to refer not to the worship of objects of wood or stone, but to adherence to any belief that is contrary to knowledge of the one true God. Brown lists ten possible referents, involving the beliefs or practice of pagan religion, sin, apostasy, or Jewish worship, which may have been considered idolatrous by Johannine Christians.[33] One attractive possibility is the meaning of the word in classical Greek ("phantom, unreality, falseness"), as some see the contrast between the reality of the one true God (v. 20) and the unreality of the deities represented by the idols (cf. 1 Cor 10:19 – 20).[34] Brown argues that the secessionists themselves had become idols.[35]

Dodd points out that Plato (*Theaet.* 150c) used the word *eidōlon* (εἴδωλον) to refer to illusory phe-

---

32. M. J. Edwards, "Martyrdom and the First Epistle of John," *NovT* 31 (1989): 164 – 71; Julian Hills, " 'Little Children, Keep Yourselves from Idols': 1 John 5:21 Reconsidered," *CBQ* 51 (1989): 285 – 310.

33. Brown, *Epistles of John*, 627 – 28.

34. J. N. Sugit "I John 5:21: ΤΕΚΝΙΑ, ΦΥΛΑΞΑΤΕ ΕΑΥΤΑ ΑΠΟ ΤΩΝ ΕΙΔΩΛΩΝ," *JTS* 36 (1985): 386 – 90.

35. Brown, *Epistles of John*, 641.

nomena contrasted with his eternal and immutable "ideas" or "forms."[36] Usage in other classical writers (e.g., Homer, *Od.* 40.476; Herodotus 5.92) and the LXX (e.g., Lev 19:4; Deut 32:21; Hab 2:18; 1 Chr 16:26) also suggests a reference to things that are unreal or illusory. In this reading of the word, the command would mean: "Reject the false and embrace the real,"[37] which functions nicely following after the statement in 5:20 that Jesus Christ "is the *true* God" (italics added). This ending would argue against many forms of heresy, and as Griffith concludes, it need not be limited to a particular form of the rejection of Jesus.[38]

In the OT, idols represented counterfeit gods as opposed to the one real God. Thus, Dodd concludes, "By idols he means not only images of the gods, but all false or counterfeit notions of God such as lead to the perversions of religion against which he has written."[39] Because false ideas about God inevitably involve sin, "the idols" may be referring to sin as a satanic power. By this reading, John's final command can be paraphrased: "Keep yourselves from sin," a thought consistent with previous exhortations in the letter.

In the historical situation of that moment, John was likely alluding to the false ideas about God that were being taught by the secessionists.[40] As Pate observes, "Most modern interpreters identify 'idols' with the idolatry of the secessionists who left the worship of the true God to follow after a false Christology."[41] Even if the specifics of the false teaching will never be known for sure, any understanding of God incompatible with John's teaching in this letter would be considered idolatry, defined as false teaching based on a nonexistent spiritual reality.[42]

This explicit mention of idols in 5:21 supports the interpretation that the opening verses (1:1 – 4) allude to the futility of knowlege of God sought from those sources that cannot see, hear, or speak (see discussion of 1:1 – 4). Such a critique of idolatry in the OT upheld God's revelation of himself to his people in opposition to the false and sinful religions of the surrounding nations. John's point in the opening verses of this letter was to establish the authority of the eyewitness testimony about Jesus Christ as the only source of true knowledge about God. His emphasis on the sensory in "what we have *heard*, what we have *seen* with our eyes, what … our hands have *touched*" not only brings the historical eyewitness of Jesus to the forefront, but also echoes OT language that derided senseless idols as being unable to provide any true knowledge about God. For unlike God, they could not see, hear, know, or speak (Deut 4:28; Pss 115:3 – 8; 135:15 – 18; Jer 10:5; cf. Rev 9:20). If this is so, the last statement of the letter (5:21), rather than being an abrupt and awkward ending, forms an inclusio with the first statement (1:1) concerning the topic of the source of true knowledge about God.

Yarbrough associates 5:21 specifically with Zechariah's new covenant prophecy concerning idols (esp. Zech 13:2): " 'On that day, I will banish the names of the idols [τῶν εἰδώλων] from the land, and they will be remembered no more,' declares the LORD Almighty. 'I will remove both the prophets and the spirit of impurity from the land.' "[43] He gives four reasons for this association: (1) John and

---

36. Dodd, *Johannine Epistles*, 141.

37. Yarbrough, *1, 2, 3 John*, 325, citing Daniel L. Akin, *1, 2, 3 John* (NAC 38; Nashville: Broadman & Holman, 2001), 215 – 16.

38. Griffith, *Keep Yourselves*, 207.

39. Dodd, *Johannine Epistles*, 141.

40. Brown, *Epistles of John*, 627 – 28; Kruse, *Letters of John*,

202; Smalley, *1 – 3 John*, 310; Smith, *First, Second, and Third John*, 137; von Wahlde, *Gospel and Letters*, 3:215; Watson, " 'Keep Yourselves from Idols,' " 298.

41. C. Marvin Pate, *The Writings of John* (Grand Rapids: Zondervan, 2011), 316.

42. Marshall, *Epistles of John*, 255.

43. Yarbrough, *1 – 3 John*, 323.

his readers live in the eschatological day Zechariah was referring to; (2) Zechariah seems to have been in John's thought in the gospel (Zech 9:9 in John 12:15; Zech 12:10 in John 19:37; Zech 13:7 in John 16:32); (3) the coming of the messianic figure banishes false prophets and spirits (cf. 1 John 4:1); (4) John's concern for a true conception of God is consistent with Zechariah's vision of God's "faithfulness and radiant purity."[44]

John recognizes what is at stake in knowledge of the one true God: nothing less than eternal life. And eternal life is the reason he wrote both the gospel (20:30 – 31) and the letter (1 John 5:13). Jesus himself said, "Now this is eternal life: that they know you, the only true God [ἀληθινὸν θεὸν, , as in 5:20], and Jesus Christ, whom you have sent" (John 17:3). Eternal life is inseparably joined to true knowledge about the one true God. Lieu writes that 5:21 is

> a warning against falling outside the place where that God is known and where eternal life is experienced.... To keep away from idols is no less than to "remain in God" (2:28).... The alternatives to this home are uncompromising: antichrist, false prophets, the devil, the evil one, and more abstractly, falsehood, darkness, and death.[45]

The Venerable Bede also sees in the idols a reference to heretical teaching about God and the possible forfeiture of eternal life. He writes:

> You who know the true God, in whom you have eternal life, must keep yourselves away from the teachings of the heretics which lead only to eternal death. In the manner of those made idols in the place of God, the heretics have corrupted the glory of the incorruptible God by their wicked doctrines which bear the stamp of corruptible things.[46]

Rather than an awkward and abrupt ending, 5:21 summarizes the point of the entire letter and challenges readers, both ancient and modern, to decide which god they will worship — the God who revealed himself in Jesus Christ or a false god conjured from human imagination.

Theology in Application

One Monday morning a man was describing his Sunday morning golf game to a group of coworkers. He paused and addressed one of his colleagues, known to be a Christian, with the comment, "You probably think I'll go to hell for playing golf on Sunday morning, don't you?" The Christian looked calmly at the man and replied, "No, I think you'll go to hell for not believing in Jesus Christ. So you might as well play golf on Sunday." Sin, belief, and the afterlife are integrally connected in religious thought, and for Christians, the nexus of these topics focuses on the person and work of Jesus Christ, God's Son. These three topics are closely bound together in this final section of John's letter, and within that context make sense of John's final command to keep away from idols.

---

44. Ibid.
45. Lieu, *I, II, & III John*, 237 – 38.
46. Bede, *Commentary on 1 John*, in Bray, ACCS 11, 229.

Knowing the One True God

John teaches throughout, but especially in 5:20, that the highest form of knowledge is knowledge of the one true God who has been revealed in Jesus Christ, for this is the knowledge by which one attains eternal life after death. This true knowledge of God in Christ stands in opposition to the many voices, views, and religions that offer God-substitutes,

> that is, idols — in the place of the living God of Christian revelation ... the worship of any God-substitute is idolatry ... whether it be a political idea, or some fashionable cult, or merely the product of [one's] own "wishful thinking."[47]

Although it is a popular belief that there are many ways to God, the only way that arrives at the destination of eternal life is through Jesus Christ. It is particularly sobering to realize that John was not writing about the idolatry of another religion; he was writing to Christian readers about the idolatry of fashioning one's own understanding of Jesus Christ that, in this case, eliminated or diminished the atonement of the crucifixion. Today, according to the U.S. Religious Landscape Survey taken by the Pew Forum in 2007, more than 78 percent of Americans self-identify as Christian.[48] But this includes Protestants, Catholics, Mormons, Jehovah's Witnesses, Orthodox, and "Other," representing a wide spectrum of religious beliefs about God and Jesus, some of which are mutually exclusive. Moreover, that same survey concludes that we find ourselves living in a "competitive religious marketplace," where movement between major religious groups is the characteristic factor, with "unaffiliated" gaining the most ground. In such a time, the message of 1 John is more needed than ever. What Marshall pointed out in 1978 has grown increasingly true:

> Today it is fashionable to imagine that religion and morality are separable and independent; one can be good and righteous without belief in Jesus as the Son of God. John would remind us that apart from Jesus Christ there is no real understanding of the truth and no power to live according to the truth.[49]

Living within a time and place when even the term "Christian" can indicate a wide variety of beliefs, how easy it is to be led astray from the true knowledge of God. And there is increasing pressure to get along with people of other beliefs, pretending that underneath all religions and religious language there is no difference. That in itself involves an assumption that there is no spiritual truth beyond what someone creates in his or her own mind, an assumption that contradicts the truth Jesus Christ came to reveal.

---

47. Dodd, *Johannine Epistles*, 142.

48. http://religions.pewforum.org/reports (accessed 25 June 2012).

49. Marshall, *Epistles of John*, 256.

But John says that there is true knowledge of the one true God and there is idolatry — false knowledge based on untrue assumptions about reality. As Calvin wrote:

> The pious mind does not dream up for itself any god it pleases, but contemplates the one and only true God. And it does not attach to him whatever it pleases, but is content to hold him to be as he manifests himself; furthermore, the [pious] mind always exercises the utmost diligence and care not to wander astray, or rashly and boldly to go beyond his will.[50]

Pray for One Another

It is within this context of the reality of both truth and falsehood that John exhorts Christian believers to pray for those fellow believers who sin, if the sin is not one that leads to death. John recognizes that even within his own church(es), there are people who self-identify themselves as "Christians," but who are on the way to spiritual death because they have rejected the historical revelation of God in the life and words of Jesus Christ. But there are also those who, though born of God and receiving eternal life, continue to live in ways that do not reflect a family resemblance to the Father. For them, John says, other believers are to pray so that their lives will conform to Christ, confirming the eternal life they have begun to live (cf. John 5:24). As for the others, they might as well "play golf on Sunday," for judgment on their sins is taken up in the judgment they will encounter for rejecting the one true God. There is sin that does not lead to death — it is that sin that has been covered by the blood of Jesus.

It is remarkable that John places a responsibility for the spiritual health of a congregation on every member, first, that they might discern truth from falsehood, and then, that they might intercede in prayer appropriately. Because death is the *outcome* of the sin that leads there, the possibility remains open that even those unwittingly on the way to such death — even the secessionists of John's day — could at some point during their lives repent and be granted eternal life through Christ's atoning death. Therefore, no one can write off another person as beyond God's saving grace. But it is also necessary to discern that not everyone who may bear the label "Christian" exemplifies spiritual truth worth following. As someone once speculated, "There will be two things that are very surprising about heaven: who's there and who's not!"

---

50. John Calvin, *The Institutes of the Christian Religion* (ed. John T. McNeill; trans. Ford Lewis Battles; Philadelphia: Westminster, 1980), 1.2.2.

Introduction to 2 and 3 John

Second and Third John are both brief letters of approximately the same length (in Greek, about 200 words), written from the same author ("the elder"). Both address the issue of denying traveling Christians the hospitality necessary to give them a hearing within the Christian congregation(s). With respect to their contents, they are two sides of the same coin: 2 John is the elder's admonition prohibiting his readers from receiving professing Christians who bring a message that deviates from that of the elder; 3 John is the elder's complaint and dilemma when the brothers he has sent out are refused hospitality and turned away by Diotrephes, a person of influence in a Christian congregation. Second John is more directly related to 1 John than is 3 John.

Living in the truth is the common theme among all three letters; it comes to its sharpest expression in the elder's concern for the health and unity of the church — especially when some are *not* living in the truth, and the nascent Christian community is at risk of being destroyed by false teaching (1 and 2 John) or by those who reject apostolic authority (3 John). Second John warns against sharing in the work of heretical teachers by extending hospitality and thereby enabling the spread of their false teaching (2 John 11). Third John warns that this must not become an excuse for failing to welcome faithful and true preachers of the gospel.

But what a confusing situation for those churches involved! For doesn't the command to love fellow believers imply that hospitality should be offered to any who profess to be Christian? So when should one extend hospitality? And when should one refuse it, lest one share in the evil works of the deceivers? The crux of the matter, then as now, rests on the issues of authority and truth that are complicated by the command to love all who are fellow Christians.

Who has the right to assert authority and claim to have the truth in today's pluralistic ethos? What are the demands of Christian love in such situations? Are all who call themselves Christians to be received? If all religious teachers are equally privileged, then how does one discern the truth among the cacophony of voices? The world into which Jesus came was similar to our own in that it too was filled with various religions and philosophies. As the gospel of Jesus Christ went out into that polytheistic and pluralistic world, the NT writers had to confront issues that in various forms still confront Christians today.

Authorship

The letter comes from a writer who identifies himself only as "the elder," a reference that must have been sufficient to identify him to his original readers. This, together with the tone, topics, and exhortations of the letter, suggests spiritual authority that is consistent with a recognized leader in the church(es). See the general introduction to all three letters and the commentary below for further discussion.

Genre and Purpose

Both 2 and 3 John are in the conventional form of a Greco-Roman letter — the one as an open letter to the church personified as the "chosen lady and her children," the other written to an individual apparently known well by the author. Both end with the conventional greetings (2 John 13; 3 John 15) and a wish for a face-to-face visit (2 John 12; 3 John 13 – 14). Differences in the character of each can be accounted for by recognizing that 2 John was intended for a wider audience and therefore had more deliberate theological language but fewer personal references.

Second John may have been the cover letter for 1 John, providing the personal address ("to the chosen lady and her children") that 1 John lacks, introducing the major themes of 1 John, and putting the major exhortation right up front — don't welcome false teachers — even before the explanation in 1 John may have been read (see Introduction to 1, 2, 3 John).

The issue of whether to welcome traveling evangelists and preachers as addressed in 2 and 3 John was pressing in the early church. The *Didache* 11:1 – 2 also addresses this issue, perhaps based on 2 and 3 John:

> So, if anyone should come and teach you all these things that have just been mentioned above, welcome him. But if the teacher himself goes astray and teaches a different teaching that undermines all this, do not listen to him. However, if his teaching contributes to righteousness and knowledge of the Lord, welcome him as you would the Lord.[1]

Ignatius also takes up the issue in his letter to Smyrna, which was written to the same geographical area as John's letters. He discusses the issue in terms similar to 2 John 10:

> Now I am advising you of these things, dear friends, knowing that you are of the same mind. But I am guarding you in advance against wild beasts in human form — people whom you must not only not welcome but, if possible, *not even meet.* Nev-

---

1. Michael W. Holmes, ed. and trans., *Apostolic Fathers* (3rd ed.; Grand Rapids: Baker Adacemic, 2007), version 1.2 accessed through Accordance.

ertheless, do pray for them, that somehow they might repent, difficult though it may be. But Jesus Christ, our true life, has power over this.[2]

The purpose of these two letters from the elder was to guard and protect the churches in that area from the false teachers who had gone out, most likely from the elder's own church (1 John 2:19). By shutting the doors of hospitality to them, the church would squelch the heresy by not allowing them a hearing in the Christian communities.

Reception and Canon

The earliest attestation of language that may be a quote from the Johannine letters is from Polycarp, bishop of Smyrna, which was in the geographical region tradition-ally associated with John. In a warning against heresy, Polycarp (not later than AD 140) uses language that evokes 1 John 4:2 and 2 John 7, "For everyone who does not confess that Jesus Christ has come in the flesh is an antichrist."[3] Even though Poly-carp does not cite 1 or 2 John by name, the similarity of language suggests that the phrasing had become familiar through previous teaching that arguably originated with the elder.

Although 1 John was widely received as an apostolic writing, 2 and 3 John, where mentioned, were questioned. Tertullian (third century, northern Africa) knows and quotes 1 John, whom he attributed to the apostle John along with the gospel of John and the book of Revelation, but he does not seem to know 2 or 3 John.[4] The eastern church also does not seem to have known about, or perhaps rejected, the shorter letters, as neither 2 John nor 3 John was translated into Syriac at the same time as 1 John. When they are first mentioned in the extant evidence, it is by Origen in the early third century, who, according to Eusebius, mentions a brief letter, and also a second and third that are disputed.[5] By the time of Jerome (AD 342 – 420), it had become common to ascribe 2 and 3 John not to the apostle John but, based on Euse-bius's reading of Papias, to a presbyter who shared the common name John. Never-theless, Jerome quotes 2 and 3 John as by the apostle John, so he apparently did not share the same opinion.[6]

There is some evidence that what we know as 1 John and 2 John may have circu-lated together in some regions. The evidence of the Council of Carthage in AD 256 is most interesting, in that one of its bishops, Aurelius of Chullabi (also in northern Africa), quoted 2 John 10 – 11 as if it were a part of 1 John.[7] Furthermore, there may be a link between 1 and 2 John within the Latin textual tradition, where the peculiar

---

2. Ibid. (Ign. *Smyrn.* 4:1; italics added).

3. Pol. *Phil.* 7.1 (in ibid.).

4. See Lieu, *Second and Third Epistles*, 6 – 35, for in-depth discussion of the evidence.

5. *Hist. eccl.* 6.25.10.

6. Lieu, *Second and Third Epistles*, 13.

7. Cited in ibid., 9.

title "to the virgin(s)" (apparently an interpretation of 2 John 1, "to the chosen lady") was somehow transferred to 1 John early in the transmission of Latin manuscripts.[8]

To add to such evidence, Irenaeus, a native of Asia Minor who became bishop of Lyon c. AD 180, quotes both 1 and 2 John, but in such a way that he seems to have known them both as a single book.[9] As Painter explains, "This evidence is consistent with the view that 2 John was a covering letter for 1 John. This being the case, 2 John did not exist separate from 1 John. Because 1 John was also used by the author in his own church where it needed no covering letter, 1 John did exist without 2 John."[10] This evidence suggests the possibility that 2 John was written at the same time as 1 John to accompany it as the cover letter to the church(es) of the original recipients, and subsequently 1 and 2 John were copied together as one.

Lieu speculates that "II John might eventually have been appended to I John in an attempt to bring its circulation beyond the original community and in recognition that I John, now being more widely read, was its god-parent."[11] However, the evidence she sees for this possibility can also be evidence for their original circulation as one. If so, what we know as 3 John may have been known in the ancient world as the *second* letter of John, which may explain why some of the early fathers (and the Muraturion canon) knew only of two letters. Scholars may have assumed that the mention of only two letters excludes 3 John.[12] This could also explain why, in those areas where scribes separated 2 John from 1 John, resulting in three letters that circulated separately, 2 John and 3 John became suspect when severed from 1 John, which was universally recognized as apostolic.

By the fourth century, both 2 and 3 John joined 1 John as canonical books. They were included in the Syriac NT of the eastern church in the sixth century, and Bede in distant Northumbria (England) attested that the consensus of the church was to receive the three letters of John as apostolic. Although many today continue to raise questions about the authorship of these books, there is no compelling reason to reject the apostolic authorship of all three.

---

8. Ibid., 29.
9. *Haer.* 1.16.3; 3.16.5, 8.
10. Painter, *1, 2, and 3 John*, 42.

11. Lieu, *Second and Third Epistles*, 165.
12. E.g., Painter, *1, 2, and 3 John*, 43.

Outline of 2 John

I. Salutation and Greeting (vv. 1 – 3)

   A. Statement Naming the Author and Recipients of Letter (vv. 1 – 2)

   B. Assurance of Future Blessing (v. 3)

II. An Exhortation (vv. 4 – 8)

   A. Cause for the Elder's Joy (v. 4)

   B. Exhortation to Love One Another (vv. 5 – 6)

   C. Reason for the Exhortation (v. 7)

   D. Warning! (v. 8)

III. A Prohibition (vv. 9 – 11)

   A. Anyone Who Does Not Hold to the Teachings of Christ Does Not Have God (v. 9)

   B. A Prohibition against Receiving False Teachers (v. 10)

   C. To Welcome a False Teacher Is to Share in Their Evil Work (v. 11)

IV. The Closing (vv. 12 – 13)

   A. Hope for a Continuing Relationship (v. 12)

   B. Greetings from a Sister Church (v. 13)

2 John 1 – 3

Literary Context

These opening verses of 2 John show it is in the conventional form of Hellenistic personal correspondence, with a statement of the author ("the elder"), recipients ("chosen lady and ... her children"), and a Christianized greeting ("grace, mercy, peace"). See also v. 13, the closing greeting.

➡ **I. Salutation and Greeting (vv. 1 – 3)**
  A. Statement Naming the Author and Recipients of Letter (vv. 1 – 2)
  B. Assurance of Future Blessing (v. 3)
  II. An Exhortation (vv. 4 – 8)
  III. A Prohibition (vv. 9 – 11)
  IV. The Closing (vv. 12 – 13)

Main Idea

The elder introduces the letter's major topics of truth (vv. 1, 2, 3, 4) and love (vv. 1, 3, 5, 6) and builds rapport with his readers through the inclusive "we" (vv. 2 – 3). God's grace, mercy, and peace are found in God's truth and love. This opening creates a substantial presence of the elder in the minds of readers and raises expectation of an authoritative message.

Translation

---

2 John 1 – 3

1a	address	The elder,
b		to the chosen lady and
		to her children,
c	expansion	whom I love in truth, and
d	expansion	not only I, but
e	expansion	also all who have known the truth,
2a	explanation of 1e	because the abiding truth is in us and
b	assertion	will be with us forever.
3a	assertion	**Grace, mercy, peace**
b		from God the Father and
c		from Jesus Christ the Son of the Father
d		**. . . will be with us in truth and love.**

Structure

The verses are structured in the conventional form of a first-century Greco-Roman letter, which resembles the format of a modern memo:

> From: The elder (v. 1)
> To: The chosen lady and her children, qualified by a relative clause, "whom I love in truth, and not only I, but also all who have known the truth, because the abiding truth is in us" (vv. 1 – 2).

The necessary and essential relationship between truth and love is introduced in this opening statement. The conventional wish occurs as an assured statement that grace, mercy, and peace from the Father and Jesus Christ are enjoyed where truth and love are present (v. 3).

Exegetical Outline

➡ **I. Salutation and Greeting (v. 1 – 3)**
    A. Statement naming the author and recipients of letter (vv. 1 – 2)
    B. Assurance of future blessing (v. 3)

Explanation of the Text

1 The elder, to the chosen lady and to her children, whom I love in the truth, and not only I, but also all who have known the truth (Ὁ πρεσβύτερος ἐκλεκτῇ κυρίᾳ καὶ τοῖς τέκνοις αὐτῆς, οὓς ἐγὼ ἀγαπῶ ἐν ἀληθείᾳ, καὶ οὐκ ἐγὼ μόνος ἀλλὰ καὶ πάντες οἱ ἐγνωκότες τὴν ἀλήθειαν). How wonderful it would have been for later readers if the elder had identified himself a bit more. But the fact that he didn't have to with the original readers indicates that they would have recognized his identity from the simple reference "the elder."

The comparative adjective "elderly" (πρεσβύτερος), used as a substantive ("elder"), was common in Greek to refer to an older man. The ancient Greek physician Hippocrates defined the next to last of seven stages of a man's life, the period from 50 to 56 years old, with the cognate noun "elder" (πρεσβύτης), distinguishing it from "old age" (γέρων).[1] Although it is common to hear that the apostle John would have been an old man at the time this letter was probably written, the designation "elder" more likely refers to his position and authority, for that title had already been in use in the church from its origin. The noun "elder" (πρεσβύτης) is used in the NT to refer to an older man (Luke 1:18; Titus 2:2; Phlm 9); the adjectival form "elder" used as a substantive (πρεσβύτερος), found here, is used dozens of times in the NT to refer to the religious leaders of Jewish congregations (e.g., Matt 21:23; Mark 8:31; Luke 22:52), and it has continued to be used to designate leaders in the Christian church (e.g., Acts 14:23; 1 Pet 5:1).

This distinction in usage between the noun and adjective likely indicates that, regardless of the elder's age, the designation implies the author's authority in the church(es) to which he writes (cf. 1 John 1:1). As Quintilian (3.8.12) states, what really carries the greatest weight in deliberative rhetoric is the authority of the speaker or writer.[2] Eusebius's inference that there were two church leaders named John, one the apostle and another the elder, is the origin of the idea that the apostle did not write this letter, but Eusebius was most likely misreading Papias (Eusebius, *Hist. eccl.* 3.39.4).[3] (See discussion of authorship, above.) The author's identification simply as "the elder" implies both the position of authority he held and the personal relationship he had with the original recipients.

The elder writes "to the chosen lady [κυρίᾳ] and to her children [τέκνοις]." Although "lady" (κυρία) is common in letters referring to either a mother or a sister or to a more exalted person, here it is most likely a metaphor for the church and those who have been reborn into it. This metaphor connotes the esteem in which the elder holds these people. The closing greeting in v. 13 also refers to the children "of your chosen sister," which, along with the absence of any personal statements in the letter, strongly tilts away from a literal reading that these are references to two individual women.

Personification such as this is usually based on the grammatical gender of the entity being personified. Thus, even though the letter doesn't mention the church (ἐκκλησία), this term is a feminine Greek noun and therefore would likely be personified as a woman, much as cities were personified as women in the ancient world, the Hebrew and

---

1. Quoted by Philo, *Opif.* 105.
2. Cited in Duane F. Watson, "A Rhetorical Analysis of 2 John according to Greco-Roman Convention," *NTS* 35 (1989): 119.

3. See Jobes, *Letters to the Church*, 406, for a discussion of Papias's references to John.

Greek nouns for "city" both being feminine. The female personification of God's people is found elsewhere in the Bible, with Jerusalem portrayed as a woman in Isaiah (and in the later apocryphal books of Baruch and 2 Esdras) and the new Jerusalem as a bride (Rev 21:1). The apostle Paul also uses female personification of the church in 2 Cor 11:2 and Eph 5:25. The closing greeting of 1 Pet 5:13 uses the feminine form of a cognate adjective "chosen together" (συνεκλεκτή), likely a reference to the church "in Babylon."

Furthermore, the content of 2 John is most apt for a congregation of Christian believers, having to do with obedience, sound teaching, and warnings about the antichrists. Note that the word for children found here (τέκνον), in distinction from its diminutive form "little children" (τεκνία), is used in the vocative only in John 13:33 and seven times in 1 John. "Child" (τέκνον) is used frequently in John's writings to refer to spiritual progeny of Abraham (John 8:39), of God (1:12; 11:52; 1 John 3:1, 2, 10; 5:2), and even of Satan (1 John 3:10).

The modifier "chosen" (ἐκλεκτῇ) would be difficult to explain if the lady and her children were not a metaphor for the Christian church(es). The thought that it is the name of an individual woman, "Eklekte" (Ἐκλεκτή), can be eliminated in light of v. 13, for it is improbable that she would have a living sister of the same name. But a metaphorical reference to the church and its members is consistent with the thought in John's gospel that Jesus' followers are chosen (John 6:70; 13:18; 15:19). Specifically in Johannine thought they are chosen "out of the world" (John 15:19), and therefore this adjective alludes to the duality drawn between those of the world and those of God (e.g., John 8:23; 17:6, 14, 15, 16; 18:36; 1 John 2:16; 4:5).

All of this adds up to the conclusion that this letter is from the elder who is located within one Christian church (cf. v. 13) but who writes with authority and goodwill to another (v. 1). Given that no location is specified, it is possible that this letter was intended for several churches, possibly the same ones in the region of Ephesus that are mentioned in Revelation (cf. Rev 2:1 – 3:22). Eusebius cites Clement of Alexandria saying that John "used to go [from Ephesus] to the neighboring districts ... in some places to appoint bishops, in others to reconcile whole churches, and in others to ordain some one of those pointed out by the Spirit."[4] This letter may have been a cover letter when 1 John was sent outside of the elder's church to outlying churches (see Introduction to 2 and 3 John).

The elder expands his description of the chosen lady and her children as those whom he "loves in truth [ἐν ἀληθείᾳ; v. 1c; cf. 3 John 1]." Although the prepositional phrase can be adverbial, meaning "truly" (cf. ἀληθῶς), the concept of truth in John's gospel and letters is closely associated with revealed truth in the gospel of Jesus Christ (see "In Depth: 'Truth' in John's Letters," at 1 John 1:6). To love "in truth" means to love in a manner consistent with the reality that Christ has brought (see The Theology of John's Letters). This nuance is confirmed in v. 1e, where the elder points out that "all who have known *the* truth" (πάντες οἱ ἐγνωκότες τὴν ἀλήθειαν) also love the lady and her children, i.e., the church. Noting the perfect tense of "have known" (ἐγνωκότες) and the definite article in "the truth" (τὴν ἀλήθειαν) tilts this statement toward a reference to Christian believers who have come to know the One who reveals reality because he is the Truth (cf. John 8:32; 14:6).

2 Because the abiding truth is in us and will be with us forever (διὰ τὴν ἀλήθειαν τὴν μένουσαν ἐν ἡμῖν καὶ μεθ᾽ ἡμῶν ἔσται εἰς τὸν αἰῶνα). Verse 2 removes all doubt that the elder here refers to

---

4. Eusebius, *Hist. eccl.* 3.23.6.

Christ and the revelation he brings, for the truth in view remains, or abides, "in us" and will be "with us" forever. This language of abiding or remaining (μένω) occurs characteristically in John's gospel and letters, for it is by remaining in the truth of the gospel (cf. v. 9) and by the truth remaining in believers that eternal life is gained and assured.

The elder's use of "us" in the opening verses communicates his assumption that his readers are in unity with him, an assumption that takes on greater significance in the historical context of disagreement and schism in which John's letters were written. He places himself within the truth, in contrast to those who left the church and may already be on their way to outlying churches, bringing false teaching with them. His use of "us" also implies that "the chosen lady and ... her children" must continue in the truth if they wish to remain in good standing with the elder.

In these first two verses the elder has introduced topics of central relevance in the body of the letter to follow. The topic of love is developed in vv. 3 – 6; the topic of truth in vv. 2 – 4, and the topic of remaining in the truth in v. 9.[5]

3 Grace, mercy, peace from God the Father and from Jesus Christ the Son of the Father will be with us in truth and love (ἔσται μεθ᾽ ἡμῶν χάρις ἔλεος εἰρήνη παρὰ θεοῦ πατρός καὶ παρὰ Ἰησοῦ Χριστοῦ τοῦ υἱοῦ τοῦ πατρός ἐν ἀληθείᾳ καὶ ἀγάπῃ). The elder's assurance in v. 3 that "grace, mercy, peace ... will be with us" employs standard Christian terminology and creates a sense of unity between the author and readers. The statement underscores that the elder's relationship with his readers is characterized by truth and love,[6] and the purpose of the letter is to ensure that the relationship remains intact. Grace (χάρις) refers to God's favor toward believers, which is truly undeserved.

Mercy (ἔλεος) means that God will not treat believers as they deserve because of sin and prior rejection of God. Peace (εἰρήνη) is not simply the absence of strife, but a personal sense of well-being despite circumstances.

The similarity of language and thought with Wisd 3:9 is striking:

> Those who trust in him will understand *truth* [ἀλήθειαν],
> and the faithful will remain [a compound of μένω] with him in *love* [ἀγάπη],
> because *grace* [χάρις] and *mercy* [ἔλεος] are upon his holy ones,
> and he watches over his *chosen* [ἐκλεκτοῖς] ones.
> (NETS, italics added)

The use of six of the same words in such a brief compass with similarity of thought expressed makes it likely that the elder is alluding to this pre-Christian pseudepigraphical writing attributed to King Solomon but likely written within two centuries before Christ. The probability of an intentional allusion is increased by noting that the context of Wisd 3:9 is about the afterlife ("the souls of the righteous are in the hand of God ... they are at peace"), which is a major theme of John's writings. Wisdom 3 goes on to describe the destiny of the impious, who "will receive punishment in accordance with the way they reasoned" — an apt comparison and warning in the context of a debate about spiritual truth and where the authority to proclaim it lies.

If the elder does indeed allude to Wisd 3:9, he goes beyond it by specifying that the grace, mercy, and peace of which he speaks are from God, the Father of Jesus Christ, and are grounded in truth and love. These very topics of truth (v. 4) and love (v. 6) form the heart of the elder's exhortation to faithfulness that follows.

---

5. Watson, "Rhetorical Analysis," 114.

6. Ibid., 115.

Theology in Application

The close connection between truth (ἀλήθεια) and love (ἀγάπη) in the Johannine writings is worth thinking about, for in our modern way of thinking truth is cognitive while love is emotional, and the two are not necessarily related. For the elder and author of 1 John, they are so closely related that they are essentially concomitant; one cannot love genuinely apart from the truth, and one does not know truth truly until one loves (1 John 3:18; 5:2). We cannot think rightly about ourselves or others until we perceive the truth that is revealed only in Jesus Christ: that we are all sinners whose sin separates us from God and from one another, and especially from those we would most wish to love. Any "love" based on something other than the reality of the human condition is merely wishful thinking, falsely based on an illusion that things are other than they are. Love may cover all wrongs (Prov 10:12), but first the wrongs must be recognized.

Genuine love is defined in John's writings as the love that God has extended to fallen human beings through the cross of Jesus Christ (John 3:16; 1 John 4:10, 19) so that we might not perish in eternity but have eternal life with God and each other. Many people mistakenly think that if God really loved us, he would simply look the other way and let us sin to our hearts' content. The idea of punishment for sin seems out of keeping with much religious thought today. Consequently, many of us do seem to look the other way and then call it love, as if it were loving to let others persist in sin. It is only through vicarious atonement that God can honor both his holiness, which demands punishment for sin, and his love for sinners. That vicarious atonement happened on the cross of Jesus Christ, the God-man, and is God's greatest expression of love for us (1 John 4:10; Rom 5:8).

It is only by recognizing the truth that all are sinners, but that all can receive God's love, mercy, and grace in Christ, that we can genuinely love ourselves and others while being fully informed about our own poor capacity for love and about the worth of others. Yes, that neighbor wronged us, but that does not disqualify them from our love, for God loves them and us, even though we are both undeserving sinners. It is only knowledge of that truth that permits us to receive God's love in Christ, and then to love others as ourselves. It is in and through such "truth and love" that the elder assures us that grace, mercy, and peace from God the Father and Jesus Christ will be with us always.

2 John 4 – 8

Literary Context

This passage opens the body of the letter with the elder's main concern: that his readers continue to believe and live out the truth revealed by Jesus Christ. His exhortation that they continue to love one another is explained within the context of false teaching, which is the opposite of love since it leads people away from eternal life that is theirs only in Christ.

I. Salutation and Greeting (v. 1 – 3)
➡ **II. An Exhortation (vv. 4 – 8)**
    A. Cause for the Elder's Joy (v. 4)
    B. Exhortation to Love One Another (vv. 5 – 6)
    C. Reason for the Exhortation (v. 7)
    D. Warning! (v. 8)
III. A Prohibition (vv. 9 – 11)
IV. The Closing (vv. 12 – 13)

Main Idea

The elder argues passionately for the truth revealed by Jesus Christ against the threat of heresy. Writing to another church at some distance, he warns his readers of those who likely went out from the elder's church(es) to spread false teaching to the Christian churches.

Translation

---

2 John 4 – 8

4a	assertion	**I rejoice greatly**
b	cause	because I have found some of your children walking in truth,
c	comparison	just as we received the command ⏿ from the Father.

5a	entreaty	And **now I ask you, lady** —
b	comparison	not as writing you a new command, but
c	comparison	[as writing a command] that we have had from the beginning —
d	content	**that we love one another.**

6a	identification	And **this is love:**
b	explanation	that we walk according to his commands.
c	identification	**This is the command,** just as you heard from the beginning,
d	identification	that you walk in it [the truth].

7a	basis	For **many** **deceivers have gone into the world,**
b	identification	those who do not confess Jesus Christ coming in flesh;
c	identification	**such a person is the deceiver and the antichrist.**

8a	exhortation	**Watch yourselves,**
b	result	so that you do not destroy what we have worked for, but
c	contrast	[that] you might receive a full reward.

Structure

The passage begins with a statement of the elder's joy that affirms his readers and ends with an imperative that warns them not to deviate from the truth. His entreaty that they love one another is followed by a definition of love (to live according to God's commands) and the reason for his exhortation (many deceivers are out and about).

Exegetical Outline

➡ **II. An Exhortation (vv. 4 – 8)**

    A. Cause for the elder's joy (v. 4)

    B. Exhortation to love one another (vv. 5 – 6)

    C. Reason for the exhortation (v. 7)

    D. Warning! (v. 8)

Explanation of the Text

4 I rejoice greatly because I have found some of your children walking in the truth, just as we received the command from the Father (Ἐχάρην λίαν ὅτι εὕρηκα ἐκ τῶν τέκνων σου περιπατοῦντας ἐν ἀληθείᾳ, καθὼς ἐντολὴν ἐλάβομεν παρὰ τοῦ πατρός). Following the contours of some types of Greco-Roman letters, thanksgiving or praise for the recipients typically follows the salutation (cf. Rom 1:8; 1 Cor 1:4; Phil 1:3; Col 1:3; 1 Thess 1:2; 2 Thess 1:3; 2 Tim 1:3; 3 John 2 – 3).

In terms of rhetorical analysis, v. 4 functions as the exordium, in which an author raises his major point by eliciting the recipients' "attention, receptivity, and good-will" toward the author and his topic, which in this case is obedience to the truth.[1] The elder elicits goodwill from the original readers by telling them how happy they have made him by walking in the truth. This implies that they would find that statement to be a valuable affirmation of their relationship with the elder and would be motivated to continue to bring him joy.

However, the prepositional phrase "some of your children" (ἐκ τῶν τέκνων) is partitive, meaning that the elder is referring only to "some" who are walking in the truth. This could be simply because he has come to know only about some of the people of that congregation, not all of them, and thus limits his evaluation accordingly. But perhaps the elder is subtly questioning some of his readers' commitment to walking in the truth. In this way the elder raises his concern that a number of his readers may have been influenced in ways that would lead them to depart from the truth.

"Walking in the truth" is a distinctively Johannine metaphor; it means to live in a way consistent with the revelation Jesus Christ has brought (cf. 1 John 1:6; 3 John 3 – 4). It is "adherence to the norms that shape the author's vision of reality."[2] More specifically here, the elder defines walking in the truth as living according the command "we" have received from the Father. The use of the first plural pronoun "we" implies the assumed unity between the elder and his readers that further establishes goodwill. The command mentioned can be defined further by 1 John 3:23, "And this is his command: to believe in the name of his Son, Jesus Christ, and to love one another, just as he gave the command to us." Walking in the truth involves both faith in Christ as God's Son and love for others (see comments 1 John 3:23).

5 And now I ask you, lady — not as writing you a new command, but [as writing a command] that we have had from the beginning — that we love one another (καὶ νῦν ἐρωτῶ σε, κυρία, οὐχ ὡς ἐντολὴν καινὴν γράφων σοι ἀλλὰ ἣν εἴχομεν ἀπ᾽ ἀρχῆς, ἵνα ἀγαπῶμεν ἀλλήλους). The elder has affirmed his joy that the "lady and her children" have been walking in the truth (v. 4), but "now" (νῦν) entreats that they continue to love one another; this phraseology suggests that the topic he is broaching has the potential of disrupting relationships. He does not issue this as a command, but frames his exhortation as an entreaty, "I ask" (ἐρωτῶ), showing esteem for his readers as he repeats the respectful vocative "lady" (κυρία).

Verse 5 echoes 1 John 2:7 – 8, "Dear friends, I am not writing to you a new command but an old command, which you have had from the beginning. The old command is the message that you have heard. Yet I am writing to you a new command, something that is realized in him and in you, because the darkness is passing away and the true light is already shining." The newness of the command has to do with the newness of a

---

1. Watson, "Rhetorical Analysis," 110 – 11.

2. Lieu, *I, II, & III John*, 249.

situation that has arisen, requiring that believers be reminded of the command to love (see comments 1 John 2:7–8).

In 1 John 2:7 it is a command that "you" have had from the beginning, but here the elder includes himself, "we have had" (εἴχομεν) from the beginning. As Watson observes, this may be meant to "buttress his relationship with the audience against possible secessionist activity which could ultimately sever it."[3]

The phrase "from the beginning" (ἀπ᾽ ἀρχῆς) recurs again and again in the Johannine letters (1 John 1:1; 2:7, 13, 14, 24; 3:8, 11). From the repeated use of this phrase we can infer that Johannine Christianity was essentially conservative, not innovative. Holding to the tradition in which the elder stood was the touchstone of right belief. As Lieu has observed, "We may say that for the Johannine Epistles an appeal to the tradition 'which is from the beginning' is fundamental for understanding what it means to be a Christian *in the present*" (italics added).[4] The elder is not bringing a new obligation or command, but a reminder of what has always stood since Jesus first gave it to his followers (John 13:34). Here this appeal aims to counteract any influence of the false teachers. In the years since, the elder's readers as well Christians today still need to be called back to the basics.

6 And this is love: that we walk according to his commands. This is the command, just as you heard from the beginning, that you walk in it [the truth] (καὶ αὕτη ἐστὶν ἡ ἀγάπη, ἵνα περιπατῶμεν κατὰ τὰς ἐντολὰς αὐτοῦ· αὕτη ἡ ἐντολή ἐστιν, καθὼς ἠκούσατε ἀπ᾽ ἀρχῆς, ἵνα ἐν αὐτῇ περιπατῆτε). The definition of love may be elusive against the clamor of the world, and the elder takes this opportunity to remind his readers that genuine love for God and others means living in the way that God has designed us to live and relating to others according to God's moral standards (1 John 5:3).

It was likely as easy then as now to claim we love others, by some subjective, relative definition of the word. But the elder grounds the concept of love in God's moral authority. The elder alternates between "the" command (love one another) and "commands," which Marshall explains "are the detailed requirements which unfold the structure of this central command."[5] Citing Rom 13:8–10, Marshall observes that "the various social commands in the second part of the Ten Commandments are summed up in the one rule of loving one's neighbor, so that love is the fulfillment of the law … the elder's point is to show that love must issue in various detailed types of actions in accordance with God's commandments."[6]

The commands in view are probably not the Ten Commandments directly, but their transposition and expansion by Jesus, which he summed up as love for God and love for neighbor (Matt 22:37–40; see comments on 1 John 2:7). John has echoed this in 1 John 4:21, "And this is the command from him: that the one who loves God must also love their brother or sister" (see comments). The apostle Paul also points to the Ten Commandments as the framework in which we understand what it means to love others; love does not steal from others, or lie about others, or murder them, or otherwise violate God's moral law (cf. Rom 13:10; 1 Cor 13:4–8).

For the first time in 2 John, the elder shifts from the first plural "we/us" to the second plural "you." Rhetorically this shift signifies his move from affirming the unity of his readers with him to exhorting them. After affirming that "some" of them are indeed walking in the truth and bringing the elder great joy, he now moves to the plural "you" as he exhorts all of these people to "walk in it."

3. Watson, "Rhetorical Analysis," 117.
4. Lieu, *Second and Third Epistles*, 176.
5. Marshall, *Epistles of John*, 67.
6. Ibid., 67–68.

The antecedent of the feminine dative pronoun "it" (αὐτῇ) in the final clause of this verse is grammatically ambiguous. It agrees with any one of the three feminine nouns in the immediate context: command (ἐντολή), love (ἀγάπη), or truth (ἀλήθεια, reaching back to v. 4, where "walking" was done "in the truth"). Wendland sees this as intentional ambiguity here that he describes as "semantic density," encompassing all three ideas to underscore their inseparability from one another.[7] Taking "command" as the antecedent produces a tautology that is less than satisfying: "And this is the command ... that you walk in the command." Lieu softens it by paraphrasing, "This, then, is the command which, as you have heard from the beginning, you should live by."[8]

The second closest antecedent is "love" (ἀγάπη), earlier in the verse: "His command is that you walk in love" (NIV 2011).[9] But love was just defined as walking in his command, still yielding a tautology, "His command is that you walk in his commands." Watson, who takes the antecedent as "love" and recognizes this as a "double tautology," points to the sequence of love – commands, command – it (love) as a chiasm.[10] However, he does not explain how this "double tautology" would contribute to the sense or rhetoric of the passage.

Kruse also takes the antecedent to be "love" (ἀγάπη) and explains that "having defined love as walking 'in obedience to his commands' (plural), the elder defines that obedience in terms of a single command: **As you have heard from the beginning, his command is that you walk in love**"

(bold original).[11] Thatcher comments that this "circular argument" highlights "the close connection between love for God, obedience to God, and love for brothers."[12]

A third reading understands the antecedent of "it" (αὐτῇ) to be "truth" (ἀλήθεια), which was mentioned in the parallel phrase back in v. 4, "walking in the truth." This would yield, "And this is the command ... that you walk in the truth," that is, live by faith in Jesus Christ. This reading follows from the prominence of the topic of obedience to the truth that was introduced in the body of the letter, to which love for others is subordinate. As Watson notes, the exordium (v. 4) raises the main point of discussion, which is obedience to the truth, even though Watson himself sees the antecedent of "it" (αὐτῇ) not as "truth" but as "love."[13]

Wendland's analysis of lexical-thematic structure also concluded that the pronoun refers back to "truth" in v. 4.[14] If the antecedent is "truth" (ἀλήθεια), this last phrase of v. 6 forms an inclusio with v. 4. Moreover, it coheres nicely with the next phrase in v. 7, "For many deceivers have gone out...." As v. 7 is giving the basis for the command, the concept of deception contrasts nicely as the antonym of "walking in the truth." Read in the context of 1 John, the truth of which the elder speaks consists of three christological points:

1. The man Jesus is the Christ.
2. The Son of God has been incarnated as a human being.
3. The death of the Son of God is atonement for sin.

---

7. Ernst R. Wendland, "What Is Truth? Semantic Density and the Language of the Johannine Epistles with Special Reference to 2 John," *Notes on Translation* 5, no. 2 (1991): 32 – 33, 56.

8. Lieu, *Second and Third Epistles*, 77; also Yarbrough, *1 – 3 John*, 339.

9. As also Marshall, *Epistles of John*, 65.

10. Watson, "Rhetorical Analysis," 121. His other observations about the rhetorical structure would apply even with a different antecedent.

11. Kruse, *Letters of John*, 208.

12. Tom Thatcher, "2 John," in *The Expositor's Bible Commentary* (ed. Tremper Longman III and David E. Garland; rev. ed.; Grand Rapids: Zondervan, 2006), 13:516.

13. Watson, "Rhetorical Analysis," 110.

14. Wendland, "What Is Truth?" 56.

Although the elder has affirmed his readers for walking in the truth (v. 4), he now points out that walking in the truth is not optional for Christian believers but is what God has commanded. "What they have heard from the beginning should go with them to the end."[15] Moreover, the elder's exhortation that they continue to love one another entails that they continue to walk in the truth. The next verse explains why aberrant teaching in the church is the opposite of love.

7 For many deceivers have gone into the world, those who do not confess Jesus Christ coming in flesh; such a person is the deceiver and the antichrist (ὅτι πολλοὶ πλάνοι ἐξῆλθον εἰς τὸν κόσμον, οἱ μὴ ὁμολογοῦντες Ἰησοῦν Χριστὸν ἐρχόμενον ἐν σαρκί· οὗτός ἐστιν ὁ πλάνος καὶ ὁ ἀντίχριστος). The need for the exhortation to love one another by walking in the truth is explained by the situation from which the elder writes: it is because many deceivers who are not walking in the truth are out and about.

This ties the elder's concern back to the same concern in 1 John (1 John 2:18 – 23; 3:7; 4:3). In all the books of the NT, only John's letters mention the word "antichrist," and that shared word ties 1 and 2 John together historically. The initial conjunction "for" (ὅτι causal) shows that the discussion of Christology is integrally related to the exhortation to love in v. 6.

The problem mentioned here is the same in 1 John: the deceivers are those who do not believe that Jesus Christ has "come in flesh" and have left the Johannine church (1 John 2:19), and we learn in this letter they are apparently trying to influence other churches in the region. It may be that the letter of 1 John was written to the church(es) who had experienced the schism, but that as those who went

out were attempting to influence other churches, it was sent to them with 2 John as a cover letter (see Introduction to 2 and 3 John).

The issue of that moment concerned the belief that Jesus was the Christ who had come in the flesh (cf. 1 John 4:2; see comments). The present participle "coming" (ἐρχόμενον) refers not to a future coming, such as the second coming of Christ, but to the past event of the incarnation.[16] Wallace identifies this anarthrous, accusative participle as indicating indirect discourse following the verb of communication "do not confess" (μὴ ὁμολογοῦντες) and offers the translations "to have come in the flesh" and "has come in the flesh."[17]

Although NT scholars have long taken the phrase as a polemic against Docetism, it is more likely involved in a broader debate about the source of true knowledge concerning God's redemptive plan. The potential for deception is directly related to this issue of revealed truth. As Moberly points out, "John's concern is intrinsic to any form of Christian faith. For where notions of divine self-revelation and corresponding human knowledge of God play a crucial role, possibilities of error and the deception of either self or others abound."[18] True knowledge of God is found only in the incarnation of Jesus Christ, for the Word became flesh specifically to reveal the otherwise invisible God (John 1:18). Therefore, everyone who has a true knowledge of God acknowledges that "Jesus Christ has come in flesh"; that is, the Son of God became a human being. Certainly this truth would argue against Docetism, but also more broadly against many forms of christological error.

The particular phrase "has come in flesh" suggests that the debate of concern to the elder probably involved the means of salvation more than the nature of Jesus Christ. De Boer has pointed out

---

15. Akin, "Truth or Consequences," 6.
16. Contra Lieu, *Second and Third Epistles*, 84.
17. Wallace, *Greek Grammar*, 645 – 46.
18. Moberly, "'Test the Spirits,'" 297.

that "the verb 'to come' in Johannine christological contexts not only means (denotes) 'to appear on the scene' but also signifies (connotes) 'to act salvifically'"[19] (see John 5:43; 7:28; 8:42; 12:46; 16:28; 18:37). While sound Christology certainly insists on the physical incarnation of Christ as fully human, Christ's full humanity was necessary *because of* his role in God's plan of salvation as the atoning sacrifice for sin.

Therefore, the confession that Jesus Christ "has come in flesh" does not simply acknowledge that Jesus was a fully human historical person (contra Docetism), but accepts the redeeming significance of his incarnate life, death, and resurrection on behalf of the human race. The elder identifies those who claim to be Christian but teach otherwise as "antichrists," because they implicitly oppose the person and work of Christ through a distorted understanding of him.

Although the elder rejoices that "the lady and her children" have been walking in the truth revealed by Jesus, he now has reason to be concerned that some of them have been, or possibly will be, exposed to false teaching that would cause them to wander from the truth; thus, he proceeds to exhort them strongly to be on their guard.

8 Watch yourselves, so that you do not destroy what we have worked for, but [that] you might receive a full reward (βλέπετε ἑαυτούς, ἵνα μὴ ἀπολέσητε ἃ εἰργασάμεθα ἀλλὰ μισθὸν πλήρη ἀπολάβητε). "Watch yourselves" is the first of three imperatives in the letter, though the third one ("do not greet" in v. 10) is an explanation of the second one, "do not receive." The purpose of being on guard, expressed in the *hina* clause, is so that "you" will not destroy what "we" have achieved.[20] As Lieu observes:

The unexpected switch to the first person plural … reinforces the seriousness of the moment. The effort has not been all their own; although the elder has endeavored to maintain a sense of the autonomy of the lady and her children, he cannot resist reminding them that they are part of a wider network and perhaps, even dependent on it.… A similar alternation between first and second person plural in verses 5 – 6 sets the audience within a larger community of the author and others … bound together by their common heritage of belief and its expression. Their loss would be to the loss of all those.[21]

While the lady and her children have brought the elder great joy, there is also the potential that they could bring him great sorrow if they do not watch out to guard the truth and live by it.

Rather than spiritual destruction, the elder wants his readers to receive a "full reward" (μισθὸν πλήρη). Both parts of the verse state the same thing, first negatively and then positively, with the rhetorical effect of amplifying the importance of this thought.[22] The language of a "full reward" is not distinctively Johannine but is common in the NT writings. Yarbrough observes that it is used frequently to refer to eschatological blessing in Matt 5:12; 10:41; Mark 9:41; Luke 6:23, 35; John 4:36; 1 Cor 3:8, 14; 9:17 – 18; Rev 11:18; 22:12.[23] This eschatological phrase heightens what is at stake in the situation against which the elder warns: nothing less than salvation to eternal life. This understanding helps to understand why he would label these errant "Christians" so harshly with the label "antichrist," and why in v. 10 he would forbid any fellowship with them. The pressing issue is not simply a matter of a difference of opinion about some unknowable religious question; it is a matter of eternal life and death.

---

19. De Boer, "The Death of Jesus Christ," 336 – 37.

20. The textual support for this reading is strong. See Yarbrough, *1 – 3 John*, 348.

21. Lieu, *I, II, & III John*, 256.

22. Watson, "Rhetorical Analysis," 124.

23. Yarbrough, *1 – 3 John*, 345.

Theology in Application

Truth, Faith, Commands, and Love

This passage forms an interesting nexus that relates truth, faith, commands, and love. Each of these terms is isolated from the others in our modern world. *Truth* is most often defined in modern society either as what can be scientifically verified or as a completely relativistic construction. As Akin observes:

> Truth is not as easy to find as it once was. Indeed it is in short supply, especially when we enter the realm of the spiritual. Atheist Richard Rorty boldly claims that truth is made, not found. Atheist Michael [*sic*] Foucault says that all truth claims are constructed to serve those in power. Deconstructionist Jacques Derrida says the author is dead and the text is dead. All meaning is the creation of the reader(s).[24]

In light of that, *faith* is often construed as merely subjective opinion — sometimes even belief against all reason. As one cynical aphorism (attributed to Mark Twain) claims, "Faith is believing what you know ain't so." *Commands* are frequently thought of as being common to all religious belief. One thinks of the Jewish Sabbath regulations or the dietary laws, of the Islamic call to prayer five times a day, or of a legalistic Christianity where faith in Christ is reduced to a list of dos and don'ts. *Love* is relegated to the realm of the emotions, and while its power to move human decisions and behavior is assumed, its best expression is seldom seen in popular society as related to God.

Faith, Truth, and Love Mutually Define Each Other

Perhaps the genius of John's writings is that he grounds truth, faith, commands, and love all in the revelation of God that Jesus Christ brought, and he redefines each in terms of the others such that one cannot have genuine faith without truth, and one cannot have truth apart from love, and one cannot love without living God's commands.

God the Father loved us first and sent the Son as a human being into this world to reilluminate the truth that the fall had darkened beyond our sight. The incarnation of Jesus Christ is the hub of the wheel from which truth, faith, commands, and love emanate. The incarnation not only attained eternal salvation through the cross, but integrates our individual beings and lives now. Without the incarnation, truth does devolve into as many relativistic opinions as there are people; faith does become a blind leap; commands are reduced to futile rules and regulations that are merely human; and love is debased by sinful hearts that are self-deceived.

---

24. Akin, "Truth or Consequences," 6.

Remaining in the Truth

It is against these maladies that the elder warns us to remain steadfast in the revelation of Jesus Christ. Not any belief about Jesus will do. Not any practice in the name of Christianity is true. The elder preserved the true revelation of God that went back to Jesus Christ himself, and which is now preserved for us in the NT. Even now as then, there are still many deceivers in the world, people who perhaps with the best of intentions speak claims of spiritual truth. The world into which Jesus came was already noisy with the clamor of religious and philosophical claims, and the cacophony has persisted through the centuries. This does not mean that there are many competing truths about God or that truth about God does not exist at all. It does mean that truth is not found in mere claims, regardless of who makes them, but only as revealed in the incarnate Son of God, who *is* the Truth.

CHAPTER 18

2 John 9 – 11

Literary Context

These verses form the climax of the letter by presenting the most pressing issue on the elder's mind: keeping false teachers from influencing other churches. Using strong language, the elder draws a sharp line dividing those who walk in the truth from those who have gone beyond the bounds of orthodoxy. He delivers a clear prohibition against giving any standing in the community to those who bring a message about God and Christ other than what the apostles have proclaimed.

I. Salutation and Greeting (vv. 1 – 3)

II. An Exhortation (vv. 4 – 8)

➡ **III. A Prohibition (vv. 9 – 11)**

    A. Anyone Who Does Not Hold to the Teachings of Christ Does Not Have God (v. 9)

    B. A Prohibition against Receiving False Teachers (v. 10)

    C. To Welcome a False Teacher Is to Share in Their Evil Work (v. 11)

IV. Closing (vv. 12 – 13)

Main Idea

Verses 9 – 11 form the center of the letter and the major point the elder wishes to communicate. His main concern is to prevent his original readers from welcoming false teachers into their community. To be a disciple of Jesus Christ, to have assurance of eternal life, to know God truly, one must continue to hold to the apostolic teaching about Jesus Christ. Furthermore, to aid and abet teaching outside the bounds of orthodoxy is to share in an evil work.

Translation

2 John 9–11			
9a	assertion	**Everyone who goes beyond and**	
b	expansion	**does not remain in the teaching of Christ**	**does not have God.**
c	assertion	**The one who remains in the teaching [of Christ],**	
d	result	this one **has both the Father and the Son.**	
10a	condition	If anyone comes to you and	
b	expansion	does not bring this teaching,	
c	exhortation	**do not receive them into a house**	
d	expansion	and **do not greet them.**	
11	result	For **the one who greets them shares in their evil works.**	

Structure

Verses 9 – 11 expound on the statement of v. 8, explaining how listening to the deceivers who have gone out destroys the apostolic work. They consist of two assertions surrounding a conditional statement, which forms the major point of the letter.

Exegetical Outline

→ **III. A Prohibition (vv. 9 – 11)**

    A. Anyone who does not hold to the teachings of Christ does not have God (v. 9)

    B. A prohibition against receiving false teachers (v. 10)

    C. To welcome a false teacher is to share in their evil work (v. 11)

Explanation of the Text

9 Everyone who goes beyond and does not remain in the teaching of Christ does not have God. The one who remains in the teaching [of Christ], this one has both the Father and the Son (Πᾶς ὁ προάγων καὶ μὴ μένων ἐν τῇ διδαχῇ τοῦ Χριστοῦ θεὸν οὐκ ἔχει· ὁ μένων ἐν τῇ διδαχῇ, οὗτος καὶ τὸν πατέρα καὶ τὸν υἱὸν ἔχει). The serious possibility of destroying one's spiritual foundation in Christ is further explained in vv. 9 – 11. Here the elder points out that those who go beyond the teaching of Christ go outside of it and do not have God.

The word rendered here as "goes beyond" (προάγων) is translated variously as "runs ahead" (NIV), "wander away from" (NLT), "goes too far" (NASB), "goes on ahead" (ESV), "goes beyond" (NJB) — all capturing the sense here in contrast to *remaining* in the teaching of Christ, a major theme in John's writings. Yarbrough abandons the metaphor of movement and translates the sense "everyone who innovates" in their beliefs.[1] In Johannine thought, remaining in the teaching of Christ is synonymous with walking in the truth, which funds the metaphor of movement beyond the bounds in the use of the verb "go beyond" (προάγων).

The genitive in "in the teaching *of Christ*" (ἐν τῇ διδαχῇ τοῦ Χριστοῦ) may be either objective (the teaching about Christ) or subjective (Christ's teaching). If subjective, it cannot be strictly limited to the teaching of Jesus during his earthly life, for Jesus himself promised that his apostles would receive further understanding from the Spirit after his death and the arrival of the *paraclete* (John 14:26; 16:14, 15). Teaching given by Jesus becomes teaching about Christ after he is no longer on earth. For that reason (and note further

that the elder specifies the teaching of Christ, not of Jesus, or even of Jesus Christ), it may be best to view the genitive as objective, the teaching about Christ, which of courses include Jesus' teaching as preserved and proclaimed by those who saw him, heard him, and touched him (1 John 1:1 – 4).

While there may be room to gain new insights throughout church history — we do need biblical scholars and theologians — not any and every teaching about God or Christ is within the bounds of apostolic orthodoxy. And as Jesus himself pointed out, "If you hold to my teaching [ἐὰν ὑμεῖς μείνητε ἐν τῷ λόγῳ τῷ ἐμῷ], you are really my disciples" (John 8:31). Only by holding to the teaching of Christ can one claim to be a follower of Jesus. Some ideas being held and taught by some segment in the Johannine church(es) at the time this letter was written were outside of the bounds of orthodoxy.

To move in one's thinking beyond the teaching of Christ is to remove oneself from relationship with God (to not have God), for the teaching that originated with Jesus, that which was illuminated by the Holy Spirit and preserved by the apostles, came from God himself (John 7:16, 17). The one who has both the Father and the Son is specified by the demonstrative pronoun "this one" (οὗτος), which refers to "the one who remains in the teaching" (ὁ μένων ἐν τῇ διδαχῇ); that is, the definite article "the" (τῇ) is anaphoric, referring back to the previously mentioned teaching, i.e., the teaching of Christ.

Here again, the elder points out the seriousness of the situation facing the people in the Johannine congregation(s). In v. 8 he warned against

---

1. Yarbrough, *1 – 3 John*, 349. See his discussion on 354 – 56 about reform movements, such as the Protestant Reformation, in light of the elder's statement.

following the deceivers' teaching and losing one's "full reward," eschatological language for eternal life after death. Here he warns that such beliefs lie outside the bounds of a relationship with God (cf. 1 John 1:3).

10 If anyone comes to you and does not bring this teaching, do not receive them into a house and do not greet them (εἴ τις ἔρχεται πρὸς ὑμᾶς καὶ ταύτην τὴν διδαχὴν οὐ φέρει, μὴ λαμβάνετε αὐτὸν εἰς οἰκίαν καὶ χαίρειν αὐτῷ μὴ λέγετε). This is the second instance of a command expressed in the imperative in the letter, in this case a double prohibition, and it is probably the reason the elder wrote this letter.

The readers must not welcome those who have gone out from the elder's church, or anyone else, who does not bring "this teaching," that is, the teaching of Christ as proclaimed by the apostles. If 2 John was a cover letter for 1 John, then "this teaching" may have the broader reference to the content of that book (see discussion in Introduction to 2 and 3 John). The indefinite pronoun "anyone" (τις) suggests that the elder is aware of the potential for false teachers to infiltrate churches. Those who went out from his church (1 John 2:19) are perhaps only one urgently pressing instance.

Hospitality for travelers was an important aspect of ancient culture; it was an essential part of Jesus' ministry when he sent out the Twelve (Matt 10:11 – 14). The gospel spread through early groups of believers who had contact with an apostle and then went on to other locations, taking the gospel with them, but likely not having adequate training to teach soundly. This spontaneous expansion of the church inevitably resulted in problems of conflicting teaching and of heresy.

Early Christianity was not monolithic; Paul's letters, John's gospel and letters, and the book of Revelation testify to the diverse nature, questions, and issues of Christianity in Asia Minor. Other forms of Christianity developed in Asia Minor as well, such as the Montanists in the province of Phrygia, who were eventually condemned in AD 177 by Apollinaris, bishop of Hieropolis. The geographical proximity of this group to the Johannine churches raises the question if their errant theology developed from false teaching similar to that of those who had gone out of the elder's church(es). The letters of Ignatius to churches in the same area (Ephesus, Magnesia on the Maeander, Tralles, Philadelphia, and Smyrna) indicate that there were many such Christian groups on the fringes of apostolic orthodoxy.

Extending hospitality in Greco-Roman culture gave one's guests a standing in the community equal to one's own standing. Therefore, to provide shelter and food for travelers was not simply a hospitable act; it had social ramifications beyond the immediate household involved. As Lieu observes, hospitality "was not only a social necessity but also established or reinforced bonds between different communities, building up the networking that was such an important feature of the growth of the early church."[2] Although the church councils were eventually necessary to reach consensus on orthodoxy, the nature of how the early church spread and developed fostered tension between individual groups of believers in one location and centers of orthodoxy where the apostles had resided.[3]

The elder's prohibition is not speaking about pagan friends or unbelieving relatives, but of those travelers who professed to be Christian in a teaching role, who may have had some standing in the church at large, but who were undermining apostolic authority and teaching. The point of the elder's strong exhortation was to deny even the

---

2. Lieu, *I, II, & III John*, 261.   3. See ibid.

slightest opportunity for false teachers to influence or infiltrate the church, especially when the church of that time was meeting not in church buildings but in private homes.

There is some debate whether the prohibition against greeting such a person (χαίρειν αὐτῷ μὴ λέγετε) meant even a simple "hello"[4] or a greeting that would acknowledge the person as a fellow Christian.[5] The infinitive "to greet" (χαίρειν) was the conventional greeting in personal correspondence (cf. Acts 15:23; 23:26; Jas 1:1)[6] and perhaps was intended to prevent any opportunity for private conversation that could infect the church. Ignatius, writing to the church at Smyrna, expresses the thought that it is better to not even meet such people:

> But I am guarding you in advance against wild beasts in human form — people whom you must not only not welcome but, if possible, *not even meet*. Nevertheless, do pray for them, that somehow they might repent, difficult though it may be. But Jesus Christ, our true life, has power over this.[7]

However, it is difficult to know how someone would be aware of what kind of teaching a traveler was bringing if there was no communication whatsoever. In either case, it would be clear to others that the false teacher was not to be given any standing in the community, making it hard for them to gain a hearing before the church (cf. Jude 3 – 4, 12, 19).

There are many extant letters of introduction requesting a friend or relative who lived in a distant place to extend hospitality to a traveler passing through who was otherwise a stranger, and 3 John is an example of such a letter (see Introduction to 3 John).[8] The elder's teaching here concerning hospitality creates an ironic contrast with the situation presented in 3 John, where it is the elder's own people who are being refused hospitality by Diotrephes and his church (see commentary on 3 John 9 – 10).

11 For the one who greets them shares in their evil works (ὁ λέγων γὰρ αὐτῷ χαίρειν κοινωνεῖ τοῖς ἔργοις αὐτοῦ τοῖς πονηροῖς). Social gestures are not always spiritually neutral acts. The elder ups the ante here with this final comment that indicts anyone who greets a false teacher as sharing in the evil works of the false teachers. Lieu comments, "The elder's injunction remains disturbingly rigorous,"[9] especially given that hospitality was considered a Christian virtue (cf. Acts 16:15; Rom 12:13; 1 Tim 3:2; 5:10; Titus 1:8; Heb 13:2; 1 Pet 4:9). Indeed, it may seem over the top when viewed from our modern social context of pluralism and ecumenical gestures.

But that was then and this is now. The Christian church with its orthodox creeds and practices has been long established, but when the elder wrote, the infant church was most vulnerable. The decentralized, scattered groups of Christians in the first century, before the NT existed, relied on itinerant teachers and preachers. Those who had "gone out" with a false message (1 John 2:19) had departed from the elder's church; that perhaps made them all the more dangerous. Their former association with the elder's church may have created a perception of good standing that could deceive the outlying

---

4. E.g., ibid., 259.

5. E.g., Kruse, *Letters of John*, 214.

6. Francis Xavier J. Exler, *The Form of the Ancient Greek Letter: A Study in Greek Epistolography* (Washington, DC: Catholic University of America Press, 1923), 23 – 68.

7. Ign. *Smyr* 4.1, in *Apostolic Fathers* (ed. and trans. Michael W. Holmes; 3rd ed.; Grand Rapids: Baker Academic, 2007), version 1.2 accessed through Accordance.

8. See Chan-Hie Kim, *Form and Structure of the Familiar Greek Letter of Recommendation* (SBLDS 4; Missoula, MT: Society of Biblical Literature, 1972); Hans-Josef Klauck with Daniel P. Bailey, *Ancient Letters and the New Testament: A Guide to Context and Exegesis* (Waco, TX: Baylor University Press, 2006).

9. Lieu, *I, II, & III John*, 262.

churches in the region; that may account for the harshness with which the elder expresses his warnings. To protect the integrity of the infant church, the issues had to be drawn in black and white, or light and darkness, to use the Johannine duality.

"Evil works" (τοῖς ἔργοις … τοῖς πονηροῖς) are mentioned elsewhere in John's writings. In the gospel, it is their "evil" works that made people reject Jesus (John 7:7) and love the darkness more than the light (John 3:19). In 1 John, Cain is held up as the paradigmatic sinner, whose works were evil and who was "of the evil one" (1 John 3:12). The elder says here that to aid and abet false teaching that is not "of Christ," even if the false teachers themselves claim to be Christian and may have all good intentions, is to "share in" (κοινωνεῖ) the works of darkness.

Not any and all spiritual teaching about God and Christ is of the truth, and what is not of the truth is of the darkness. To give credence and aid to false teaching is to keep people in darkness and, to that extent, to forfeit fellowship in the light. For genuine Christian fellowship with the elder, the Father, and Jesus Christ is based on embracing the proclamation of those who have seen, heard, touched, and perceived the true significance of Jesus' earthly life (1 John 1:1 – 3). True fellowship with God and with one another is based not on shared personal opinion or common social factors, but on walking in the truth, on remaining in the teaching of Christ.

Theology in Application

Ecumenical or Not?

We live in a pluralistic age animated by an ecumenical spirit. We also live at a time when we possess the complete NT and long after Christian orthodoxy has been established by the historic church councils. But the church today needs discernment no less than it did when the elder wrote. While the church at large is probably not in danger of being destroyed, individual lives and congregations are still at great spiritual risk.

It is interesting that of all the NT writers, the Johannine author repeatedly stresses the need for Christians to love one another as an expression of their love for God. But it is the same author who so boldly prohibits social interaction with professing Christians who do not embrace the orthodox, apostolic message. Is it not unloving to shun another professing Christian? Apparently the elder does not think that love, as paramount as it is to the Christian life, trumps truth — and that is perhaps the great sin of our age.

Modern society and even some churches do believe that love is the ultimate parameter that trumps even the orthodox doctrines and practices that have stood for millennia. In fact, claims to truth are often in our times accused of being mere power plays to suppress other people, an act that, if this accusation is true, is the opposite of love. But in John's thought, truth and love are inseparably wed. One cannot have truth without love, nor can one truly love without truth. For it is not loving to encourage someone to wander from the truth or to allow them to persist in the deception of sin.

We do not know precisely what was happening in the Johannine church(es) that motivated the elder to write such strong words, but it is clear that whatever it was, threatened the heart of the gospel (cf. Jude). It does seem clear that the pressing situation involved an errant Christology that rejected Christ as "coming in flesh" (2 John 7; cf. 1 John 4:2) and coming in both water and blood (1 John 5:6). It was apparently an example of Calvin's claim that worldly people "do not therefore apprehend God as he offers himself, but imagine him as they have fashioned him in their own presumption."[10] And the world is full of such people today.

The Need for Discernment in a Pluralistic Age

Christians need to exercise discernment, and particularly Christian leaders who are the gatekeepers to our churches. At the same time, so much infighting among Christian leaders about things that are not essential to the heart of the gospel has taken the focus off those issues where truth is at stake. And when every issue is defined as a life-or-death struggle for the gospel, the force of the elder's prohibition is blunted and the command to love others is violated.

One of the clearer issues today is the prevalent assumption that all monotheistic religions must be worshiping the same God by different names. This is an ecumenical impulse that reaches to embrace the world's great religions — Christianity, Judaism, and Islam — into one brotherhood. While there may be common values and practices shared by these three (and other) religions, the NT example of a similar ecumenical impulse cautions us. When the Greek and Roman cultures met, each was worshiping a pantheon of gods and goddesses. In an ecumenical spirit to embrace the other, the pantheons were simply equated. "You Greeks call him Zeus and we Romans call him Jupiter, but it's all the same." However, when the apostle Paul encountered the Greco-Roman pantheon, he did not simply say, "The Greeks call him Zeus and the Romans call him Jupiter, but we know him as Yahweh or Jesus Christ." To the contrary, Paul responded to the pagan religious zeal of his time with the rebuke, "turn from these worthless things" (Acts 14:15). And so we should be wary of too quick an application of monotheism that would, without nuance, equate the God of the Muslims and/or the God of the Jews with the Father of Jesus Christ.

Jesus Is Not Just Another Prophet

Christians also need to be wary of those religions who honor Jesus in some way, such as Mormonism, Jehovah's Witnesses, and Christian Scientists, but who have gone beyond the teachings of Christ by supplementing or revising the NT with religious ideas by much later thinkers such as Joseph Smith, Charles Taze Russell, and

---

10. Calvin, *Institutes of the Christian Religion*, 1.4.1.

Mary Baker Eddy, respectively. These groups may well represent a modern instance of what the elder was arguing against in his time, for they emerged in the nineteenth century by deviating from orthodox Christian doctrine. To be clear, the elder's prohibition does not give anyone license to be unkind or uncivil to coworkers, neighbors, or relatives who practice these religions. But the elder would prohibit us from endorsing their teaching, giving them a platform in our churches, or supporting them financially.

A case closer to home for Protestants is the Reformation. As the church developed from the ancient world to the medieval, the Roman Catholic magisterium, composed of the bishops and headed by the Pope, became the authoritative body charged with discernment and teaching. But when Martin Luther and other Reformers recognized the magisterium had gone beyond the teachings of Scripture in the sixteenth century, particularly on the issue of salvation, there was nothing left to do but disassociate.[11]

The unstoppable flow of history has brought, and always will bring, with it complex issues, intractable questions, and painful situations that confront Christ's church. But in the midst of all this, true disciples of Jesus Christ in every generation must not lose sight of the elder's main point: that truth has been revealed by God in Christ and that anything other than that brings spiritual destruction to those who embrace it. Belief about God is not mere personal preference, nor do all religions lead to God even if practiced sincerely. Thankfully the Spirit remains with us, the Spirit whom Jesus promised would guide future disciples into all truth (John 16:13). And the Spirit bears witness to the One who was born for the very purpose of bearing witness to the truth (18:37). Everyone who is "of the truth" will hear his voice, and in that promise the church's future rests secure.

---

11. See Yarbrough, *1 – 3 John*, 354 – 56, for a fuller discussion of the complexities of innovative teaching in the church throughout its history.

2 John 12 – 13

Literary Context

These final verses bring the elder's letter to a conventional close with a greeting that echoes the salutation in v. 1.

I. Salutation and Greeting (vv. 1 – 3)

II. An Exhortation (vv. 4 – 8)

III. A Prohibition (vv. 9 – 11)

➡ **IV. The Closing (vv. 12 – 13)**

    A. Hope for a Continuing Relationship (v. 12)

    B. Greetings from a Sister Church (v. 13)

Main Idea

The elder raises the possibility of a face-to-face visit, perhaps testing the water to see if the original readers would still welcome him and affirm their unity with him. The final greeting with its repetition of "chosen" and personification of the church as a "sister" indicates that at least two churches, and possibly more, were known to and in communication with elder.

Translation

(See next page.)

Structure

Though conventional in form, these verses connect the closing to the salutation, bringing the churches into familial relationship and expressing hope for the joy of a continuing relationship. Verse 12 anticipates joy if and when the elder visits the

2 John 12 – 13

12a	concession	I have many things to write to you,
b	contra-expectation	but **I do not wish [to write] with pen and ink;**
c	contrast	rather, **I hope to be with you and**
d	expansion	**to speak face-to-face**
e	result	so that our joy might be full.
13a	greeting	**The children of your chosen sister greet you.**

sister church, forming an inclusio on the topic of joy that is motivated by walking in the truth (v. 4). The metaphorical mention of "your chosen sister" in v. 13 forms an inclusio with the opening salutation in v. 1, "to the chosen lady."

Exegetical Outline

➡ **IV. The Closing (vv. 12 – 13)**
    A. Hope for a continuing relationship (v. 12)
    B. Greetings from a sister church (v. 13)

Explanation of the Text

12 I have many things to write to you, but I do not wish [to write] with pen and ink; rather, I hope to be with you and to speak face-to-face so that our joy might be full (Πολλὰ ἔχων ὑμῖν γράφειν οὐκ ἐβουλήθην διὰ χάρτου καὶ μέλανος, ἀλλὰ ἐλπίζω γενέσθαι πρὸς ὑμᾶς καὶ στόμα πρὸς στόμα λαλῆσαι, ἵνα ἡ χαρὰ ἡμῶν πεπληρωμένη ᾖ). Having issued the warning against receiving false teachers, the elder closes his letter with the conventional hope to speak with his readers face-to-face (Gk. "mouth-to-mouth"). He mentions full joy, forming an inclusio with his previous statement that it gives him great joy to find them walking in the truth (v. 4). The thought of "our full joy" (ἡ χαρὰ ἡμῶν πεπληρωμέν) in the Johannine writings denotes a fellowship characterized by unity in belief and mission in the Christian gospel.

John the Baptist had full, or completed, joy when he heard of Jesus' early public ministry (John 3:29). Jesus intends a completed joy for his disciples when he exhorts them to remain in his love by keeping his commandments (15:11) and to petition the Father in Jesus' name (16:24). Jesus prayed that his disciples would have a "full measure of my joy" (17:13). John's first letter was also written with the intent that joy may be made complete (1 John 1:4). As Lieu notes, "this is an 'eschatological' joy not limited to human emotions but marking the fulfillment of God's purposes as when the pain of childbirth reaches its goal in the joy of the child that is born."[1]

Although the elder's hope to see them does not necessarily imply imminent travel plans, two inferences might be made here: (1) the elder, as old as he

---

1. Lieu, *Second and Third Epistles*, 99.

may be, was still able enough to travel the distance between him and his original readers so as to not make the statement ludicrous; (2) his statement of hope might be testing the waters to see if the sister church was still open to receive him, that is, whether they had not been contaminated with the problem documented in 3 John. There the elder had written to a church that was under the influence of a leader named Diotrephes, and the church refused to receive his letter or those who carried it. One wonders if that church may have been "the chosen lady and her children" who rebuffed the elder, making 3 John the sequel to the story of 2 John. But if the lady and her children, after receiving this letter, were still in unity of belief and mission with the elder and so would welcome his visit, his joy would be complete.

13 The children of your chosen sister greet you (Ἀσπάζεταί σε τὰ τέκνα τῆς ἀδελφῆς σου τῆς ἐκλεκτῆς). The letter ends in the conventional way of personal greetings,[2] with a close parallel in 1 Pet 5:13. The metaphor of the church as a chosen lady and her children continues here with the greetings sent from "the children of your chosen sister." The female personification here is not simply the general "lady" but the more specific, and familial, "sister." This forms an inclusio with v. 1 and reinforces the likelihood that the letter is addressed to another church in the region rather than to an individual woman.

Theology in Application

The Success of the Gospel Creates Problems for the Church

The historical moment that gave rise to 2 John was a unique time in the history of the Christian church. The NT was not yet in existence; only its individual books were in circulation in various geographical regions. (It took until the fourth century for all apostolic writings to be known by the churches in all areas.) Many, if not most, of the eyewitnesses of Jesus' earthly life, ministry, and resurrection had passed on. The missionary impulse of the church in its first decades had been remarkably successful, planting small groups of Christian believers throughout most of the Mediterranean world. As Lieu observes, "The New Testament and early Christian literature reflects the very high degree of mobility among Christians whether in service of the Gospel or for more secular or commercial reasons."[3] This mobility meant that various understandings of the significance of Jesus and applications of the apostolic message traveled among the churches, some of them sound, many of them not. Therefore, keeping Christian belief within the bounds of orthodoxy, when orthodoxy had yet to be articulated in any universal or codified form (such as the Nicene Creed), was a pressing and difficult task.

In the last half of the first century, heresy was one of the major problems that threatened the gospel, especially because the world to which the message of Jesus Christ went out heard that message through the din of many different pagan religions and philosophical worldviews. The leaders of the church quickly saw the need

---

2. Exler, *Form of the Ancient Greek Letter*, 112 – 16.   3. Lieu, *Second and Third Epistles*, 125.

to draw the geographically, ethnically, and theologically diverse congregations into a uniform system of belief that was faithful to the message and meaning of Jesus Christ. The development of the ecclesiastical hierarchy, the gathering and publication of the NT writings, and the great church councils with their representatives from the far-flung churches arose in answer to that early situation.

We do not live in such a time when the beliefs and practices of Christianity are in such flux. Or do we? The one ecclesiastical hierarchy has been splintered into many, many denominations, with the Catholic pope a reminder of an ecclesiastical unity that, for good reason, the church has never been able to sustain. The NT has been translated and published in every corner of the world, yet the church continues to debate its interpretation and application to modern issues that the NT writers could never have imagined. The creeds of the great church councils stand as statements of orthodoxy for many Christians, but they have been rejected by whole segments of the church throughout its history. It seems the more things change, the more they stay the same.

The Family of God

It is significant to note that after the elder makes his bid to the original readers to reject and rebuff those self-professing, traveling Christians who bring a teaching different from his own, he sends greetings from "the children of your chosen *sister*" (τὰ τέκνα τῆς ἀδελφῆς σου τῆς ἐκλεκτῆς). He reminds his readers of their familial and spiritually genetic relationship to one another as children of the heavenly Father.

That is a reminder that the Lord's churches around the world still need to hear today. We are family. The organic unity of the Christian churches is not found in looking to one, ultimate, superior human leader but in the spiritual rebirth as God's children. If God is our Father, we are spiritual siblings. Contrary to the liberal Protestant view of the brotherhood of man by virtue of God as our Creator, John and the rest of the NT writers insist that only those who know God as their *Father* through faith in his Son Jesus Christ are his children (cf. John 1:12 – 13). Furthermore, not even everyone who claims to be a Christian is "of us," as 1 John 2:19 so poignantly observes (cf. Matt 25:31 – 46). What was at stake then, as it is now, is what constitutes the truth about the person and work of Jesus Christ. We need both a defining center of that truth and a circumscribing boundary that delimits what lies beyond the truth.

The Elder's Spiritual Authority

The elder insisted that he was a bearer of the apostolic tradition that defined both the center and boundaries of the truth about Jesus Christ. His insistence that any other teaching be rejected was not a power play or the insufferable arrogance of one man's personality. In the time before the apostolic writings were gathered and published as the NT, only the eyewitnesses whom Jesus himself chose and their direct associates had the knowledge and the authority to define the center and the circumference of the truth against all upstart voices. It was not a simple or quick task, and there were disputes even among the apostles, such as the one that gave rise to the Jerusalem Council (Acts 15). It has never been easy to be the church.

But today we do have the NT, and we have the Nicene Creed and other confessional statements that have stood the test of time. We have much less to argue about. And yet the language and tone of our religious and theological discourse has become at times so harsh and so polarized that we need to hear the elder's reminder that, despite many legitimate and important differences of opinion, genuine believers in Jesus Christ are *family*, organically connected with one another by the Spirit. Since only God truly knows the heart of a person, it behooves us to give a professing Christian every benefit of our doubt until it is clear without doubt that they have moved beyond the boundary of orthodoxy.

The definition of orthodoxy is not at stake in many (most?) of the church's squabbles today, and it is a sad state when every issue is polemicized, and opponents demonized, as if it were. It is disingenuous to talk about things such as the mode of baptism, the charismatic gifts, the ordination of women, accuracy in Bible translation, music in worship — and others you can probably add — in tones and terms that demonize brothers and sisters in Christ who hold an equally high view of the authority of the Bible. Yes, we must call each other to walk in the truth of the gospel of Jesus Christ, but as we do so, let's remember to address the other as our "chosen sister."

Introduction to 3 John

We should become increasingly familiar with the NT, but we should not let that familiarity dull the amazing truth that when we read 3 John, we are reading an actual letter involving real Christians that was written nearly two thousand years ago! Third John documents the names of three Christians from the first century who, along with the author of the note, "the elder," were involved in an actual situation that exemplifies issues of authority, truth, and love — issues that in their more abstract form fill the pages of 1 and 2 John.

At just under two hundred words in its original Greek, 3 John comes to us as the shortest book of the NT. The autograph would have fit on one sheet of papyrus, the "paper" typically used in the first century (cf. 2 John 12). It was originally written as a letter of introduction requesting hospitality for the bearer of the letter, a man named Demetrius. But if that were all there was to it, this brief personal note probably would not be in the Bible. When this letter was written, much more was at stake — the very truth about Jesus Christ.

Third John is the only NT book that does not mention Jesus by name (though see commentary on v. 7). But given the brevity and specific purpose of the note as a letter of introduction (as opposed, for instance, to a theological discourse or evangelistic presentation), this is not too surprising. Most Christians today write many notes and emails to believing friends that allude to their shared faith without explicitly mentioning Jesus. While the content of 3 John lacks the theological material of, for instance, John's gospel or Romans, it does not deserve to be neglected by preachers or in Bible studies. Much less warranted is the conclusion that it lacks edifying material and is of only historical interest today. The evangelical, Protestant doctrine of Scripture does not allow any book of the Word of God to be dismissed as unworthy of our attention.

But to understand 3 John, we must also understand its relationship to the other Johannine writings and the historical moment for which it was written. Despite its brevity and the specificity of its message, 3 John is a treasure that provides a glimpse into early church dynamics, provides a much-needed exhortation to Christians today, and makes a significant theological claim about where the truth of the gospel of Jesus Christ is to be found.

The Genre and Structure of 3 John

The highest level of the form and structure of any text is necessarily defined by the genre of the text. Because 3 John is an actual note from one person to another, it exhibits many features of first-century Greek letters, its epistolary structure being the most obvious of them. In fact, it is closer in form and structure to other extant personal notes from the ancient world than any other book. Just as there are various types of letters in the modern world that take different forms depending on their purpose and the relationship between the writer and the recipient — compare a business form letter to a chatty email from a close friend — different kinds of personal correspondence from the ancient world are known among the extant documentary papyri.[1]

Among such letters are those that functioned as letters of introduction or recommendation (known in the ancient world as ἐπιστολὴ συστατική, cf. 2 Cor 3:1).[2] It is clear from 3 John 12 that this letter functioned to introduce Demetrius to Gaius, but that is not its only, or even its primary, purpose. Recognizing that this is an actual note helps us to bring appropriate assumptions to our reading and interpretation.

For instance, we cannot fault the author for not telling us more about his relationship with Gaius or Diotrephes, because that lack represents information that was shared between the author and Gaius and needed no formal description. We have no warrant to read elements of the text as allegories or poetic features when they can be understood more literally as communicating information between the writer and the recipient. The significance and meaning of the text is not to be sought by lifting it out of its historical moment, but by contemplating how that moment provides insight into the spiritual issues of the time, which are still issues today.

Various methodologies can be brought to bear on NT epistles, each contributing something to our understanding. Third John can be analyzed according to categories of classical Greco-Roman rhetoric,[3] according to the conventions of Hellenistic letter writing,[4] and according to modern linguistic principles of discourse analysis,[5] each producing somewhat different outlines of the text. The rhetorical function of each part of a Greco-Roman letter overlays the discourse structure, which at its highest level is governed by the form of Hellenistic letters; but within its body it exhibits vari-

---

1. The documentary papyri are those actual documents and letters from the ancient world that were amazingly preserved, primarily in the sands of Egypt, and then recovered by archaeologists. There are thousands published in various collections. The most accessible in English are those published by the Harvard University Press in the Loeb Classical Library, *Select Papyri*; in Adolf Deismann, *Light from the Ancient East* (trans. L. R. M. Strachan; New York: George H. Doran, 1927; repr. Peabody, MA: Hendrickson, 1997). Many papyri have been put on online and can be viewed at www.papyri.info.

2. Kim, *Form and Structure*.

3. Watson, "Rhetorical Analysis," 479 – 501.

4. Klauck and Bailey, *Ancient Letters*; Stanley K. Stowers, *Letter Writing in Greco-Roman Antiquity* (Philadelphia: Westminster, 1986).

5. Sherman and Tuggy, *Semantic and Structural Analysis*; Clark, "Discourse Structure in 3 John," 109 – 15; Floor, "Discourse Analysis of 3 John," 1 – 17.

ous discourse markers that are based on syntax and depend on the subject and the style and flow of thought of the writer. Therefore, an exact correspondence between the segments in a rhetorical outline of 3 John and those of a discourse outline should not be expected, though there should be some corroboration between the results of various methodologies.

Although exegesis of 3 John shows that the letter functioned to introduce Demetrius to Gaius, the letter really isn't about Demetrius; rather, it is about the elder's concern for Gaius's continued faithfulness to the truth in light of Diotrephes's previous rejection of the elder's envoys (see comments on v. 11). The elder employs only subtle persuasion, for he is hoping against hope that he is right to assume that Gaius remains a coworker for the truth. A more polemic tone would have had to assume a greater alienation than was warranted. But if Gaius were beginning to waver, the rhetoric of this letter would function to call him back to the truth while simultaneously presenting a practical test of Gaius's faithfulness to the elder's cause.

Outline of 3 John

    I. The Letter's Address and Greeting (vv. 1 – 4)
       A. The Address of the Letter (v. 1)
       B. A Wish for Well-Being (v. 2)
       C. Basis of the Elder's Confidence (v. 3)
       D. Implicit Exhortation (v. 4)
    II. The Reason for Writing (vv. 5 – 8)
       A. An Affirmation of Gaius's Hospitality (vv. 5 – 6a)
       B. An Exhortation to Do Right (v. 6b – 8)
   III . The Problem with Diotrephes (vv. 9 – 11)
       A. He Does Not Receive Exhortation from the Elder (v. 9)
       B. He Publicly Makes Disparaging Remarks about the Elder (v. 10a – e)
       C. He Does Not Welcome Fellow Christians Endorsed by the Elder (v. 10f-h)
       D. He Throws Those Who Do So out of the Church (v. 10i)
       E. A Command to Do What Is Right (v. 11)
    IV. Introducing Demetrius (v. 12)
       A. Demetrius Is Affirmed by All Who Know Him (v. 12a-b)
       B. Demetrius Is Affirmed by the Truth Itself (v. 12c)
       C. The Elder Personally Recommends Demetrius (v. 12d)
       D. The Elder Reasserts the Reliability of His Knowledge of the Truth (v. 12e-f)
    V. Closing (vv. 13 – 15)
       A. There's More to Be Said If and When the Elder Visits (vv. 13 – 14)
       B. A Blessing of Peace during a Troubling Situation (v. 15a)
       C. An Exchange of Greetings (v. 15b-c)

3 John 1 – 4

Literary Context

These verses form the conventional Greco-Roman letter opening in a manner that makes 3 John more similar to ancient secular letters than any other book of the NT. The address of a letter was always the first line of a letter, identifying both the writer and the recipient. The writer of 3 John identifies himself only as "the elder" and writes to a dear acquaintance whose name is Gaius. Knowing that this book originated as personal correspondence provides a key to interpreting its message because we can be assured that the issues it addresses and the names it mentions refer to authentic people and that the given situation was real.

Unlike poetry or apocalyptic literature, this note gives no indication that the author wishes his writing to be understood symbolically or allegorically. There is no reason to believe that the situation depicted here is anything but actually true at the time the note was written. Because we lack sufficient historical background to know with certainty who and where the elder was and more precisely who Gaius was, where he lived, or what were the specifics of the situation that gave rise to this letter, such historical background must be reconstructed largely by inference from the letter itself. Any such reconstruction must necessarily be held with the exegetical humility of acknowledged uncertainty. Nevertheless, while we don't know everything we might wish we knew about the origin of 3 John, we do know enough to understand the significance of its message for Christians in other times and other places.

As rhetorical analysis indicates, these opening verses (vv. 1 – 4) comprise the *exordium*, which introduces the main topic of the discourse and prepares Gaius to be receptive for what follows in the letter. Specifically, the elder focuses on Gaius by praising his faithfulness to following the truth, as exemplified by his previous practice of Christian hospitality.

Main Idea

The opening verses of this letter introduce its major concern, "the truth" (ἡ ἀλήθεια), which is mentioned four times in the first four verses. The elder finds no greater joy than hearing from others that his spiritual children are living faithfully in the truth of the gospel, which takes the topic of truth out of the abstract and makes it intensely personal.

Translation

3 John 1 – 4

1a	address	The elder,	
b		to my dear friend Gaius, whom I love in the truth.	
2a	greeting	Dear friend,	
b	desire	**I hope that in all ways you are**	**well and are healthy —**
c	comparison		as well as your soul is.
3a	basis	For **I rejoice greatly**	
b	circumstance	when brothers come and tell	of your truth —
c	expansion		how you are walking in the truth.
4a	assertion	**I have no greater joy than**	**these times**
b	identification		when I hear that my children are walking in the truth.

Structure

As noted under Literary Context, these opening verses exhibit the standard Hellenistic letter opening. The author identifies himself only as "the elder" (ὁ πρεσβύτερος) and the recipient as Gaius. The standard address is amplified with a term of affection for Gaius, which indicates the apparently warm personal acquaintance between him and the elder. The conventional wish for health that is typical in Hellenistic letters is personalized by the elder's knowledge based on good reports he has heard that Gaius is spiritually healthy.[1]

Though couched in the form of a Hellenistic letter greeting, the elder reminds Gaius that his faithfulness to the truth is bringing great joy to the elder and serves as a gentle and implicit exhortation that Gaius will continue to bring the elder joy by remaining faithful to the truth.

Exegetical Outline

→ **I. The Letter's Address and Greeting (vv. 1 – 4)**
   A. The address of the letter (v. 1)
   B. A wish for well-being (v. 2)
   C. Basis of the elder's confidence (v. 3)
   D. Implicit exhortation (v. 4)

Explanation of the Text

1 The elder, to my dear friend Gaius, whom I love in the truth (Ὁ πρεσβύτερος Γαΐῳ τῷ ἀγαπητῷ, ὃν ἐγὼ ἀγαπῶ ἐν ἀληθείᾳ). In this standard form of Hellenistic letters, the writer identifies himself with a word in the nominative case and the name of the person to whom he is writing in the dative case.

Although the Greek term "elder" (πρεσβύτερος) can be used in a general sense to refer to an older man in his senior years, in the NT the term most often refers to an office of oversight in the local church.[2] Because the structure of first-century Greco-Roman society held a special place for the patriarch of a family (the *pater familias*), the leader of an assembly might typically have been an older man, collapsing the distinction between the two senses of the word "elder."

In the case of the early church, local groups of believers typically met in a home whose owner may or may not have been the spiritual overseer of the church but who was obviously influential in the life of the congregation. The tone and content of 3 John show that the elder was a spiritual leader whose authority extended beyond one local house church, for he evidently felt free to exhort Gaius and seems confident that his words will be well received, even though Gaius is clearly not a member of the elder's local home church. Furthermore, the fact that the author of this letter refers to himself only as "the elder" without specifying his name implies that Gaius knows his identity. It also suggests that the letter is to be read as more than a note between friends; it comes with some ecclesial

---

1. For instance, P.Oxy. 292 (Loeb, p. 297), "Before all else I pray that you may have health and the best of success"; B.G.U. 423 (Loeb, p. 305), "Before all else I pray for your health and that you may always be well and prosperous." See also P.Giess. 17 (Loeb, p. 309 – 10); B.G.U. 846 (Loeb, p. 317). The examples are too numerous to list.

2. D. Lake, "Elder (NT)," *ZEB*, 2:290 – 91; also Hermann W. Beyer, "ἐπίσκοπος," *TDNT*, 2:608 – 22; Günter Bornkamm, "πρεσβύτερος," *TDNT*, 6:651 – 81.

authority, an authority that Gaius is expected to recognize.

Some interpreters argue against apostolic authorship by taking the author to be one of the presbyters whom Papias calls the bearers and transmitters of the apostolic tradition (see Eusebius, *Hist. eccl.* 3.39.3), though it is debatable whether or not his categorization would exclude an apostle.[3] Moreover, the word "elder" (πρεσβύτερος) had been widely used over a long period of time to refer to the leader of an assembly, first by Jewish writers and later by Christian writers, and therefore it cannot be used as evidence that the letter dates to after the lifetime of the apostles when a certain form of ecclesial hierarchy emerged with a more clearly defined office of elder. The author's self-designation as "the elder" is also found in 2 John 1, and both letters have similar closings (2 John 12; cf. 3 John 13). Taken together with the similar style, vocabulary, and themes of the letters, this letter strongly suggests that both came from the same person. (See the discussion of authorship in the Introduction to 1, 2, and 3 John.)

Unless Gaius can be identified with other men of the same name mentioned in the NT, nothing is known of him except what can be inferred from this letter. He is a Christian man considered by the elder to be true to the faith (vv. 3–4), who was personally known by the elder, who was apt to offer hospitality of a substantial nature (vv. 5–8), who was widely respected (v. 3), and who exercised a degree of influence in the church (vv. 2, 5, 6a). The personal nature of Gaius's relationship to the elder is attested by the remark that the elder has much more on his mind as he writes and hopes to visit Gaius soon (vv. 13–14).

The warm tone of this note is set when the elder places "to my dear friend Gaius" (Γαΐῳ τῷ ἀγαπητῷ) in the address of the letter. Various forms of the verb for "love" (ἀγαπάω) or its cognates are used by the apostle Paul (Rom 12:19; 1 Cor 10:14; 15:58; 2 Cor 7:1; 12:19; Phil 2:12; 4:1), James (Jas 1:16, 19; 2:5), Peter (1 Pet 2:11; 4:8, 12; 2 Pet 3:1, 8, 14, 17), Jude (Jude 3, 17, 20), and the author of Hebrews (Heb 6:9) to describe their relationship to the Christian recipients of their letters. But forms of the verb "to love" are especially frequent in the letters of John (1 John 2:7; 3:2, 21; 4:1, 7, 11; 3 John 2, 5, 11).

Given the widespread use of this term by several Christian authors in reference to so many fellow Christians, it appears to be a conventional Christian term (though nonetheless sincere) and cannot be used here to speculate on the distinctive nature of the elder's relationship with Gaius. Forms of ἀγαπάω are found centuries later in the opening address of letters between Christians, often alongside a form of "brother" (ἀδελφός), which indicates that the apostolic correspondence found in the NT shaped subsequent Christian letter writing.[4]

The verb for "love" (ἀγαπάω) is adverbially modified by the prepositional phrase to specify a love that is "in the truth" (ἐν ἀληθείᾳ). It is syntactically identical to the phrase in the relative clause in 2 John 1, addressed to "the chosen lady and her children, whom I love in the truth" (οὓς ἐγὼ ἀγαπῶ ἐν ἀληθείᾳ). Note the emphatic use of the personal pronoun "I" (ἐγώ) and the anarthrous noun for "truth" in the phrase in both letters.

If this were the only reference to "truth" in 3 John or in the Johannine corpus, Bultmann would probably be right that it should be read as synonymous with the adverb "truly" (ἀληθῶς), meaning "in reality, authentically."[5] In that case it would refer simply to the sincerity of the elder's

---

3. Bultmann, *Johannine Epistles*, 95.

4. E.g., P.Oxy. 1162 ; P.S.I. 208; see also Kim, *Form and Structure*.

5. Bultmann, *Johannine Epistles*, 95–96.

love. But in Johannine thought, love is closely associated with truth defined as the revelation of God, for God's revelation in Christ reveals God's love for those he came to save (see "In Depth: 'Truth' in John's Letters" at 1 John 1:6). On that basis those whom Christ has saved are taught to love one another as God loves them (cf. 1 John 4:11). This expression of love for Gaius in the opening salutation of 3 John refers to their shared faith in Christ as the basis of their relationship, and the elder's hope that it will continue undisrupted.

Gaius is addressed three more times with the vocative of "dear friend" (ἀγαπητέ; vv. 2, 5, 11),

emphasizing the bond of Christian fellowship between him and the elder. In the context of conflict within the Johannine community, the emphatic pronoun "I" (ἐγώ) here in v. 1c (also in 2 John 1) signals the elder's continuing regard for Gaius, perhaps in contrast to how other Christians of influence, such as Diotrephes, might view Gaius in light of his hospitality to those sent by the elder. This repetition of "dear friend" and the emphatic "I" reinforce the elder's relationship with Gaius, since the elder is about to ask Gaius to do what would undoubtedly put him into tension, if not outright hostility, with Diotrephes and his followers.

IN DEPTH: Which Gaius?

The Latin name "Gaius," which means "rejoicing," was common in the Greco-Roman world.[6] The name occurs five times in the NT, referring probably to three different men (Acts 19:29; 20:4; Rom 16:23; 1 Cor 1:14; 3 John 1). In Acts 19:29, a man named Gaius is mentioned as one of Paul's traveling companions "of Macedonia," who was seized along with Aristarchus during the Ephesian riot over Artemis in AD 56. A man named Gaius is also mentioned in Acts 20:4 as among Paul's cohorts returning from Corinth to Jerusalem in the spring of AD 58. But that Gaius is there said to be from Derbe ("the Derbian," Δερβαῖος), calling into question whether it could be the same man, though Derbe is in eastern Asia Minor.

In Rom 16:23, Paul refers to a man named Gaius who extended hospitality to the apostle and to the Corinthian church about the year AD 58 and who previously had been baptized by Paul in the early 50s (1 Cor 1:14). The hospitable nature of the Gaius in Corinth resembles the Gaius to whom 3 John is addressed, who was probably living somewhere in the region of western Asia Minor.

According to a tradition recorded in the fourth century, the apostle John made Gaius of Derbe, who had traveled with Paul, the first bishop of Pergamum, a city of western Asia Minor, and it is this man to whom 3 John is addressed (*Apostolic Constitutions* 7.46.9). Probably based on that tradition, the Venerable Bede believed the recipient of 3 John was probably the same man Gaius mentioned by Paul in Rom 16:23 as his host.[7]

Given the ease of mobility in the Roman world, it is not implausible that

---

6. Smalley, *1, 2, 3 John*, 344.

7. Bray, ACCS 11, 240.

only one man named Gaius could have throughout his lifetime moved around, as these NT verses suggest if all references were to just two or three different men. Nevertheless, most modern commentators take the NT occurrences of the name "Gaius" to refer to four different men: Gaius of Macedonia, Gaius of Corinth, Gaius of Derbe, and the Gaius of Asia (to whom 3 John was addressed).[8]

2 Dear friend, I hope that in all ways you are well and healthy — as well as your soul is (Ἀγαπητέ, περὶ πάντων εὔχομαί σε εὐοδοῦσθαι καὶ ὑγιαίνειν, καθὼς εὐοδοῦταί σου ἡ ψυχή). The affection the elder has for Gaius is repeated as he addresses him with the vocative adjective translated "dear friend" (Ἀγαπητέ). The wish for health was a standard part of the Hellenistic letter, found frequently in the conventional form, "Above all I pray that you are healthy" (πρὸ πάντων εὔχομαί σε ὑγιαίνειν), but among NT letters it occurs only here, although with the preposition "about" (περί) instead of "before" (πρό; see below).[9] The earliest extant appearance of the phrase is in a letter that dates from about AD 25, where it is placed at the end, and it continued to be used in letters throughout the second and third centuries.[10]

Because the verb "I pray" (εὔχομαι) is part of the conventional phrase, it should not be pressed for a more specific Christian or theological meaning. Its use is similar to the English "good-bye," which virtually every English speaker uses without knowing that it is a contraction of the phrase "God be with you." Just as it would be a misunderstanding to think that everyone who says "good-bye" is pronouncing a blessing, it is probably wrong to overload "I pray" with meaning here, even though the same term was used in the some contexts to refer to praying to a deity. Nevertheless, one cannot argue that because a *Christian* English speaker uses the parting phrase "good-bye" with no thought of its original meaning, he or she would be disinclined to so bless a friend. Similarly, the fact that "I pray" cannot be pressed does not mean that the elder did not or would not pray for Gaius. But that isn't strongly in view here. Given the idiomatic nature of the expression, prayer should not be made the main exegetical point of the passage.[11]

Similarly, the fact that the health wish was part of an epistolary convention also means that "I pray you … are well" (εὔχομαί σε … ὑγιαίνειν) should not be taken to mean that Gaius was ill or weak, as some interpreters have previously done.[12] Nor should it be spiritualized as a prayer specifically for spiritual health, as Carrie Judd Montgomery did at the turn of the twentieth century.[13] Such examples

---

8. Brown, *Epistles of John*, 703; Bultmann, *Johannine Epistles*, 95; Marshall, *Epistles of John*, 81; Smalley, *1, 2, 3 John*, 344; Stott, *Epistles of John*, 217; John Christopher Thomas, *The Pentecostal Commentary on 1 John, 2 John, 3 John* (Cleveland: Pilgrim, 2004), 21.

9. See *Select Papyri*, vol. 1 (Loeb), for the following examples: P.Oxy. 292 (p. 296), *Class. Phil.* xxii (p. 302), B.G.U. 423 (p. 304), P.Giess. 17 (p. 308), B.G.U. 846 (p. 316).

10. Exler, *Form of the Ancient Greek Letter*, cited by Robert W. Funk, "The Form and Structure of II and III John," *JBL* 86 (1967): 425.

11. E.g., Andrew Whitman, "3 John: Helping or Hindering with the Spread of the Gospel?" *Evangel* (Summer 1997): 37 – 38. Though Whitman should not put such exegetical weight on 3 John 2, he makes many valid points about prayer.

12. For instance, John Bird Sumner, *A Practical Exposition of the General Epistles of James, Peter, John, and Jude* (London: J. Hatchard & Son, 1840), cited in H. L. Landrus, "Hearing 3 John 2 in the Voices of History," *JPT* 11, no. 1 (2002): 78.

13. Carrie J. Montgomery, "The Sacredness of the Human Body," *Triumphs of Faith* 30 (July 1910): 167.

show how biblical interpretation can go awry when texts are not understood within their original linguistic and cultural context.

Third John 2 differs from the conventional phrase in the choice of a different preposition (περί instead of πρό), expressing the sense "concerning all things," or in more idiomatic English, "in every way." The Greek text is stable here, and there are no textual variants to support a conjectural emendation to "above all" (πρό), which have been proposed from time to time.[14] Even if there were textual variants, the reading "concerning/in" (περί) is the more difficult reading, which scribes would likely change to conform with the standard form; thus, "concerning/in" should be accepted as original. More conclusively, another first-century letter from Arsinoites, Egypt (BGU 3 885) contains almost the exact phrasing, "In all ways I pray you ..." (περὶ πάντων εὔχομαί σε), including the preposition "concerning/in" (περί).[15]

Some English versions translate the other infinitive as "prosper" (εὐοδοῦσθαι; e.g., NKJV, NASB), leading some readers to think of material wealth. The "health and wealth gospel" assures 3 John a place in the modern history of interpretation. One morning Oral Roberts opened the Bible for a word from God and read the first verse his eyes fell upon, which happened to be 3 John 2. He took this verse to be a prompting of the Spirit to begin a ministry of "whole-person prosperity."[16] Over time this verse became what Roberts called the "master key" of his ministry, for he read it to say, despite the Greek, that God desires *above all* things that Christians have the fullness of prosperity here and

now, an interpretation that corrected his previous view of the virtue of Christian poverty. Kenneth Hagin followed Oral Roberts in using 3 John 2 as a direct promise from God to all Christians.[17]

Against this interpretation, a study of the Greek verb "to prosper," which occurs again immediately in v. 2 in reference to the soul (also in Rom 1:10 and 1 Cor 16:2), confirms what Albert Barnes wrote about this word in the mid-nineteenth century: it "seems to refer to the journey or passage of life" and could refer "to any plan or purpose entertained," not just material wealth.[18] Of course, to enjoy favorable financial circumstances is not excluded from the elder's wish "concerning all things" (περὶ πάντων) for Gaius, and "prosper" is used in the context of finances in 1 Cor 16:2a.

The wish for health and good circumstances in everything is compared to the good state of Gaius's spiritual health ("as well as your soul is"; καθὼς εὐοδοῦταί σου ἡ ψυχή), which the elder knows because others have testified that Gaius is faithful to the truth and continues to live by it (v. 3). The ancient interpreter Oecumenius comments that Gaius is doing well *because* he is living according to the truth of the gospel.[19] However, spiritual health does not necessarily imply well-being in every circumstance of life. Especially in the first century, fidelity to Christian faith could in fact result in various forms of suffering, persecution, and even execution (cf. 1 Pet 2:21). The elder knows that Gaius is doing well spiritually because those to whom he previously extended hospitality have returned and given a good report about him. Because the elder is going to ask Gaius to continue to

---

14. J. Rendel Harris, "A Study of Letter-Writing," *The Expositor*, 5th series, 8 (1898): 167; Funk, "The Form and Structure of II and III John," 425 n7.

15. See http://papyri.info/hgv/9398/?q=transcription_ngram_ia%3A%28Θεόκτιστος+++++%29 (accessed 2 August 2012).

16. Landrus, "Hearing 3 John 2," 81.

17. Ibid.

18. Albert Barnes, *Notes: Explanatory and Practical on the General Epistles of James, Peter, John and Jude* (New York: Harper & Brothers, 1854), 422, cited in Landrus, "Hearing 3 John 2," 79.

19. Bray, ACCS 11, 240.

express his faithfulness to the truth by continuing to receive the elder's envoys, the elder alludes here to Gaius's past faithfulness in this regard. With this, the letter transitions to material that will form the background of the elder's request in v. 6.

Unlike the apostle Paul's letter openings, this one contains no prayer or wish for "grace," "mercy," or "peace," though the elder does send a wish for peace in the closing (v. 15a).

3 For I rejoice greatly when brothers come and tell of your truth — how you are walking in the truth (ἐχάρην γὰρ λίαν ἐρχομένων ἀδελφῶν καὶ μαρτυρούντων σου τῇ ἀληθείᾳ, καθὼς σὺ ἐν ἀληθείᾳ περιπατεῖς). The elder knows that Gaius is spiritually well (v. 2) because some "brothers" have come to the elder and have testified that Gaius is "walking in the truth" (καθὼς σὺ ἐν ἀληθείᾳ περιπατεῖς). The English equivalent of "just as" (καθώς), learned in first-year Greek, will not serve well here. This adverb should be construed as either "the extent to which" or "because."[20] The frequently occurring noun "truth" (ἀλήθεια) is found in the Johannine writings in both anarthrous and articular constructions without distinction in meaning and in context should be translated with the English article to connote the truth of the gospel (cf. 3 John 3, 4).

Note the emphatic pronoun "you" (σύ): "You, Gaius, are walking in the truth," which in the context of schism and conflict contrasts with others known to the elder who are not. The verb "to walk" (περιπατεῖν) is used metaphorically to refer to how one lives one's life, occurring five times in 1 John (1:6, 7; 2:6 [2x], 11), three times in 2 John (vv. 4, 6 [2x]), and twice in 3 John (vv. 3, 4). Because it is clear to others that Gaius is living his life consistently with the truth revealed in the gospel of Jesus Christ, the elder hopes that all the circumstances

of Gaius's life are going well and that he is in good health (v. 2). The plural noun and participles in the genitive absolute ("brothers coming and testifying"; ἐρχομένων ἀδελφῶν καὶ μαρτυρούντων) suggest an unspecified number of brothers who had previously enjoyed Gaius's hospitality, perhaps on a number of different occasions.

The word "brother" (ἀδελφός) is used throughout the NT to refer to fellow Christians, and in the plural is a generic masculine used even where women are included in the group (e.g., Rom 1:13; 1 Cor 1:11; Eph 6:23; 1 Thess 1:4; Heb 13:22; Jas 1:2). Though it is not clear whether women believers are among the "brothers" mentioned here, women in the first century did travel between churches, such as Priscilla with her husband, Aquila (Acts 18:18), and Phoebe, who carried Paul's letter from Corinth to Rome (Rom 16:1). Here in 3 John the "brothers" are most likely traveling preachers and teachers associated with the elder and sent out from his church with his blessing. The fact that women traveled with Jesus and the Twelve (Luke 8:1 – 3) opens the possibility that women may have been among the earliest evangelists and teachers in the wider church, but little work has been done to confirm this. If the elder is the apostle John, his presumably advanced age might have made it difficult for him to travel.

The elder "rejoices greatly" (ἐχάρην ... λίαν) when he hears reports that believers are living their lives in accord with the gospel of Jesus Christ as received and taught by the elder. The phrase "I rejoice greatly" is another conventional expression in some Hellenistic letters in response to a letter or to good news.[21] However, here it is more than a platitude as v. 4 makes clear. In a time of conflict created by the teaching of the antichrists (1 John 2:18 – 25) and the rejection of Diotrephes (3 John 9 – 10), the loy-

---

20. BDAG, s.v. καθώς 2, 3.

21. Kim, *Form and Structure*, 131. For an example, see Deismann, *Light from the Ancient East*, 184.

alty of those who remained faithful to the apostolic teaching would be important to the elder.

The verb "to testify" (μαρτυρέω) is often found in letters of recommendation during the Roman period, though with a somewhat different use than here.[22] Kim points out that letters of introduction may attempt to motivate the recipient to receive and do something on behalf of the introduced individual so that "he may bear witness to me," acknowledging that the recipient of the letter has done what was requested. In other words, testimony that the recipient has complied with the request of the writer closes the loop of communication, so to speak. In 3 John the previously sent envoys have done just that; they have "spoken well" of Gaius's welcome in the past, and "before the church" at that (v. 6).

4 I have no greater joy than these times when I hear that my children are walking in the truth (μειζοτέραν τούτων οὐκ ἔχω χαράν, ἵνα ἀκούω τὰ ἐμὰ τέκνα ἐν τῇ ἀληθείᾳ περιπατοῦντα). The specific instance of joy caused by Gaius's faithfulness (v. 3) is generalized here in v. 4 to all who are faithful to the truth. The separation of the comparative adjective "greater" (μειζοτέραν) from the noun it modifies, "joy" (χαράν), marks semantic prominence of the phrase, which is further emphasized by its position in front of the negated verb. This emphatic construction indicates that while the phrase in v. 3, "for I rejoice greatly," may be conventional to the letter form, it is certainly not mere platitude.

Note that the comparative genitive is plural (τούτων), even though most English translations render it as the singular "this" to achieve good English style. The plural demonstrative pronoun is probably a reference to the several times when the

elder has heard a good report about his children (τὰ ἐμὰ τέκνα, plural) in the next clause. The elder apparently is thinking of the great joy he takes each time he hears of a faithful believer.

The *hina* clause is appositional, defining the cause of joy. As Wallace notes, this use of a *hina* clause is almost idiomatic in the Johannine corpus.[23] Also characteristic of Johannine writing is the use of the possessive adjective "mine" (ἐμά) instead of the more common genitive personal pronoun "of me" ([ἐ]μου).

Despite any differences with 1 and 2 John, the criterion of the elder's joy is the same — seeing Christians living out the truth of the gospel of Jesus Christ, as defined by the tradition in which the elder stands (cf. 1 John 1:1 – 4). There is nothing that pleases the elder more than to see Christians faithfully adhering to the apostolic teaching about Christ. The Venerable Bede's comment on this verse continues to resonate with pastors and others in Christian leadership: "There is no greater joy than to know that those who have heard the gospel are now putting it into practice by the way in which they live."[24]

The elder apparently views his spiritual oversight paternally, for he refers to his "children" (τέκνα), of which Gaius is apparently one prime example. The apostle Paul also referred to those he led to faith in Christ as his "children" (1 Cor 4:14; Gal 4:19; Phil 2:22), but in the Johannine letters the phrase seems to have a broader sense of those over whom the elder has spiritual oversight (1 John 2:1; 2 John 1, 4, 13). The two thoughts are not, of course, mutually exclusive.

The elder's declaration of what gives him the greatest joy is at the same time an implicit exhortation that his dear friend Gaius will continue to give him joy by continuing to walk in the truth. This

---

22. Kim, *Form and Structure*, 85.
23. Wallace, *Greek Grammar*, 475.

24. Bray, ACCS 11, 240.

implicit exhortation prepares Gaius to respond positively to the elder's request that follows in v. 6 and culminates in v. 11, where the only imperative verb in the body of the letter is found. (The other imperative form "greet" [ἀσπάζου] in v. 15 is formulaic for letter closings.)

Theology in Application

Truth and Love, Again

In 3 John 1 – 4, the noun "truth" (ἀλήθεια) is mentioned four times, making it the central theme of a passage that functions rhetorically to introduce a major theme of the letter and joining it to what is said about truth in the other Johannine writings. The closely associated theme "love" (ἀγαπάω and its cognates) is mentioned three times in these verses. These opening verses make clear that the basis for such a bond of *love* between believers is the shared value of living one's life in accordance with the *truth* of the gospel of Jesus Christ, who is himself the Truth (John 14:6). Even though 3 John does not mention "Jesus" or "Christ," the truth in view is clearly the Christian gospel, not only because the rest of the Johannine corpus is so explicitly centered on Jesus Christ, but also because the itinerant teaching in view in 3 John is being done for the sake of "the Name" (v. 7, see comments), an allusion to Jesus Christ and the only name in which salvation is found (Acts 4:12) and to which all will one day bow (Phil 2:9 – 10).

Centered in the gospel of Jesus Christ, John's teachings define the nature of both truth and love and their relationship to one another, concepts that had to be redeemed in the first century and that are terribly abused and distorted in our times as well. As Wilson notes:

> Love is a terribly debased term today, almost beyond rescue as a description of the good news of the kingdom come in Jesus Christ. . . . We must work to recover an understanding and practice of love. . . . Salvation is living in the way of love.[25]

The concept of truth also fares poorly in a postmodern age that revels in relativism and pluralism. By referring to the gospel of Jesus Christ as "the truth," the elder is making a bold claim in his time (cf. John 18:38). The early church lived in a world that was possibly even more pluralistic than ours, with a plethora of religions and philosophies vying for the hearts and minds of people. The elder identifies the gospel of Jesus Christ as truth, not simply in the cognitive sense, but as the existential reality that demands to be lived out by those who call themselves followers of Christ. The elder considers his apostolic ministry to be successful only when those over whom he has spiritual influence are living their lives in a manner consistent with that truth in such a way as can be observed and affirmed by all who know them. The elder

---

25. Wilson, *For God So Loved the World*, 131.

rejoices that Gaius is no closet Christian, whose religion is so private that it finds no public expression, but is known by others for his faithfulness to the truth because of his way of life.

This brief note to Gaius exposes the nature of the relationship between Christian truth and Christian love as it is brought to bear on the topic of Christian hospitality later in the letter. Although hospitality may initially seem a rather mundane issue in light of the awesome realities revealed by Jesus Christ, it is in the details of living that the elder looks for an understanding of the gospel that keeps truth and love in right relationship in times of conflict and schism.

If love and truth are visualized as two concepts weighed on a balance scale, with the goal of keeping them in balance, they will always be in conflict to some extent in our thinking. In our modern ethos, defending the truth and loving others are often put in opposition by a postmodern view that argues that any claim to truth is a power play that insults, and perhaps oppresses, those with a differing viewpoint. Christians who think that love trumps truth tend to argue for acceptance — or at least tolerance — of beliefs and practices that are clearly in conflict with scriptural truth, and they are buying into the ethos of relativism more than they perhaps realize.

By contrast, some Christians, convinced that they have God's truth, tend to defend it, especially against other Christians, by using the most vitriolic and mean-spirited tactics. The distance from virtue to evil is sometimes not great. I've heard it said that it is a small step from being willing to die for the truth to be willing to kill for it — a thought that looms large in the wake of religiously motivated terrorists convinced they know God's truth. Therefore the biblical relationship between truth and love must be understood and held together in our thinking. Holding that love and truth are in tension shows an inadequate and unbiblical view of both concepts.

Love Doesn't Trump Truth

Contrary to the values of modern society, the NT teaches that it is not loving to encourage someone to live in ways counter to the truth that God has revealed, that is, to aid and abet someone in their sin, especially those who claim to be Christian (1 Cor 5:2). Whether the sin is wrong belief about Christ or disobedience to the way of life Christ commands, the elder does not want Christians to be a part of it. Christians today need to hear the elder clearly on this relationship between truth and love and to think carefully about what supports the truth. The matter comes down to discerning truth from falsehood.

The Johannine letters are exhortations to remain faithful to the truth revealed by God through Jesus, who then commissioned his apostles to proclaim it. Where is that truth to be found today? Although some denominations today wish to retain the office of "apostle," there must be a clear distinction between divinely inspired writers of the NT and anyone who claims the title of apostle today. At the time 3 John was written, the NT did not yet exist; thus, it was important to know whom to listen to, and it no doubt was confusing. But today the apostolic teaching about Christ is found within the pages of the NT. Only those who teach and preach the divinely inspired message of the NT stand in the apostolic tradition today. That excludes those — especially who call themselves Christian — who reject the Bible as God's Word and take it to be just an ancient book whose content is mostly irrelevant to modern issues.

The elder is still exercising his apostolic oversight through the words of this letter. Gaius becomes an "everyman" of the Christian faith with whom we can identify as we hear the elder's words exhorting us also to live our lives in faithfulness to the gospel of Jesus Christ. The positive example of Gaius, who was widely known for living out the Christian faith by putting his resources into service for others, is a model worthy of imitation. As Christian apologist Josh McDowell once asked, "If we were on trial for being a Christian would there be enough evidence to convict us?"[26]

---

26. This is the central thesis of a popular book by Josh Mc-Dowell, *Evidence That Demands a Verdict* (San Bernardino, CA: Here's Life, 1972).

3 John 5 – 8

Literary Context

The elder now moves quickly into the purpose for which he is writing to Gaius. In the modern world we would send a note requesting hospitality in advance of showing up. But without email, telephone, or a public postal system in the ancient world, the elder must request hospitality via this letter; it was probably carried by those standing on Gaius's doorstep who needed it.[1]

Rhetorical analysis suggests that vv. 5 – 6 function to give background information that sets up the main point(s) that follow(s).[2] In epistolary rhetoric this section (the *narratio*) of a letter specifies why the letter is being written. If the *narratio* mentions a person, praise is given if the person is considered to be on the side of the writer, which illuminates the reconstruction of the situation.[3] In 3 John the transition to the *narratio* is marked by the vocative form of the adjective "dear friend" (ἀγαπητέ) and the praise of Gaius's previous hospitality and loyalty. This probably indicates that the elder assumes Gaius to be on his side and not persuaded by Diotrephes or others who would alienate Gaius from the elder. There is no lead-in discussion of background information, which suggests that the relationship between the elder and Gaius is relatively current. This reference to past hospitality prepares Gaius for the central request of the letter in vv. 7 – 12, namely, the urgent need to extend hospitality to those sent by the elder because Diotrephes refuses to do so.

---

1. The Romans did have a well-organized postal system, but it was used only to carry imperial mail. See A. M. Ramsay, "The Speed of the Roman Imperial Post," *JRS* 15 (1925): 60 – 74.

2. Watson, "Rhetorical Analysis," 491, 493; Barth L. Camp-

bell, "Honor, Hospitality and Haughtiness: The Contention for Leadership in 3 John," *EvQ* 77 (2005): 331.

3. Watson, "Rhetorical Analysis," 491.

Main Idea

The plea in v. 6, "Please send them on their way in a manner worthy of God," is the main point of this passage. This no doubt refers to Christian workers sent by the elder who have arrived in the vicinity of Gaius's home, probably led by Demetrius (v. 12).

Translation

3 John 5 – 8

5a	address	Dear friend,
b	assertion	**you are doing a faithful deed**
c	reference	in whatever you do
d	advantage	for your fellow Christians
e	concession	even [if they are] strangers.
6a	assertion	They speak well of your love before the church.
b	entreaty	**Please send them on their way**
c	manner	**in a manner worthy of God**.
7a	basis of 6b	For **they set out on behalf of the Name,** taking nothing from those who are not Christians.
8a	exhortation	Therefore, **we ought to support such people**
b	result	so that we might be fellow workers for the truth.

Structure

These verses open the body of the letter (vv. 5 – 12) and focus on Gaius and his faithful hospitality in the past. The esteem and affection of the elder for Gaius are emphasized by the repetition of the vocative "dear friend" that appears in both the opening (v. 5) and closing (v. 11). The next section (vv. 9 – 10) focuses on Diotrephes and contains five assertions describing his behavior. The elder's troubles with Diotrephes is sandwiched between the implicit exhortation for Gaius to provide hospitality on this occasion (v. 6b, 8) and the command that Gaius do what is right in order to remain on the side of truth and love (v. 11). This structure invites Gaius to see himself in contrast to Diotrephes and to be persuaded not to follow his example.

Exegetical Outline

II. The Reason for Writing (vv. 5 – 8)
    A. An affirmation of Gaius's hospitality (vv. 5 – 6a)
    B. An exhortation to do right (vv. 6b – 8)

Explanation of the Text

5 Dear friend, you are doing a faithful deed in whatever you do for your fellow Christians even [if they are] strangers (Ἀγαπητέ, πιστὸν ποιεῖς ὃ ἐὰν ἐργάσῃ εἰς τοὺς ἀδελφοὺς καὶ τοῦτο ξένους). "Dear friend" (Ἀγαπητέ), the second of three occurrences of this vocative adjective, opens a new discourse unit. The verbs switch from the first person singular in vv. 1 – 4 to the second person singular as the elder begins to present his request to Gaius.

The elder emphasizes his esteem and affection for Gaius because what Gaius is doing for the "brothers" reflects his faithfulness. What's more, Gaius has been extending hospitality not on the basis of personal friendship, but even for fellow believers unknown to him personally. The elder's acknowledgment of Gaius's reputation as a generous host based on previous hospitality to Christian brothers prepares Gaius to respond favorably to the request to host Demetrius also, whom he apparently does not know personally. The repetition of terms of affection and friendship might be intended both to confirm the elder's belief that Gaius has been a good friend and to express his hope that Gaius will not turn from his friendship with

the elder because of the growing tensions with Diotrephes or the confusion caused by the apparent problem in the elder's church (see 1 John 2:19).

The neuter singular accusative adjective "faithful" (πιστόν) functions as a substantive object fronted before the verb for emphasis, "a faithful deed you are doing," affirming that what Gaius had previously done for the brothers was indeed a faithful deed — should there be any question about that. Bauer's translation followed by Bultmann, to "act loyally" is *ad sensum*, for he offers only 3 John 5 as evidence for this sense.[4] The Venerable Bede comments, "Gaius's loyalty is the result of his faith. What John means is that Gaius is doing all these things because he is a believer and wants to show faith in the things that he does."[5]

The phrase "whatever" (ὃ ἐάν) implies an unspecified number of instances where Gaius has acted for the benefit of fellow Christians, showing his faithfulness to love and to truth. The aorist subjunctive "you do" (ἐργάσῃ) is used because of the contingency of "whatever" and therefore means "whatever you do" on behalf of fellow Christians — in the past, the present, or the future. In the Johannine corpus the verb ἐργάζομαι refers to works

---

4. BDAG *s.v.* πιστός 1b; see also Bultmann, *Johannine Epistles*, 98 n8.

5. Bray, ACCS 11, 241.

done either by God (John 5:17) or by those serving God (6:27, 28, 30; 9:4; 2 John 8), though this sense is difficult to capture here in smooth English.

The preposition translated "for" (εἰς) in the phrase "for your fellow Christians even [if they are] strangers" (εἰς τοὺς ἀδελφοὺς καὶ τοῦτο ξένους) bears the sense of "with reference to" or "for."[6] The phrase raises the question of the relationship between the "strangers" (ξένους) and the "brothers" (ἀδελφούς). Are these two categories of people whom Gaius has done good deeds for — brothers and strangers? Or are they one category composed of brothers some of whom are strangers to Gaius?

The syntax is further complicated by the neuter, singular demonstrative pronoun "this" (τοῦτο). While this word might at first glance be taken as an accusative object of the elided but implied verb "you do," it almost certainly is one of the twenty-two instances in the NT of an adverbial use of the pronoun. BDF (§290 [5]) considers the construction "even this" (καὶ τοῦτο) to have the concessive sense "although," which would mean Gaius has extended hospitality to one category of people, fellow Christians, *although* they were strangers to him. Wallace also takes "this" (τοῦτο) to have an adverbial sense meaning "especially," but he takes the conjunction (καί) to be copulative, applies an extension of the Granville Sharp rule, and defines the second substantive, "strangers," as a subset of the first ("brothers").[7] Wallace's construal conveys the sense that Gaius was hospitable to fellow Christians, *especially* to those who were strangers to him.

The syntax does not allow for certainty, but either way it is read, the point is clear that the elder considers it a good and faithful deed for Gaius to extend hospitality, not just to fellow Christians he knows but even to those he doesn't. Given that the elder apparently needs to introduce and commend Demetrius (v. 12), who is probably the bearer of the note, the concessive sense of "even this" (καὶ τοῦτο) may be a somewhat better fit. The elder wishes Gaius to welcome Demetrius *although* he is a stranger, as he has apparently welcomed other fellow Christians in the past.

The elder's emphatic commendation of Gaius for extending hospitality to strangers suggests that hospitality to strangers was not a commonly expected practice in the Greco-Roman world.[8] Extending hospitality to strangers was considered a virtue in ancient societies as reflected in both the OT and NT (e.g., Gen 18 and 19; Rom 12:13; Heb 13:2). However, the fact that Joseph and Mary did not find shelter in Bethlehem, that hospitality to strangers had to be instructed, and that it was highly praised when it did occur suggests that it was not practiced by the majority of the population.

Hospitality in Greco-Roman society had a somewhat different form and function than the English word connotes in our times, and the practice was governed by different values and expectations. To us, "hospitality" usually refers to entertaining family and friends for a meal or brief overnight stay. Such customs are good and right, but that isn't what hospitality involved as referred to in 3 John. Hospitality in the ancient world generally meant taking a visiting stranger under one's temporary care, thereby transforming their social status from stranger to guest in the community and consequently giving them a social status that reflected one's own standing in the community.[9] A stranger could become part of the community even

6. BDAG, *s.v.* εἰς 5.

7. Wallace, *Greek Grammar*, 271, 335.

8. For an analysis of the sociology of this practice, see Bruce J. Malina, "The Received View and What It Cannot Do: III John and Hospitality," *Semeia* 36 (1986): 171 – 89. See also Abraham J. Malherbe, "The Inhospitality of Diotrephes," in *God's Christ and His People: Studies in Honour of Nils Alstrup Dahl* (ed. J. Jervell and W. A. Meeks; Oslo: Universitetsforlaget, 1977), 222 – 32.

9. Malina, "III John and Hospitality," 181 – 83.

temporarily only through a personal bond with a member of the community.

This practice had the potential of putting the host at some risk, because one's own social standing and reputation could be affected, depending on the behavior and character of the stranger to whom one extended or refused hospitality. Thus, hospitality was not a casual matter, and although it was considered a virtue in Greco-Roman society, the motive for it contrasted with Christian hospitality. For the moral philosophers such as Cicero, the "houses of illustrious men should be open to illustrious guests."[10] Rather than creating a social advantage for the host, Christian hospitality was to be offered to even lowly people without expectation of benefit (cf. Rom 12:13; 1 Tim 3:2; Titus 1:8; Heb 13:2; 1 Pet 4:9).

The form of hospitality that welcomed overnight guests into one's home was needed in Roman society because there was ample opportunity for travel on an extensive system of roads by land and on large fleets of ships by sea, but inns were not pleasant places to stay.[11] It was common for travelers to seek shelter with the mutual acquaintances of family or friends. Because the earliest churches were most often located along the major travel routes, Christian travelers sought hospitality from fellow believers through the local house churches. Because the practice involved some risk for the host, a letter of introduction from a mutual acquaintance was often written to put the host's mind at ease and to avoid abuse of the practice.

6 They speak well of your love before the church. Please send them on their way in a manner worthy of God (οἳ ἐμαρτύρησάν σου τῇ ἀγάπῃ ἐνώπιον ἐκκλησίας, οὓς καλῶς ποιήσεις προπέμψας ἀξίως τοῦ θεοῦ). This subordinate clause (cf. the relative pronoun translated "they" [οἵ]) joins this thought to the preceding clause, thus forming one sentence in Greek, but preserving it as one sentence in translation makes the English too unwieldly. The antecedent of this relative pronoun refers to those fellow Christians to whom Gaius has previously extended hospitality ("your fellow Christians even [if they are] strangers") and who have testified before the elder's church(es) of Gaius's love.

Some have argued that the verb ἐμαρτύρησαν (often translated "they testified") has a connotation that suggests a more formal public report, but the verb can mean simply "to affirm in a supportive manner" or "speak well of."[12] Moreover, the recipients of a favor given as the result of a letter of recommendation often acknowledged their appreciation by speaking well of their benefactor to the person who wrote the letter.[13] Therefore, this verb says less about the circumstances behind the letter than some interpreters wish to make of it. For instance, it puts too much weight on the verb to suggest that the elder had sent out a delegation to all the churches to determine which ones had fallen to the antichrist heresy (cf. 1 John 2:18 – 23) and had formally received their testimony.[14] Since the circumstances that gave rise to this letter are knowable only in broad strokes, the verb should probably be construed only with the degree of specificity appropriate to our lack of knowledge. The point is simply that the elder had heard good reports about Gaius's hospitality, with perhaps an implication that should Gaius refuse hospitality to Demetrius, that refusal would also become known to the elder and the church. Malherbe observes that in some

---

10. Christine D. Pohl, *Making Room: Recovering Hospitality as a Christian Tradition* (Grand Rapids: Eerdmans, 1999), 17 – 18.

11. R. C. Stone, "Inn," *ZEB*, 3:313.

12. BDAG, *s.v.* μαρτυρέω 2.

13. Kim, *Structure and Form*, 85.

14. E.g., Tom Thatcher, "3 John," in *Expositor's Bible Commentary* (ed. Tremper Longman III and David E. Garland; rev. ed.; Grand Rapids: Zondervan, 2006), 13:532.

extant letters of introduction, the subsequent testimony of those being introduced is noted as partial motivation for the host's compliance.[15]

The prepositional phrase "before the church" (ἐνώπιον ἐκκλησίας), found instead of a dative indirect object, may suggest the testifying was during the gathering of the church, even as many churches today have times of "testimonies" in their services when members share thoughts and experiences with the congregation. Brooke observes, "The anarthrous phrase [ἐνώπιον ἐκκλησίας] denotes a meeting of the Church at which the witness was borne."[16] Notably 3 John is the only Johannine work to refer to the "church" with the Greek word ἐκκλησία (vv. 6, 9, 10; see comments on v. 9 for further discussion of this term in 3 John).

The hospitable deeds of Gaius are referred to here as expressions of his love (τῇ ἀγάπῃ). This alludes to the conundrum Gaius faced, wanting to express love for Christ and for fellow Christians on the one hand but also facing questions of authority and truth on the other. Third John offers guidance on holding love and truth together. The very fact that this note was written suggests the elder feared that Gaius would be influenced to abandon such expressions of love in the face of contested truth about the authority of the elder and his proclamation of Christ (cf. 1 John 2:19; 2 John 9). This close relationship between truth and love in the Johannine tradition is attested in the variant reading here, "testifying of your *truth and* love" (ἀληθείᾳ καὶ ἀγάπῃ) in a few manuscripts from the twelfth through fourteenth centuries.

The elder states his specific request in the relative clause translated here as a separate sentence, "Please send them on their way in a manner wor-

thy of God" (οὓς καλῶς ποιήσεις προπέμψας ἀξίως τοῦ θεοῦ).[17] The phrase (lit.) "you will do well" (καλῶς ποιήσεις), followed most often by an aorist participle as here, is an idiom used from the third century BC through the NT period as a polite introduction to a request, much as "please" functions in English.[18] It should not be construed as a commendation ("you do well"), any more than the English idiom "good-bye" should be understood etymologically as "God be with you."[19]

The future tense "you will do" in the idiom shifts the discourse from affirming Gaius's past practices to introduce a request that Gaius once more do (for Demetrius et al., v. 12) what he has a reputation in the church for doing — extend generous hospitality. The relative pronoun οἵ subordinates this clause grammatically to the main clause in v. 5, "you are doing a faithful deed in whatever you do for your fellow Christians." The aorist participle "send on their way" (προπέμψας) functions adverbially as probably modal, specifying an instance of "doing a faithful deed." In this context the verb "send forth" (προπέμπω) refers to a request for assistance with food, money, arranging transportation, and so forth.[20] The object of the participle is the plural accusative relative pronoun "them" (οὕς), the antecedent of which is "fellow Christians" in the main clause of the sentence. This clause is a hinge looking back to the good report of previous recipients of Gaius's hospitality while making a polite request for the practice to continue in the immediate future. Since the next opportunity to extend hospitality is probably to Demetrius, who brought this letter to Gaius, the plural of the relative pronoun implies either that the request extends to all future occasions for hospitality or that Demetrius was not

15. P.Osl. 55, P.Flor. 173, P.Oxy. 1064 and 1424 in Malherbe, "Inhospitality of Diotrephes," 226.

16. Brooke, *Johannine Epistles*, 184.

17. Campbell, "Honor, Hospitality and Haughtiness," 331–32.

18. E.g., Ps.-Eup. 2:12; Josephus, *Ant.* 11.279; *Let. Aris.* 39, 46; P.Tebt. 56; P.Oxy. 294.

19. LS, *s.v.* καλός C.5; Funk, "Form and Structure of II and III John," 427–28.

20. BDAG, *s.v.* προπέμπω 2.

alone (for which one would expect the relative pronoun ὅν).

The exact meaning of the adverbial phrase "worthy of God" (ἀξίως τοῦ θεοῦ) is debated, but it specifies the manner in which the assistance is to be provided (cf. Col 1:10; 1 Thess 2:12). It may echo the custom that those carrying the gospel in the ancient world were to be received as the Lord Jesus himself, though for this one might expect "worthy of the Lord" (ἀξίως τοῦ κυρίου). Reflecting this concept, *Didache* 11:4 – 6 comments:

> Let every apostle who comes to you be welcomed *as if he were the Lord* [δεχθήτω ὡς κύριος]. But he is not to stay for more than one day, unless there is need, in which case he may stay another. But if he stays three days, he is a false prophet. And when the apostle leaves, he is to take nothing except bread until he finds his next night's lodging. But if he asks for money, he is a false prophet.[21]

Alternatively, the phrase may refer to providing for visitors in such a way that God would approve[22] or treating the travelers in a manner that respects and validates the dedication to God that moved them to leave the safety and comfort of their homes (v. 7).[23] While none of these ideas is mutually exclusive, this last one seems likely given the explanation for this exhortation that immediately follows in v. 7. In any case, Gaius's Christian hospitality is to reflect the gracious and generous character of the God he worships.

7 For they set out on behalf of the Name, taking nothing from those who are not Christians (ὑπὲρ γὰρ τοῦ ὀνόματος ἐξῆλθον μηδὲν λαμβάνοντες ἀπὸ τῶν ἐθνικῶν). The elder now gives the basis for his request to Gaius (γάρ) — because the travelers set out from their homes "on behalf of the Name," and they will receive no help from unbelievers along

the way, as was the practice of disciples of Jesus. Given that Christians were relatively few, it was especially important for believers to be willing to feed and shelter Christian workers as they traveled.

The reference to "the Name" (τὸ ὄνομα) occurs also in Acts (Acts 5:41; 9:16; 15:26; 21:13) and in Paul's letter to the Romans (Rom 1:5). Ignatius uses the phrase in his letter to the Ephesian church: "For even though I am in chains for the sake of the Name" (Ign. *Eph.* 3:1). Clearly, the "Name" is a metonymy for Jesus Christ (cf. Acts 15:26, which refers to men who have risked their lives for "the name of our Lord Jesus Christ"). This mention of "the Name" is the closest the elder comes to mentioning Jesus in 3 John; this makes it clear that these travelers are *Christian* workers. Far from calling into question whether 3 John is actually a Christian letter, this unqualified reference to "the Name" shows that the elder and Gaius must have been familiar with this way of referring to Jesus.

One purpose of this letter of introduction is to confirm to Gaius that these strangers are indeed fellow believers in the Lord Jesus Christ known to the elder and that the very reason for their travel is on behalf of the Lord. The exact nature of their work is unknown, though most likely they were sent from the elder for evangelization and discipleship through preaching and teaching. This situation created a dire need for believers like Gaius to extend hospitality even to those Christians who were strangers. This was such an important practice in the early church that beginning with Jesus himself, both the NT and other early Christian writings provide instructions for the practice (e.g., Matt 10:8; 1 Cor 9:14; 2 Cor 12:14; 1 Thess 2:9; *Did.* 11:4 – 6).

8 Therefore, we ought to support such people so that we might be fellow workers for the truth

---

21. Michael W. Holmes, ed. and trans., *Apostolic Fathers*, 263 (italics added).

22. Smalley, *1, 2, 3, John*, 350.

23. Westcott, *Epistles of St. John*, 238.

(ἡμεῖς οὖν ὀφείλομεν ὑπολαμβάνειν τοὺς τοιούτους, ἵνα συνεργοὶ γινώμεθα τῇ ἀληθείᾳ). The request for hospitality in v. 6b is restated here as an assertion of moral obligation — "we ought [ἡμεῖς . . . ὀφείλομεν] to support" the Lord's work; note the switch to a first person plural and the emphatic use of a personal pronoun.

The verb translated "support" (ὑπολαμβάνειν) has a broad semantic range in the NT ("suppose, take up, reply"), but here means to take someone under one's care as a guest.[24] The adjective "such" (τοιούτους) refers to those mentioned in v. 7, namely, the sort of people who travel for the sake of the gospel not knowing ahead of time where, or even whether, they will find lodging and provisions among the Christian communities. Such people are deserving of the hospitality of their brothers and sisters in Christ.

The *hina* clause expresses "purpose-result," indicating "*both the intention and its sure accomplishment*."[25] The purposeful *intent* of Christians who support traveling gospel workers should be to share in the work of truth and hospitality extended, so that, *as a result*, they share in the work of the gospel.

In v. 7a the travelers are said to have gone out on behalf of "the Name" (i.e., Jesus Christ); here in v. 8 they are further called "fellow workers for the truth [τῇ ἀληθείᾳ]." This confirms that the elder uses the word "truth" to refer to the gospel of Jesus Christ, who is himself the Truth sent by God the Father (John 14:6) (see "In Depth: 'Truth' in John's Letters" at 1 John 1:6). The elder's choice of "truth" to refer to the gospel was probably motivated by the situation in which he was writing, when many so-called Christians had gone out with false teaching contrary to the truth (1 John 2:19). Consequently,

when the elder claimed to love Gaius "in the truth" (v. 1), he was referring to that bond of Christian love shared by those who are joined to Christ and consequently to each other.

This love is not an emotion — though emotional bonding may be involved — but is a commitment to treat others, as Jesus himself taught, in a manner that one would be wish to be treated (Matt 7:12; Luke 6:31). When the elder affirms Gaius's faithfulness to "walking in the truth" (v. 3), he is recognizing that Gaius embodies both the love and truth of the Lord Jesus Christ. It gives the elder greatest joy to see his spiritual children "walking in the truth," that is, living out the gospel with love and truth (v. 4).

The verb "we might be" (γινώμεθα) does not have the sense of *becoming* fellow workers for the truth; rather, it means to show oneself *to be* a fellow worker in the gospel.[26] The original setting of the letter bears this out, for the elder has sent Demetrius (and his entourage) to Gaius with this note. The implication is that should Gaius refuse to provide the hospitality requested, his intent of continuing as a fellow worker for the gospel of Jesus Christ would, in the elder's judgment, be called into question. This implicit test is put into stark relief by vv. 9 – 10, where Diotrephes is reported to have recently done just that — refused hospitality to traveling Christians sent by the elder. One can almost feel Gaius's tension rising as he reads the note.

The elder stipulates only one qualification for traveling Christian workers to receive support — they must be "workers for the truth," and those who aid and abet their work by providing provisions for their travel also share in that work. Not only does support make the work possible, but the fact that someone supports those who preach and teach the gospel of Jesus Christ also validates the

---

24. BDAG, *s.v.* ὑπολαμβάνω 2.
25. Wallace, *Greek Grammar*, 473 (italics original).
26. BDAG, *s.v.* γίνομαι 7; also Brown, *Epistles of John*, 714;

Bultmann, *Johannine Epistles*, 99; Schnackenburg, *Johannine Epistles*, 296.

gospel message in the eyes of unbelievers, making them more open to receive it.

Material support for itinerant preachers and teachers was a necessity in the early church, but it also presented a dilemma, as we glimpse in 2 John. Second John 9 – 11 warns that to support those who are *not* preaching and teaching the truth is to "share in their evil works." Many who considered themselves Christian went out preaching and teaching a message that opposed the truth of Christ (the "antichrists" in 1 John 2:18 – 21). Such false teaching is a lie that did not come from the truth (2:21). The letters of John were written at a confusing time when Christians were expected to host and support traveling Christians, even those they did not personally know, but they were also expected to refuse hospitality to those who preached a false message (2 John 10 – 11). The consequences were dire, for extending hospitality made one a participant in the work, whether for good or evil. Therefore, the authority and standing of anyone who wrote a letter of introduction took on great significance as a guide for when to open one's home and when not to do so. This confusing situation is the background against which to understand what the elder will say about Diotrephes in 3 John 9 – 10.

Will Gaius receive these strangers because he believes the elder's teaching about Jesus Christ that Demetrius and company are spreading is the truth? Or has the truth about Christ become so confused by conflicting voices that Gaius will pull back from hospitality out of a fear of supporting the wrong message? If honor and shame were major motivators in the relationships between the elder, Gaius, Diotrephes, and Demetrius, then the stakes are higher than most modern Western readers would discern.[27] Gaius has a big decision to make.

Theology in Application

Christian Hospitality

The major exhortation of this passage that we must hear today is about Christian hospitality. As Amy Oden points out,

> the word "hospitality" has lost its moral punch over the recent centuries. Reduced to connoting refreshments at meetings or magazine covers of gracious living, the moral landscape in which it resides has all but faded into the background. Yet it is this moral and spiritual landscape that the early Christian voices can help us recover.[28]

The elder of 3 John is one of the original apostolic voices to speak on this subject. He writes in v. 8 that "we ought" to show hospitality to people traveling for the sake of the gospel so that we may work together with them for the truth. The inclusive "we" refers to all who consider themselves to be within the sphere of apostolic influence. Not all are called or gifted for evangelism, preaching, or teaching, but all can provide assistance to some extent as allowed by their means and situation.

The need for material sustenance to be provided on a person-to-person basis

---

27. See Campbell, "Honor, Hospitality and Haughtiness"; Malina, "III John and Hospitality," 171 – 93.

28. Amy G. Oden, *And You Welcomed Me: A Sourcebook on Hospitality in Early Christianity* (Nashville: Abingdon, 2001), 15.

is not as pressing today in North American society as it was in the first-century Greco-Roman world when 3 John was written. Hotels and restaurants are plentiful now, and they do not turn away anyone because of one's religious convictions. But in many parts of the world where Christians are few or food and shelter are not readily available, the situation corresponds more directly to that in which the elder wrote 3 John. Moreover, the Christian church in modern North America has developed many various organizations to sponsor evangelism and discipleship, and financial support for their workers is collected and disbursed from a central point. Christians are still under a moral obligation to materially support those who spend their daily lives in Christian service.

Moreover, even person-to-person hospitality continues to have a place. From time to time a local church today may ask members of its congregation to open their home to a visiting preacher or missionary. This is another modern expression of hospitality offered in faithfulness to Christ that would no doubt please the elder of 3 John.

Hospitality Is Different from Entertaining

Third John also invites us to reconsider what we mean by hospitality. Hospitality, in whatever form it takes today, should not be offered only to our friends in the Lord, but even to strangers whose faith in Christ and work for the gospel our Christian leaders have validated. The Christian church is not to be a social club of cliques. The church is composed of all who have come to faith in Jesus Christ, regardless of their race, ethnicity, social position, or economic standing. Wherever and whenever those engaged in the work of the gospel have need of life-sustaining provisions in order to continue their work, they should be able to count on the generosity of their fellow Christians, who will send them on their way "in a manner worthy of God." Generously supporting those sent out in the name of Christ is not primarily a tax deduction; it is a spiritual work that enables one to participate in the work of the gospel. Those who spend their lives representing Christ should be supported not luxuriously but well, as a testimony to God's goodness and as an affirmation of the truth of the gospel. To put our money where our mouth is shows the world our commitment to the gospel of Jesus Christ.

But as Wilson observes, "Our prosperity may also undermine the practice of hospitality by enabling us to meet the needs of others without actually having to encounter them."[29] Encountering the other is a practice that is sorely absent from today's modern life. Were the elder of 3 John alive today, he would no doubt lament

---

29. Jonathan R. Wilson, *Gospel Virtues: Practicing Faith, Hope, and Love in Uncertain Times* (Downers Grove, IL: InterVarsity Press, 1998), 165.

the loss of community that the amenities of modern society and our prosperity have brought about. Why is it that in many churches someone could worship for years and not be invited into the home of another? And those who open their homes to someone in need of a home, with all of the risk and inconvenience that may entail, are truly exceptional in this day and age. Can you imagine your doorbell ringing late one evening and there stands a stranger with a note in his or her hand allegedly from a mutual acquaintance asking you to take the person in for a stay? Such a scenario helps us to appreciate the risk that Gaius and other Christians faced in the first century.

What we practice as hospitality today has been so redefined that it is no longer viewed as central to our lives as Christians. Although the practice of hospitality is no longer central in the life of the church, the elder of 3 John seems to be saying that it is close to the heart of the gospel. As Wilson argues, the neglect of hospitality among Christians is a reflection of a cultural resistance to hospitality in our society, a place where Christians have assimilated unbiblical values and need to hear the call of the gospel once more. "When we understand hospitality as a practice of the gospel, it is one of the primary means by which we learn and teach love."[30] Through 3 John the elder speaks as powerfully today as he did in the first century on the question of Christian hospitality as it relates to truth and love.

Alienation in Modern Living

Most of us have probably experienced living in a neighborhood, sometimes for years, and never meeting one's neighbors, much less knowing them in any significant way. We pull into our driveways, open the garage door with a remote opener, park our car inside, and never even have to so much as wave to a neighbor. Email and voicemail have contributed to the convenience of avoiding others. In some ways modern life has become psychologically reclusive. Twenty-some years ago I had a pleasant, weekly chat with the owner of a gas station who pumped gas into my car week after week. It barely counted as a relationship, but it did add a routine person-to-person encounter to my day. Now self-service pumps have replaced such human contact.

Modern life has conspired to make us all strangers, allowing us to choose to encounter only those with whom we feel comfortable, those who are similar enough to ourselves. Such alienation breeds a suspicion of strangers, which is a tendency rooted in our fallen human nature that is reflected throughout human history.[31] Rather than feeling naturally open toward strangers, most today are uncomfortable with the risks that a stranger presents, even to the extent that it deters someone from

---

30. Ibid., 164. Cf. also Pohl, *Making Room.*

31. For a sociological analysis of the stranger, see Malina, "III John and Hospitality."

approaching the stranger at church with a friendly handshake. We often rationalize our discomfort by an appeal to our busy schedule or our perception that we would be intruding on another's privacy.

Wilson suggests that "modernity's stress on the dominance of individualism and the quest for autonomy has turned us all into strangers." He continues, quoting Henri Nouwen:

> Our society seems to be increasingly full of fearful, defensive, aggressive people anxiously clinging to their property and inclined to look at their surrounding world with suspicion, always expecting an enemy to suddenly appear, intrude and do harm.[32]

Wilson goes on to comment on Nouwen's observation about individualism and autonomy: "If my 'self' is all that I have and all that really counts, then everything else is an enemy. As a result modernity is marked by attempts to control others and protect ourselves."[33] Interestingly, it was Diotrephes's need to control others and protect his power in the church that was his fatal flaw. Whether or not modernity can be blamed for our culture's resistance to the practice of hospitality, the attitude of autonomy and the need to be in control that destroyed Diotrephes's Christian community are at work just as potently in churches today.

Hospitality Builds Christian Community

If such is the society in which we live, the elder of 3 John calls us to be builders of Christian community through hospitality. Hospitality begins with an attitude of openness and generosity that allows us to appropriately share ourselves and our resources with whomever God brings into our day. Rather than being the person who habitually isolates himself or herself inside their home, would it not be a better witness for the gospel to be the person who welcomes the new family to the neighborhood with a friendly introduction and a basket of muffins? We cannot love others as Jesus commanded without being open to them.

An openness to others that frees us to be hospitable does involve a degree of vulnerability and risk. Christine Pohl argues that "it is, in part, the hosts' own sense of vulnerability that allows them to offer recognition and respect to other vulnerable persons."[34] Moreover, Pohl observes that sometimes what is offered as hospitality is really a form of condescension:

> Friendship, solidarity, and commensality occur among equals, and this requires an appreciation for what the guest might bring to the relationship. Persons who have

---

32. Henri J. M. Nouwen, *Reaching Out: The Three Movements of the Spiritual Life* (Garden City, NY: Doubleday, 1975), 46, quoted in Wilson, *Gospel Virtues*, 167.

33. Wilson, *Gospel Virtues*, 167.

34. Christine D. Pohl, "Hospitality from the Edge: The Significance of Marginality in the Practice of Welcome," *The Annual of the Society of Christian Ethics* (1995): 135 (quoted in Wilson, *Gospel Virtues*, 166).

never experienced need or marginality find it easier to be hosts than guests, and the deepest condescension may be expressed in their unwillingness to be a guest, an unwillingness to allow the relationship to be mutual.[35]

Such "hospitality" cannot be a sure foundation for Christian community. Thus, while the amenities of our modern society may eliminate the need for the specific form of hospitality that the elder requested of Gaius, we nevertheless have ample opportunity to welcome the stranger.

35. Pohl, "Hospitality from the Edge," 135.

3 John 9 – 11

Literary Context

Verses 9 – 11 form the second major section of the body of the letter (vv. 5 – 12). From the perspective of Greco-Roman rhetoric, vv. 9 – 12 are the *probatio* of the letter,[1] developing the topic(s) previously discussed by "introducing new and related matters" for amplification of the topic.[2] In this case, the need for hospitality is amplified by the unfortunate extenuating circumstances of Diotrephes's refusal to provide it.

I. The Letter's Address and Greeting (vv. 1 – 4)

II. The Reason for Writing (vv. 5 – 8)

➡ **III. The Problem with Diotrephes (vv. 9 – 11)**

    A. He Does Not Receive Exhortation from the Elder (v. 9)

    B. He Publicly Makes Disparaging Remarks about the Elder (v. 10a – e)

    C. He Does Not Welcome Fellow Christians Endorsed by the Elder (v. 10f-h)

    D. He Throws Those Who Do So out of the Church (v. 10i)

    E. A Command to Do What Is Right (v. 11)

IV. Introducing Demetrius (v. 12)

V. Closing (vv. 13 – 15)

Main Idea

The elder presents a negative characterization of a Christian man named Diotrephes and introduces the question of authority in the church. The elder implies that by turning away those who brought the apostolic teaching, Diotrephes was not a fellow worker for the truth; he thus calls into question his loyalty to apostolic authority and orthodoxy. The implications of this segment of the letter speak on

---

1. Watson, "Rhetorical Analysis," 491, 493; Campbell, "Honor, Hospitality and Haughtiness," 332.

2. Watson, "Rhetorical Analysis," 493.

the important question of where authoritative Christian truth is found and how to discern those who are truly brothers and sisters in the faith.

Translation

---

3 John 9 – 11

9a	event	**I wrote something to the church,**
b	contrast	but **Diotrephes,**
c	apposition	who loves to lord it over them,
d	result	**…does not welcome us.**
10a	basis	Because of this,
b	event	if I come,
c	assertion	**I will bring up his deeds that he is doing**
d	means	by disparaging us
e	means	with evil words.
f	assertion	and not satisfied with that,
g	assertion	**he himself does not welcome the brothers,**
h	expansion	and **[he] prevents** those who wish [to do so],
i	expansion	and **throws [them] out of the church.**
11a	address	My friend,
b	exhortation	**do not imitate what is evil** but
c	contrast	[imitate] what is good.
d	assertion	**The one who does good is from God;**
e	assertion	**the one who does evil has not seen God.**

Structure

This pericope extends the body of the letter, giving the reason for the note that was begun in v. 5. All of the verbs are in the first person and third person singular, focusing this paragraph on the elder ("I") and Diotrephes ("he"). After a negative introduction describing Diotrephes's character, a litany of examples of his bad behavior is given. The elder's major concern that motivated the letter is expressed in v. 11, which contains the only imperative within the body of the letter, "do not imitate" (μὴ μιμοῦ; the imperative "greet" [ἀσπάζου] in v. 15 being formulaic in letter closings). This exhortation is expanded in v. 11d-e as antithetical parallels constructed by the contrast between doing good and doing evil, in parallel with being of God and not having seen God, respectively.

Exegetical Outline

→ **III. The Problem with Diotrephes (vv. 9 – 11)**

    A. He does not receive exhortation from the elder (v. 9)

    B. He publicly makes disparaging remarks about the elder (v. 10a – e)

    C. He does not welcome fellow Christians endorsed by the elder (v. 10f-g)

    D. He forbids those in his local church to welcome Christians endorsed by the elder (v. 10h)

    E. He throws those who do so out of the church (v. 10i)

    F. A command to do what is right (v. 11)

Explanation of the Text

9 I wrote something to the church, but Diotrephes, who loves to lord it over them, does not welcome us (Ἔγραψά τι τῇ ἐκκλησίᾳ, ἀλλ᾽ ὁ φιλοπρωτεύων αὐτῶν Διοτρέφης οὐκ ἐπιδέχεται ἡμᾶς). The focus of the letter shifts to a problem of authority. An influential Christian named Diotrephes has, for some reason unknown to us, taken a stand against the elder, and apparently also against those affiliated with him, by refusing hospitality to those the elder sent with a previous letter. The elder has just advised Gaius that to assist the traveling Christians with hospitality is to be a fellow worker for the truth of the gospel. Therefore, Diotrephes's refusal to extend hospitality calls into question his allegiance to the truth.

In v. 9, the elder switches to the first person singular, "I wrote" (ἔγραψα). The indefinite pronoun "something" (τι) possibly refers to a letter of introduction requesting hospitality of Diotrephes, or it may be that the elder had sent 2 John, with or without 1 John, expecting its message and those who carried it to be welcomed by Diotrephes.[3] This assumes, of course, a possible sequence to the three letters. Perhaps Diotrephes had in fact read 2 John, was disaffected by the elder's opposition to what he defined as a christological heresy in that letter, and then refused to welcome the elder's envoys on their

next visit. Interpreters must admit that we simply do not know the facts.

The elder had written to "the church" (τῇ ἐκκλησίᾳ), a term found only here in John's gospel and letters (though it is used in Revelation). Painter argues, probably rightly, that the referent of "church" in 3 John "lies somewhere between the Pauline use in 1 and 2 Corinthians and the reference to the universal church" and refers not to a particular house church, but to the network of Johannine churches under the elder's authority.[4] Although the schism may have happened in only one church (cf. 1 John 2:19), it had potential repercussions throughout the network of outlying churches the elder refers to as "the church."

If the church is so understood, the previous letter could have been 2 John, which seems to be a circular letter intended for any or all of the "sister" churches, given its unusual address, "to the chosen lady and her children." The alternative reading of the definite article would limit the previous letter to the specific local church of which Diotrephes was a part.

The description of Diotrephes as one "who loves to lord it over them" hints that as Diotrephes goes, so goes his church. The adjectival substantive participle "who loves to be first" (ὁ φιλοπρωτεύων)

---

3. Yarbrough, *1 – 3 John*, 377; Painter, *1, 2, and 3 John*, 53.   4. Painter, *1, 2, and 3 John*, 53 – 54.

occurs only here in the NT, but the cognate adjective (φιλόπρωτος) is found more widely in Greek writings with the sense of loving to lead by controlling others.[5] This stands in sharp contrast to Jesus' teaching that the one who wishes to be first must be the servant of all (Matt 20:27; Mark 9:35; 10:44). We don't know if Diotrephes was a rightly ordained leader of the church or just a member with a forceful personality, but it hardly matters. Motivation for leadership borne from a need for control over others is always destructive in a church community, and ordination is no excuse for it.

The verb "welcome" (ἐπιδέχεται) occurs twice in vv. 9 – 10 and probably bears the same sense in both places. Mitchell has traced the lexicographical history of the word and has argued convincingly that it means simply to welcome or receive here.[6] English translations that render "he does not welcome us" (οὐκ ἐπιδέχεται) as "he rejects our authority" or something similar are providing an interpretation of his motivation, which in context is likely a true insight into the relationship between the elder and Diotrephes. Nevertheless, the verb itself does not include the sense of authority and therefore should be understood as referring to a refusal to welcome those sent by the elder, regardless of the motivation. Notice the present tense here, which implies that the elder is aware that Diotrephes's decision to refuse hospitality is ongoing.

Given the protocol of hospitality in the wider society that one welcomes a guest as one would have welcomed the writer of the letter of introduction, Malherbe points out that the refusal to welcome those sent by the elder was understandably taken to be a rejection of the elder himself and expressed ill will.[7] Mitchell further describes the refusal within the larger context of diplomatic relations.[8] The diplomatic envoy was to be received with all the same honors and privileges as the one who sent him. To honor a king, one must host his envoy in royal fashion. Conversely, the envoy of a king was to behave and speak not as an individual with his own interests, but only as the king himself would have. To refuse to welcome an envoy was not only an affront to the sender but a signal that diplomatic relations were severed.

Such is the cultural background against which the major theme of being "sent" in John's gospel should be interpreted, and it is of relevance for 3 John 9. Consider these verses against the background of the Greco-Roman protocol of receiving envoys:

John 3:17: "For God did not send [ἀποστέλλω] his Son into the world to condemn the world, but to save the world through him."

John 3:34: "For the one whom God has sent [ἀποστέλλω] speaks the words of God."

John 5:23b: "Whoever does not honor the Son does not honor the Father, who sent [πέμπω] him."

John 6:29: "Jesus answered, 'The work of God is this: to believe in the one he has sent [ἀποστέλλω].'"

John 12:44 – 45: "Then Jesus cried out, 'Whoever believes in me does not believe in me only, but in the one who sent [πέμπω] me. The one who looks at me is seeing the one who sent [πέμπω] me.'"

John 13:20: "Very truly I tell you, whoever accepts anyone I send accepts me; and whoever accepts me accepts the one who sent [ἀποστέλλω] me."

John 14:24: "Anyone who does not love me will not obey my teaching. These words you hear are not my own; they belong to the Father who sent [πέμπω] me."

---

5. BDAG, *s.v.* φιλοπρωτεύω.

6. Margaret M. Mitchell, "'Diotrephes Does Not Receive Us': The Lexicographical and Social Context of 3 John 9 – 10," *JBL* 117 (1998): 299 – 320.

7. Malherbe, "Inhospitality," 227 – 28.

8. Mitchell, "Diotrephes," 318; see also Margaret Mitchell, "New Testament Envoys in the Context of Greco-Roman Diplomatic and Epistolary Conventions," *JBL* 111 (1992): 655 – 58.

Jesus was sent to earth as an envoy by God, the King of all creation. This way of conceptualizing Jesus' relationship to the Father serves John's defense of monotheism as he explains how Jesus can speak and act as God himself and yet there be only one God. It also heightens the tragedy of Jesus' rejection, for to refuse to accept and welcome Jesus is to refuse God, who sent him (see John 1:11).

Jesus deputized his apostles in John 13:20 and 20:21 to be his official envoys (cf. Gal 4:14b). In its first-century linguistic context the word "apostle" (ἀπόστολος) was widely used to refer to one sent as an envoy, a sense largely lost to modern readers, who understand "apostle" in only a religious sense. This cultural background explains why the elder takes Diotrephes's refusal of his envoys not only as a personal affront but also as a rejection of the teachings of Christ, which Christ's apostles bear. In other words, while the topic of 3 John is about hospitality, in that cultural context refusing hospitality to the *elder's* envoy meant rejecting the authority of the elder himself. It is therefore apt that the elder uses the plural "he does not welcome *us*" (οὐκ ἐπιδέχεται ἡμᾶς) rather than the singular "he does not welcome *me*," for he links himself with all those who are bearers of the apostolic teaching (cf. 1 John 1:1–4).

Whether or not he has an official office with authority over the church, Diotrephes apparently has the power to refuse hospitality to those sent by the elder. This strongly suggests that he was the host of a house church, for homes large enough to accommodate a group for worship would most likely also have the space and resources to put up overnight guests. The extent to which the host of a house church had spiritual authority is an interesting question, but even without ecclesial office, the host would clearly exert great influence on the practices of the church, perhaps as we see happening in 3 John.

10a-e Because of this, if I come, I will bring up his deeds that he is doing by disparaging us with evil words (διὰ τοῦτο, ἐὰν ἔλθω, ὑπομνήσω αὐτοῦ τὰ ἔργα ἃ ποιεῖ λόγοις πονηροῖς φλυαρῶν ἡμᾶς). The causal phrase "because of this" (διὰ τοῦτο) is anaphoric, pointing back to the main clause of the preceding sentence, "he does not welcome us," as the cause of the next statement, "I will bring up his deeds" (ὑπομνήσω αὐτοῦ τὰ ἔργα). Both Smalley and Marshall suggest that the elder intends to schedule a public showdown between himself and Diotrephes, not simply that he'll mention the problem during some future visit.[9]

It is debated whether the third class conditional (also called a general condition) represented by "if" (ἐάν) implies an uncertainty in the elder's visit ("if I come") or a temporal sense, expressing uncertainty only of when the visit will be ("whenever I come"). Brown thinks the elder is uncertain whether he will make the trip because he is not sure the church will side with him against Diotrephes.[10] Culy, following Brown, observes that in v. 14 the elder "hopes" (ἐλπίζω) to see Gaius soon (see comments).[11] Smalley states, "The force … is temporal ('*when* I come'), and does not necessarily imply that there is any doubt about his arrival."[12] Smalley sees this as a promise to visit the congregation of Diotrphes in person. Given the exigencies of travel, the elder perhaps must wait to see how Gaius receives Demetrius to know if Gaius is open to hosting a visit from the elder himself, since the church of Diotrephes will not. If so, this may hint

---

9. Smalley, *1, 2, 3 John*, 357; Marshall, *Epistles of John*, 90–91.

10. Brown, *Epistles of John*, 718.

11. Culy, *I, II, III John*, 164.

12. Smalley, *1, 2, 3 John*, 357 (italics original); cf. Westcott, *Epistles of St. John*, 240.

that Gaius lives within a day's travel to and from the church of Diotrephes.

Malina argues that this threat of a personal visit is necessary for the elder to regain his honor, and that simply overlooking the insult of Diotrephes could not be tolerated in a society where every interaction was framed by the issue of honor and shame.[13] The largest flaw with such a sociological interpretation is that it does not take into consideration the Holy Spirit's transformation of the character and motives of Christ's apostles and followers. While it may be true that all Greco-Roman social interactions were controlled by the zero-sum dynamic of honor and shame, we must assume that the writers of the NT letters were men transformed by the Holy Spirit, which calls into question to what extent they followed the social conventions and protocols of pagan society.

For example, one can imagine an apostle overlooking a personal insult that a pagan would not have overlooked because of a Christ-motivated humility. Rather than explaining the elder's intent to expose what Diotrephes was doing as an attempt to regain honor, we would do better to see the elder's reaction as illumining the serious consequences of Diotrephes's behavior on the unity and even survival of the nascent Christian church. The elder cannot overlook behavior that threatens the survival of the truth of Jesus Christ in the churches.

The subordinate clause "that he is doing by disparaging us with evil words" helps confirm that the well-being of the truth of the gospel is the elder's motivation. Notice the shift from the first person singular verbs in the main clause to the first person plural direct object here (ἡμᾶς). The elder is not the only one being insulted by Diotrephes; so also are those associated with the elder — those he has sent out as his envoys of the truth. It may be an allusion to all those who carried the apostolic teachings of Christ throughout the empire (cf. 1 John 1:1 – 4).

The verb "disparage" (φλυαρέω) occurs only here in the NT, but elsewhere in extant Greek writings it means to make outrageous statements or malicious gossip about someone. The damaging works that Diotrephes is doing through malicious gossip are expressed in "evil words" (λόγοις πονηροῖς). Diotrephes is not spreading slight inaccuracies about the elder but serious accusations that the elder characterizes as "evil." In v. 11 the elder will strongly exhort Gaius not to imitate "the evil" (there τὸ κακόν), which likely alludes back to this statement. The elder does not wish Gaius to side with Diotrephes, thereby validating those "evil words" about the elder. Notice the present tense of the verb (ποιεῖ) and the participle (φλυαρῶν), which suggests that these problems are ongoing.

No one knows why Diotrephes has rejected the elder or what precisely he was saying about the elder, and much ink has flowed on whether Diotrephes was disapproving the teachings of the elder and his associates or their character and behavior. While it would be informative to know this, it is not essential for understanding the main point of the elder's concern.

The elder first mentions Diotrephes in v. 9 without any further explanation, so Gaius must have already known who Diotrephes was. If Gaius was a member of the same church as Diotrephes, the elder would be asking Gaius to defy Diotrephes and risk being thrown out of the church by hosting Demetrius and his entourage. But if so, it would seem unnecessary for the elder to describe in such detail what Diotrephes had been doing. Even if Diotrephes had kept the elder's previous letter a secret, Gaius would have almost certainly known about those thrown out of the church because they

---

13. Malina, "III John and Hospitality," 187; so also Campbell, "Honor, Hospitality and Haughtiness," 334.

wished to extend hospitality to the elder's people. Thus, Gaius was likely the host of another house church in the same general area and is being asked to provide a base of operation for those the elder sends out, possibly for his own future visit. By doing so, Gaius would of course be taking the elder's side against Diotrephes in the developing conflict.

There is much we would like to know about this situation. We don't know the specific nature of the conflict between the elder and Diotrephes or the relationship between Gaius and Diotrephes. As Lieu insightfully observes, "the ambiguity of the relative positions of the Elder and Diotrephes lies at the heart not simply of our problem of interpretation, but of the original problem itself."[14] Those were confusing times in the early church, and it was probably obvious that the apostolic message would prevail. The fact that 3 John has survived with 1 and 2 John indicates not only that the elder saw himself as the defender of the true gospel with the authority to address the churches in his purview, but that his view did win over the secessionists (1 John) and Diotrephes (3 John).

It isn't necessary to have our questions about the historical specifics answered before we can understand the message and value of 3 John. It is necessary only to observe that Diotrephes failed to recognize the authority of apostolic teaching and failed to exercise Christian love, and did both because of his need to be a controlling person. In contrast to Gaius's faithfulness to the truth expressed by extending hospitality to those the elder sent, Diotrephes's behavior calls into question his apprehension of the truth.

Regardless of why Diotrephes decided to refuse the elder's envoys, the elder perceives Diotrephes as a threat to the truth of the gospel and as a source of confusion in the church, and so he has to be confronted. Jesus promised punishment to religious leaders who love to make a show of their piety for the sake of self-interest (Mark 12:38 – 40). The elder recognizes the serious and damaging impact of the deeds Diotrephes was doing, and with the authority of Jesus he acts to call Diotrephes to account and repentance and to prevent others from being misled.

IN DEPTH: What Was the Problem with Diotrephes?

There have been three general theories concerning the reason for Diotrephes's accusations about the elder and his associates and his refusal to extend hospitality to them:

1. a differing view of church authority and polity
2. a differing view of what constituted true doctrine and teaching
3. a strictly personal issue between the elder and Diotrephes
4. some combination of the above

The third theory, while plausible, cannot be reconstructed without resort to sheer speculation. We simply cannot know if Diotrephes had a personality clash with the elder. The fact that the letter has been preserved in the canon of the church suggests something more is going on here. The first two theories are in-

14. Lieu, *Second and Third Epistles of John*, 157.

timately entwined with various scholarly reconstructions of the circumstances in the Johannine community and depend on the dating of these letters.[15]

The late nineteenth-century German scholar Adolf von Harnack famously represents the first theory.[16] Harnack saw in the Johannine writings a snapshot of a period in early church history when the model of church polity built on the presbyter-bishop was emerging in Asia Minor and argues for a conflict between the elder and Diotrephes that is essentially political. In the earliest phase of the expansion of the Christian church, itinerant preachers such as the apostles and those associated with them went throughout the Mediterranean world evangelizing and teaching, as Jesus commanded (Matt 28:18–20) and as the book of Acts attests. As the gospel of Jesus Christ succeeded to convert clusters of people, house churches formed over which the founders of the church appointed elders, following the pattern of Jewish synagogue polity.

At some point as the number of house churches in any one area multiplied, a "monarchical bishop" was put over the elder(s) of the house churches, a model we see reflected in Christian writings from the early second century onward. Harnack theorized that Diotrephes is the first monarchical bishop known to us, and his refusal to welcome the itinerant preachers happened at a critical transition point. Well-established local churches, led by the elders and the bishop over them, wanted control over what was taught and preached. The house churches no longer needed itinerant evangelists for "pulpit supply," as in earlier days. According to Harnack's theory, the traveling envoys sent out by the elder of 3 John were simply part of a passing age regardless of doctrinal agreement or disagreement, and Diotrephes was asserting his rightly ordained authority to shepherd the churches entrusted to his care.

Variations of this theory discuss whether the authority of the elder was superior, inferior, or equal to the office held by Diotrephes. What is common to all such discussions is the assumption of Diotrephes's rank and role as an official in the church and certain assumptions about the development of church ecclesiology. The text of 3 John does not give a clue about this, of course, and it is prudent to not build large reconstructions on speculation.

A variation on the theme of conflict over the form of church polity argues that Diotrephes was not a rightly ordained elder or bishop but was instead a charismatic church leader who resisted formal offices, such as that represented by the elder, on the grounds that the Holy Spirit himself should be the only revealer of truth to the church. Though this may have points of contact with the later development of Montanism, all forms of this theory simply go far beyond the evidence permitted by the Johannine texts themselves.

---

15. For a thorough survey of the variations on these theories, see Brown, *Epistles of John*, 732–39.

16. Adolf von Harnack, *Über den dritten Johannesbrief* (Leipzig: Hinrichs, 1897).

The second theory about the conflict between the elder and Diotrephes centers on a doctrinal dispute. This view perhaps has more textual support if 1 and 2 John are allowed to be brought into the conversation, for both those letters are emphatically concerned with the false teaching of those "antichrists" who have gone out from the elder's church(es) with heretical Christology (1 John 2:18, 22; 4:3; 2 John 7). In all of the Johannine writings, 3 John no exception, the emphatic repetition of "truth" implies that its opposite, falsehood, may have been the context for the elder's thoughts.

But while we can be sure that heresy was a major issue when the letters of John were written, there is little evidence in 3 John that the elder counts Diotrephes among the heretics. Diotrephes's faithfulness to the truth and loyalty to the elder have come into question, but he does not accuse Diotrephes of heresy. Nevertheless, Walter Bauer has argued that Diotrephes was the most active representative of those holding the heretical views condemned in 1 and 2 John.[17] In fact, those who interpret the indefinite pronoun "something" (τι) of v. 9 as a reference to 2 John often assume that Diotrephes refused hospitality to those bearing that letter because he was personally offended by the elder's condemnation of the views he himself held. Because in 2 John the elder exhorted the churches to refuse hospitality to the traveling false preachers, Diotrephes's refusal to welcome those sent from the elder was simply following that principle. Bauer was following an ancient understanding of Diotrephes as heretical, reflected for instance in the commentary of the Venerable Bede:

> It seems that Diotrephes was a leading heretic of those times. He was proud and insolent, preferring to gain control of the church by preaching something new and different rather than by following humbly the old commandments which John had already given them.[18]

The biggest weakness with this view, ancient as it may be, is that of everything the elder says about Diotrephes, he does not call him an "antichrist" or a false teacher or suggest that his doctrine is wrong. The elder represents him as a powerful man with a character flaw, not with a heretical view of Christ. Thus, although Diotrephes may well have been a heretic or been on his way to becoming one, the text does not explicitly say that or necessarily imply that.

Käsemann's novel theory proposed in 1951 turns Harnack's theory upside down and makes the elder a heretic whom Diotrephes had excommunicated.[19]

17. Walter Bauer, Robert A. Kraft, and Gerhard Krodel, *Orthodoxy and Heresy in Earliest Christianity* (Philadelphia: Fortress, 1971), 93.

18. Bray, ACCS 11, 242.

19. Ernst Käsemann, "Ketzer und Zeuge," *ZTK* 48 (1951): 292–311.

In this theory, Diotrephes becomes the faithful church leader protecting his flock from the false teaching of the elder. The same criticisms of Bauer's view apply here, plus the serious implications concerning the nature of the NT books. If Diotrephes were the orthodox party in this conflict, one would expect on both historical and theological grounds that his views would have been canonized rather than those of the elder. The fact that the elder's writing in 3 John is so consistent with three other books of the NT (John's gospel, 1 John, and 2 John) poses a serious difficulty for the unity of the Johannine corpus and an insurmountable problem for Käsemann's theory, at least among those who adhere to the infallibility of Scripture.

If the conflict between the elder and Diotrephes was neither over church authority and polity nor over doctrinal disputes, it is possible that in a time of rampant heresy when truth and false teaching were so easily confused, Diotrephes, wanting to be a good shepherd of his flock, simply demanded that his church refuse hospitality to any and all traveling preachers, so that they didn't find themselves to be coworkers in heresy (cf. 2 John 11). Against this theory we note that the elder describes Diotrephes not in neutral terms but as actively spreading malicious talk about the elder and his associates, whereas such a description of Diotrephes would be unwarranted if he were simply confused and defensive. Moreover, even if Diotrephes *was* confused about the truth, his refusal of the apostolic messengers indicates a serious deficiency in his understanding of the gospel of Jesus Christ — that the truth about Christ was to be found in the teaching and preaching of the apostles Christ chose and those immediately associated with them.

Whether the elder was the apostle John or a close associate of the apostle (analogous to the relationship between Paul and Luke or Peter and Mark), Diotrephes did not rightly know the truth if he didn't know that Christ was to be found only in the apostolic tradition that the elder represented (cf. 1 John 1:1 – 4). While confusion about discerning the truth is understandable when one is presented with conflicting teachings, one should stand with those sent out from apostolic authority even if one cannot evaluate and decide on the merit of the teaching itself.[20] Thus, even when Diotrephes is viewed in this relatively admirable light, he still should have known that to reject apostolic teaching was to reject the truth of the gospel and therefore to commit an egregious act against Christ and his church.

20. This view assumes my view that while there may have been differing perspectives in the teaching of various apostles, there was no inherent contradiction. Heresy was still distinct from apostolic orthodoxy. Some biblical scholars today argue for little unity in the teachings of the NT and that what has survived as orthodoxy resulted only from the assertion of political power in the fourth century.

10f-i And not satisfied with that, he himself does not welcome the brothers, and [he] prevents those who wish [to do so], and throws [them] out of the church (καὶ μὴ ἀρκούμενος ἐπὶ τούτοις οὔτε αὐτὸς ἐπιδέχεται τοὺς ἀδελφοὺς καὶ τοὺς βουλομένους κωλύει καὶ ἐκ τῆς ἐκκλησίας ἐκβάλλει). The subordinate clause "not satisfied with that" refers back to v. 10d-e, where Diotrephes is said to be making outrageous accusations expressed in evil words against the elder. The participle "satisfied" (ἀρκούμενος) expresses satisfaction (here negated) with something (expressed in the dative case) and occurs frequently in the NT and the LXX.

However, only here do we find this verb followed by the preposition "with" (ἐπί). Were it merely a stylistic variant, as Culy suggests,[21] one would expect to see a few more instances elsewhere. While "with" can mark the cause or reason for a subsequent state or event, the verb "satisfy" (ἀρκέομαι) with the dative already carries that sense, making the preposition (ἐπί) superfluous if that were its sense. The preposition probably contributes semantically by nuancing the construction to mean "not content with the circumstance of speaking evil words."[22] Although the preposition doesn't change the translation, it does heighten the sense of provocation. That is, Diotrephes is not content to leave his opposition of the elder a matter of talk alone, but has escalated the provocation to actions, even to the extent of actions involving others.

The construction "he himself ... and" (αὐτὸς ... καί) is probably used to join two thoughts, the first negative (οὔτε) and the second positive.[23] Diotrephes *both* does not welcome the brothers *and* does prevent those who wish to do so. This construction heightens the progression, as the elder heaps up accusations and builds his case against Diotrephes (and hopefully for Gaius's hospitality).

So great is Diotrephes's enmity against the elder that it overflows even against those Christians who have come from another church with the elder's endorsement and who are in need of Christian hospitality to make their travel on behalf of the gospel possible. Where hospitality is withheld, the work of the gospel will be stunted in that area. Diotrephes allows his issues with the elder, whatever they may have been, to justify his refusal to welcome those affiliated with the elder. Going even a step further, Diotrephes not only refuses to extend Christian hospitality himself, but he forbids others in his congregation from doing so and thereby completely shuts the elder's envoys out of the region under his influence.

The present tense of "throws out" (ἐκβάλλει) suggests that this was not a onetime lapse of judgment but has become Diotrephes's policy or custom. The direct object of the verb must be inferred. Syntactically, it is likely to be "those who wish" (τοὺς βουλομένους) from the previous clause. If so, this is a harsh situation, where Diotrephes throws people out of the church for merely *wanting* to extend hospitality. This does not necessarily imply that Diotrephes held ecclesiastical office or powers of excommunication, for if the church met in his home, he could assert power over who was admitted and who was not.

By spreading his dissension to others in the church, Diotrephes has drawn a line in the sand. Now it is not just a matter between him and the elder, for everyone in the house church must decide either to follow Diotrephes on this issue or to be refused fellowship in the house church. At a time when there was not a Christian church on every corner, to be put out of the local church was extremely serious, as it cut a believer off from the fellowship and teaching needed to sustain the

---

21. Culy, *I, II, III John*, 165.
22. LS, *s.v.* ἐπί B.I.1.i.

23. LS, *s.v.* οὔτε II.4.

Christian life in a hostile pagan society and put their salvation at risk.

In sum, Diotrephes has single-handedly wreaked damage on the elder by slandering him, on the traveling teachers and preachers by refusing them sustenance, and on the local church by causing a conflict that could spread to other churches. Such a serious situation documented in such a brief letter!

The tone and content of this letter imply that the elder perceives himself to have greater authority in determining what supports the work of the gospel than Diotrephes has. Although referring to himself simply as an "elder," even if Diotrephes is the pastor of his church, the author is clearly an elder of a different order of magnitude if 3 John is read in the context of 1 John. The elder bears the apostolic witness of

> what was from the beginning, what we have heard, what we have seen with our eyes, what we have perceived, and our hands touched … about the Word of Life. The Life appeared, and we have seen [it], and testify [to it], and proclaim to you the eternal Life, which was with the Father and has appeared to us. What we have seen and have heard, we proclaim also to you, so that you also may have fellowship with us. And indeed our fellowship is with the Father and with His Son, Jesus Christ. And these things we write so that our joy may be complete. (1 John 1:1–4)

The role the elder assumes in 3 John, both for determining the truth consistent with the gospel of Jesus Christ and in rebuking a leader of a distant church, corroborates the apostolic identity of the author of 1 John, whether the author is the apostle John or a close associate (such as Luke was to Paul or Mark to Peter). When the situation is read in this light, it is not simply a dispute between two Christian men of equal authority, but between an apostolic leader and a church leader whose character weaknesses have gotten the better of him.

11a-c My friend, do not imitate what is evil but [imitate] what is good (Ἀγαπητέ, μὴ μιμοῦ τὸ κακὸν ἀλλὰ τὸ ἀγαθόν). The elder now turns his thought back to Gaius with the third occurrence of the vocative "dear friend" (Ἀγαπητέ). This verse is especially semantically marked because it contains the only imperative verb in the book (except for the last sentence) and states the elder's major concern, "Do not imitate evil." The object of the verb "imitate" is neuter (τὸ κακόν), not masculine, so this is not a direct reference to Diotrephes himself, but alludes to what Diotrephes has done (cf. v. 10d-i). The positive command of the strong contrast is to imitate "what is good" (τὸ ἀγαθόν), with the elided imperative verb (μιμοῦ) supplied from the previous clause and again a neuter singular object.

In the context of the request in v. 6b-c, the command to do good calls Gaius to continue to be the elder's ally and to receive his envoys, in spite of whatever power or influence Diotrephes may be exerting. But given the significance of withholding hospitality to the elder's envoys and the damage Diotrephes is causing to the work of the gospel, the command takes on a much larger scope, as the rest of the verse goes on to say.

11d The one who does good is from God (ὁ ἀγαθοποιῶν ἐκ τοῦ θεοῦ ἐστιν). The "one who does good" (ὁ ἀγαθοποιῶν) occurs only here in the Johannine corpus but is found elsewhere in the NT referring to those who live for God (Luke 6:35; 1 Pet 2:15, 20; 3:6, 17). The preposition ἐκ indicates the origin and motive of the person who does "the good." This statement is a functional definition meaning that the one whose motives and behavior are for "the good" is of God. "The good" is to be understood in contrast to "the evil" that Diotrephes is speaking about the elder, and consequently about the truth of the gospel.

The preposition ἐκ is used in the Johannine letters to allude to the duality between God and the world that was constructed in the gospel (e.g., 1 John 2:16, 19, 29). Christian believers, like Jesus, are "of God" (ἐκ θεοῦ; e.g., John 1:13; see "In Depth: Being of God (ἐκ) in John's Letters" at 1 John 2:15) and not "of the world" (ἐκ τοῦ κόσμου; e.g., 8:23; 15:19; 17:6, 14, 16) or "of the devil" (8:44). Third John 11d reflects the Johannine duality expressed, for instance, in 1 John 3:8 – 10:

> The one who does sin is of [ἐκ] the devil, because the devil has been sinning from the beginning. For this reason the Son of God appeared, so that he might destroy the works of the devil. No one who has been born of [ἐκ] God sins, because his [God's] seed remains in them, and they are not able to sin because they have been born of [ἐκ] God. In this way the children of God and the children of the devil are distinguished: Everyone who does not do what is right is not of [ἐκ] God, even the one who does not love his brother and sister.

In this way Gaius is exhorted to remain on the side of truth and God by siding with the elder.

11e The one who does evil has not seen God (ὁ κακοποιῶν οὐχ ἑώρακεν τὸν θεόν). This sentence forms an antithetic parallel to v. 11d by the antonyms "doing good" (ἀγαθοποιῶν) versus "doing evil" (κακοποιῶν) and "being of God" (ἐκ τοῦ θεοῦ ἐστιν) versus "not having seen God" (οὐχ ἑώρακεν τὸν θεόν). "Seeing God" is a major theme in John's gospel and is closely associated there with knowing God, as in John 14:7 – 9:

> "If you really *know* me, you will *know* my Father as well. From now on, you do *know* him and have **seen** him."

Philip said, "Lord, **show us** the Father and that will be enough for us."

Jesus answered: "Don't you *know* me, Philip, even after I have been among you such a long time? Anyone who has **seen** me has **seen** the Father. How can you say, 'Show us the Father'?" (italics and bold added)

Therefore, in the Johannine context, not having seen God means that one does not truly know God and is therefore not truly Christian. Those who do evil even while calling themselves Christian, such as Diotrephes exemplifies here, are self-deceived. Therefore, with v. 11 the elder places before Gaius a choice: either to do what is right and stand with the apostolic tradition and those who bear it, or to behave like Diotrephes and become someone who is self-deceived, doing evil out of their own need for power. What at first glance seems a simple issue of hospitality is at its root a choice between standing for the truth and not doing so.

Verse 11 is the main thought of the letter and is much in keeping with the call to be on the right side of the Johannine duality found throughout John's gospel and 1 and 2 John. The unfortunate situation that Diotrephes has stirred sets two courses of action in sharpest relief. The elder wants Gaius and others to make a right decision, so he must expose the true character of the issue. The one who sides with the apostolic testimony is motivated by God, and the one who does not has not made even the first step toward God, for it is only through the witness of those who heard, saw, and touched the Word of Life that the truth about Jesus Christ can be known.

Theology in Application

Spiritual Confusion

The elder's plea to imitate the good and not the evil is the major point of exhortation in the letter, not only for Gaius but also for readers today. For those who accept the spiritual authority of the NT writers it is a direct command to Christians today. All Christian readers of 3 John stand where Gaius stood so many centuries ago, with a decision to make about what spiritual authority they will submit themselves to whenever they encounter conflicting voices.

In the letter's original setting, the specific way the elder expected Gaius to reject evil and do good was to continue to offer hospitality to the elder and those he sent. Christians today more than ever need to pay attention to the call for hospitality as directly related to the heart of the gospel (see Theology in Application on vv. 5 – 8). But there is a deeper sense of the elder's plea in v. 11 that concerns the foundational issue of spiritual authority. The elder wants Gaius to reject Diotrephes's influence and to continue to accept the elder's spiritual authority concerning the truth of Jesus Christ. If Gaius also chooses to refuse those sent by the elder, he will be imitating Diotrephes and doing evil, not good. Therefore Diotrephes, at least in this one act recorded in 3 John, represents the evil of rejecting apostolic authority. Gaius, like every Christian, must continually decide under what spiritual authority he will live. Authentic and true spiritual authority is the overarching issue in 3 John.

Historically the church grew from the foundation of the apostles, whom the Lord Jesus Christ himself appointed and sent out to be witnesses to the revealed truth that his incarnation embodied. Christ's apostles, as they preached the gospel and founded churches throughout the Roman world, appointed elders who received the apostolic witness and kept the local churches centered in that truth. Successive generations of leaders of the local churches were expected to bind themselves to the truth that had been passed down to them (cf. 1 Cor 15:3; 2 Tim 1:13; 2:2).

That apostolic witness was recorded in the Gospels and letters that eventually were gathered into the NT. But when the elder wrote to Gaius and for some time after, the NT did not yet exist, even though its individual parts were circulating.

Furthermore, the first century was no less confusing about spiritual truth than is our own time. Many different voices vied in first-century Greco-Roman society for the hearts and minds of the people, just as they do today. It was a pluralistic, polytheistic society in which various philosophies and religions competed for acceptance. Christians could not readily access the writings of the apostles when evaluating whether the teachings they heard were true or false. Therefore, one's alignment with a spiritual leader became a defining issue of greatest importance. Today, a Christian's choice of a spiritual leader is still of great importance, but more foundational is the decision to accept the apostolic authority found the NT and then to affiliate with like-minded Christians. This was essentially the decision the elder called on Gaius to make.

Christians today, and especially those who lead churches or Christian organizations, must be servants of the apostolic truth handed down through the ages as links in a mighty chain that stretches from Jesus Christ through our moment in history and into the future to the last generation. The chain must be anchored in Christ. There are many different philosophies and religions making appeals to Christians that must be evaluated against the authoritative teachings of the Bible. The role of the church leader as an elder or pastor is to conserve apostolic truth and apply it to contemporary situations, not to be the entrepreneur of his own religious organization.

But as we know, many church leaders and laypeople today call themselves "Christians" and yet do not live in submission to the apostolic authority of Scripture. Deliberately or not, they are going the way of Diotrephes when he rejected the elder's teaching and refused to be a fellow worker with the truth. Regardless of why a "Christian" rejects the authority of Scripture — and many reasons could be given — they are severing themselves from the truth of Jesus Christ.

Was the Elder Unloving?

Some today could perhaps accuse the elder of 3 John of being unloving toward Diotrephes and, given the repeated call to love one another in the Johannine corpus, a hypocrite — a popular accusation made against Christians in general and church leaders in particular. Those who claim to revere Scripture but nevertheless align themselves with causes and practices that Scripture clearly prohibits most often justify it by claiming that the biblical command of love trumps obedience to those practices that our society finds intolerant and offensive. "After all," some say, "God is love" (1 John 4:8, 16; see comments).

But love as God defines it does not approve of sin, for it is not loving to encourage someone to live with a false view of the spiritual reality for which he or she will one day have to give an account to the Judge of all. Christians who live as if love trumps truth need to hear John's message that truth and love are two sides of the same coin. One cannot be sacrificed for the other, and neither can be played off against the other.

Thus, if we accept the spiritual authority of the elder as a divinely inspired author, he must be allowed to define the terms of Christian love. As Burge observes, 3 John teaches that in order to hold love and truth together, confrontation is sometimes necessary.[24] He notes that the existence of this letter proves that the elder was persistent and unwilling to let Diotrephes or his church go their own way without confrontation. There comes a time when a tolerant acceptance is not love. Diotrephes had

---

24. Burge, *Letters of John*, 251 – 54.

come to that time. It is not a loving attitude to allow someone to wander from the truth without confrontation, as difficult as confrontation may be. And it is especially important for spiritual authority to confront those who can lead whole congregations astray. The elder intended to meet personally with Diotrephes, even though it was potentially an unpleasant prospect and may even have been ineffective (cf. Paul's confrontation in Corinth that did not go well, 2 Cor 2:1).

Vigilance for Truth and Love

The inevitable consequence of a lackadaisical "live and let live" attitude in the church regarding doctrine and morality is the dilution of the truth. It is certainly biblical to overlook an insult (e.g., Prov 12:16) and to be forbearing and patient with one another as we allow the fruit of the Spirit to ripen in each other's lives (Gal 5:22 – 25). Moreover, not every point that arises in the life of a congregation warrants confrontation. But when the truth of the gospel is at stake, conflict avoidance that masquerades as Christian piety is not spiritual strength.

In Johannine thought, love does not trump truth, nor does truth trump love. We have all probably known Christians who wield truth like a club to browbeat others into submission to their own viewpoint. But even if that viewpoint is correct, their manner imitates Diotrephes's heavy-handed form of leadership. When we remember that the truth we claim is not "ours" but Christ's, we need not defend our egos by battling others to the death. "Do not imitate what is evil," the elder says to Christians today (v. 11).

The insistence that truth and love are closely bound in God's economy is not unique to John's writings. As the apostle Paul puts it:

> Then we will no longer be infants, tossed back and forth by the waves, and blown here and there by every wind of teaching and by the cunning and craftiness of people in their deceitful scheming. Instead, speaking the *truth* in *love*, we will grow to become in every respect the mature body of him who is the head, that is, Christ. (Eph 4:14 – 15, italics added)

In today's postmodern, relativistic world, anyone who claims to have the truth about God or morality is at risk of being thought arrogant and manipulative when he or she will not accept spiritual and moral truth from a variety of religious or philosophical sources. The smorgasbord approach to religion is much in vogue, and the exclusive claim of the gospel sounds offensive. But the exclusivity of the truth Christians claim is not from us but from Jesus Christ, who said, "I am the way and the truth and the life. *No one comes to the Father except through me*" (John 14:6, italics added). Christians need only be sure that our *manner* of upholding the truth is not arrogant or manipulative. All Christians — not just church leaders — must be willing to stand for truth and act in sincere, courageous love so that the church of Christ will not be compromised.

Leadership of the Church

Verses 9 – 11 in 3 John also invite readers today to contrast Gaius and Diotrephes as we consider how we are involved in the church and the consequences of our involvement. Gaius had been a partner with the elder in the gospel in a quiet, behind-the-scenes role. Although evidently a man of means, he put himself and his resources into the service of others in the church rather than trying to control others. Those served by his hospitality saw Christ shining in his life, making Gaius widely known as someone who practiced the truth of his Christian faith with love.

In contrast, the elder characterizes Diotrephes as the type of leader Jesus warned against, the type who loves to lord it over others (Matt 20:25; Mark 10:42; Luke 22:25). The question of whether Diotrephes held a duly appointed office in his church or not is moot, for such leadership is fatally flawed whether exercised by a duly ordained officer of the church or a personally influential layperson. Ordination does not license one to reject authority or abuse the flock. As Marshall warns, never confuse personal ambition with zeal for the gospel.[25] Those with experience of life in the church can probably recall situations where issues of personality and character were asserting themselves as claims for orthodoxy or orthopraxy. Each of us involved in the church must examine ourselves to see what motivates our service and leadership, whether we hold ordained office or not.

By rejecting the elder who linked the churches to the apostolic tradition, Diotrephes is making himself autonomous in his leadership, which is always a dangerous position for anyone in Christ's church. Moreover, rejecting the authority and teaching of the apostles of Jesus Christ can only eventually lead to heresy and unorthodox practices.

As Diotrephes is presented in this letter (and we must allow that he may have repented of his need to put himself first and been restored to fellowship with the elder), he remains a negative example for Christians today. As Jackman writes:

> Because his heart was wrong, Diotrephes erred both from the truth and from Christian love.... The picture John draws of this domineering man is horrific. Destroying unity, flaunting authority, making up his own rules to safeguard his position, spreading lies about those whom he has designated his enemies, cutting off other Christians on suspicion of guilt by association. This is what happens when someone who loves to be first decides to use the church to satisfy his inner longing for a position of pre-eminence, for his own personal aggrandizement.[26]

Clearly a major moral lesson from 3 John is that no one in Christ's church should serve out of such motives, whether in ordained leadership or lay service. From time to time we must ask ourselves these questions:

25. Marshall, *Epistles of John*, 90.

26. David Jackman, *The Message of John's Letters: Living in* the Love of God (The Bible Speaks Today; Downers Grove, IL: InterVarsity Press, 1988), 197 – 98.

- Does my way of being in the church foster community or destroy it?
- Do I equate leadership with being in control?
- Am I hospitable to everyone or am I exclusive about whom I extend myself to?
- Do I have my ego wrapped around every activity, meeting, and issue?
- Do I always have to be right?
- Do I avoid those who disagree with me, or even worse, try to alienate them from others as well?

Christians today are called, just as Gaius was, to imitate the good, to stand on the side of truth and love, and to be fellow workers for the cause of the gospel of Jesus Christ. Lord, make us the courageous people of faith you have called us to be!

CHAPTER 23

3 John 12

Literary Context

After praising Gaius for his previous faithfulness and hospitality, and after describing the evil Diotrephes has done by refusing hospitality to those sent by the elder, the elder introduces Demetrius, the one who most likely brought the letter to Gaius. This letter, therefore, is a letter of introduction.

I. The Letter's Address and Greeting (vv. 1 – 4)
II. The Reason for Writing (vv. 5 – 8)
III. The Problem with Diotrephes (vv. 9 – 11)
→ **IV. Introducing Demetrius (v. 12)**
    A. Demetrius Is Affirmed by All Who Know Him (v. 12a-b)
    B. Demetrius Is Affirmed by the Truth Itself (v. 12c)
    C. The Elder Personally Recommends Demetrius (v. 12d)
    D. The Elder Reasserts the Reliability of His Knowledge of the Truth (v. 12e-f)
V. Closing (vv. 13 – 15)

Main Idea

Gaius apparently does not know Demetrius personally, and so the elder gives a glowing recommendation of the man who most likely brought this letter to him. Although Demetrius needs hospitality, the letter is not about Demetrius. The main point is about Gaius and the decision put before him.

Translation

3 John 12

12a	assertion	Regarding **Demetrius, he has been affirmed**
b	means	by all and
c	means	by the truth itself.
d	assertion	And **we also testify,**
e	assertion	and **you know**
f	content	that our testimony is true.

Structure

Demetrius has been confirmed as an honorable Christian in good standing with the elder's church. Two prepositional phrases with "by" (ὑπό) give the means by which the confirmation has happened. The elder as writer of the letter also adds his own personal testimony, which was required in a letter of recommendation. The verse refers to three character witnesses: "everyone," "the truth itself," and "we also."

Exegetical Outline

→ **IV. Introducing Demetrius (v. 12)**

    A. Demetrius is affirmed by all who know him (v. 12a-b)

    B. Demetrius is affirmed by the truth itself (v. 12c)

    C. The elder personally recommends Demetrius (v. 12d)

    D. The elder reasserts the reliability of his knowledge of the truth (v. 12e-f)

Explanation of the Text

12a-c Regarding Demetrius, he has been affirmed by all and by the truth itself (Δημητρίῳ μεμαρτύρηται ὑπὸ πάντων καὶ ὑπὸ αὐτῆς τῆς ἀληθείας). The name "Demetrius" is in the dative case, likely a dative of respect or reference, hence "regarding Demetrius." This does not follow the convention in extant letters of introduction, where the name of the person being introduced is given in the nominative case followed by an articular participle further identifying the person (usually a present or perfect form of ἀποδίδωμι, ἀναδίδωμι, κομίζω, παρακομίζω, φέρω, προσφέρω, or καταφέρω). The formula is completed by a form of the verb "I am" (εἰμί) with a predicate that identifies the relationship of the person being introduced by the writer.[1] However, there is considerable variation among the extant letters. This verse is clearly meant to introduce and recommend Demetrius to Gaius. It

---

1. Kim, *Form and Structure*, 38 – 53.

makes sense only if Demetrius is present to Gaius, probably as the bearer of the letter from the elder.

It is interesting that the name "Demetrius" is also found together with the name "Gaius" in Acts 19:23–41. There, a silversmith named Demetrius living in Ephesus caused uproar over the preaching of Paul, Gaius, and Aristarchus. Because the name was common, these two are probably not the same man, though the ancient interpreter Andreas wrote: "In my opinion this Demetrius is the same man who made silver idols of Artemis and who once led a riot against the apostle Paul."[2] Ephesus was a large city of about 200,000 people, and there were probably many men named Demetrius and Gaius. But if Demetrius is the same person as in Acts 19, one could certainly understand why Gaius would need a letter confirming Demetrius's Christian faith! And it would be evidence of contact between the Pauline mission in Ephesus and the later ministry of John.[3] Even so, it is a curiosity that both a Demetrius and a Gaius are referred to in both Acts 19 and in 3 John, and that both texts are associated with the city of Ephesus.

The verb "has been affirmed" (μεμαρτύρηται) means to be thought of good reputation and spoken well of, in this case, "by all" (ὑπὸ πάντων).[4] Together with "by the truth itself," it forms a phrase used in law and later adopted by Christians. Citing the early Greek orator Aeschines (mid-fourth century BC, *Against Timarchus* 90), Lieu explains that this is "the language of the law court, where the case for or against someone is — so it is argued — beyond questioning."[5] The phrase was taken up in early Christian literature to refer to someone who was beyond reproach and deserving to be imitated or given church office. The perfect passive form

here indicates that Demetrius has attained that good reputation in the past, which stands unquestioned in the present. Demetrius has a reputation for fidelity to Christ in his way of life.

Clearly, the qualifier "who know him" is presumed after "all"; that is, everyone in the Johannine community (of Ephesus?) thinks highly of Demetrius. Lieu claims the verb "has been affirmed" doesn't necessarily mean doctrinal fidelity, "for such testimonies have their parallels in purely secular or civic contexts of those worthy of office or of honour."[6] While Lieu may be right that the formula per se was widely used and does not mean doctrinal fidelity, its referent in any given occurrence must be determined from its context, and given the context of this recommendation, it can hardly mean anything other than Demetrius's faithfulness to the truth as expressed in the conduct of his life and the soundness of his belief.[7]

The second form of approval, by "the truth itself," moves the affirmation away from the opinions of people and focuses on the requirements of the gospel itself. "The truth" is probably not a direct reference to Jesus or to the Holy Spirit here, as we find no reference to how the ascended Jesus or the Spirit made such an approval known (cf. Acts 13:1–3). More likely Demetrius so clearly and publicly lived his life according to God's word of truth that when measured by that standard, his faith was confirmed in the quality of his character and devotion to Christ. Demetrius's love for others in response to the gospel of Jesus Christ speaks well of him.

12d-f And we also testify, and you know that our testimony is true (καὶ ἡμεῖς δὲ μαρτυροῦμεν,

---

2. Bray, ACCS 11, 243.

3. For a discussion of the interaction of various Christian communities in Ephesus and its environs, see Trebilco, *The Early Christians in Ephesus*.

4. BDAG, *s.v.* μαρτυρέω 2.b.

5. Lieu, *I, II, & III John*, 279.

6. Lieu, *Theology of the Johannine Epistles*, 10, but she gives no citations.

7. Brown, *Epistles of John*, 722–24.

καὶ οἶδας ὅτι ἡ μαρτυρία ἡμῶν ἀληθής ἐστιν). The elder himself is the third confirming character witness for Demetrius. All letters of recommendation needed to bear the personal recommendation of the writer, who was usually a relative or close friend of the person being introduced.[8] It is interesting that the social standing or personal credentials of the person being introduced are not found in extant letters of recommendation, but only the person's relationship to the writer, so it was on the basis of trust in the sender's credibility that the guest was to be received. But here Demetrius's credentials are presented and related first to the Christian community and to the gospel before the elder gives a personal endorsement. It is first and foremost a fellowship with other Christians based on the truth of Jesus Christ that recommends Demetrius to Gaius.

The elder affirms his personal knowledge by adding "we also testify" (ἡμεῖς δὲ μαρτυροῦμεν). The sense of the first person plural pronoun used here is, of course, related to this characteristic mark of the Johannine corpus (see discussion of authorship in Introduction to 1, 2, and 3 John and comments on 1 John 1:1 – 4). If "we" (ἡμεῖς) is genuinely plural, it likely refers to those who bear the apostolic teaching of what was seen, heard, and touched during Jesus' earthly life. More likely it refers to the elder alone, who is asserting his authority to judge Demetrius's conformity to the truth.

Since a threefold affirmation of the person being introduced and recommended is not conventional in the letter of recommendation, it may reflect the Jewish practice referred to in Deut 19:15, "A matter must be established by the testimony of two or three witnesses" (cf. 1 John 5:8).

The statement "you know that our testimony is true" alludes once again to the confusing situation concerning the truth when this letter was written. It is an oblique exhortation to Gaius to remain committed to the truth as the elder teaches it, since the elder by virtue of his apostolic role has the authority to adjudicate what is truth and what is not, and therefore to judge who is aligned with the truth and who is not (cf. 1 John 2:18 – 27). The use of the first person plural "our" (ἡμῶν) is likely intended to remind Gaius that, by virtue of the elder's role with respect to the apostles, his testimony is the apostolic testimony; therefore, the elder affirms that Gaius already knows that such testimony is true.

Note that the elder uses the first person singular eleven times in 3 John in instances that refer to him alone, but when speaking of his testimony to the truth, the plural likely ties the elder to the tradition borne by the apostles of Christ. The shift to the second person singular verb "you know" (οἶδας) functions as a mild exhortation that the elder presumes is true — that Gaius has not departed from that truth as Diotrephes has done.

Theology in Application

There is probably no better balm for one's soul than to hear that others think highly of you. Demetrius was blessed in having won the approval of all who knew him in the Johannine Christian community. It was a high compliment that the elder could send him out in confusing times with the full confidence that Demetrius would represent the gospel of Jesus Christ well. If you were traveling to a Christian

---

8. Kim, *Form and Structure*, 49 – 51.

community in a foreign place with a letter of introduction in hand, what would you want it to say about you? Do you live out the gospel so consistently that everyone who knows you could affirm your commitment to Christ and love for others? Most people can even in their own strength do a sprint for Christ, but the life to which we are called is a marathon, not a sprint — that "long obedience in the same direction."[9]

Demetrius was courageous to go out as an emissary from the elder into an area where his welcome was in doubt. To be refused hospitality — as Diotrephes had previously done — left a traveler in an uncomfortable, and possibly downright dangerous, situation. Yet not knowing for sure where he would sleep or where his next meal was coming from, Demetrius was willing to travel for the cause of Christ in uncertain times. He stood with the elder and those who stood with him in spite of the rejection and criticism of Diotrephes. We know virtually nothing else about Demetrius, but perhaps there is nothing more that we need to know.

To what extent are we willing to take risks for the work of the gospel? Are we willing to risk our reputations by siding with the apostolic truth found in the passages such as 3 John? Are we willing to trust and content ourselves with the generosity of other Christians? Or does our pride prevent our ability to receive from others? And what would we do if late some evening our doorbell rang and there stood a stranger bearing a letter from a distant Christian friend asking us to receive the stranger as a guest?

The letter of 3 John is brief and in some ways enigmatic, but it shows us an authentic situation in the early church and the real people involved in it. While we may not know the names and numbers of the countless, anonymous believers around the world and throughout the centuries who were faithful bearers of the gospel in confusing and risky times, we are in their debt. And we each have the opportunity today to be one of them.

---

9. Cf. Eugene H. Peterson, *A Long Obedience in the Same Direction: Discipleship in an Instant Society* (Downers Grove, IL: InterVarsity Press, 1980).

3 John 13 – 15

Literary Context

With these verses we reach the closing of this brief letter. Every Hellenistic letter had a closing generally similar to this, where the writer sent good wishes to the recipient and greetings to others to end the note.

I. The Letter's Address and Greeting (vv. 1 – 4)

II. The Reason for Writing (vv. 5 – 8)

III. The Problem with Diotrephes (vv. 9 – 11)

IV. Introducing Demetrius (v. 12)

→ **V. Closing (vv. 13 – 15)**

    A. There's More to Be Said If and When the Elder Visits (vv. 13 – 14)

    B. A Blessing of Peace during a Troubling Situation (v. 15a)

    C. An Exchange of Greetings (v. 15b-c)

Main Idea

The elder has many things on his mind that are best said in person rather than by letter. After expressing a hope to see Gaius soon, probably dependent on Gaius's response to this letter, he sends personal greetings.

Translation

> **3 John 13 – 15**
>
> | 13a | assertion | **I have many things to write to you,** |
> | b | contrast | but **I do not wish to write to you** |
> | c | means | with ink and pen. |
>
> | 14a | desire | **I hope to see you very soon,** |
> | b | assertion | and **we will speak face-to-face.** |
> | 15a | wish | **Peace be to you.** |
> | b | assertion | **The friends greet you.** |
> | c | exhortation | **Greet the friends by name.** |

Structure

The letter closes with two statements (vv. 13 and 14) followed by closing greetings.

Exegetical Outline

➡ **IV. Closing (vv. 13 – 15)**

    A. There's more to be said if and when the elder visits (vv. 13 – 14)

    B. A blessing of peace during a troubling situation (v. 15a)

    C. An exchange of greetings (v. 15b-c)

Explanation of the Text

13 – 14 I have many things to write to you, but I do not wish to write to you with ink and pen. I hope to see you very soon, and we will speak face-to-face (Πολλὰ εἶχον γράψαι σοι ἀλλ᾽ οὐ θέλω διὰ μέλανος καὶ καλάμου σοι γράφειν· ἐλπίζω δὲ εὐθέως σε ἰδεῖν, καὶ στόμα πρὸς στόμα λαλήσομεν). After reasserting his apostolic testimony to the truth in v. 12, the elder switches to the first person singular "I have" (εἶχον, imperfect tense). The thought of many more things to say echoes Jesus' words to his disciples in John 16:12, "I have much more to say

to you, more than you can now bear." This suggests the elder's sense that he owes more of an explanation to Gaius, as opposed to just wanting casual conversation with him.[1] The use of the imperfect tense may express the idea that the elder has had, and will continue to have, these many things on his mind for a while.

The elder hopes to see Gaius soon, which indicates that the elder believes the situation calls for his personal presence. However, if Gaius decides to sever ties with the elder by refusing hospitality

---

1. BDAG, *s.v.* ἔχω 7.a.d.

to those he sent, it would also preclude a visit from the elder. Reading between the lines, the elder may be testing the waters to see if Gaius will remain his ally and provide a place for him to stay when he comes to call Diotrephes to account. It may be some uncertainty about Gaius's response that gives v. 10 its conditional quality (see comments).

The idiom "mouth-to-mouth" (στόμα πρὸς στόμα) cannot, of course, be translated "literally," for in English its sense is expressed by "face-to-face." The modifier "with ink and pen" is not to suggest there were other means of writing, but to form a rhetorical contrast with "mouth-to-mouth," which expresses the inadequacy of writing for the elder's purposes.

Note that the closing of 2 John contains an almost identical statement (2 John 12), which suggests that the situation caused by confusion, strife, and heretical teaching called for more than could be said in these brief notes.

15a Peace be to you (εἰρήνη σοι). If Gaius was confused by the situation in which he found himself and perhaps even pressured by Diotrephes, this note from the elder would put him on the spot, forcing him to take a stand. The elder wishes him the peace of the Lord as he decides whether to welcome Demetrius and the elder himself. The Christian wish for "peace" that developed from

the Semitic greeting (šālôm) is a prayer of blessing, "peace be to you." The elder's peace blessing expresses hope for a continued Christian fellowship with Gaius, even while recognizing the tense situation his request will cause.

15b-c The friends greet you. Greet the friends by name (ἀσπάζονταί σε οἱ φίλοι. ἀσπάζου τοὺς φίλους κατ᾽ ὄνομα). One might expect "brothers" (ἀδελφοί) where the text reads "friends" (φίλοι), and this expectation no doubt explains the textual variant found here, as a scribe would be motivated to change "friends" to "brothers." The elder perhaps chooses to name those who send greetings as "friends" because they personally know Gaius, whereas "brothers" would include strangers who were Christian believers.

The exhortation to greet others personally on behalf of the writer is frequently found in other letters of the NT (e.g., Rom 16:3 – 23; 1 Cor 16:19 – 20; 2 Cor 13:12; Phil 4:21 – 22; Col 4:12, 14 – 15; Titus 3:15; Phlm 23; Heb 13:24; 1 Pet 5:13, 14) and extant secular letters.[2] Note that the elder sends greetings from "the friends" not to the church congregation but to Gaius, for the "you" is singular (σε). The idiom "by name" (κατ᾽ ὄνομα) means individually and is found in secular notes.[3] This strongly implies that the elder and Gaius have several mutual friends.

Theology in Application

What We Do and Don't Know

The elder closes his letter with the hope of visiting soon, if Gaius is willing to have him. Had v. 15 ended at "peace to you," there would be no clue that the elder and Gaius were each members of communities bonded by several personal relationships. Apparently the elder represents a community of Christians on behalf of whom he

---

2. See Klauck and Bailey, *Ancient Letters*; Exler, *The Form of the Ancient Greek Letter*; John L. White, *Light from Ancient Letters* (Philadelphia: Fortress, 1986).

3. For instance, P.Iand. 9(42); P.Oxy. I.123 (190); cf. Loeb, *Select Papyri*, 334, 376.

sends greetings to Gaius. He wishes Gaius to give greetings to other Christians the elder knows by name. Although this letter was from one individual to another, their relationship was within the bond of Christian communities, separate and yet joined in a common calling.

Our lack of knowledge about the situation in the Johannine churches has led biblical scholars to speculate and reconstruct scenarios built on speculations; after all, this is part of what biblical scholars get paid to do. There are endless debates about whether Diotrephes was a legitimately appointed elder and whether Gaius was in the same local house church as Diotrephes. Who is "the elect lady and her children" in 2 John, and what is her relationship to the men named in 3 John? There are various theories about the order in which the three letters of John were written, for there is no reason to assume their canonical sequence represents their chronological sequence, and whole books have been written about the Johannine community and the Johannine "school" (see the Introduction to 1, 2, and 3 John).

At this point in the history of Johannine scholarship, there is a top-heavy reconstruction of the original historical situation that rests on slight evidence, a multitude of inferences, and much speculation. Thus, any exegesis that depends on a particular reconstruction of the Johannine community should be held lightly. True, we would more clearly understand the text if we had more background information, but even though not all our questions are answered, we are not prevented from taking its message to heart.

Since 3 John was canonized in spite of the questions it has always raised, once it began circulating beyond its original setting, we are reminded that we do not need to understand the origins of the biblical books exhaustively or even to our own satisfaction in order for Scripture to accomplish its purposes. The points about accepting or rejecting apostolic authority, the relationship between truth and love in Christian living, and the significance of hospitality as a Christian hallmark — these are important messages from this letter that do not stand or fall by any hypothetical reconstruction of the original historical setting. They do, however, require that we view the elder as an authentic apostolic voice for the truth of God's revelation in Christ (see the discussion of authorship in the Introduction to 1, 2, and 3 John).

The Good Old Days?

In the spiritually confusing times in which we live, it may be appealing to think nostalgically that in its earliest days, the Christian church was a tranquil place of unity, joy, and peace, which only gradually became fragmented and contentious as the centuries rolled on. The history of the church is indeed primarily a history of disagreements and schisms that have led to the three major segments of Christianity we see today — Protestantism, Roman Catholicism, and Eastern Orthodoxy — and to hundreds of denominations and groups within each. John's three letters evidently give us a glimpse of one of the earliest schisms, and we don't know with certainty the consequences it held for the development of the Christian church in Asia Minor and more broadly throughout the Mediterranean world.

Third John is enigmatic because we have so many unanswered questions and because we don't know what happened after it was written. We don't know if Gaius received Demetrius, or if the elder did visit and confront Diotrephes face-to-face, or whether Diotrephes repented or persisted to lead his church into heresy and apostasy — which is the only place to go when one departs from the apostolic teaching. There is no guarantee that the elder's efforts ensured his desired outcome (cf. Paul's frustrated ministry with the Corinthian church). The fact, however, that 3 John was canonized and was titled as a Johannine writing hints that, when push came to shove, Gaius did stand with elder and that the church preserved this letter as a memorial of his faithfulness and an example for subsequent generations who faced similar challenges.

The Church Has Never Been Perfect

Third John shows us that even from the earliest days of its existence, the Christian church has been made up of imperfect people whose attitudes and actions cause confusion about what is true and about hard feelings between spiritual brothers and sisters, and consequently such attitudes can damage the spread of the gospel and the health of the church. The church will always have within its ranks those like Gaius and those like Diotrephes. Thus, when 3 John is viewed in the long span of church history, it should inspire us with confidence and encouragement. Here we are, nearly two thousand years after the elder wrote, and the gospel of Jesus Christ is still alive and active, still reconciling people to God and transforming their lives as they read the NT. What a wonder! What a testimony that the work is the Lord's and the power is the Spirit's!

The Theology of John's Letters

The preeminent theological point of John's letters is consistent with the overarching message of the NT in general: that Jesus Christ, God's Son, has come from God the Father to die as the atoning sacrifice for sin, and on the basis of his self-sacrifice, to create for God a new covenant people who will both know him and enjoy eternal life with him. This theological point is an interpretation of the historical events of Jesus' birth, ministry, crucifixion, and resurrection. Just as the statement "Jesus Christ died on a cross in Jerusalem for your sins" is an interpretation of "Jesus of Nazareth died on a cross in Jerusalem," John's letters interpret the significance of the historical events concerning Jesus' life and death. Because the significance of the life, death, and resurrection of Jesus is an interpretation, the authority and credentials of the interpreter are of paramount importance to those who seek to know the truth.

Spiritual Authority

It is on this point of spiritual authority that 1 John begins, with its assertion in 1:1 – 4 that only "we" who have heard, have seen, have touched, and have understood the one who was "from the beginning," but who has appeared in human history, have the authority to rightly interpret the significance of his appearing. This starting point was no doubt necessary because unnamed people, who were not included in the "we" of 1:1 – 4, but who had "gone out" from "us" (2:19), were offering a different understanding of the significance of Jesus, possibly making his death all but irrelevant to the spiritual "truth" they preached.

Before his death, Jesus gave his closest associates the authority to testify about him and promised them that the Paraclete who would come — the Spirit of truth (John 14:16 – 17) or Holy Spirit (14:26) — would give them the necessary knowledge and understanding accessible only after the crucifixion and resurrection. This promise could be interpreted to mean that everyone who has the Spirit has an equal claim to the authority to define the truth about God as revealed in Christ, were it not that the promise is limited to those whom Jesus chose who were with him from the beginning (15:26 – 27).

The emphatic statement that the author of these letters stood with the authority of that apostolic group (1 John 1:1 – 4) suggests that the root of the false teaching was an unauthorized and unwarranted claim to spiritual authority that challenged the role and teaching of the elder. The elder's assumed responsibility for and influence over the churches and individuals to whom he wrote 2 and 3 John suggests that he was working from a position of authority that was being called into question by the secessionists and Diotrephes, though perhaps for different reasons.

The question of who has the authority to declare the truth about Jesus is not a bad starting place even for theological conversations today, for we live in a world full of not only a variety of religions, but also a cacophony of "Christian" voices with a wide range of opinions about who Jesus was and about his relevance for the times in which we live. It is important for those who minister God's Word to realize that spiritual authority is not vested in themselves, by any credential or merit, but is vested in the truth of the One whose Word they proclaim.

Eternal Life

The author of 1 John considers the stakes to be high for those who must decide to whom to listen when it comes to the significance of Jesus Christ, for the appearance of Christ in history signals that eternal life, which was with the Father, has been revealed to "us" earthbound mortals (1 John 1:2; cf. John 1:1 – 18). While "the eternal Life, which was with the Father" (1 John 1:2), may primarily refer to the eternal preexistence of the Son who has appeared as a human being, the point of his appearance is to bring eternal life after physical death to all who believe in him (2:25; 3:14, 15; 5:11 – 13, 20; cf. John 3:15 – 16, 36; 4:14; 5:24, 28 – 29, 40; 6:40, 47, 54; 10:28; 11:25; 12:25; 17:2 – 3; 20:31). This long list of citations in the Johannine writings indicates the primacy of eternal life in John's thinking.

The truth about Jesus' role in attaining eternal life is central to the letter's stated purpose in 1 John 5:13, "These things I write to you who believe in the name of the Son of God so that you might know that you have eternal life." Eternal life, and how to attain it, is at the heart of both John's letters and gospel (cf. John 20:31). Jesus defines eternal life in terms of knowing God: "Now this is eternal life: that they *know* you, the only true God, and Jesus Christ, whom you have sent" (John 17:3, italics added). If eternal life rests on knowing God and knowing Jesus Christ whom he has sent, there can be no assurance of eternal life apart from a true and genuine knowledge of God in Christ. This is why the concept of truth is so central to both John's gospel and letters, in which the Greek words for "truth" or "knowing" are mentioned almost two hundred times. From this we can infer that John is zealous to defend and protect the truth he has received from and about Jesus Christ against competing and conflicting claims to truth that have begun to infiltrate the churches.

Theologically speaking, is any topic of greater importance? While theology brings us many blessed insights for this life about God's being, character, and work in the world, if death were the end of all benefits from knowing about God, of what transcendent importance would it be? Since the greatest gift Christ offers is life after death, it is of greatest importance to know the truth about him, and therefore, the source of that truth becomes a primary concern in the quest for our knowledge of God. The author of 1 John argues hard to warn his readers away from voices who might seem to offer truth, but whose teaching does not lead to eternal life in Christ (1 John 2:19 – 25). These were people who talked about God but, because they denied that Jesus is the Christ, had no true knowledge of God the Father. First John characterizes them in strong language, calling them "liars" (2:22). Thus, the source of true spiritual knowledge is a major theological point of John's letters.

People today also need to understand that spiritual truth about God and eternal life is not a matter of personal opinion, where one person's thoughts are as good as another's. There is spiritual truth and there is spiritual error and falsehood, and the difference between them is the difference between life and death.

Sin and Atonement

The question of attaining eternal life, which occupies such a prominent place in John's thinking, comes because the entire human race — each and every person — is born already dead in sin. This tragedy of cosmic proportion occurred in the garden of Eden, when the entire human race — at that time one man and one woman — rebelled against God and broke fellowship with him (Gen 3, especially v. 3). Because God himself is the source and sustenance of all life, to be a law unto oneself and consequently to walk away from God is by definition to die. When one turns away from the source of life, there is no other place to go but death.

That first rebellion against God is the source of all sins that have plagued human life ever since. Sin is the issue that breaks fellowship with God (cf. 1 John 1:3), and in its multitudinous expressions, sins break the fellowship of one person with another. Because sin resulted in death to all and we are all helpless to expunge its consequences, God himself had to deal with the problem of sin or to leave humanity in death, eternally separated from fellowship with him.

God's love for the human race, however, led him not to leave us in death, eternally separated from him, but to put into play a plan of redemption that is *the* story the Bible tells in all its various books. When Adam and Eve were cast out of the garden, they were not cast into hell but into history, where God works out the plan of his redemption. John clearly sees that God's love for his fallen creation culminates in the execution of his Son, who became a man to die on the cross. This brought God's plan of redemption to its ultimate fruition in atoning for the sin of the fallen world.

It was in the life, death, and resurrection of Jesus that eternal life appeared in history (1 John 1:1 – 2), and is offered to all who agree with God that they are sinners in need of deliverance from death. The world's great religions might offer moral and wise guidance for how to live this life, but only Jesus Christ by virtue of his resurrection offers eternal life after death.

Therefore, the topics of sin and the significance of Jesus Christ are inextricably entwined in 1 John, forming two of the major theological themes of the letter. Spiritual truth can be found only through right thinking about both. Some of the issues pertaining to mistaken understandings of sin and Christ's atoning death may have arisen in the context of a misreading of the gospel of John, if it was written first, or of the Johannine tradition in its oral form.

John's original readers had been exposed to false teaching from those who eventually left the Johannine churches. Even if 1 John 1:5 – 10 is not a direct reflection of that false teaching, right thinking about sin was apparently an issue in the wake of the departure that John needed to address. The character of God is the basis for all definition of sin. "God is light" (1:5), and in him is no darkness. Therefore, God himself defines the moral standard by which the human race is to live; there is no independent standard by which we can judge God. Because of that, those who profess faith in Jesus Christ must agree with God that there is such a thing as sin, that those who walk in ways contrary to God's nature are in darkness and have no fellowship with God, and that each of us is a sinner (1:5 – 10). To say otherwise is to call God a liar.

However, even those who have accepted God's greatest gift of eternal life in Christ by agreeing with God about their sin and claiming Jesus' atonement for their forgiveness still live in a fallen world with a fallen nature, which is in the process of being transformed by the Holy Spirit. True, genuine Christians do still commit sins, in both word and deed, in both commission and omission. The proper response to that sin is not to deny it or to rationalize it, but to confess it and to claim God's forgiveness in Christ.

Remaining in Christ

John writes his letters to people who have already professed faith in Jesus Christ; therefore, his major exhortation is to remain in the truth by continuing to hold to the true significance of Jesus' life, death, and resurrection (cf. John 8:31; 15:4 – 7; 1 John 2:24, 27 – 28; 4:13; 2 John 9). Forgiveness of sin and assurance of eternal life are found only by remaining in Christ, that is, by continuing to understand and believe that Jesus atoned for sin, the obstacle that separated humanity from God. Therefore, the apostolic message about who Jesus Christ is and what he has done are crucial aspects of the theology of 1 John.

The two aspects of Christology that John's letters underscore are that (1) Jesus Christ "has come in flesh" (1 John 4:2; 2 John 7), and that (2) he "came … not in water alone — but in water and in blood" (1 John 5:6). Those who professed to be Christians but are not believers ("they have gone out from us, but they were not of us"; 2:19) are "antichrists" and "liars" because they did not continue in the truth about Christ that the elder represented (2:22). As discussed in the commentary, the issue seems to involve a dispute about the significance of Jesus' earthly life, most particularly his death on the cross, with respect to atonement, salvation, and eternal life. The dispute about the significance of the cross is likely related to John's emphasis on sin, for the concepts of sin and atonement are so closely related in Christian thought as to be inseparable. He links the two in 2:2, "He himself is the atoning sacrifice for our sins," in the immediate context of the extended discussion about sin and its denial (1:5 – 2:8).

The comment that the "antichrists" deny that "Jesus Christ has come in flesh" (1 John 4:2; 2 John 7) suggests that they held an inadequate view of the significance of the incarnation of the Word who became flesh. Perhaps they held docetic tendencies that denied the physicality of Christ. Or perhaps they claimed Jesus' promise in John's gospel for "another Advocate [*paraclete*]" (John 14:16, 26; 15:26; 16:7) to mean that Jesus himself predicted he would diminish in importance once the Holy Spirit came. The rather meager references in John's letters to the Holy Spirit's role compared to the extensive discussion about the Paraclete in John's gospel may corroborate the inference that the schism involved false claims made in the name of the Spirit.

Rather than discuss the Holy Spirit directly, John takes another approach to teach who has the Spirit and who does not, showing that the Spirit speaks in concert with the cross of Christ. The apostle considers any diminishment of Christ's life and death to be sub-Christian, for the incarnation provided the human being necessary to atone for the sin of human beings, and the Holy Spirit convicts us of our need for atonement, applies the blood of Jesus to each one of us, and reassures the believer of the central truth of the gospel, that Jesus' death and resurrection provide the entrance to eternal life.

The second false claim cited above is related, for John asserts that Jesus Christ has come "*not* in water alone — but in water *and in blood*" (1 John 5:6, italics added), where blood alludes both to Jesus' human body and to his death on the cross. This suggests that the false teaching involved a "water only" gospel, one that eliminated or diminished the significance of the cross of Jesus. Since the cross of Jesus is where God's love for the human race is most clearly expressed, any beliefs that take as a starting point the neglect of the cross can lead only to theological error. Because the cross of Jesus at its core is about God's love for us, it follows naturally that the topic of love should be among the major topics of John's letters.

Love for God, Love for Others

Because the clearest expression of God's love is found on the cross of Jesus, remaining in that truth entails the response of love for God. Sin alienated humanity's relationship with God, and the atonement for that sin through Christ's atoning death implies the restoration of fellowship with God (1 John 1:3). Within that context of that restored relationship, the appropriate response to God's love of us is our love for God. On this point, John is similar to the Synoptic writers, who report Jesus saying that the greatest moral demand, the greatest commandment, is to love God with all one's being — with all one's heart, soul, mind, and strength (Matt 22:37; Mark 12:30; Luke 10:27). Then, Jesus quickly adds, the second commandment is to love your neighbor as yourself (Matt 22:39; Mark 12:31; Luke 10:27). John understands that the second is an entailment of the first and that it is spiritually impossible to love God but not to love others (1 John 2:9 – 10; 3:10, 14, 16, 23; 4:7, 8, 11, 20 – 21).

Many of us live in societies that define love as an emotion that can be held in our hearts, whether or not it is acted upon. By that definition, one could claim to love God but not show it outwardly, and who could refute the claim? But the NT in general, and John in particular, defines love not as an emotion but as treating others as we would want to be treated (cf. the parable of the good Samaritan, Luke 10:25 – 37). Love for God means extending ourselves and our resources to meet the needs of others (1 John 3:16 – 18). This is based on the example of God's love, for he did not simply love the fallen human race in his heart; he acted at greatest cost upon that love, extending himself to us through his Son to deliver us from sin (4:9).

In the specific situation in which 1 John was written, this principle to love others is applied specifically to love for other Christians, the "brother or sister." It is not that John wishes to narrow the love command to exclude the unbelieving neighbor, but simply that his concern at that moment was how believers were treating each other within his churches. "The one who says, 'I am in the light,' and hates their brother or sister is still in the darkness [i.e., sin]. The one who loves their brother or sister remains in the light" (1 John 2:9 – 10). The one ethical command John gives is that Christians should "love one another" (3:11; see also 4:7, 11 – 12; 2 John 5) even if the "world" hates us (1 John 3:13).

Christians must not hate one another, for hate is the response of the "world" to the gospel. Hate for others can never express love for God, even if it is based on a self-righteous understanding of how those others might be offending the God we love. Although some interpreters have seen the love command as so broad and general as to be practically worthless for ethical guidance,[1] it is arguably a reference to Jesus' summary of the OT law and prophets as love for God and love for others

---

1. E.g., Meeks, "The Ethics of the Fourth Evangelist," esp. 317 – 18.

(Matt 22:36 – 40; Mark 12:28 – 31; Luke 10:27; see Theology in Application at 1 John 4:17 – 5:3 for a fuller discussion).

An important point of John's theology for our age of relativism is that love, as John defines it, does not trump truth. It is not loving to allow others to continue in their sin and ignorance about God. The necessary relationship between love as God defines it and truth as Christ brought it binds the messages of John's second and third letters to the teaching of 1 John. In those books the elder must explain why refusing to extend hospitality to those who do not bring the truth into a community is not an unloving act (2 John 10 – 11), even while exhorting his readers to extend hospitality to his own associates (3 John 8 – 11). The discernment to distinguish which situation calls for which response is rooted in knowing the truth about God in Christ, which brings the reader of these letters back to the issue of knowing the truth with certainty.

In sum, John's letters teach that certainty of the truth that results in eternal life and a properly defined love for others rest on three pillars: (1) the significance of the life, death, and resurrection of Jesus Christ; (2) the trustworthiness of the apostolic witness to interpret the significance of Jesus Christ; and (3) the anointing of the Holy Spirit, which confirms the truth to Jesus' followers (1 John 2:20).

Scripture Index

2 John

3 John

Jude

Revelation

Apocrypha Index

Subject Index

Author Index